SURVEYS OF APPLIED ECONOMICS

Volume 2

W0193178

CONTRIBUTORS

A. D. Bain, Professor of Economics, University of Warwick

I. B. Kravis, Professor of Economics, University of Pennsylvania, Philadelphia

David Laidler, Professor of Economics, University of Western Ontario

David Morawetz, Professor of Economics, Hebrew University of Jerusalem

J. M. Parkin, Professor of Economics, University of Western Ontario

John Williamson, Professor of Economics, University of Warwick

SURVEYS OF
APPLIED ECONOMICS

THE ROYAL ECONOMIC SOCIETY
THE SOCIAL SCIENCE RESEARCH COUNCIL

VOLUME 2

SURVEYS I–V

PALGRAVE MACMILLAN

Library of Congress Catalog Card Number: 2–73–82638
First published in the United States of America in 1977
ISBN 978-1-349-01865-9   ISBN 978-1-349-01863-5 (eBook)
DOI 10.1007/978-1-349-01863-5

CONTENTS

FOREWORD

THE articles which appear in this volume are the second in a series of Surveys specially commissioned by the Social Science Research Council and the Royal Economic Society and originally published in the *Economic Journal*. Each of the articles is designed to provide a comprehensive review of research in a major area of applied economics, including reference, where appropriate, to relevant theoretical work. Each is written by a specialist but aimed at the general economist rather than other specialists in the field covered.

The first of the articles reprinted here, " International Liquidity " by John Williamson, was originally published in the September 1973 issue of the *Economic Journal*, but has been brought up to date (December 1975) for this volume. The next article, " Flow of Funds Analysis " by Andrew Bain, appeared in the December 1973 issue of the *Economic Journal* and has likewise been brought up to date (January 1976). David Morawetz's article " Employment Implications of Industrialisation in Developing Countries " appeared in the September 1974 issue, and was updated in December 1975. The last two articles, " Inflation " by David Laidler and Michael Parkin and " International Comparisons of Productivity " by Irving Kravis, appeared in the December 1975 and March 1976 issues respectively, and have, therefore, been modified in minor detail only.

This volume, together with its predecessor, which appeared in 1973, represents a continuation into the field of applied economics of *Surveys of Economic Theory*, Volumes I–III, 1965–6, published by Macmillan and St Martin's Press for the Royal Economic Society and the American Economic Association.

DONALD WINCH

May 1976

I

INTERNATIONAL LIQUIDITY[1,2]

John Williamson

I. Introduction

It has long been customary to contrast the aesthetic rigour of the pure theory of international trade with the superior journalism of international monetary economics. No doubt such a contrast still exists, but in recent

[1] This is the fifth of a series sponsored jointly by the Social Science Research Council and the Royal Economic Society.

[2] The views expressed in this paper are those of the author and do not necessarily reflect those held in the International Monetary Fund. The same caveat is, of course, applicable to the large number of economists who provided valuable comments on a previous draft, of whom special mention should be made of R. N. Cooper, J. M. Fleming, J. A. Frenkel, H. G. Grubel, H. R. Heller, F. G. Hirsch, P. M. Oppenheimer and J. J. Polak.

years the latter field has increasingly followed the trend that has been evident in economics for some two centuries, and a serious technical literature has emerged alongside the profuse writings of a more traditional character.   This development has affected both balance-of-payments theory and international-liquidity theory, where the latter is conceived of as that part of international monetary economics that is not confined to establishing what does (or should) determine an individual country's balance-of-payments position (or policy).   The primary aim of this article is to provide a guide to this technical literature, hopefully by casting it into a coherent theoretical framework.

The subject is a part of applied economics, not in the spurious sense of spurning theory, but in the sense that the work done is closely related to the evolving problems of the system that is being studied.   It would be impossible to divorce the literature from its historical context, because the literature has in large measure been prompted by concern for the particular policy questions that have arisen.   In the period since 1959 there have been three major questions:

   (a) Is there a need for additional liquidity?
   (b) What are the desirable characteristics of reserves?   In particular, how should one design a fiduciary reserve asset?
   (c) In what quantity should reserves be provided?

This survey concentrates on the period since 1959.   The system underwent something of a transformation at the end of 1958: restoration of convertibility of the European currencies and termination of the European Payments Union marked a watershed between the problems of dollar shortage and post-war reconstruction and those of dollar glut and management of a growing, interdependent international economy.   This change in the facts of the situation rapidly provoked a response from economists, in particular in the form of Triffin's two modest articles (1959) which subsequently formed the core of *Gold and the Dollar Crisis* (1960).   Since the breakdown of the gold standard in 1914, there had been no real theory of how the contemporary international monetary system operated.   Triffin provided one: it claimed that the demand for reserves was growing faster than the supply could do unless the United States ran a deficit that would progressively undermine confidence in the dollar, so that the world was faced with a dilemma between a growing liquidity shortage that would threaten the expansion of the international economy and a collapse reminiscent of 1931.   The subject of international-liquidity theory grew up around this thesis.

It is obligatory to preface a survey on international liquidity by a clarification of the terms being used.   " Reserves " are virtually always defined in terms similar to " those assets of [a country's] monetary authorities that can be used, directly or through assured convertibility into other assets, to support its rate of exchange when its external payments are in deficit " (Group of Ten (1965), p. 21). At present, therefore, reserves consist of gold, convertible foreign exchange, Reserve Positions in the International Monetary Fund (I.M.F.), and Special Drawing Rights (S.D.R.s). Foreign exchange is counted gross; *i.e.*, no deduction is made on account of liabilities, even if these constitute reserves to some other country. The assets included are restricted to those held by the monetary authorities. The term " international money " has recently been adopted by a number of authors to include private, as well as official, holdings of internationally-liquid assets (Heller (1968), McKinnon (1969)).

The term (unconditional) " international liquidity " is most often used as a synonym for reserves, and this usage was endorsed by that invaluable clarification and classification of the issues that emerged from the first meetings of the Bellagio group (Machlup and Malkiel (1964), p. 31). In addition, conditional liquidity consists of the possibility of borrowing reserves through inter-central bank swap agreements or from the credit tranches at the I.M.F. It should be noted that the distinction between owned and borrowed reserves differs from that between unconditional and conditional liquidity in two respects: by the proportion of reserves tied up in " backing " the domestic money supply, and by automatic borrowing rights (I.M.F. (1964), p. 26). There is a persistent undercurrent of thought which seeks to go much further than this in adopting a " functional " definition of international liquidity (Arndt (1948), Brown (1955), Woodfine (1958), Clement (1963), Williamson (1963), Kane (1965)). The basic idea is that liquidity—or a country's " liquidity position," as Arndt termed it—should provide a measure of a country's ability to finance a payments deficit without resorting to adjustment measures. It has therefore been argued that a country's reserve holdings should be supplemented by its reserve-borrowing possibilities (Arndt, Williamson); part of the foreign-exchange holdings of its commercial banks (Arndt, Brown, Clement); inventories of foreign-trade goods (Woodfine); the extent to which its own currency would be held by foreigners in the event of a deficit materialising (Brown, Woodfine, Clement, Williamson); and the extent to which " innocuous " [1] interest-rate manipulations would attract a capital inflow (Arndt, Brown, Woodfine, Williamson). But liquidity is reduced by the existence of cover requirements (Nurkse (1944), Arndt, Clement) and some deduction needs to be made for the existence of foreign liquid liabilities, either by deducting a percentage of them (Arndt, Clement) or by postulating that the minimum reserve level needed to maintain confidence is dependent on their size (Williamson). The most promising approach to integrating these diverse factors into a single measure has been suggested by Kane (1965), who proposed defining a country's international liquidity as

---

[1] A major problem with this approach is bound to be the difficulty of drawing the line between adjustment measures and the mobilisation of liquidity.

a weighted sum of its foreign assets, liabilities, commitments and credit lines. The weights would represent the authorities' estimates of the fractions of the various instruments or credits that they could expect to activate or have drawn. This measure has the virtues of making world liquidity the sum of the liquidities of the individual countries, provided the same expectations are held in each country, and of recognising that liquidity is influenced by changes in expectations as well as financial flows. A purist might object that it may be rational for actions to be influenced by higher moments of a probability distribution than the first, but this is not a constructive criticism given that the alternative currently used involves weights of zero and one. It is sad to record that Kane's framework has not yet been utilised in empirical work.

One further semantic point concerns the distinction between the positive and the normative. The viewpoint is that of the managers of the international monetary system. Hence the optimal reserve-holding policy of a single country is placed in II, in positive theory—just as the traditional approach to the theory of the firm involves studying the optimal profit-maximising policy of a firm as a way of generating positive predictions about the way that it will react to changes in its environment. Normative questions are those concerned with management of the system.

II. POSITIVE THEORY

1. *The Demand for Reserves*

The literature on this subject has already been surveyed three times—by Clower and Lipsey (1968), by Niehans in I.M.F. (1970) and by Grubel (1971a). It is hoped that the present treatment will complement rather than compete with these: it concentrates less on detailed exposition and evaluation and more on sketching the evolution of the theory and the results it has yielded.

In 1802 Henry Thornton argued that a country's gold stock should be related to the potential benefits of being able to mitigate internal fluctuations by financing trade deficits, as well as to the size of the domestic money supply (Thornton (1802), pp. 111, 153). Thereafter the gold standard triumphed, and attention was focused on the tie between reserves and the stock of money until Keynes ((1913), pp. 166–70; (1930), pp. 275–8) reintroduced the importance of the external factor. By 1943 there was general recognition that reserves were relevant for international purposes rather than for backing the money supply, and the Keynes Plan for an International Clearing Union (Cmd 6437 (1943)) applied this by proposing that bancor quotas—which would have been the main source of liquidity— be related to the value of trade. Triffin (1947) carried the argument a stage further by arguing that the demand for reserves could normally be expected to grow in line with trade, so that the reserves/imports ratio (R/M)

could be taken as a measure of reserve adequacy. This measure was subsequently used by Harrod (1953), the I.M.F. (1953) (1958), Franks (1958), Stamp (1958) and Triffin (1960), so that by 1960 it was regarded as the standard approach to the subject. (Incidentally, the postulate that the demand for reserves grows in line with trade has often been referred to as the international quantity theory. Those who regard the quantity theory as more than just a theory of the demand for money will understand why that term has here been reserved for a theory to be discussed in II.4 below.)

One criticism of the use of the reserves/imports ratio stems from ideas initially advanced by Johnson (1958, p. 157) and Scitovsky (1958, pp. 106–8). These represent a revival of the tradition of relating reserves to the money supply. Johnson argued that, on welfare grounds, reserves should be large relative to the money supply so as to permit the public to execute a desired shift out of money into goods without obliging the authorities to intervene to prevent a payments crisis, which would frustrate the public's profit- and utility-maximising decisions. The difficulty with the argument is that the object of demand-management policy is precisely that of frustrating the desires of the public to shift between money and goods, with their inevitable consequence of destabilising income.[1] It is of course possible that countries may actually determine their reserve holdings with reference to their money supplies even if this is an irrational act based on traditional superstitions, but there is no persuasive evidence that they do (Machlup (1966), Lamfalussy (1968)).

A second criticism of the use of the reserves/imports ratio stems from recognition of the fact that reserves are used to finance deficits, not trade. The point was first emphasised by Nurkse (1944, p. 13), who also quantified the variability of different countries' imbalances that reserves were required to finance. His measure (p. 91) was calculated for 18 countries and was $(T_{max} - T_{min})/\bar{M}$, where T_{max}, T_{min} and $\bar{M}$ are respectively the algebraically largest and smallest trade balances, and the average imports of each country over the period 1925–29. This measure was substantially larger for primary-producing countries than for industrial countries. An updating of the measure to the period 1950–56 by Woodfine (1958) indicated greater instability of imbalances in the 1950s than in the 1920s. Although Nurkse's work was subsequently ignored, it would be wrong to suppose that the users of the R/M measure were unaware that reserves are actually used only to settle imbalances. Triffin (1947) was quite explicit, and concluded that countries with large export fluctuations required higher ratios (p. 70). The importance of trade variability was at least partially recognised by the I.M.F. from its inception, since export variability was one of the elements

[1] Scitovsky's argument was limited to the members of an exchange-rate union, and is therefore not subject to the same objection because the countries have, by assumption, foregone independent demand-management policies. The corollary is that it provides no rationale for including the money supply in demand-for-reserves functions of countries that are not members of an exchange-rate union.

that entered the formula on which quotas were based (Horsefield (1969), p. 95). The Fund's first study (1953) on the adequacy of reserves listed the factors that would influence the adequacy of a given R/M as the size of seasonal and random fluctuations, the variability of import and export prices and of export demand, the " compressibility " of imports, inventories of import and export goods, reserve-borrowing facilities, and the non-availability of reserves because of internal reserve requirements. Only Harrod (1953) and I.M.F. (1958) can really be charged with uncritical use of R/M.

Nevertheless, Harrod and the I.M.F. were sufficiently influential to provoke a good deal of wrath, starting with that of Balogh (1960). In due course this gave birth to some very constructive developments. Brown (1964) suggested that one should measure the adequacy of a country's liquidity by dividing its reserves by the absolute value of its payments imbalance in a particular year. This is clearly unsatisfactory—a country with reserves so low that it was compelled to eliminate a deficit at great cost could score a near-infinite measure of " reserve-adequacy." The problem is partly that no account is taken of the simultaneity problem posed by the fact that realised imbalances depend *inter alia* on the adjustment measures taken in response to reserve shortages or surpluses (Cooper (1968), p. 627; this is a problem that remains present in much subsequent work), and partly that it attaches an inappropriate importance to the realised outcome as opposed to the probability distribution of potential outcomes from which it was drawn. The second point indicates the need for a stochastic approach to the subject—a need that was promptly filled by Kenen and Yudin (1965), who postulated that each country's reserve changes could be described by a simple Markov process

$$\Delta R_t = \rho \, \Delta R_{t-1} + \epsilon_t \text{ where } 0 < \rho < 1 \text{ and } \epsilon_t \text{ is } N(\bar{\epsilon}, \sigma_\epsilon^2).$$

They estimated the parameters ρ, $\bar{\epsilon}$ and σ_ϵ^2 from monthly data for 14 countries over the period 1958–62. Subsequent writers have been critical of the stochastic specification. Streeter (1970) found that using monthly data for the period 1958–67 there was significant autocorrelation in only 13 out of 40 cases, while in 16 cases the data were consistent with having been generated by a normal distribution. Using quarterly and annual data there was virtually no support for the autoregressive hypothesis and strong evidence for the normality hypothesis (p. 69). This is a striking result which seems at odds with the casual observation that prolonged imbalances, or " fundamental disequilibria," have been frequent. Archibald and Richmond (1971) again found little support for the Kenen–Yudin specification from monthly data for 14 countries over the period 1961–67, but their proposed alternative statistical representation again involved autocorrelation. There is little doubt that the problem of giving a correct statistical description of reserve behaviour merits further investigation.

Once one has obtained (or assumed) a statistical description of the behaviour of reserves over time, there appear to be three possible ways of proceeding. The first, adopted by Kenen and Yudin, is to proceed directly to the estimation of a demand-for-reserves function by an international cross-section regression of average reserves on the estimated values of ρ, $\bar{\varepsilon}$ and σ_ε^2. A second approach, adopted by Archibald and Richmond,[1] is to use the statistical estimates to calculate the probability of reserve depletion occurring over some period. This was a difficult exercise in the case of their statistical specification. Ideally one would wish to use the results of this type of calculation as an input to the third approach, which involves assuming that countries choose their (average) reserve level by a rational optimising decision. The approach was pioneered by Heller (1966), who identified the factors relevant to the optimisation as the probability of reserve depletion, the cost of the adjustment which would be entailed by depletion, and the opportunity cost of reserve holding. Heller's stochastic specification was too crude to give his calculation great interest, but the approach has subsequently been developed by Clark (1970a), Kelly (1970), Streeter (1970), Agarwal (1971) and Britto and Heller (1973).

A typical example of this approach, which has the virtue of being illustrated by an easily-comprehensible four-quadrant diagram overleaf, is that of Clark. He assumes that each country optimises by simultaneously choosing a target (and therefore average) level of reserves, R^*, and an adjustment parameter γ which measures the proportion of any discrepancy between R^* and its actual reserve level in the preceding period that the country aims to eliminate in the current period. (It will not in general succeed in this aim because the payments balance is subject to exogenous normally-distributed shocks.) There exists a locus of combinations of R^* and γ, shown in the S.E. quadrant, which are consistent with the maintenance of a constant probability of reserve depletion: how this " acceptable " probability is chosen is unspecified. The problem of optimisation is viewed as that of determining the best point on this curve, taking account of the effects of the choice on both the level and variability of income. A higher average level of reserves involves a sacrifice in the expected level of income (N.E. quadrant) because reserves are lower-yielding assets than the alternative possible forms of investment. A higher value of γ (more rapid adjustment) involves a greater variance in income (S.W. quadrant) because the assumed method of adjustment is demand management; e.g., a reserve deficiency implies deflation so as to cut imports, and this must be more severe the greater the

---

[1] Streissler (1969) also constructed models, based on a priori assumptions about the nature of the underlying stochastic process, aimed at calculating reserve-depletion probabilities. His two-country analysis suffered from a misplaced concern with the probability that one country will suffer depletion before the other rather than with whether it will suffer depletion over a fixed time horizon, and this was presumably responsible for his curious result that an increase in the number of international transactions (of constant size) required no increase in reserve holdings to maintain a constant security level.

chosen speed of adjustment. These three curves therefore trace out a trade-off between the expected value of income and its variability (shown as the solid curve in the N.W. quadrant) implied by the choice of a combination of $R*$ and γ. The country makes this choice on the basis of a conventional quadratic utility function (dotted curve in N.W. quadrant). The model predicts that average reserves (the speed of adjustment) will vary positively (negatively) with wealth and the inherent variability of payments, and negatively (positively) with the marginal propensity to import and the opportunity cost of holding reserves.

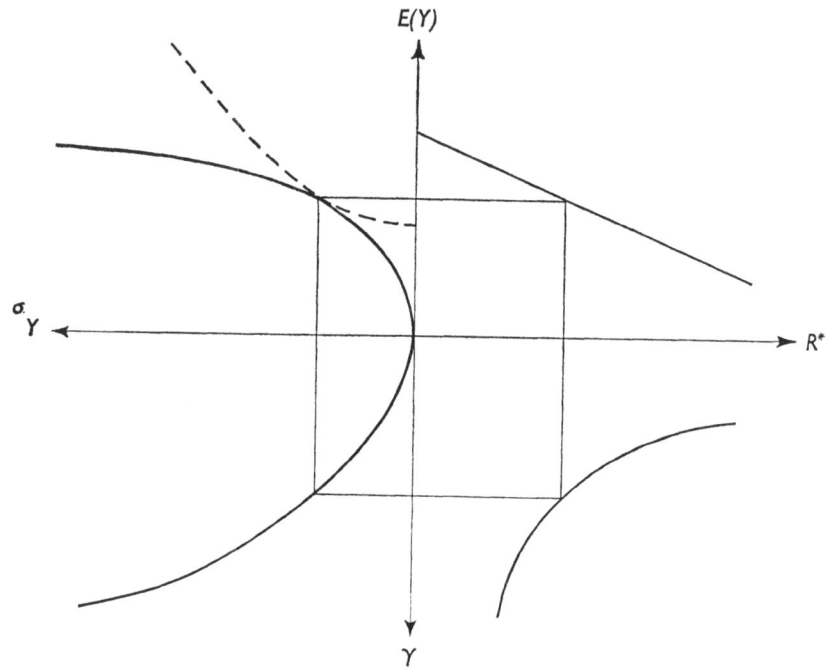

These models still suffer from important limitations. One is that they do not address themselves to the special problems of banker countries. Another is the assumption that expenditure-changing techniques are always used, in preference to expenditure-switching ones, for payments adjustment. This has been relaxed by Britto and Heller (1973) and also by Frenkel in Aliber (1974), who considered a model at the other extreme where adjustment was always effected by expenditure switching induced by price changes. The principal implication of this assumption is that optimal reserves will vary *positively* with the propensity to import provided that the income elasticity of the demand for money exceeds a critical value which is less than unity. A third limitation is the assumption that payments imbalances are basically random. In the first place, there are some imbalances that tend to be reversed automatically: to this extent reserve holding enables a country to raise the average level of income and not just to reduce its variance. Second, there are some imbalances that are prolonged and become "fundamental disequilibria," which in the present context may be defined as a situation where the expected imbalance, $E(\epsilon_t)$, is not equal to zero [1] for a constant exchange rate and any acceptable set of values for the other policy variables. The more sophisticated models recognise that even random imbalances require the systematic application of adjustment measures if reserve depletion and saturation are to be avoided, but this does not fully portray the value of reserves in their role of permitting the process of adjustment that is necessary in a situation of fundamental disequilibrium to be effected less rapidly (if that is desirable, which need not always be the case).

Incorporation of the possibility of fundamental disequilibrium into the analysis requires an inter-temporal model, since $E(\epsilon_t)$ depends not merely on the current values of the policy variables but also on their past history. An exploration of what is involved in an intertemporal optimising approach was made by Niehans in I.M.F. (1970, pp. 53–7). He was mainly concerned to clarify concepts. At any particular time he supposed that a country's authorities have in mind an economic strategy, stretching into the indefinite future, which represents their assessment of the optimal policies that are feasible subject to current and anticipated future constraints. One of these constraints is provided by the current level of reserves. A windfall gain of a unit of reserves at time zero would permit the country to recast its optimal strategy so as to increase utility; this utility gain is the marginal utility of reserves. An analogous exercise is suggested for defining the marginal cost of reserves: this is the utility loss (consisting of both holding and acquisition costs, where the latter may be negative—*e.g.*, in an inflationary situation) that would result from the country being obliged to acquire and then forfeit a unit of reserves. The optimal reserve level is, of course, where marginal utility is equal to marginal cost.[2] Iyoha (1973) applied a similar conceptual framework in constructing an inter-temporal stochastic model of a small economy, which he solved for the optimal policies by dynamic programming in a series of simulation exercises. The behaviour of reserves is then determined simultaneously with the whole range of macro-economic and adjustment policies. Iyoha's results confirm that optimal reserves are a positive function of export instability and the rate of interest on reserves. He also concluded that adjustment via deflation is more costly than that via import restriction, but the generality of this is critically dependent on his assumption that deflation does nothing to improve competitiveness even in the long run.

[1] In a growing economy, fundamental equilibrium would be characterised by the possibility of setting $E(\epsilon_t)$ equal to the desired long-run rate of reserve growth.

[2] One puzzle is the relation between Niehans' concepts of marginal utility and marginal cost and the shadow price of reserves that would be thrown up by solving the relevant inter-temporal model.

There is a distinguished list of sceptics who are unconvinced of the possibility of providing rational explanations of reserve-holding behaviour, either in terms of the R/M measure or of the preceding optimising models. Perhaps the most common criticism, made particularly forcefully by Yeager (1959) and Sohmen in I.M.F. (1970), is that liquidity requirements depend critically upon the adjustment policies pursued. In the extreme case of freely floating exchange rates with no official intervention of any kind, there would be no need for reserves, except perhaps as a " war chest "; more generally, the need for reserves will decline as exchange rate flexibility increases. In the presence of capital mobility the need for reserves depends on the willingness to direct monetary policy to external aims and the willingness to thwart capital flows by controls; if capital flows were sufficiently great the variability of current account imbalances might be of insignificant importance. Machlup (1966) must also be ranked as a sceptic: having demonstrated that the ratios of reserves to a wide range of possible explanatory variables showed vast international variations, he suggested that the demand of central bankers for reserves, like that of women for clothes, is a simple desire for a little more than last year (the " Mrs. Machlup's Wardrobe Theory "). It is paradoxical that the economist who so vigorously resisted the suggestion that businessmen are satisficers should have so readily assumed that central bankers are! The sceptics also include Clower and Lipsey (1968), who seem to assume that systematic analysis must necessarily be restricted to analysing the reserves needed to finance regular and random current-account fluctuations; this would mean excluding the role of reserves in financing capital-account imbalances, adjustments to fundamental disequilibria, and speculative flows. In fact, much of the quantitative work includes the capital account. In a world such as ours, where speculative flows are largely the product of expectations of parity changes, this provides a double reason for wanting to see fundamental disequilibria incorporated into the analyses. Only time will tell whether this will be rewarding in practice, but there seems no reason for dismissing it as impossible in principle. Niehans' scepticism (I.M.F. (1970)) stems from the fact that, having outlined the context he deemed proper for analysing the problem, he concluded that the difficulties it posed were too intractable to raise hopes of useful results. Flanders (1971) found that her empirical results were a " dismal failure," and therefore became a sceptic on empirical grounds.

Whether this scepticism is justified can be sensibly decided only after reviewing the empirical results that have been obtained. The variables that have emerged as important in the optimising models are some measure of payments variability, the propensity to import, and the opportunity cost of holding reserves. In addition, it is of interest to examine the present status of the hypothesis that the demand for reserves varies with imports.

There are now six studies that have used some measure of payments variability to attempt to explain the demand for reserves. Kenen and

Yudin (1965) used $\hat{\sigma}_\epsilon$, along with $\hat{\bar{\epsilon}}$ and $\hat{\rho}$. They found that $\hat{\sigma}_\epsilon$ had the expected (positive) sign and was highly significant, while $\hat{\rho}$ had the right (positive) sign but was insignificant and $\hat{\bar{\epsilon}}$ was insignificant with the wrong (*i.e.*, positive) sign. This may have been the result of a simultaneity problem, since a country with an underlying surplus is likely to accumulate a high level of reserves despite its *willingness* to see these run down. Clark (1970b) first estimated an equation

$$R_t = \gamma R^*_t + (1 - \gamma) R_{t-1} + \epsilon_t$$

to test the hypothesis that countries did respond to departures of R_t from a target level. (R^*_t was assumed to be growing at a constant rate, so that the actual estimating equation contained a constant term, time, and R_{t-1}.) He used monthly data for 38 countries over the period 1958–67. His results were rather satisfactory, γ being in the expected range between 0 and 1 in 37 cases out of 38, and significantly different from zero in 21 cases despite the fact that γ was, as common sense would suggest, usually rather small. His estimate of σ_ϵ was then used in a cross-country regression analysis to explain average reserves and proved highly significant, even after the data were deflated by the value of trade to prevent spurious correlation due to size. Streeter (1970) used the standard deviation of the change in reserves, and again found a significant coefficient with an elasticity close to unity. Kelly (1970), using data for 46 countries over 13 years, employed the standard deviation of exports (which has the advantage of reducing the simultaneity problem posed by the fact that some parts of the payments balance—*e.g.*, imports—are influenced by adjustment policies rather than being exogenous as supposed in the theory, though this advantage is bought at the cost of ignoring other causes of instability), again with a significant positive result and an elasticity close to the predicted value of unity. Frenkel in Aliber (1974), with data covering 55 countries for 5 years, used the trend-adjusted average absolute reserve change, and found significant positive elasticities of around 0·5. Frenkel (1972) found the relationship held for both developed countries and less-developed countries considered as two separate groups; the effect of variability was greater for the developed countries. The only failure to find a significant relationship was that of Flanders (1971), who used several measures of export instability and also $\sigma_R/\bar{R}$ in attempting to explain R/M. It should be noted that, while the results of Kenen and Yudin, Streeter, and Kelly could simply be spurious correlation with size (so that imports would work just as well, as Flanders found), both Clark and Frenkel allowed for this and found that variability made an independent contribution to explaining the demand for reserves. These results seem to provide adequate evidence to recommend the sceptics to reconsider their position.

The second variable which the optimising models suggest to be relevant is the propensity to import. It has generally been argued that it is the

marginal propensity that is theoretically relevant, but Frenkel in Aliber
(1974) derived the relationship using the average propensity, and this
has in fact invariably been used in empirical work. It was included in
their cross-section multivariate regressions by Clark, Streeter, Kelly and
Frenkel. All of them found that the propensity to import tends to be
positively associated with reserve holding, rather than negatively associated
as their theoretical models (Frenkel's excepted) would suggest. But this
does not necessarily refute the hypothesis that reserve behaviour is rationally
determined. It could be taken as evidence that expenditure-switching
policies play a more important role than expenditure-changing policies in
effecting adjustment. Alternatively, Clark (1970b, p. 592) has pointed out
that this would also be rational if payments shocks originate primarily
from domestic rather than external sources. A third possible explanation
is that the import propensity acts as a proxy for the openness of the economy
and, therefore, its susceptibility to external disturbances (Cooper (1968),
pp. 629–30).

The third variable to have been widely tested is the opportunity cost of
reserve holding. Various proxies for this, such as the growth rate and the
interest rate on reserves (Flanders), the domestic bond rate (Streeter), *per
capita* income (Clark and Kelly) and international indebtedness (Kelly), have
been tried, with uniform lack of success. Possible explanations are that the
proxies chosen are not good ones, that there is not in fact sufficient variation
in the opportunity cost of reserve holding to permit statistical estimation,
and that the interest elasticity of demand for reserves is low.

The question that remains is whether the growth of trade will raise the
demand for reserves. There cannot really be serious doubt that it will:
even Flanders' otherwise-negative results yielded a significant coefficient
for imports, while Frenkel found that both the level of imports and the
variability of payments made independent contributions.[1] The controversial question is whether demand can be expected to grow in proportion
to trade. All of the optimising models [2] agree that reserve demand should
grow in proportion to the standard deviation of the inherent instability of
the payments balance. The question therefore becomes whether payments
imbalances tend to grow in line with the level of trade. Salant (in Murphy
(1964), p. 22) argued that there was an *a priori* assumption of such proportionate growth unless countries are constrained by decreasing reserve ease
into adjusting more rapidly, while Cooper (1968) argued that *ex ante* disturbances were likely to grow more rapidly because of the trend to increasing
international integration. On the other hand, Olivera (1969) derived a
square root law, analogous to the Baumol–Tobin theorem on the demand for

[1] The statistical results of Courchene and Youssef (1967) and Thorn (1967) might be cited as
additional evidence, but their use of time-series analysis to explain the holdings of a buffer stock
whose control is indirect and subject to very long lags seems quite misplaced. See Niehans in
I.M.F. (1970), pp. 77–8.

[2] Except that of Streeter, but his model building appears to be deficient.

money (although relying on a different rationale), which stated that the demand for reserves would grow in proportion to the square root of trade.[1] Similarly, Streissler (1969) used results from the theory of stochastic processes to demonstrate the existence of scale economies in reserve holding.

The empirical evidence on the point is also pretty mixed. Archibald and Richmond (1971) postulated and estimated a constant rate of growth of the standard deviation of the payments disturbance term; they found evidence of such growth for all countries except one, but their techniques precluded derivation of point estimates and their range of growth rates between 0·5% *per annum* and 10% *per annum* is too wide to be very useful. Rhomberg (1966) found that there was no evidence that imbalances were growing less rapidly than trade, but Bhattacharya (1968) argued that this conclusion involved brushing aside evidence of a structural break in 1958. A subsequent Fund study which updated Rhomberg's work to 1968 found that imbalances had grown considerably less rapidly than imports (4·2% *per annum* against 7·3% *per annum*—I.M.F. (1970), pp. 475, 481). Bhattacharya found no correlation between imbalances and trade, which is an extreme result that is unsupported elsewhere. Kelly (1970) found that export variance had grown at 5·8% *per annum* as against 7·6% *per annum* for imports—and his reserve-demand function is dominated by the imbalances term. Frenkel in Aliber (1974) found an elasticity of about 0·6 on imports and 0·5 on imbalances; allowing for the fact that increased trade will also increase imbalances, these figures imply that scale economies exist if imbalances grow at less than 80% of the rate of trade growth. Finally, Flanders' coefficient relating reserves and imports was close to unity (1971, p. 47). All things considered, therefore, Polak's judgment (I.M.F. (1970), p. 512) that the ratio of the rates of growth of payments fluctuations to trade is unlikely to be greatly below unity (" or, say 0·8 ") is rather brave.

2. *The Composition of Reserves*

The dilemma of the gold-exchange standard as posed by Triffin (1960) was that either liquidity would become progressively more inadequate as elimination of the United States deficit restricted reserve growth to the net supply of new gold, or else a continued deficit would lead to a progressive deterioration in the United States reserve ratio, thereby undermining confidence in the dollar and eventually provoking massive attempts to convert dollars into gold with the result that the system would again collapse as it did in 1931. The first part of Triffin's thesis, the need for increasing liquidity over time, stimulated the literature on the demand for reserves that was reviewed in the previous section. The danger of the system collapsing through attempts to alter the composition of reserves has also provoked a

---

[1] The scale economies apply only to increased trade volumes, and not to increased trade values caused by inflation.

considerable theoretical and empirical literature, which forms the subject matter of the present section.

A formal model of the development of the gold-exchange standard as envisaged by Triffin was constructed by Kenen (1960). He postulated a world in which reserves consisted exclusively of gold (G) and dollars (D), and in which countries other than the United States determined the composition of their reserves according to a simple portfolio theory. Specifically, he assumed that their desired ratio of dollars to total reserves (D/R) was an increasing function of the interest rate on dollars and a decreasing function of the risk of a devaluation of the dollar against gold, and he took as a proxy for the latter the ratio of D to the United States gold stock. He then inquired how the system would evolve over time if interest rates were constant and the American deficit were large enough to satisfy the reserve-accumulation objectives of the rest of the world so as to prevent a liquidity shortage materialising. He showed that, even if desired reserve growth exceeds the increment in the supply of monetary gold, collapse is not inevitable. If the ratio of incremental gold supplies to desired reserve growth, dG/dR, exceeds a certain critical value (less than unity), then the ratio of the global gold stock to rest-of-world reserves (G/R) would approach dG/dR and the system could expand without the United States reserve ratio declining beyond a certain acceptable level. But he did not argue that this possibility provided much reassurance. The probability of collapse is greater the higher are reserve-accumulation objectives and the lower is the supply of new gold; it is increased by introducing foreign private dollar holdings into the analysis; and a stable growth path is impossible if countries want to accumulate reserves at a constant compound (rather than absolute) rate of growth unless the supply of gold is also growing at the same compound rate. This theory therefore leads to a strong presumption that the gold-exchange standard will not be viable indefinitely.

The model has been embellished by later writers, notably Gilbert (1968), who divided the development of the gold-exchange standard into four Rostovian stages: that of adequate new gold, a shortage of new gold, zero growth of monetary gold, and negative new monetary gold. He was particularly concerned to emphasise that the later stages would bring severe problems of inconsistency of countries' payments objectives.

An alternative to the portfolio theory has become known as the " signalling theory." An early trace of it can be found in Posthuma (1963), who argued both that the economic function of the right to convert dollars into gold was to enable Europe to goad the United States into adjustment, and also that actual conversion would be dictated by " sound banking principles " (meaning the portfolio theory). There is no such half-hearted compromise in the writing of the theory's chief expositor, Mundell (1968, Chapter 20). He assumed that Europe's portfolio choice is determined by its views as to whether world income should expand or contract. A desire to restrict income is signalled to the United States by conversion of dollars into gold. This forces the United States to restrict monetary expansion so as to restore its reserve ratio, and since United States monetary policy is viewed as determining world income this has the effect the Europeans desire. But Mundell shows that " assigning " income stabilisation to Europe and maintenance of the United States reserve ratio to America could result in instability. Reversing the assignment—requiring the United States to select a monetary policy appropriate to the needs of world income stabilisation, while Europe selects a dollar/gold reserve mix that will maintain the United States reserve ratio—results in strong stability. But as Whitman noted in her Comment on Mundell's paper in Mundell and Swoboda (1969), this amounts in substance to Europe abdicating a role in income stabilisation by passively validating the monetary policy chosen by the United States, as under a dollar standard. Niehans in Johnson and Swoboda (1973) argued that the essence of the gold-exchange standard is that Europe indeed abandons any control (other than through consultations with the United States) over short-run monetary policy, but that it retains the right to exercise gold convertibility as a constraint on secular inflation. A pure gold standard leaves no degree of freedom to monetary policy; a pure dollar standard places no restraint on United States monetary policy; the gold-exchange standard is viewed as a sophisticated compromise in which Europeans are willing to engage in perfect substitution between gold and dollars within certain limits, which provides a certain range of flexibility to accommodate short-run monetary policies. But the system is not consistent with secular inflation, because that results in the supply of monetary gold growing less rapidly than all other variables of the system and therefore in the acceptable limits on reserve composition ultimately being violated. This can be viewed as its strength, if one believes that monetary policy both can restrain secular inflation and should be used for that purpose, or its weakness, if one doubts the ability of monetary policy to restrain inflation at an acceptable cost or the willingness of the United States to be constrained.

A different form of signalling theory has been advanced by S. D. Cohen (1970), a political scientist who studied the S.D.R. negotiations as a case study in international relations. He argued that the European preference for holding gold was an essentially political phenomenon explained by a desire for power and disregard for income. He interpreted power as the ability to avoid being obliged to pursue adjustment policies, so that the European motive in converting dollars into gold was that of furthering a long-run campaign to restore symmetry to the adjustment process.

A third theory starts out by questioning the assumption, which is particularly important in the portfolio theory, that countries act independently in determining their reserve-composition policies, rather than recognising their interdependence. Kenen (1963a) first suggested that the major reserve holders might be modifying their policies to reduce the danger of the system collapsing. Both Johnson (1967, p. 25) and Machlup (1968a, p. 100) claimed that the dominant concern of the large countries is avoidance of a confidence crisis; Sohmen (in I.M.F. (1970), p. 29) termed the traditional concern that central banks would try to switch into gold the " lemming syndrome." The most ambitious attempt to formalise these ideas is to be found in the second of two papers by Officer and Willett (1969) (1970). They assume that the utility functions of the major countries have as components both the disutility of the system collapsing (u) and the disutility of abandoning optimal portfolio-management policies (v). Each country seeks to minimise the expected value of disutility $= pu + (1 - p)v$, where p is the probability that their individual action will provoke collapse. (The probability that the system will collapse irrespective of their action is one of the determinants of v.) The main implication of the model is that the survival prospects of the gold-exchange standard are (or were) better than suggested by the traditional portfolio model, because an increase in the " v-incentive " for gold conversion would be accompanied by an increase in p, and might therefore prompt the adoption of a more conservative strategy. The system can become more stable deeper in the " crisis zone " because of a reduction in the scope for successful " free riding."

The other important topic concerns the effect on the system of introducing S.D.R.s. The subject was first taken up by Aliber (1967). He adopted the portfolio theory; assumed that the new reserve unit (N.R.U.) would be a closer substitute for the dollar than for gold, since he thought it would be likely to pay interest but not have a gold-value guarantee; and also assumed that the N.R.U. would be a preferable reserve asset to the dollar, because it would carry a guarantee against a dollar devaluation unaccompanied by a general gold revaluation. Gresham's Law would therefore lead to N.R.U.s displacing dollars in official portfolios. This would produce a viable system (though one that need not be in the United States interest), provided that the N.R.U. was sufficiently attractive relative to gold to prevent the rate of N.R.U. creation having to be depressed below the desirable level in order to preserve confidence in the gold/N.R.U. exchange rate. In a Comment, Goldstein (1969) took up a point that Aliber had relegated to a footnote: the possibility that S.D.R.s (as N.R.U.s had by then solidified into) would be better substitutes for gold than for dollars and so decrease the perceived risk of a dollar devaluation and increase the attractiveness of dollar holding. Aliber's Reply (1969b) suggested there was no convincing reason for assuming one thing rather than the other about comparative substitutability, but Hirsch (1971) argued that the gold denomination and low interest yield of S.D.R.s are likely to make them a considerably closer substitute for gold than dollars. He developed a theme first introduced by Holtrop in I.M.F. (1961, pp. 114–15), who argued that the willingness of central banks to hold a mixed portfolio of gold and dollars was conditional on the existence of uncertainty as to future changes in the price of gold.

An infinitely-elastic supply of gold substitute at the existing price would eliminate any fear (or hope) of gold revaluation and consequently any motive for holding gold in preference to interest-bearing dollars. If the S.D.R. did not dominate both the dollar and gold, an S.D.R. standard (in which S.D.R.s constitute the bulk of the reserve stock) on the lines anticipated by Aliber (1969b) would be unlikely to develop. Rather, Hirsch argued, S.D.R.s would mainly be absorbed by the reserve centres, and their rate of creation would in the long run be governed by the need to give the reserve centres enough reserves to preserve confidence. In short, the world would move to an S.D.R.-exchange standard, unless action was taken to make S.D.R.s more attractive relative to reserve currencies.

Attempts at empirical testing have centred on the portfolio theory: advocates of the other theories have preferred enunciation to demonstration. But some evidence has been accumulated as a by-product of the tests of the portfolio theory.

The first study was that of Kenen (1963a). He used quarterly data covering 61 countries during the 1950s. He tried to discover whether countries aimed (a) to hold the bulk of their reserves in gold with a mere working balance in foreign exchange; (b) to hold gold and foreign exchange in constant proportions; or (c) to hold a basic reserve in gold (a " war chest "?) and the bulk in foreign exchange. The first pattern implies a large, and the third pattern a small, marginal propensity to hold gold. The evidence proved ambiguous. There was little sign of the proportionality pattern (b), but some evidence for both of the other patterns. The majority of countries appeared to fall in class (c), but the working-balance hypothesis fared much better when a stock-adjustment model was specified. Kenen also investigated whether there had been a trend towards increased gold holding during the 1950s, and found some evidence that there had. Finally, he used both his estimates of the reserve composition of individual countries and a set of conditional frequencies of gold purchases and sales to test whether central banks participated in the gold rush during the fourth quarter of 1960. He found fairly strong evidence that the peripheral central banks participated, but the major central banks did not and may even have been particularly restrained in their gold-conversion policy. This conclusion was endorsed by Høst-Madsen (1964), who found that the actual gold outflow from the United States to 12 high-reserve countries in the fourth quarter of 1960 was in line with the prediction derived from extrapolating average reserve-holding behaviour in the past, despite the presence of special circumstances that would have suggested an above-average loss of gold.

Greene in Kenen and Lawrence (1968) started off by updating Kenen's approach. She recalculated Kenen's individual country equations for the Group of Ten (plus Switzerland minus United States) for the sub-period 1957(1)–1960(3) with similar results to his, except for the absence of any trend towards gold. She repeated the estimation for 1960(4)–1964(2) and again found evidence of restraint in gold purchases in 1960(4), and also in 1961(1); in addition, the recomputed equations showed a poorer fit, lower propensities to buy gold, and lower predicted gold purchases for given reserve changes than in the earlier period. The analysis was then extended into the first real portfolio model. Gold purchases were postulated to be dependent on the difference between a target gold stock and current gold holdings, and the target was initially postulated to be a function of the level of reserves, time, United States interest rates and working-balance requirements. Reasonably satisfactory results were reported for 8 of the 10 countries; they suggested the absence of a trend towards gold (and a fall-off after 1960), weak interest elasticity and the importance of working-balance requirements. Efforts to introduce a proxy for the risk of dollar devaluation (the United States deficit, gold loss and reserve ratio) proved unsuccessful. Her major finding is substantial evidence of a shift towards restraint, of the sort discussed by Officer and Willett, after 1960.

Another portfolio model was estimated by Hagemann (1969). He computed stock-adjustment equations for 11 major countries on quarterly data between the " early 1950s " and 1965(4), trying a wide range of explanatory variables. Like the other investigators, he found overwhelming evidence that adjustment was far from instantaneous. He found the United States reserve ratio to be highly significant in all cases, while the interest rate was significant in only two. United States short-term assets and liabilities (an alternative proxy for the weakness of the dollar) were significant in five cases, and the long-term debt position in two. The foreign-exchange position of a country's commercial banks was significant in three cases (with foreign indebtedness tending to increase the holdings of dollars). The United States deficit was significant only for Japan, which tends to contradict Mundell's version of the signalling theory. Reserve composition was close to the computed values in 1960(4), except for Spain. Unfortunately there was no test of the hypothesis that portfolio behaviour underwent a longer-run shift towards restraint in 1960, but evidence of a shift *towards* gold in 1965 was found (presumably attributable to uncertainties over Vietnam and sterling). Hagemann also computed a cross-sectional model explaining the percentage of reserves held in dollars by 18 major countries in 1964. He found a strong negative relationship between United States direct investment and the proportion of reserves held in dollars, thus providing some empirical support for one version of the signalling theory. There was also a positive relation with United States portfolio investment, the current-account deficit, exports to the reserve-currency countries, G.N.P., and G.N.P. *per capita* and a negative relation to Reserves/G.N.P.

Stekler and Piekarz (1970) also estimated a stock-adjustment portfolio model for 12 major reserve holders using annual data over the period 1951–66. They assumed that the need for working balances rose in proportion to the square root of imports; this must be considered questionable in view of the meagre support for the square root law noted in II.1. Changes in the gold proportion were primarily attributed to the increasing reserve adequacy that this measure implied, with significant contributions from the United States reserve ratio (as a proxy for the risk factor) for three countries and interest rates for only one country.

Yet another stock-adjustment portfolio model was estimated by Makin (1971a). This has two novel features: the use of a cubic utility function (the intuitive appeal of which is not universal), and use of the forward premium on gold futures in Zürich as a measure of the expected return on gold. The model was estimated for 13 countries using monthly data over the period 1961–68. The variables suggested by the cubic utility function, the variance and the skewness of the return on gold, did not perform impressively, although skewness was significant in three cases. But the return on dollars and the expected return on gold both proved highly significant. Neither the United States deficit nor United States inflation had any explanatory power, which would again seem to refute Mundell's version of the signalling theory. In another paper, Makin (1971b) found that the expected return on gold had a significant effect in inducing countries to add to their holdings of gold substitutes in the form of swaps and Roosa bonds.

The evidence would therefore suggest that rational portfolio-management considerations play a considerable role in determining the composition of reserves. But there is also evidence, largely from Greene's work—no-one else has sought to retest the question—that co-operative restraint of the sort hypothesised by Officer and Willett has played a role in modifying behaviour. There is also some evidence that gold acquisition policy is influenced by the desire to signal displeasure to the United States, but none to confirm that the initiating factor is short-term United States monetary policy.

It is pleasing to reflect that anyone who had made a careful survey of the empirical literature would have been led to conclude that the gold-exchange standard would have been unlikely to survive the strains to which it was subjected by the United States deficit of 1970–71. It is even more pleasing to reflect that the long-predicted breakdown of the system in August 1971 did not bring in its wake the descent into economic warfare that had sometimes been predicted. The co-operative instincts were not strong enough to prevent breakdown, but they were strong enough to prevent breakdown turning into disaster.

One final reflection on this subject concerns the fact that all of the reported empirical work concerns dollar holdings. But the world still contains a second reserve currency, and it is one whose varied experiences over the past decade—speculative runs, devaluation, dollar guarantees and floating—should provide an ideal set of data to test the portfolio theory. It is to be hoped that serious work on this subject will be attempted.

3. *The Supply of Reserves*

From the Genoa Conference of 1922 until quite recently there may well have been more written about the supply of reserves than about any other single topic covered in the present survey.   Much of this material is now of rather limited interest, owing to the recent revolution in the reserve-supply mechanism constituted by the introduction of S.D.R.s and its (arguable) consequence, the splitting of the monetary and private gold markets agreed in Washington in March 1968.   The fact that one component of the nominal supply of reserves is under conscious international control means that the most interesting questions about reserve supply are now the normative questions discussed in III.4 rather than the positive questions of the present section.

The Genoa Conference was convened because of the " shortage " of gold.   The gold scarcity arose because of the desire to restore the pre-war gold standard with largely unchanged parities despite the intervening inflation.   The suggested solution was to economise on gold, partly by supplementing gold reserves by convertible foreign exchange and partly by withdrawing gold from monetary circulation.   From then on the supply of monetary gold was a topic of regular interest, with fears of scarcity in the 1920s giving way to concern over the " golden avalanche " that eventually resulted from the gold revaluation of the 1930s.   Concern over a possible gold shortage re-emerged in the 1950s: the results of a careful survey of the probable future supply of monetary gold by Altman (1958) were adopted by Triffin (1960) in his prognosis of a future liquidity shortage resulting from termination of the United States deficit.   By the late 1960s there seemed to be a consensus that production had peaked so long as the price remained at $35 per ounce (Busschau (1967), Briffaux (1968), Hirsch (1968)).   Machlup (1969) maintained that output still exceeded non-speculative private demand by a wide margin, but subsequent assessment (Fells (1972)) suggests that the rapid expansion in the demand for gold for fabrication resulted in private non-speculative demand for gold overtaking output in 1968, the year of the Washington Agreement.   If this is so it implies that the free-market price of gold will remain in excess of the monetary price, so there will be no significant accretions to the stock of monetary gold even through the Agreement of December 30, 1969, between the Fund and South Africa.   Neither will there be significant decreases in the stock of monetary gold so long as the two-tier system continues to be observed in its present form.   Gold will remain a constant element in reserves.

Reserves are also provided through the I.M.F.   Since 1970 the Fund has provided unconditional liquidity to (most of) its members in the form of S.D.R.s, in parallel to its traditional activities which are principally directed to the provision of conditional liquidity.   Special Drawing Rights are, as Machlup (1968a) has emphasised, something of a novelty in monetary practice: they are claims that derive their acceptability solely from their transferability to other participants (who are obliged to accept them within specified limits); they dispense with the " fiction of a central debtor " whose liabilities they are and whose assets constitute backing for the claims. However, the force of this innovation is diminished to the extent that the countries initially receiving S.D.R.s are subsequently required to provide the interest servicing. To create S.D.R.s, the Fund credits the accounts of the participating countries in the Special Drawing Account. To use S.D.R.s the account of one country is debited and that of another is credited, with the second providing foreign exchange in one of the major international currencies to the first in return. There are of course a host of technical provisions, which are well described by Machlup (1968a), Polak (1971) and Fleming (1971a), but the basic idea is simple. Since S.D.R.s are created by a decision of the Fund (in quantities which are normally to be determined for five-year periods although the allocations are annual), the supply of S.D.R.s is a topic in normative economics and is deferred to III.5.

The General Account of the Fund exists primarily to provide conditional liquidity to members, but unconditional liquidity is a by-product. Early decisions of the Fund resulted in members' access to their borrowing rights being conditional (contrary to Keynes' proposal), although in 1952 this policy was modified by making access to the gold tranche automatic, and there are also limited provisions for automatic drawings to offset export shortfalls by primary producers (Mookerjee (1966); Horsefield (1969), Vol. II, Chapter 18). Each country has a quota, 25% of which (the gold tranche) is subscribed in gold and 75% (the credit tranche) in its national currency. This subscription gives it a right to borrow (technically, to purchase) foreign exchange up to a value of 125% of its quota, subject to the consent of the Fund. Since consent to withdraw the gold tranche is automatic, the gold tranche is counted as a part of a country's Reserve Position in the Fund and is therefore included in the country's measured reserves. When country A makes a drawing of country B's currency, so that the Fund's holdings of B's currency fall below 75% of quota, B acquires additional claims which are part of its Reserve Position in the Fund. The same is true when B's currency is provided through a loan to the I.M.F. under the General Arrangements to Borrow rather than out of B's quota. Unlike subscriptions of gold, which create Reserve Positions in the Fund at the cost of destroying an equal volume of gold reserves, the creation of Reserve Positions as the counterpart to I.M.F. lending operations results in a net increase in unconditional liquidity, a fact first noted by Ezekiel (1966) in the course of a careful accounting analysis of the system. Thus, in analogy to the rise in the money supply as a result of commercial-bank borrowing from a central bank, reserves increase as a result of an initiative by borrowers (Ahtiala in I.M.F. (1970)). The net result of I.M.F. operations on reserves in the period 1960–69 (together with all other sources of reserve growth) can be found in I.M.F.(1970, pp. 329, 445).

The other reserve component is foreign exchange, which consists principally of dollars. One can distinguish three theories about the mechanism governing the supply of dollar reserves. The traditional theory, expounded by Triffin (1960) and repeated by him and many others on innumerable subsequent occasions, treats the supply of dollars as determined by an essentially capricious United States deficit, minus such portion of that deficit as those accumulating reserves choose (or chose) to convert into gold. The deficit is viewed as capricious in the sense of bearing no systematic relationship to the reserve-accumulation objectives of other countries; it results from a complex of such factors as demand-management policies in the United States and the rest of the world and historically-determined relative cost levels. This is a supply-oriented theory of the supply of dollar reserves.

The second theory is, in contrast, a demand-oriented theory. (The useful distinction between supply- and demand-oriented theories is due to Aliber (1969a)). It was first articulated by Johnson (1964) and subsequently became an integral part of the case for a dollar standard (see in particular Kindleberger (1965); Despres, Kindleberger and Salant (1966); McKinnon (1969); Krause (1970).) The theory claims that the United States deficit is primarily a residual which is determined by the reserve-accumulation desires of the rest of the world; any American effort to reduce the deficit would be countered by adjustment policies on the part of other countries designed to re-establish their desired rate of reserve growth. A measured United States deficit is not necessarily a symptom of disequilibrium but can be a result of mutually-beneficial financial intermediation, and United States capital controls are likely to impede the working of the system by reducing the sensitivity with which the United States " deficit " can respond to the liquidity desires of the rest of the world. This would imply that the ability of the I.M.F. to control the rate of S.D.R. creation will not give it the power to control the total rate of reserve growth, but only to influence reserve composition (McKinnon (1969), p. 28).

A third theory has recently been advanced by Ahtiala in I.M.F. (1970). He treats gold and I.M.F. Reserve Positions as international base money and foreign-exchange reserves as derivative liquidity; if one assumes that the peripheral countries maintain a constant ratio of base to derivative liquidity and the reserve centres maintain a constant ratio of liabilities to (base) assets, a given quantity of derivative liquidity will result from a given level of base liquidity through a monetary expansion process analogous to the customary bank deposit multiplier. This theory evidently requires that the deficit of the reserve centre be supply-determined and adjusted with a view to maintaining its assets/liabilities ratio at the desired level. Ahtiala does not claim that there is likely to be sufficiently sensitive control of payments positions to result in great stability of the assets/liabilities ratio, but the existence of some forces making for such stability is essential to the theory. Causal empiricism would not seem to provide much support for such stability, but the hypothesis perhaps deserves more serious empirical investigation.

Mundell (1971, Chapter 16) suggested that the supply-oriented and demand-oriented theories could be reconciled by recognising that the United States deficit will be influenced by the rate of credit expansion relative to real growth [1] in both the United States and the rest of the world, with the supply-oriented theory emphasising the dependence on United States actions and the demand-oriented theory emphasising dependence on rest-of-world policy. This misses the point; the supply-oriented theory has never adopted the absurd position of claiming that the United States deficit was immune to European actions, but simply contended that the deficit was not a mere reflection of the liquidity desires of the rest of the world. In the normal classification Mundell's model falls squarely in the supply-oriented category.[2] Since simple reconciliation of the two theories fails, there is a need to discriminate between them on the basis of empirical evidence. Unfortunately the available evidence is somewhat meagre. Aliber (1969a) went the furthest in assembling evidence for the demand-oriented theory, pointing to the fact that the series of measures taken during the 1960s to remedy the deficit had failed (but so did British measures prior to devaluation!). He also claimed that few countries had had larger reserve increases than they desired (which was more convincing in 1969 than subsequently), and that the sum of desired reserve accretions exceeded the reserve growth that would have occurred without the United States deficit. Williamson (1971) argued, on the basis of a casual inspection of the time series on the United States deficit, that it showed every sign of being supply-determined in the short run, but conceded that it was probably influenced by the desire for reserves in the long run. Machlup (1968b) examined the statistical record much more deeply and concluded that marginal changes in net financial flows had consistently led to variations in real transfers almost as large; however, there remained a persistent transfer gap of something under $2·5 billion. He attributed this gap to United States monetary policy being relaxed prematurely whenever the deficit was significantly reduced (a supply-determined theory), and demonstrated that the facts seemed consistent with this interpretation. But he did not consider the alternative possibility that foreign policies were tightened whenever the rate of foreign reserve growth declined (the demand-determined theory). The question is therefore still open.

There remain three secondary questions concerning the supply of foreign-exchange reserves. The first is the influence of the Euro-dollar

---

[1] These are the only factors conceded to have any important influence on the payments outcome in the monetarist world.

[2] Oppenheimer suggested verbally an alternative reconciliation: that the deficit is the maximum of that which would be suggested by the demand-determined and supply-determined theories, since the rest of the world would adjust to eliminate inadequate reserve growth but would passively accept a growth rate in excess of this minimum.

market on the supply of reserves. This seems to have been discussed first by Mayer (1970, p. 13), who reasoned that a switch of reserves from New York to the Euro-dollar market would result in the sum switched being loaned by the Euro-dollar banks and thence converted into non-dollar currencies, so that the supply of reserves would rise by the amount of the switch. However, Hirsch (1972) concluded that in normal circumstances the supply of reserves would rise by rather less than the sum switched, because of leakages caused by lending to United States borrowers and because conversion into non-dollar currencies involves the Euro-dollar borrowers holding an open position between dollars and local currency. The second topic is the effect of activated swaps in increasing the reserves of the creditor: this became an important source of reserve growth in the late 1960s: (see Gilbert in Bosman and von Geusau (1970), Fleming in I.M.F. (1970) especially pp. 340–1). The increase in the creditor's reserves (of a sort commonly regarded as qualitatively inferior to other reserve assets) is a by-product of reserve borrowing, as with reserve borrowing from the Fund. The third topic concerns the supply of secondary reserve currencies, notably the pound sterling. Hirsch (1974) pointed out that, now that all the secondary reserve centres hold the bulk of their marginal reserves in dollars, a shift of reserves to such a centre (even from the Euro-dollar market) will add an extra layer to the reserve currency pyramid and thereby expand the volume of reserves. Total sterling holdings are presumably demand determined, by the interaction of the total reserve holdings and the portfolio policies of the Overseas Sterling Area. (This does not mean that the United Kingdom deficit is demand-determined, because sterling is merely a regional rather than a global reserve currency.) In the absence of any systematic knowledge of O.S.A. portfolio policies it is difficult to say more.

4. *Reserves and Adjustment*

The subjects just discussed were the mechanisms that govern the supply of nominal reserves. But there is a school of thought, originated by Yeager (1959) and recently developed by Johnson in I.M.F. (1970) and Mundell (1971), which argues that control of the nominal supply of reserves may be no more effective in providing control of the level of real reserves than control of a country's nominal money supply is in exerting control over the real stock of money. Those who regard the quantity theory of money as a general equilibrium theory which predicts that changes in the money supply will (except in the very short run) affect prices rather than output will find it natural to refer to this as the international quantity theory. The questions it raises are (1) whether an inequality between the demand for and supply of reserves precipitates payments adjustment; (2) what forms such adjustment takes; and (3) what implications these adjustment mechanisms have for the operation of the international monetary system. These questions involve some trespassing into the province of balance-of-payments theory, but they do not require detailed consideration of the mechanisms involved.

The international quantity theory assumes that reserve changes still have a dominant influence on national monetary policies, as prescribed by the gold-standard " rules of the game." The assumption that payments adjustment is prompted, with considerable reliability, by reserve changes can also be based on other grounds; in particular, it is implied by the existence of a well-defined demand-for-reserves function of the character postulated by Clark (1970a, b) and Kelly (1970), and by the view of most of the dollar-standard proponents that countries other than the United States can and normally do achieve their reserve targets (see e.g., McKinnon (1969) and Krause (1970)). The opposing view is not that reserves *never* precipitate adjustment—that would clearly be an untenable hypothesis, since the threat of reserve depletion compels adjustment, at least for non-reserve-currency countries—but that reserves constitute a *constraint* rather than an *objective*. This view was expressed forcefully by Machlup (1966); Mrs. Machlup is indifferent to the size and growth rate of her wardrobe, provided the latter is positive. Similarly, Corden constructed a model in Mundell and Swoboda (1969) which postulated that policy is directed solely to the preservation of " internal balance " unless this is infeasible due to reserve depletion. A number of other writers, including Triffin (1968, p. 89), have expressed the view that the reserve level is not a high-priority target so long as it exceeds a critical minimum.

Compromise views are of course possible. In his comprehensive review of the effects of reserves on adjustment, Cooper in I.M.F. (1970) lists the various possible reactions to a reserve change and includes the possibility that some countries (" reserve taps " or " reserve sinks ") will not in fact react, at least over a wide range of reserve levels. An alternative compromise might argue that reserves act only as a constraint in the short run, but that long-run adjustment policies (defined as those intended to influence $E(\epsilon_t)$) are directed towards the maintenance of target reserve levels.

The second question is what form adjustment takes, when it occurs. The traditional way of handling this question is to list the various forms that adjustment can take; careful taxonomies can be found in the papers by Cooper and Rhomberg in I.M.F. (1970). (It is generally agreed that the major effects of reserve changes arise indirectly as a result of the attention paid to reserves in the formulation of government policy, although Rhomberg also mentions that reserves can have a direct effect on payments flows by influencing confidence.) Any such list would include higher domestic demand, lower interest rates, revaluation, and relaxation of restrictions on the import of goods and the export of capital, among the responses to a gain in reserves; any of the opposite responses might be prompted by a reserve loss. Further possibilities, like the level of aid and the extent to which it is tied, can be added, although these are often subsumed in the " restrictions " category.

Two types of asymmetries in the adjustment process have been postulated; both of these have important implications for the way in which the international monetary system operates.   The first, which advocates of a dollar standard generally believe is important, is an asymmetry between the United States and the rest of the world (R.O.W.).   The R.O.W. can and does adjust by one or more of the above mechanisms, with interest rates characteristically given pride of place as the weapon permitting sensitive control of reserve levels.   But, partly because the United States sets the world level of interest rates while other countries essentially select interest differentials (Despres, Kindleberger and Salant (1966)) and partly because the United States is presumed to be unable to influence its exchange rate *vis-à-vis* other currencies, the United States lacks the power to adjust its balance of payments, which is demand-determined.[1]   The theory implies that the supply of reserves adjusts to the demand for them.

The second asserted asymmetry is between the response of a reserve-gaining and that of a reserve-losing country.   This is based on the fact that there is some definite limit to the sustainable reserve loss, set by the threat of reserve depletion; whereas there is no (relevant) limit to the reserves a country can accumulate.   The assumption is therefore commonly made that a country gaining reserves is under less pressure to adjust than one losing reserves (*e.g.*, Cooper in I.M.F. (1970)), which imposes a deflationary bias on the system if adjustment takes place via income changes or a devaluation bias if adjustment takes the form of exchange-rate changes. The presumption that an asymmetry in possibilities or motives is sufficient to produce an asymmetry in behaviour has been challenged by Roper (1972). His model assumed that the authorities prefer operating with a below-equilibrium exchange rate for two reasons: because of the greater political muscle of producer interests as opposed to consumer interests, and because reserve shortages impose greater penalties than excess reserves.   Despite this, equilibrium in his model is only attained when the exchange rate is in equilibrium, for the obvious reason that a sub-equilibrium exchange rate implies a payments surplus and is therefore not consistent with equilibrium. As reserves accumulate, the country is eventually persuaded to abandon its attachment to undervaluation by the growing resource waste that is involved. The system provides additional reserves either because the supply of reserves is demand-determined or because the real value of reserves is bid up by successive devaluations (or, in principle, by price deflation).   A devaluation bias—or a deflationary bias—is therefore an inherently transitory phenomenon, and whether it—or its opposite, a revaluation bias—is present at a particular point in time depends on the existing size of the real reserve

---

[1] Rueff (1961) agrees that there is an important asymmetry, but argues that it is not caused by the United States deficit being demand-determined, but by the fact that a United States deficit does not cause a contraction of the United States credit base because the dollars continue to be held in New York.

stock relative to the effective demand for reserves as influenced *inter alia* by the supposed causes of an inherent devaluation bias. Perhaps the only circumstances in which the system *qua* system—as opposed to the current supply of reserves—imposes a bias is when a reserve centre exploits a reserve-currency standard by pursuing inflationary policies designed to secure an " inflation tax " (Mundell (1971), pp. 145, 160), in which case the bias is an inflationary or revaluation bias.

Asymmetries aside, the reaction of the system to an excess demand for, or supply of, reserves will depend on which of the several possible adjustment mechanisms is in fact typically employed. The theorising which has been done on this topic tends to assume that only one mechanism will be involved. The best known of the theories, the international quantity theory, assumes that reserve changes influence monetary policy on gold-standard lines and that monetary policy produces changes in nominal income that reflect price rather than quantity changes except in the very short run. The principal conclusion of the theory is that the real level of reserves cannot be manipulated through variations in the quantity of nominal reserves created because of the reactions of those confronted with excess or deficient reserve holdings. It is further argued that an increase in the rate of nominal reserve creation need not, in the long run, lead to an increase in reserve ease but is more likely to do the reverse (Mundell (1971), Chapter 14). The logic is that reserve creation leads to monetary authorities trying to dispose of the excess reserves they now find themselves holding, which they do by inflating. This is assumed to drive down the real return on reserve-holding and therefore to *reduce* the real level of reserves the authorities wish to hold. In the new equilibrium, when the system has adjusted to a faster rate of reserve creation, crises and their associated restrictions and forced devaluations will be more and not less frequent than before because reserve holdings are less adequate.

The international quantity theory treats the international monetary system as a straightforward parallel to a national monetary system, and it can be challenged on the ground that this ignores three major differences. First, domestic money characteristically consists of non-interest bearing assets, whereas important parts of the supply of reserves bear interest; to the extent that nominal interest rates rise in line with inflation, the effect of inflation in providing an incentive to cut real reserve holdings will therefore be blunted (Fleming in I.M.F. (1970), p. 524). Second, the authorities will be constrained in adopting policies to run down their reserve holdings by the fact that doing so involves jeopardising other policies, notably internal stabilisation objectives. Fleming constructed a model to analyse the implications of this difference and concluded that whether a permanent acceleration of reserve growth would ultimately increase or decrease real reserves is ambiguous, but that there is some presumption that it would increase them (I.M.F. (1970), p. 535); Howle (1974) endorsed this conclusion. Third, there is the fact that the authorities have other policies besides the level of expenditure which they can use to effect adjustment.[1] These other adjustment mechanisms lead to distinct theories of how the system operates.

One such theory postulates that the main adjustment mechanism involves exchange-rate changes. The main contribution to constructing a coherent theory based on this premise has been made by Howle (1974). He assumed that countries select their inflation rates on internal grounds and therefore need periodically to alter their exchange rates in order to offset the effects of differential inflation rates on external competitiveness. Both devaluing and revaluing countries are assumed to engineer their exchange rate changes so as to preserve a certain average reserves/imports ratio, this ratio being higher for the revaluing countries. An increase in the rate at which nominal reserves are created, assuming they are distributed " neutrally," will initially ease the pressure to devalue or intensify the pressure to revalue on all countries. The ultimate effect of this would be to raise the " pivot," *i.e.*, the dividing line between the devaluing and revaluing countries. In the new equilibrium real reserves would rise no more rapidly than before, but the *level* of world real reserves would be greater because of the larger number of revaluing countries with their higher average reserve levels.

The other category of adjustment mechanisms involves the use of various types of restrictions and controls on both current and capital accounts. If these are the principal adjustment mechanisms, an increase in reserve creation will lead to a multilateral relaxation of restrictions which will stimulate trade and capital flows. This will increase the demand for reserves, and equilibrium will be restored when the demand has risen to match the increased supply. The supply of reserves determines the degree of openness of the world's economies, rather than the levels of demand and inflation (Cooper in I.M.F. (1970), pp. 128–40; La Pittus (1970); Howle (1974)).

There is not a great deal of empirical evidence (other than the traditional anecdotes) with which one can judge between the competing hypotheses that have been outlined. The strongest evidence favouring the hypothesis that countries do have reserve targets, and that deviations from these do prompt adjustment, is Clark's success (1970b) in estimating functions which embody precisely this hypothesis. Michaely (1970) used N.B.E.R.-type methods to examine whether in the post-war period the major countries (Group of Ten less Canada) adjusted their demand-management policies in response to reserve changes as required by the gold-standard rules of the game. He found evidence that this occurred in some countries, with respect to some indicators of monetary policy, notably discount rates and the

[1] Fleming also pointed out that it would be paradoxical if one and the same event caused both an intensification of restrictions and a more expansionary demand-management policy (I.M.F. (1970), p. 523). But presumably this paradox could materialise if different weapons of adjustment policy are influenced by different aspects of the external situation rather than just an overall state of reserve ease.

growth of the money supply. He also found that the countries which re-acted most regularly were those with the weakest reserve positions, that the E.E.C. countries reacted more in the 1950s (when their reserve position was relatively weak) than in the 1960s, and that responses to deficits were more regular than to surpluses—all of which findings suggest that there is some-thing in the notion that reserves act as a constraint rather than a target. He also found (and this was confirmed by McClam, and Argy and Kouri, in Aliber (1974)) that payments flows are typically partially—but only partially—sterilised.[1] This provides evidence that one of the mechan-isms envisaged by the international quantity theory is present. One inter-pretation of the finding of a positive relationship between the propensity to import and the demand for reserves (see II.1 above) is that expenditure-switching rather than expenditure-changing policies play the major role in adjustment—which is consistent with either the quantity theory hypothesis that income variations consist predominantly of price changes or with the view that exchange rates or restrictions are the principal adjustment mech-anism. These findings are fragmentary and it would be premature to start drawing firm conclusions from them: the major work remains to be done.

There is also scope for important theoretical work in constructing and analysing the behaviour of models of the international monetary system *qua* system. Perhaps the major contribution of the international quantity theorists will turn out to be their role in pioneering this type of analysis. There is scope for generalising their framework by including the possibility of several adjustment mechanisms simultaneously; Howle (1974) has already made a start in this task. One may conjecture that the international quan-tity theory will emerge as a limiting case of such a generalised model. Even if that is so, its construction will remain an important milestone in the evolution of a satisfactory world-macro model.

III. NORMATIVE THEORY

1. *Alternative Proposals for Increasing Liquidity*

During the 1950s Harrod (1953), Franks (1958), Stamp (1958) and Day (1960) all advanced proposals to increase international liquidity. But what had been an unfashionable British-based speciality prior to 1960 was transformed into a widely-dispersed growth industry following Triffin's diagnosis of a prospective liquidity shortage and his proposed remedy. Much of the resulting writing was of somewhat ephemeral interest, and coverage of it will therefore be less comprehensive than hitherto. An excellent survey of the earlier plans can be found in Machlup (1964), and a valuable collection of original papers is contained in Grubel (1963). The

---

[1] This is similar to results found for the pre-1914 and inter-war periods by Bloomfield (1959), p. 50, and Nurkse (1944), p. 69 respectively.

main plans will be briefly described in the present section, but their evaluation is postponed to III.2.

One possible method of increasing liquidity for which provision was made in the I.M.F. Articles was a " uniform increase in par values," or gold revaluation. (Gold revaluation needs to be distinguished from a dollar devaluation, such as was embodied in the Smithsonian Agreement in December 1971: both involve a change in the gold/dollar parity, but gold revaluation is directed to changing the relationship between gold and currencies in general while dollar devaluation changes the relation between the dollar and other currencies while leaving that between gold and currencies essentially unchanged.)   This method has never been utilised, but a number of economists have argued that it should be.   A few (e.g., Busschau (1961)) still regard gold as the only form of real money or " money proper " and conclude that the greater is the credit pyramid erected on the basis of a given gold stock, the more illiquid the system is, from which it follows that gold revaluation is the only possible way of increasing liquidity.   But the important support for gold revaluation stems from less archaic reasoning. On the one hand, there are those who wish to restore a fully-functioning gold standard and who recognise that to do this without a preliminary period of severe deflation would require an increase in the price of gold; the most influential of these are Rueff (1961) and Heilperin (1962).   On the other hand, there are those who are convinced of the existence of a serious liquidity shortage and are unconvinced that the creation of fiduciary reserves in the necessary quantities is politically feasible.   The most consistent spokesman for this position has been Harrod (see especially Harrod (1953), (1966) and Johnson's summary of Harrod's evolving views in Eltis et al (1970)).   Johnson (idem and (1969)) provided influential but apparently temporary support, while Gilbert (1968) and Oppenheimer (1969) placed their emphasis on the need for higher reserve growth rather than an increase in the stock of reserves, but nevertheless argued that this required a once-for-all gold revaluation.   Wonnacott (1963) agreed in the diagnosis but inferred that the appropriate remedy was a crawling increase in the price of gold.

Gold is not the only commodity that can form the basis of a commodity money, although it is the only one that has functioned successfully in this role in recent history.   The alternative that has commanded a certain amount of support in recent years is a commodity reserve currency.   Under this proposal money would consist of warehouse receipts issued in exchange for a composite bundle of storable basic commodities combined in fixed proportions.   The idea of basing currencies on this principle was originated by Jevons (1875) and received spasmodic subsequent support.   Hart, Kaldor and Tinbergen (1964) have most recently revived the idea, in the form of a proposal for an international I.M.F.-managed reserve asset. Kaldor (1971) subsequently suggested that the I.M.F., in its role as stockpiling agency, should buy and sell individual commodities rather than only dealing in a composite bundle. The classic analysis of the monetary principles underlying the proposal is by Friedman (1951).

The remaining proposals involve the creation of credit money rather than commodity money. The least ambitious approach was that which was initially adopted: the expansion of conditional liquidity through increased I.M.F. quotas, the General Arrangements to Borrow, and the creation of the swap network. These measures, together with such other expedients as Roosa bonds, the gold pool and multilateral surveillance, became known as " ad hoccery." An optimistic account of their potential was given by their chief architect, Roosa (1962).

In the same article, Roosa indicated that the United States intended that the swap network should expand into a multiple-currency system when the United States balance of payments moved back into surplus (an event that was anticipated with some confidence). This followed the proposals of Zolotas (1961) and Lutz (1962) (1963) that the circle of reserve currencies should be expanded to include other major convertible currencies so that countries would hold their reserves in the form of gold and a (freely-chosen) mixed bag of currencies. Posthuma (1963) suggested formally limiting the freedom to vary the gold/currency mix in which deficits are settled. When such restrictions are pursued very far, this proposal merges into that for a composite reserve unit.

Enthusiasm for the multiple-currency standard was short-lived, but the claim that the system was evolving, or had already evolved, into a satisfactory pattern based on existing national currencies found a new form in the mid-1960s. Specifically, it was asserted that the world had been moving unconsciously towards a dollar standard and that this was capable of providing an efficient monetary standard if the system was allowed to work properly and not sabotaged by continued conformity to the behaviour patterns required by the now-defunct gold-exchange standard. Kindleberger (1965) argued that the concern over the measured payments deficit of the United States was misplaced since the deficit was a reflection of balance-of-payments accounting conventions which were inappropriate to the position of a banker country engaged in mutually-profitable financial intermediation; if accounting practices were revised in line with economic realities, it would be seen that the dollar was strong and the system could continue to expand in line with need. The more fundamental claim was that implicit in Despres, Kindleberger and Salant (1966) and first fully articulated by McKinnon (1969): that the passive American balance-of-payments strategy that is implicit in a full dollar standard and permitted by the lack of any obligation on the part of the United States to convert dollars into primary reserve assets would be in the best interests of the rest of the world because it would permit other countries to have access to an elastic supply of reserves that could be tapped according to need.

The remaining group of proposals all involve deliberate international action to create some form of fiduciary reserve asset. The earliest recorded proposal in this class was made by a German economist, Julius Wolf, in 1892 (Schumpeter (1954), p. 1076), but it was not until the early 1930s that significant support emerged (Keynes (1930), Henderson (1932)). Keynes (1933) urged the World Economic Conference to create an international agency that would issue gold certificates up to a value of $5 billion, so as to relieve central banks of external constraints on reflationary monetary policies. He was also responsible for the wartime British proposals for the post-war monetary system (Cmd 6437 (1943)). These envisaged an International Clearing Union issuing an international currency, bancor, that would not be convertible into gold but would be accepted as an alternative method of settling international debts. Bancor balances could have been increased only through sale of gold to the I.C.U. or use of the overdraft facilities with which each country was provided in proportion to its quota, but the scale of the I.C.U. would have been increased automatically (from its large initial size of quotas of around $26 billion) by quota increases tied to the growth in trade. During the 1950s Franks (1958) and Day (1960) urged that such proposals be revived, and the latter's views were endorsed by the Radcliffe Committee (Cmnd 827 (1959), para. 678).

The first essentially different proposal was that of Stamp (1958), who proposed that the I.M.F. should issue Fund certificates that would be " backed " solely by the agreement of all I.M.F. members to accept them in settlement of international debts—a principle whose unacceptability to dimwitted bankers was vociferously proclaimed by numerous economists until it was discovered that the S.D.R. agreement embodied precisely that principle. Stamp proposed that these Fund certificates should be introduced by distributing them in the first instance to the I.B.R.D. for investment in less-developed countries, which is an idea now known as " the link " and discussed in III.3. The Triffin Plan (1960) was technically closer to the Keynes Plan in that it envisaged converting the I.M.F. into a deposit-issuing institution, but it differed in proposing that I.M.F. deposits be convertible into gold and in adding open-market investment in member countries and international institutions like the I.B.R.D. to overdrafts and gold sales as methods of expanding deposits. Triffin proposed to wind up the reserve-currency system by having the dollar and sterling balances traded in for I.M.F. deposits. He also proposed that a minimum proportion of reserves (initially 20%) be held in deposits. The main rival to the Triffin Plan in the early discussions proved to be Bernstein's proposal (1963) for Composite Reserve Units (C.R.U.s), which would have been created by a limited group of key-currency countries depositing their currencies in a special account at the I.M.F. and receiving a corresponding number of reserve units. These would have been used to supplement gold in settling deficits within the limited group, who would have agreed to accept and

hold units up to a specified percentage of their gold holdings.   Other plans—
the " also-rans "—were advanced by Angell (1961), Harrod (1961),
Maudling in I.M.F. (1962), Giscard d'Estaing (1965), Roosa (1965),
Modigliani and Kenen (1966), Scitovsky (1966) and Mundell (1969).
Invaluable taxonomies were provided by Machlup (1964) and the Ossola
Report (Group of Ten (1965)).

   An alternative way of solving a problem of shortage is to decrease
demand instead of increasing supply.   One of the (minor) attractions of
floating exchange rates is that they would have this effect.   Another possibility, which Whittlesey (1964) argued still had great potential, is to release
reserves from their ritual role of providing backing for the domestic money
supply.

2. Desirable Characteristics of Reserve Assets

   The range of rival plans offered to the managers of the international
monetary system presented them with quite a choice problem.   The role of
economists in helping them to choose rationally is not above criticism: far
too much of the early writing suffered from a preoccupation with a single
issue to the exclusion of all others, or a failure to relate the technical details
to the substantive economic issues that lie behind them.   Only Triffin (1960)
and Yeager (1961) identified and discussed all three of the substantive issues
that ultimately emerged as fundamental: the prevention of instability due
to the confidence problem, the control of the volume of liquidity in the
interest of stabilisation, and the size and distribution of the resource benefits
(or costs) yielded by monetary reform.   It is to these three issues that the
bulk of the present section is devoted.

   At the risk of being more controversial, one might also fault a number of
the most eminent economists in the field for a dogmatic use of *ad hoc* hypotheses about political motives and relationships.   Specifically, it has
repeatedly been taken as axiomatic that politicians and/or officials are
motivated by an essentially irrational attachment to national sovereignty,
and that gold is a guarantor of national autonomy.   The first proposition is
never deduced from any more general principles of human behaviour nor
substantiated by more than anecdotal evidence, which usually refers to
de Gaulle; while the abundant experience of countries negotiating limited
surrenders of sovereignty clearly contradicts the hypothesis.   The second
hypothesis seems entirely based on what de Gaulle once said at a press
conference.   Both the explicit analyses of the question, by Cassell (1965)
and Hirsch (1969), concluded that an international monetary order based
on gold involved just as much loss of autonomy as one based on credit, and
no-one has yet given an example of a national action that would be permitted by an increase in the gold price but prevented by the creation of an
equivalent value of S.D.R.s.   Yet one continues to read that the central
issue in selecting between gold and credit money is the " determination of

the proper and acceptable line between national autonomy and world institutions " (Johnson in Eltis *et al.* (1970) p. 292).

The assumption about political motivation that underlies the following analysis is the one that seems the natural extension of economists' customary postulates about human motivation; that is, it is assumed that countries pursue their material self-interest in the most effective way possible; where international spillover effects are significant this implies that they may agree to a mutual limitation of sovereignty. A plausible alternative hypothesis which merits comparison and testing is that countries aim to maximise national power rather than national wealth (S. D. Cohen (1970)).

(a) *The Confidence Problem.* One of the three major problems of the international monetary system identified in Machlup and Malkiel (1964) is that of confidence in reserve media. The confidence problem (which may be regarded as a special case of the oldest proposition in economics to have been dignified by the title of " law," Gresham's Law) consists in the danger that reserve holders will seek to substitute one reserve asset for another and so place unbearable strains on the reserve centre and/or the total volume of liquidity. An important part of Triffin's thesis (1960) was that the gold-exchange standard was vulnerable to a confidence crisis which could cause a collapse of the system parallel to that of 1931. The subsequent literature on reserve composition (see II.2 above) sought to test whether central-bank portfolio policy was motivated by independent portfolio management or whether it was dominated by co-operative restraint intended to prevent a breakdown of the system. It was concluded that the evidence showed both factors to be present, but that co-operative restraint was insufficiently dominant to allay fears of the " lemming syndrome." It follows that the mere fact that the asset-holders in question are central banks rather than private agents is insufficient to justify overruling the ordinary presumption of monetary theory that the monetary system should be designed to minimise the danger that asset shifting will lead to a change in the volume of liquidity and so turn the monetary system into a source of instability (Friedman (1951)).

The confidence problem can be eliminated by resorting to a single form of money, either in the guise of a strict commodity standard or a single form of fiat money (*idem.*). Both Rueff (1961) and Triffin (1960) rated the risk of a credit collapse as very real, and therefore sought to guard against the threat. Rueff's solution of a full gold standard would be satisfactory for the purpose (provided it was not eroded—see III.2(*c*)). But many early critics of the Triffin Plan questioned whether his solution would not merely shift the locus of the confidence problem. Triffin proposed to convert the dollar and sterling balances into claims on the I.M.F., so as to eliminate shifting into and out of reserve currencies. He relied on the gold denomination of I.M.F. deposits for the incentive for countries to refrain from exercising their right to convert their deposits (above the minimum 20%) into gold.

Several writers (*e.g.*, Altman (1961), Angell (1961)) concluded that the Fund would be likely to suffer a run if its ability to convert deposits into gold came under suspicion, especially if it were so reckless as to issue assets that were backed only by the debts of less developed countries. The obvious solution was to abandon the right of gold conversion, so establishing I.M.F. deposits as the ultimate form of international money (Angell (1961), Yeager (1961)). And the ultimate monetary unit requires no backing (Machlup (1968a)). Triffin's failure to carry his proposals to their logical conclusion seems to have arisen from an attempt to make them politically palatable while equating political aversion to loss of sovereignty. Since restricting reserve composition involves a minor encroachment on sovereignty, he assumed that countries had to be tempted into holding a fiduciary reserve asset by the ability to convert it into their traditional reserve medium at will. But in fact there is a clear potential for mutual gain through a joint renunciation of conversion rights, so that countries which pursue their material self-interest in a rational way might be expected to agree to such a sacrifice of sovereignty.

Most of the other proponents of particular plans gave rather less emphasis to the confidence problem. The advocates of a dollar standard were particularly relaxed because they viewed the ultimate result of a shift out of dollars into gold as an ending of the United States convertibility obligation (either before or on exhaustion of the United States gold stock). This would produce a single form of money and therefore a solution to the confidence problem. The equanimity of the advocates of a multiple-currency standard was more puzzling. Lutz (1963) emphasised that the new reserve centres would have very favourable reserve ratios for a long time, and also claimed that the holding of several reserve currencies would so spread the risks as to reduce the incentive for shifting. Others (Machlup (1962), Williamson (1963)) thought that any multiplication in the number of reserve assets could only be expected to intensify the danger of shifting. In that event one might regard gold guarantees on all official currency balances—as advocated by Zolotas (1961)—as essential. The proposal for gold or exchange guarantees was also discussed in the context of an unreformed gold-exchange standard. Roosa (1962) opposed the suggestion on the grounds that it amounted to an assurance that devaluation would not occur; he argued that such an assurance was unnecessary if the dollar was strong and unbelievable if it was weak. Kenen (1963b) and Halm (1965) replied that guarantees were intended to provide insurance against devaluation and not assurance of its impossibility; the real resource cost of implementing a guarantee was not such as to threaten its credibility, but was a price worth paying to restore the right to change the parity without dishonour. But it also emerged that bilateral guarantees raised greater technical problems than initially assumed, such as whether one compensated for a devaluation that was matched by the reserve-holding country (matched within what period of time?) or for a change that was initiated by it (Beza and Patterson (1961), Halm (1965)). No doubt these were among the reasons that caused the multiple-currency proposal to be transmuted into the form of C.R.U.s.

Most of the other proposals that were discussed—gold revaluation without eliminating the gold-exchange standard, a partial commodity-reserve currency, C.R.U.s and S.D.R.s—would have left the confidence problem largely unchanged, because there would still have been multiple reserve assets with values that were not rigidly welded together. The S.D.R. scheme involves gold denomination (without gold convertibility) and a system of " guided transferability " where the I.M.F. designates the country to receive S.D.R.s in accordance with a complicated set of rules designed to ensure their equitable distribution subject to maximum required holding limits. (See Machlup (1968a) Chapter 3 for details.) This should ensure the peaceful co-existence of gold and S.D.R.s,[1] but there remains the problem of the reserve currencies. As noted in II.2, there is an argument (due to Goldstein (1969) and Hirsch (1971)) that the ready availability of a supply of gold substitute at a fixed price will gradually reduce expectations of gold revaluation to vanishing point and thereby consolidate the position of the dollar. In one sense a temporary " solution " to the confidence problem was found in 1971 by the suspension of dollar convertibility and the operation of Gresham's Law, which resulted in gold ceasing to be used in international settlements. A number of economists have urged a more permanent solution in the form of a Reserve Settlement Account, under which all reserves would be pooled in the I.M.F. and countries would hold some form of I.M.F. deposits as their sole form of reserves (Joint Economic Committee (1968), Mundell (1969)). The same object could be attained by funding operations which would make the S.D.R. into the sole reserve asset (Fleming (1971a)). Permanent elimination of the confidence problem will presumably be one of the aims of the attempt to reconstruct the international monetary system (Krause (1971)).

(b) *Stabilisation.* All schools of economic thought are agreed that the prime criterion of an efficient monetary system is its performance in contributing to the stabilisation of the level of economic activity and either the level or trend of prices. A classic expression of what this implies in the international sphere was that of Keynes:

> " We need a *quantum* of international currency, which is neither determined in an unpredictable and irrelevant manner as, for example, by the technical progress of the gold industry, nor subject to large variations depending on the gold reserve policies of individual countries; but is governed by the actual current requirements of world commerce,

[1] This confidence is not universally shared. Both Kaldor (1971) and Mundell (1971, Chapter 17) have argued that international organisation or trust are insufficiently developed to support a pure fiduciary asset like the S.D.R.

and is also capable of deliberate expansion and contraction to offset deflationary and inflationary tendencies in effective world demand." (Cmd 6437 (1943).)

There are three partially distinct desiderata that are involved: the avoidance of those monetary shocks that have periodically generated hyper-inflations and slumps, counter-cyclical operation and provision for an optimum long-run rate of monetary growth.

Monetary shocks can arise for two sorts of reasons: because of shifts between assets altering the total volume of liquidity, and because of permissive or deliberate monetary (mis)management. The primary cause of liquidity variation through asset shifting in the international context has normally been assumed to be the confidence problem discussed in the previous section, with a secondary source arising from payments imbalances between countries with different policies regarding reserve composition. Both sources of instability would be eliminated by reserve consolidation. In fact, however, the experience of the early 1970s has demonstrated that asset shifting on the part of the private sector under a reserve currency system has the potential to lead to an explosive growth in official reserves. The full implications of this have not yet been explored.

The danger of shocks arising from monetary mismanagement is excluded by a strict commodity standard, which is claimed as one of the major virtues of the gold standard by those like Heilperin (1962) who believe that geology is less untrustworthy than governments. The trouble with this argument is that it assumes that governments would obey a self-denying ordinance committing them to a gold standard but that they would not obey a self-denying ordinance on deliberate liquidity creation, such as Triffin's suggestion (1960) that reserve growth in excess of 3% should only be possible with progessively larger weighted majorities in favour. The S.D.R. scheme requires an 85% vote in favour of S.D.R. creation, which would seem to be a fairly powerful safeguard against irresponsible reserve expansion. The most serious threat of this type of mismanagement would seem to be posed by a dollar standard, since this would entrust monetary policy to a single country with a seigniorage interest in inflation and no constraints from the rest of the world.

One of the virtues claimed for the gold standard from the time of Ricardo onwards is the contra-cyclical effect of variations in the profitability of gold mining. In fact this mechanism is at best weak, because of the very small proportion of world resources devoted to gold mining (c. 0·1% according to Hart et al. (1964), p. 528). One of the main claims for a commodity-reserve currency is that it would vastly strengthen the anti-cyclical potential of commodity money, by increasing the proportion of world output eligible for monetisation to 5% to 10% (idem.). A tendency towards recession would produce a decline in commodity prices that would provoke large sales to the I.M.F.'s buffer stocks, which would be paid for by newly-created reserves. There can be little doubt that this would provide a powerful built-in stabiliser. Although Friedman (1951) argued that one could construct a fiat currency standard with even stronger stabilising properties, none of the proposals for international fiat money involves any attempt in this direction. Even the idea of running a discretionary anticyclical reserve policy has been dismissed on the grounds that the responses to reserve changes are too complicated (Yeager (1961)) or too slow (I.M.F. (1966), p. 10; Polak in I.M.F. (1970), p. 520). A question that might merit investigation is whether the elastic reserve supply that would result from a dollar standard (and perhaps from a multiple-currency standard as well) would destroy the stabilising negative feedbacks of the customary rules of monetary management in the same way that the real-bills doctrine would (Williamson (1971), p. 11).

The third desideratum is that of providing for an optimum long-run rate of growth of reserves. There is a consensus that it is desirable for countries to be able on average to accumulate reserves (see, for example, Triffin (1960), Machlup (1966), Gilbert (1968)), and this is only possible if the supply of reserves is growing. It was the inability of the gold-exchange standard to support long-run reserve growth which provoked the various proposals for supplementing liquidity, and so it is not surprising to find that all of them provide the ability to manufacture reserves. The clumsiest instrument to this end is gold revaluation, because although a higher gold price would increase reserve growth through higher production and less hoarding (Oppenheimer (1969)), one cannot alter the flow addition to reserves without also changing the stock of reserves, and gold production cannot be manipulated to respond to changes in the desired rate of reserve growth. It was traditionally assumed that control of the process of creation of fiduciary reserve assets would give control of the rate of reserve growth, subject to the ability to predict correctly the largely exogenous variations in the supply of other reserve assets (see I.M.F. (1970), especially Fleming on pp. 321–49). However, Johnson questioned whether control of S.D.R. creation really gives any control over the stock of reserves so long as United States monetary policy is not constrained by the same need to maintain adequate reserves as is monetary policy in other countries (I.M.F. (1970), p. 149). The central issue underlying the continuing controversy over restoration of a United States convertibility obligation is therefore whether control of the world stock of reserves should be placed under collective international control through I.M.F. decisions on S.D.R. creation, or whether it should be in the hands of those who influence the size of the deficit on the United States balance of payments. McKinnon (1969, pp. 29–34) argued that a major benefit of the dollar standard would be its ability to reconcile inconsistent payments objectives by having the United States act as the residual supplier of reserves through adoption of a passive balance-of-payments strategy.[1] One contrary argument points to the danger of the United States being tempted to exploit the inflation tax (Johnson (1972a), p. 86); another to an asserted reduction in total adjustment costs if S.D.R. creation is at the level that will reconcile payments objectives but the United States does not withdraw from participation in the adjustment process (Williamson (1971), pp. 10–15). It is not clear that these exhaust the considerations relevant to the choice between unilateral and collective controls of the world liquidity base.

(c) *The Social Saving and Seigniorage.* The production of commodity money is costly, and the substitution of fiat money therefore produces a social saving of the resources that would otherwise have been absorbed in the production of money. In so far as the money supply industry is a competitive one, this social saving will be distributed to the holders of money —*e.g.*, through the payment of interest. In so far as the issuer of money enjoys monopoly power, it is able to extract the difference between the value of produced money and the cost of producing it as " seigniorage." (Historically, seigniorage meant the mint charge for turning metal into money, but in the modern context it refers to the net value of the resources accruing to the issuer of money.) (Grubel, Johnson, Mundell and Schmidt in Mundell and Swoboda (1969).)

The following questions are suggested naturally. (1) How large. is the cost of producing commodity money and therefore the potential social saving? (2) How and to whom would the social saving be distributed under alternative monetary arrangements? (3) Is it desirable to reap the social saving? (4) If so, how and to whom should it be distributed? The last question involves, of course, the desirability of an aid link.

It might be thought that the resource cost of producing a growth in reserves of (say) $2 billion each year in the form of commodity money would be $2 billion per annum, but matters are not so simple. Consider first the case of gold, where storage and depreciation costs are negligible. Oppenheimer (1969) estimated that the additional resources required in gold mining to support an annual reserve growth of $2 billion would be only $600 million–$1 billion, with the remainder of the increment in value consisting of a reduction in gold consumption (which implies a loss of consumer surplus) and a transfer payment to gold producers. Laidler (1969) attempted to estimate the additional social cost involved in continuing to

---

[1] McKinnon termed this a resolution of the " redundancy problem." Actually, this term as defined by Mundell in Mundell and Swoboda (1969, p. 29) referred to the " problem " of which country could be excused a payments constraint in a world where achievement of payments equilibrium by $(n-1)$ countries implies equilibrium of the nth country, and what use should be made of the " redundant " policy instrument. Since there is no theorem which asserts that attainment of equilibrium is likely to be obstructed by n countries pursuing n mutually consistent targets, it is not obvious that a redundant instrument should cause concern. But Oppenheimer (1973) has argued that the assumption of consistency in payments objectives is acceptable only in the case of a classical gold standard with rigidly fixed exchange rates, money supplies tied to reserves, and flexible internal prices. In the real world, McKinnon's problem is the real one.

withhold existing monetary gold from private consumption, which he conservatively valued at $1·9 billion per annum. The pure theory of the size of the social saving was studied by Johnson in Mundell and Swoboda (1969): in Johnson's world any trace of cost inflation is conspicuous by its absence, and therefore Laidler's element of cost is the only necessary one because the desired increase in real reserves can equally well be engineered by a falling price level. In total, the resource cost of a gold standard would seem to be in the range of $2 billion to $5 billion per annum, if the desirable rate of reserve growth was $2 billion per annum.

A commodity-reserve-currency is generally assumed to be even more expensive because it involves expenditure on storage, maintenance and depreciation of the stockpile. This was estimated at 3% to 3½% per annum by Harmon (1959); Grubel (1965) argued that this was conservative, but Hart (1966) replied that his substitute figure of 6% was casual in the extreme. Hart, Kaldor and Tinbergen (1964) pointed out that at least some of the operating costs could be covered by the difference between the buffer stock's buying and selling prices. They also claimed that some two-thirds to three-quarters of the stockpile would represent a diversion from existing inventories rather than a net addition to stocks, which would make the resource cost quite moderate. But this would only remain true so long as the commodity-reserve-currency was a marginal addition to the stock of reserves. A full commodity standard would unquestionably be expensive: comparable assumptions to the gold standard case would suggest an order of magnitude of $6 billion–$8 billion per annum.

There are therefore substantial social savings under a system of credit money. For some years the world has been on a mixed commodity/credit standard, so that some social saving has been realised. Part of the saving accrued to the reserve centres as seigniorage and part was paid to the reserve holders in the form of interest. There is a considerable literature on the costs and benefits of operating a reserve currency (Day (1954), Aliber (1964), W. A. Salant (1964), Grubel (1964), who provoked comments by Aliber (1965), Goldstein (1965), Kareken (1965) and Kirman and Schmidt (1965); Karlik in Kenen and Lawrence (1968), Green (1969), and B. J. Cohen (1971a), (1971b)). It is a rather unsatisfying literature in that this is one of those cases (like assessing the economic effects of British entry to the E.E.C.) where the reasonably quantifiable has to be weighed against the highly subjective. In this case it is the costs that are highly subjective, since these stem principally from the additional constraints on national economic policy (particularly regarding the exchange rate and monetary policy) that supposedly arise from operating a reserve currency. The benefits are principally the seigniorage-type benefits of having been able to borrow more cheaply from the rest of the world in the past than would otherwise have been possible, and the prospect of being able to finance future deficits without the prior necessity of tying up resources in low-yielding reserves. These benefits appear to be significant,[1] but not large enough to outweigh even quite modest constraints on the freedom to pursue appropriate macro-economic policies. Everything therefore depends on one's judgment of whether the reserve-currency role has in fact distorted policy. The one thing that is clear is that a country that can enjoy the seigniorage gains without being subject to the constraints—as the United States could under a dollar standard —stands to gain. (An amusing discussion of these gains, which concludes that they roughly reimburse the United States for Marshall Aid, can be found in Kolm (1970).) Another entertaining paper is Mundell's short history of colonialism in terms of the mother country's attempt to maximise its seigniorage gains: see Claassen and Salin (1972).

Machlup (1965) (1968a) and Grubel in Mundell and Swoboda (1969) analysed who would get the benefit of the social saving under alternative plans for international monetary reform. In so far as international fiat money pays interest, the saving accrues to the countries which hold reserves. To the extent that interest is below the rate that the first recipient of newly-created reserves would have had to pay to borrow the same sum, the saving accrues as seigniorage to that first recipient. Thus the Stamp Plan would have distributed seigniorage to the poor; multiple currency schemes and Bernstein's C.R.U. would have given it to the rich (and the dollar standard to the very rich); Giscard's C.R.U. would have given it to the conservative, who already held large (gold) reserves; Triffin's I.M.F. would have distributed it between the " broke " who needed to borrow reserves, the rich who had money markets able to absorb I.M.F. open-market purchases, and the poor who borrowed from the I.B.R.D.; gold revaluation would have given it to the conservative who held large gold reserves and the mining companies who would have made bigger profits; and the S.D.R. scheme gives it to those who are net users of S.D.R.s. To the extent that I.M.F. quotas are a measure of countries' long-run demands for reserves, countries will on average be neither net users nor net holders of S.D.R.s in excess of their cumulative allocations and the S.D.R. scheme will be distributionally neutral in the same sense that distributing the social saving via interest payments is.

Is it desirable to reap the social saving? Other things being equal, the answer is obviously yes; but there are at least three reasons why some would claim that other things are not equal. First, there is the claim made by Harrod that it is politically inconceivable that adequate liquidity will

[1] The seigniorage benefit to the United States was estimated as $420 million in 1963 by Aliber (1964, p. 447) and $1·8 billion in 1961 by Grubel (1964, p. 205). That to the United Kingdom was estimated at £286 million in 1962 by Kirman and Schmidt (1965, p. 102), but their use of gross sterling liabilities was criticised by Green (1969, Chapter 7) as involving double counting. Green gave an average gain in the early 1960s in the range of £110 million to £165 million and B. J. Cohen (1971a, p. 197) a round figure of £100 million for the late 1960s. Cohen (1971b) claimed that a gain of the same order of magnitude was offset by the financing charges, leaving a zero net benefit; but this rests on a misinterpretation of the results of the Reddaway Report (1968), which already includes an allowance for financing charges (p. 335).

be created without gold revaluation.   Even if recent history did not enable one to dispute the contention that liquidity is unlikely to be increased as much as Harrod would want through any other mechanism, he is rather isolated in desiring such a large increase (see III.5).   Second, there is the claim of Rueff and Heilperin, and Hart, Kaldor and Tinbergen, that reliance on commodity money would more than justify the cost because of the benefits in terms of the elimination of confidence problems and/or improved stabilisation performance.   The fundamental error in this argument would seem to be that it ignores the fact that the costliness of commodity money provides a strong economic incentive to substitute credit money (Friedman (1951)), which in the international context leads to a pure commodity standard being superseded by a commodity-exchange standard.[1]   Unless one can devise and enforce sanctions that will prevent individual countries benefiting themselves by substituting reserve currencies for the prescribed commodity money in times when confidence is strong, commodity money provides no solution to the confidence problem.   Similarly, there is a danger of the anti-cyclical benefits of commodity-reserve money being swamped by pro-cyclical swings in the ratio of credit reserves to commodity reserves.   Third, Mundell (1971, Chapter 17) has argued that it is foolish to try to go straight to 100% fiat money backed by nothing but general acceptance obligations, because this is possible only where complete trust exists.   Where there is no trust, 100% commodity money is needed.   Where (as now) there is incomplete trust, partial commodity money is necessary, and the appropriate strategy is to reduce this backing gradually as trust develops.   The counter argument is that 100% fiat reserves represent a game-theoretic equilibrium point; i.e., that it is to no country's individual advantage to break the agreement to accept such reserves.

Assuming that the case for fiat money is accepted, the questions are how and to whom the social saving is to be distributed.   The two methods of distribution are via interest paid on reserve holdings and via the distribution of new reserve assets.   There are three arguments in favour of distributing the saving via interest payments.   The first is that failure to pay a market interest rate will result in the maintenance or re-emergence of reserve currencies because the economic incentive which in the past led to credit money supplanting commodity money will still be present.   As Hirsch (1971) argued, the maintenance of low interest rates on S.D.R.s is liable to lead to an S.D.R.-exchange standard rather than an S.D.R. standard. While the S.D.R.-exchange standard might be less prone to confidence crises than the gold-exchange standard, because of the ability to create additional S.D.R.s, it could not simultaneously secure ultimate international control of international monetary policy.   The second advantage of paying

---

[1] Giscard d'Estaing acknowledged the force of this when he argued that one of the main objections to gold revaluation was that it would increase the leeway for the gold-exchange standard (Mundell and Swoboda (1969), p. 12).

market interest rates is supposed to be that this would provide the incentive for countries to hold the socially-optimal quantity of reserves—the analysis being parallel to that which in the domestic context is called the theory of the optimum quantity of money. (See Johnson (1967), in Mundell and Swoboda (1969), in Eltis *et al* (1970); Mundell (1971), Chapter 17; Grubel (1971b); Clark (1973).) However, Tower and Willett (1972) have pointed out that the rather fundamental criticisms of the theory, on the grounds that its application would be prone to result in macro-economic instability, apply in the international context as well. The third argument that has been advanced in favour of paying market interest rates is that this is distributionally neutral. According to Machlup (1968a, p. 53) it should be a canon of international liquidity creation that it leads to no unrequited long-run resource transfer. Grubel tried to justify the canon by pointing to the absence of a government with world-wide taxation authority (Mundell and Swoboda (1969), p. 277). This is a somewhat odd argument because one would have thought that the lack of a government with world-wide taxation authority would lead to a strong presumption that the provision of international public goods and the extent of international income redistribution is sub-optimal, and if a tax on reserve holding is a politically feasible way of partially remedying this then it is highly probable that it would yield a welfare gain. The other argument against market interest rates is that they would weaken the incentive for surplus countries to play a role in the adjustment process (Scitovsky (1965), p. 12).

If the whole of the social saving is not distributed through interest payments, there remains a potential seigniorage gain whose distribution is determined by the initial allocation of reserve assets. It is still possible to achieve distributional neutrality, as the S.D.R. scheme aims to do, by distributing S.D.R. issues in proportion to the presumed long-run demand for reserves. Triffin (1971) has argued that, because the social saving arises through collective international action, it should be used to support collectively-agreed purposes (stabilisation, aid, etc.) rather than accrue to countries individually: the logic of this does not seem compelling. What has seemed convincing to many is the argument that the saving should go to the poor, through an aid link.

3. *The Aid Link*

The proposal for an aid link—*i.e.*, to give the benefit of the social saving to the less-developed countries, either by allocating them new reserves in excess of their estimated holding needs or by initially placing the new reserves in the hands of an international financial intermediary like the I.D.A. or I.B.R.D.—was anticipated by a casual reference in the Keynes Plan (Cmd 6437 (1943)) and by Kalecki and Schumacher (1943). They suggested permitting industrialising countries to obtain bancor credits by borrowing from a special Investment Account in the International Clearing Union, and argued that this would strengthen the defences against the expected post-war deflation. The Stamp Plan (1958) initiated the considerable literature that has grown up on the link.

The principal argument for the link has already been developed. The international community has few instruments to improve the world distribution of income, and therefore it should utilise such opportunities as arise. One of these is the seigniorage resulting from the production of fiduciary reserve assets. There is a long and unfortunate tradition in economics of dismissing this type of argument just because it involves a value judgment additional to that embodied in the Pareto criterion. The degree of egalitarianism needed to justify preference for the link rather than neutrality is minimal, given the existing facts on world income distribution.

However, most supporters of the link have sought other, supposedly more objective, arguments. Two of these are in the Paretian tradition: they argue that the link would improve the position of the developing countries without requiring any worsening in that of the developed countries. Thus, it has sometimes been argued that the link would permit increased aid to be effected without imposing any burden on the developed countries. This is true if the " burden " referred to is the balance-of-payments burden (Maynard (1972)), but the more relevant concept is the resource burden and this would be zero only if the relevant alternative to increasing liquidity through linked S.D.R.s were increasing it through the production of commodity money rather than through the creation of non-linked S.D.R.s. Second, it has been argued that the balance-of-payments objectives of the developed countries cannot be made consistent by unearned S.D.R. allocations because these countries wish to run current account surpluses, which they would be permitted to do through the aid link (Haan (1971), p. 99; Maynard (1972)). Some will remain sceptical about an argument which assumes that developed countries prefer earning additional reserves to receiving them as a free issue, but others are impressed by the durability of mercantilist modes of thought.

A third argument for the link rests on the assumption of an insufficiency of world demand, which could be ameliorated by distributing reserves to those who could be relied on to spend them (UNCTAD (1965)). As Polak has observed, this argument would indeed be powerful in an era of deflation but is unconvincing in recent circumstances (I.M.F. (1970), p. 518). A fourth argument is that the developing countries suffer from particular difficulties related to their economic structure—export instability, import incompressibility, debt servicing, lack of confidence—which impose greater adjustment burdens on them than on developed countries, so that world efficiency would be maximised by distributing new reserves to the less-developed countries so as to reduce their need for adjustment (B. J. Cohen (1966), Márquez in I.M.F. (1970, pp. 104–11)). It might be counter-argued that, if countries are rational, they will choose to hold average reserves which are related to their adjustment costs, in which case distribution of the social saving through interest payments would be a more sophisticated way of taking account of relative adjustment costs.

A number of arguments have been advanced against the link, some of which appear equally uncompelling. Machlup (1965) and Johnson (1966) argued that the major interest of the developing countries lay in a well-functioning system that would discourage deficit-induced restrictions and enable them to benefit from general world prosperity. As Corden commented (Mundell and Swoboda (1969), p. 283), this is true, but irrelevant, because they would benefit even more if they obtained the seigniorage as well as the prosperity. The two are in conflict only if (as Mohammed asserted, in I.M.F. (1970), p. 113, was in fact the case) an essential condition for the political acceptability of a scheme to create fiduciary reserves is the avoidance of unrequited long-run resource transfers. An unproven political constraint should not, however, be dignified as an economic argument.

A second common observation of the critics is that development aid and liquidity creation are different things (Group of Ten (1965), para. 138; Johnson (1966)). The logical force of this observation may not be immediately evident: driving a car and listening to the radio are indisputably different activities, but this is not generally judged a compelling reason for not installing radios in cars. A reader of the first draft of this paper retorted that one does not install TV sets in cars. The moral is surely that, while being different is *per se* irrelevant, it is crucial to examine whether the activities are competitive. One form of competitiveness that has often been feared by opponents of the link is that its institution would result in the need for aid becoming a determinant of the volume of liquidity creation, despite the avowals of the link's supporters (*e.g.*, UNCTAD (1969)) that no such effect is intended. Even if this were avoided, variations in the world's liquidity needs would subject the aid flow to irrelevant shocks (Group of Ten (1965)). To this it has been answered that I.D.A. replenishments are already subject to at least an equal degree of uncertainty (UNCTAD (1969)) and that it is in any event intended that reserve creation be planned on a long-term basis (Haan (1971), p. 117).

A third objection used to run in terms of the inadequate backing that would be provided by the obligations of less-developed countries (Altman (1961); Angell (1961); Machlup (1964); Group of Ten (1965), para. 138). Machlup's conversion (1965) to being the prime proponent of the irrelevance of backing deprived that argument in its crude form of serious support, but a related point is that an aid link could conceivably create a risk of default on the interest payments (Williamson (1972)). So long as there is a continuing flow of S.D.R.s being distributed, however, these could be collected by deduction.

A fourth argument concerns the danger of inflation. There are two points here. The first is that the first-round impact on world aggregate demand of a given volume of reserve creation will be greater if one distributes S.D.R.s to those who would plan to spend them rather than to hold them. This is true, but, it might seem, easily countered through an offsetting change in the quantity of S.D.R.s created. If, however, reserve creation is intended to persuade countries to ease payments restrictions rather than to stimulate demand, the counter would be at best incomplete (Polak in I.M.F. (1970), pp. 517–18). The second point concerns the effect that the link would have on the volume of S.D.R.s whose creation countries were prepared to sanction. The initial argument was that the rate of reserve creation might be pushed up through the desire of the less-developed countries for development finance or the desire of the industrialised countries to minimise the amount of aid for which they needed to seek legislative authorisation (Group of Ten (1965), para. 138). An alternative worry is that creditor countries might be unwilling to sanction adequate S.D.R. creation if they were going to have to earn the S.D.R.s with real resources (Fleming (1971a)). Stamp (1965, p. 15) and Haan (1971, pp. 122–27) agreed that S.D.R. creation would be restrained if the majority of countries had to earn their reserve increases, but they would have welcomed this as a desirable restraint on the inflationary potentialities of fiduciary reserve creation.

Fifth, it has been said that the link will increase aid only if it succeeds in " tricking " national Parliaments, since a Parliament which understands what is happening will promptly reduce conventional aid by an equal sum (Salin in I.M.F. (1970), p. 120; Haberler (1971); Johnson (1972b)). But, in so far as aid is a public good to the advanced countries, Parliaments might be willing to participate in a collective increase in aid even when they would resist a unilateral increase, particularly in view of the fact that this would largely obviate the normal terms-of-trade cost. It is only in so far as this is not true that democrats with a cosmopolitan welfare function who doubt whether other forms of aid would in fact be cut equivalently (a question not within the professional competence of the average economist) may suffer from divided loyalties.

Sixth, Haberler (1971) pointed out that the link would alter the distribution of the aid burden between countries. Reserve holdings might provide an even more arbitrary tax base than the 1% aid target. This might be thought a stronger argument if the 1% target was more widely honoured.

Finally, there is the argument developed in III.2(c) above regarding the desirability of paying market interest rates on reserves. An analogous point is that it would be difficult to reduce the quantity of reserves, should this prove desirable in the interests of international monetary management, if this involved calling in loans to developing countries (I.M.F. (1965), p. 18). Both these factors reduce the sums that could safely be dispensed on aid-link principles. But payment of interest equal to that on short-term dollar assets would still leave an element of seigniorage because most countries are unable to borrow long term at short-term dollar interest rates, so there would remain scope for a restricted aid link (Grubel (1972), Williamson (1972)). Another suggestion is that the payment of market interest rates on S.D.R.s could be reconciled with the link by combining high-yielding I.B.R.D. bonds and low-yielding I.D.A. loans in appropriate proportions in the I.M.F.'s portfolio (Haan (1971), p. 107).

As with other proposals for international monetary reform the aid link has spawned a number of variants. One may distinguish three bases of differentiation. First, there is the question as to whether the reserve assets to be made available to the developing countries in excess of their estimated needs should be paid to them directly, or whether they should be placed in the hands of an international financial intermediary such as the I.D.A. or I.B.R.D. which would thus obtain the resources to expand its lending activities. Second, there is the distinction between the " organic link " under which the I.M.F. would change the allocation rules so that S.D.R.s are initially credited to the I.D.A./I.B.R.D. or less-developed countries (Stamp (1958) (1962) (1965) and Triffin (1960)), and the " voluntary link " under which the advanced countries would pay part or all of their S.D.R. allocations either directly, or indirectly by payment of the national currency counterpart of allocations, to the I.D.A./I.B.R.D. (Colombo in I.M.F. (1968), Fried (1969), UNCTAD (1969)). Third, there is the question as to whether these S.D.R.s should be freely usable on the first round of spending (the " untied link "), or whether the developing countries should be restricted to spending them on the goods of those countries that indicate their willingness to accept additional S.D.R.s (the " tied link," proposed by Scitovsky (1966) and Karlik (1969)).

It is only the third of these questions that raises interesting issues of international monetary economics. The argument in favour of tying is that it avoids intensifying the pressure of demand in fully-employed economies, since it is assumed—perhaps questionably—that only countries suffering from unemployment would declare themselves eligible for expenditure from the proceeds of newly-created reserves. The real cost to the world of enabling countries to avoid payments-induced output losses is, Scitovsky argues, zero or negative. The main criticisms of the proposal stem from the fact that tying is unlikely to be very effective (since the I.D.A. could divert its non-tied funds to support purchases from those countries that were not eligible for tied expenditure); that tying is in any case restricted to the first round of expenditure, so that reserve increases would still indirectly intensify the pressure of demand in fully-employed countries; and that the availability of reserves on " preferential " terms to deficit countries would impair operation of the adjustment process (Haan (1971), p. 145).

4. *The Normative Theory of Reserve Supply*

Ever since the early 1920s economists have been comparing estimates of the " need " for reserves with projections of the future supply of reserves, with a view to making recommendations that would change the supply—by generalising the gold-exchange standard, changing the gold price, creating an International Clearing Union, increasing I.M.F. quotas, introducing new fiduciary reserve assets or (latterly) determining the rate of S.D.R. creation. The analysis has become more sophisticated in recent years, as is best appreciated by studying the proceedings of the conference convened by the I.M.F. to explore the subject in 1970 (I.M.F. (1970)).

The predominant standpoint at that conference (adopted *inter alia* by Kemp, Polak, Rhomberg, Salant and several of the I.M.F. staff papers printed as appendices) was to follow Fleming (1961) (1967) in viewing reserve creation as a policy instrument in the hands of the international authorities, which should be set with the aim of maximising a world welfare function. The maximisation is, of course, subject to a set of constraints imposed by the positive way in which the world economy operates, *including* the reaction patterns of the various national governments. In principle this requires that one should give a precise specification of the world welfare function, as well as construct and estimate a positive model that predicts how national governments would react to changes in reserve ease and how the international economy would respond to these variations in national policies. The obvious infeasibility of approximating this ideal procedure does not mean that the approach is incapable of generating operationally useful guidelines. Virtually any positive theory of the behaviour of national governments will lead to the prediction that greater reserve ease will generate some or all the various effects listed in II.4, such as more expansionary demand-management policies and fewer restrictions. The optimum rate of reserve growth is characterised by beneficial effects in the form of higher employment and fewer restrictions being equal at the margin to the untoward effects of inflation and the resource misallocation implied by larger reserve flows. If one could find a period when demand policies seemed in general to be about right, when restrictions and controls were low and declining, and so on, this could be taken as indicative of a desirable degree of reserve ease. The question then becomes one of extrapolating the reserve growth needed to perpetuate the same degree of reserve ease.

One approach which might be taken as competitive with the above " welfare-maximising approach " could be termed the " target-reconciliation approach." This goes back at least to Day in Joint Economic Committee (1961) and was developed explicitly by Argy in I.M.F. (1970, pp. 255–9). Its essence is the claim that the optimum rate of reserve growth is that which will permit the simultaneous satisfaction of the payments objectives of all countries. Argy demonstrated this in the context of a two-country world in which payments equilibrium is consistent with full employment in both countries, but in which desired reserves exceed actual reserves. He then showed that all the possible reactions to this situation—competitive increases in interest rates, competitive devaluations, deflation and restrictions

—are unambiguously inferior to the outcome that would occur if one created sufficient S.D.R.s to eliminate the excess demand for reserves.[1]   He therefore concluded that the major objective of reserve-creation policy should be that of reconciling targets, and hence a liquidity shortage or surplus should be established by seeking evidence of target incompatibility.   Unfortunately it is not clear that the conclusion can legitimately be generalised from a two-country world to an *n*-country world, because in the latter an increase in liquidity that would *permit* all countries to achieve their payments objectives would not necessarily result in all countries *actually* achieving them.   The increased liquidity may end up with those who have enough rather than those with a shortage: the latter may simply be relieved of the need to pursue adjustment with the vigour that would otherwise have been required, and the welfare of surplus countries may accordingly be reduced.   Under such conditions there seems no alternative but to attempt to weigh the benefit to one country against the loss to another (as under the welfare-maximising approach).   But if there is a mechanism that ensures that adjustment actually occurs, the target-reconciliation approach is quite acceptable because it is equivalent to the welfare-maximising approach: an increase in reserve creation which enables one country to satisfy its preferences without thwarting another will have that result, and that is unambiguously beneficial under any welfare function in which world welfare is a positive function of national welfare levels.

If targets are not consistent, then the system will suffer from an inflationary (or revaluation) bias or a deflationary (or devaluation) bias (see II.4 above).   Thus Scitovsky in Joint Economic Committee (1961) and Tobin (1963) argued that the optimum rate of reserve growth should be sought by examining whether the existing reserve situation is placing equal pressure to adjust on both deficit and surplus countries.

A third approach, which might be termed the price-stabilisation approach, comes in several variants.   Their common feature is that they propose that the rate of reserve creation be determined with a view to stabilising some particular price index.   Mundell (1965) (1968, Chapter 13) has in effect proposed that the appropriate price index is a weighted average of final output prices in the various countries, with weights equal to real output levels: both a dearth and an excess of liquidity should be avoided because they would impose general deflationary or inflationary pressure. This could be viewed as a special case of the welfare-maximising approach in which one assumes that reserve ease mainly influences demand-management policy and in which no problems of cost inflation arise to threaten adoption of a zero price trend target.   Mundell used his criterion to deduce that the proper division of the burden of adjustment is in inverse proportion to the size of countries, which is similar to the Scitovsky/Tobin position.

---

[1] The only possible exception would be if one preferred the distributional result of increasing liquidity through gold revaluation resulting from competitive depreciation to that of S.D.R. creation.

A second variant of the approach is that of Modigliani and Kenen (1966), who proposed that the objective should be stabilisation of an index of foreign trade prices in terms of the reserve asset; they advocated accomplishing this by reducing liquidity creation when inflation occurred, and vice versa. (Countries would, however, have been allowed to overcome the deflationary effect of the restriction of liquidity by devaluation.) This approach regards stability in the purchasing power of the numeraire as an end in itself, and does not seem to be related to any of the ideas previously discussed. A third variant of this approach, due to Marris (1970, p. 58) and Williamson (1971, pp. 15–22), was proposed as an adjunct to a crawling-peg system of parity changes; it suggested that the rate of S.D.R. creation should be varied so as to stabilise an index of currency parities. The logic of this is that if parities are changed when and only when countries are dissatisfied with their rate of reserve accumulation, parity changes provide a test as to whether payments targets are consistent. An excess of devaluations over revaluations provides evidence of a reserve shortage which is leading countries to compete for the existing stock of reserves, so increased reserve creation is indicated by the target-reconciliation approach. Since the crawling peg is envisaged as providing the adjustment mechanism to ensure that adjustment actually occurs, this is claimed to be a case in which satisfaction of the target-reconciliation approach implies welfare maximisation as well.

In the preceding discussion the phrase " reserve ease " has been used deliberately. The reason is that Fleming (1967) [1] argued that the attitudes of a country towards its external position—and therefore its balance-of-payments policy—would be governed jointly by its stock of reserves and its rate of reserve growth. Most of the literature on the demand for reserves (see II.1) assumes that it is the stock of reserves alone that determines reserve ease, although a minor role would be attributed to reserve growth in those models that postulate positive auto-correlation in reserve changes. In strong contrast, a number of writers (*e.g.*, Machlup (1966) and Gilbert (1968)) placed their emphasis entirely on reserve growth. This extreme position is unpersuasive, partly because indifference to the level of reserves gives rise to an indeterminacy akin to that of the price level in a general equilibrium system that omits the demand for cash balances (Niehans in Johnson and Swoboda (1973), p. 53) and partly because of the historical examples of high-reserve countries that viewed reserve losses with equanimity (the United States in the 1950s or certain primary producers on attaining independence). Fleming's compromise is much more appealing, and would be consistent with the generalisation of the demand-for-reserves models sketched at the end of II.1, in which the expected value of the payments outcome is a state variable which could be changed through time by measures that might impose some welfare loss. The main doubt about this conception

_____
[1] Fleming actually used the term " balance-of-payments ease."

is Streeter's (1970) empirical finding of virtually no support for the auto-regressive hypothesis concerning quarterly and annual reserve changes.

Knowledge of individual countries' demand-for-reserves functions can play an important role in aiding application of the above approaches to determining the global supply of reserves, but it is less crucial than most of the early work supposed. This is primarily because the target-reconciliation approach, for which knowledge of the national demands for reserves would be essential, has tended to lose ground to the welfare-maximising approach, which relies primarily on evidence provided by the state of the world economy. As Niehans pointed out in I.M.F. (1970, pp. 83–4), domestic monetary policy relies on macro-economic symptoms and not on judgments of the adequacy of individual cash balances. Nevertheless, the fact that reserve policy operates with long lags and is determined by laborious and lengthy international negotiations means that observations of excessive reserve ease or stringency cannot be translated into prompt monetary responses as in the domestic context. It is therefore necessary to extrapolate the reserve growth needed to perpetuate a desired degree of reserve ease that was observed in some past period, and it is for this purpose that know-ledge of demand-for-reserves functions can be particularly valuable. Specifically, a tendency for the demand for reserves to grow in proportion to imports—or in any other systematic relationship, such as by the square root law—can permit the desirable rate of reserve growth to be deduced from forecasts of trade growth. This is essentially the way in which the I.M.F. staff used the various " quantitative criteria for the assessment of reserve needs " in estimating the need for S.D.R. creation (see the appendices to I.M.F. (1970)).

5. *The Adequacy of Reserves*

Prior to 1960 the discussion of reserve adequacy tended to be centred in Britain, where there was an apparent consensus that a world liquidity shortage existed and was growing worse. (See Harrod (1953) (1958), Day (1954) (1960), MacDougall (1957), Franks (1958), Stamp (1958) and the Radcliffe Report Cmnd 827 (1959). In due course Hawtrey (1962) differed sharply.) Two international reports on the subject (U.N. (1952) and I.M.F. (1953)) shared the predominant British conception of the prob-lem, in which reserve adequacy tended to be measured in terms of the ability of the non-dollar world to withstand a United States recession of the severity of 1937–38. This approach precluded recognition of the fact—which is so crucial in retrospect (Polak in I.M.F. (1970) p. 512)—that a *world* liquidity shortage could hardly be said to exist so long as there was a dominant country with vastly excessive reserve holdings available for redistribution. The next major investigation of the subject (I.M.F. (1958)) was no longer dominated by the fear of " Europe catching pneumonia if the United States sneezed." It assumed a normal reserve need of 30% to 50% of annual imports, which implied that the existing reserve supply was adequate. More controversially, it also claimed there was a reasonable prospect of meeting the growth in the demand for reserves until the mid-1960s without radical institutional change.   The fact that some countries continued to suffer from inadequate reserves was attributed to their unwillingness to take the necessary adjustment measures rather than to a deficiency of supply.

Triffin (1960) was critical of the complacent tone of the I.M.F. report. He cited (as the British writers had done) the decline in the reserves–imports ratio, which had fallen to 35% (outside the reserve centres) by 1957.   But he did not make the mistake of treating any decline as a self-evident misfortune: he examined the experience of countries that had suffered lower ratios and concluded that below 20% their situation had been desperate, and below 30% they had felt compelled to adjust.   (It is a curious fact that this promising method of evaluating the usefulness of the reserves–imports ratio has been little further utilised, although I.M.F. (1966, p. 14) contains a brief reference.)   Hence a 35% average was close to the minimum safe level.   But Triffin's chief attack was centred on the assertion that the prospective reserve growth would prove adequate over the period 1958–67; he argued that the Fund had both under-estimated the growth in demand and over-estimated the safe supply of dollars.

The initial reaction of the authorities to Triffin's warnings was to affirm that the system was basically sound and could be further strengthened by the *ad hoccery* described in III.1.   In particular, there was little inclination to accept the diagnosis of an existing liquidity shortage and considerable support for the opposite view that reserve ease was excessive and causing inflation.   But this gradually became coupled with acceptance of the probability that a reserve shortage would emerge after the United States deficit had been eliminated, and this led to the contingency planning for the creation of a new reserve asset.   It was regarded as contingency planning because of the official view in the mid-1960s that reserves were at that time adequate.   (See Group of Ten (1964) (1965) and the Annual Reports of the I.M.F. from 1963 to 1966.)   When presenting the case for activating S.D.R.s, the I.M.F. took the view (based on the welfare-maximising approach described in III.4) that reserve ease had certainly been satisfactory up till 1965 and largely so up till 1968 (see I.M.F. (1970), pp. 465–6, 494).

Academic opinion was more varied (or, at least, its variation was more apparent).   At one extreme was Lutz (1965), whose views would have pleased the most anti-inflationist central banker.   Triffin (1961) revised his views on the existing inadequacy of liquidity, and even suggested it might have been growing too rapidly.   The majority of academic opinion probably endorsed this view, although with less conviction than the authorities.   And the academics were more rapidly convinced that it would be necessary to devise new arrangements to cope with future reserve growth. Furthermore, an increasing number, headed by Johnson (1964), adopted the view that one could not leave the creation of a new reserve asset until after the United States deficit had been corrected, because in that event the deficit—being at least in part demand-determined—never would be eliminated.

There was a minority view which continued to hold that a serious liquidity shortage already existed. One adherent of this view was Scitovsky ((1965), and in Samuelson (1969)), who judged that the surplus countries were almost entirely escaping any pressure to participate in the adjustment process and regarded that as conclusive evidence of a liquidity shortage (see III.4). Presumably this implied that the Continental complaints of imported inflation were regarded as a mere diplomatic ploy, a diagnosis suggested to some by their failure to revalue their currencies. The other adherents, Harrod (in Harris (1961), (1966)), the Brookings Report (1963) and Salant in Murphy (1964), all based their view on the desirability of permitting countries to adjust very slowly. There are two possible criticisms of their position. The first is that, even if it is true that countries in general will not abuse liberal reserve facilities by inflating so as to obtain unrequited resource transfers from the rest of the world—and Harrod in particular denounced any such supposition with a conviction that must be deemed questionable in view of the empirical results surveyed in II.1 and II.2—this does not mean that inflation will not result. The mere avoidance of deflation in the deficit countries will have expansionary consequences in the surplus countries. The second is the doubt as to whether " slow adjustment " does not really mean " no adjustment." Harrod advocated incomes policy, and waiting two or three years to see whether things would reverse themselves naturally, as the ideal adjustment methods: those recommended by the Brookings Report inspire little greater confidence. Their world looks dangerously like that portrayed by Flanders (1969), where countries are indifferent to the opportunity costs of reserve holding, refuse to change exchange rates, and have identical Phillips curves but different tastes for inflation, so that the optimal stock of international liquidity is infinite in order to finance the ever-increasing payments imbalances.

Round about 1965, the international monetary system underwent—by common consent—a profound change. In the stages of the gold-exchange standard portrayed by Gilbert (1968), one lurched from Stage II to Stage III—the stage of zero gold growth—and then to Stage IV—the stage of negative gold growth. Others emphasised that voluntarily-held dollars also started to decline and that the sole component of reserve growth became the counterpart to the negotiated credits extended to the reserve centres (Triffin (1967), Lamfalussy (1969)). The long trend towards decreased restrictions and controls was checked and in some areas—notably those relating to capital movements—reversed. There was sharply increasing dissatisfaction with adjustment performance, which some attributed to the consequences of the Vietnam war and others (e.g., Salant (1969)) to a liquidity shortage in combination with the unrecognised position of the United States deficit as demand-determined. The sterling devaluation of 1967 and the two-tier gold market of 1968 marked the end of an era.

It was therefore in an atmosphere of considerable uncertainty and confusion, and accompanied by sudden discussion of long-forbidden subjects like exchange-rate flexibility, that the S.D.R. agreement ground its way to ratification and discussions on activation commenced. These resulted in activation on a considerably larger scale ($9·5 billion over 3 years) than had been envisaged during the negotiations to create the S.D.R. facility. It would seem that this was the joint product of three factors. First, virtually all the methods employed by the I.M.F. to extrapolate the reserve ease prevailing up to the mid-1960s into the early 1970s suggested there would be a substantial shortfall in liquidity in the absence of S.D.R.s: this largely reflected the fact that reserves had scarcely grown between 1965 and 1968. (See the appendices to I.M.F. (1970).) Second, the conviction had been growing in the I.M.F. (it was first noted in I.M.F. (1966), p. 10) and presumably in other official circles that the main response to payments stringency was to be found in restrictions and controls rather than demand-management policy, so that the conflicting signals for reserve policy provided by the simultaneous intensification of restrictions and inflation were resolved in favour of the former (I.M.F. (1970), pp. 495–6). Third, the temporary United States official settlements surplus resulting from acute monetary stringency produced a liquidity famine in Europe that provided both a perceived need for additional reserves and an occasion for contending that the condition of S.D.R. activation regarding the prior elimination of the United States deficit had been satisfied.

The second of these reasons has since been challenged by Johnson (1972a). After a brief flirtation with the idea of gold revaluation to relieve the acute liquidity shortage (1969), and in Eltis (1970), Johnson (1972a) has asserted that the threat of a liquidity shortage is " an exact inversion of the real problem, which is to establish international control over the magnitude and rate of growth of international reserves and use it to restrain the rate of growth of those reserves to a non-inflationary pace " (p. 86). It will doubtless be worth watching the controversy that develops on this issue.

IV. Conclusion

The literature surveyed in the preceding pages may be interpreted as providing the basis for an approach to the study of the international monetary system similar in philosophy to the conventional way of analysing national economies. The material covered in II.1 and II.2 posed the prior question as to whether the actions of individual countries are sufficiently influenced by maximising behaviour to make it profitable to construct models of the system based on the postulate of rationality. It was concluded that there is sufficient evidence to justify such an approach. Section II.4, and parts of II.2 and II.3, explored the progress that has been made in constructing such models of the international economy and exploring their implications for the functioning of the system. The understanding gained from this analysis is an essential input into the evaluation of alternative methods of creating and distributing new liquidity, and of regulating its supply (Section III).

There remains ample scope for theoretical work in integrating the disparate strands of analysis into a more coherent general framework than has yet been achieved. But the potential benefits of more systematic applied analysis may well be even greater. In a number of cases different views are attributable to economists adopting competitive hypotheses that can only be chosen between on empirical grounds. The field has started to generate serious empirical work (II.1 and II.2), but there remains ample scope for more. To begin with, the fact that there are plenty of data should not obscure the fact that there are certain crucial gaps: no attempt has been made to construct a liquidity series on the more sophisticated concept developed by Kane (1965), or to develop performance indices of the system as suggested by Salant in I.M.F. (1970), or to measure adjustment costs. Statistical description of reserve-change series needs to be further pursued. Models of the demand for reserves need developing to include fundamental disequilibria. The hypotheses on reserve composition could be further tested on sterling holdings. There is an urgent need to discriminate between the demand-oriented and supply-oriented theories of the United States deficit. It is equally urgent to gain systematic knowledge about the form in which countries' policies typically react to changes in reserve ease. And it would be interesting to have a test of whether governments' policies are principally motivated by national wealth, national power or an incurable attachment to sovereignty. The future usefulness of international monetary economics is likely to be determined by its success in providing correct and convincing answers to such questions.

JOHN WILLIAMSON

University of Warwick, Coventry
and International Monetary Fund, Washington.

BIBLIOGRAPHY

J. P. Agarwal (1971), " Optimal Monetary Reserves for Developing Countries," *Weltwirtschaftliches Archiv*, 1971.

R. Z. Aliber (1964), " The Costs and Benefits of the US Role as a Reserve Currency Country," *Quarterly Journal of Economics*, August 1964.

—— (1965), " The Benefits and Costs of Being the World Banker: Comment," *National Banking Review*, March 1965.

—— (1967), " Gresham's Law, Asset Preferences, and the Demand for International Reserves," *Quarterly Journal of Economics*, November 1967.

R. Z. Aliber (1969a), *Choices for the Dollar*, National Planning Association, Washington, D.C., 1969.

—— (1969b), " Gresham's Law and the Demand for NRUs and SDRs: Reply," *Quarterly Journal of Economics*, November 1969.

—— (1974), ed., *National Monetary Policies and the International Financial System*, University of Chicago Press, Chicago, 1974.

O. L. Altman (1958), " A Note on Gold Production and Additions to International Reserves," I.M.F. *Staff Papers*, April 1958.

—— (1961), " Professor Triffin on International Liquidity and the Role of the Fund," I.M.F. *Staff Papers*, April 1961, reprinted in Grubel (1963).

J. Angell (1961), " The Reorganisation of the International Monetary System: an Alternative Proposal," ECONOMIC JOURNAL, December 1961, reprinted in Grubel (1963).

G. C. Archibald and J. Richmond (1971), " On the Theory of Foreign Exchange Reserve Requirements," *Review of Economic Studies*, April 1971.

H. W. Arndt (1948), " The Concept of Liquidity in International Monetary Theory," *Review of Economic Studies*, October 1948.

T. Balogh (1960), "International Reserves and Liquidity," ECONOMIC JOURNAL, June 1960.

E. M. Bernstein (1963), " A Practical Program for International Monetary Reserves," *Quarterly Review and Investment Survey* of Model, Roland and Co., 1963(4).

S. T. Beza and G. Patterson (1961), " Foreign Exchange Guarantees and the Dollar," *American Economic Review*, June 1961.

D. Bhattacharya (1968), " International Liquidity: Is There a Problem of Current and Prospective Shortage?," Wayne State Ph.D., 1968.

A. I. Bloomfield (1959), *Monetary Policy Under the International Gold Standard: 1880–1914*, Federal Reserve Board, New York, 1959.

H. W. J. Bosman and F. A. M. Alting von Geusau (1970), eds., *The Future of the International Monetary System*, A. W. Sijthoff, Leyden, 1970.

J. P. Briffaux (1968), " Un point de retournement dans le mouvement long de la production mondiale d'or," *Recherches Économiques de Louvain*, May 1968.

R. Britto and H. R. Heller (1973), "International Adjustment and Optimal Reserves," *International Economic Review*, March 1973.

Brookings Report (1963), *The United States Balance of Payments in 1968*, Joint Economic Committee, U.S. Congress, Washington, D.C., 1963.

W. M. Brown (1955), " The Concept and Measurement of Foreign Exchange Reserves," ECONOMIC JOURNAL, September 1955.

—— (1964), *The External Liquidity of an Advanced Country*, Princeton Studies in International Finance No. 14, Princeton 1964.

W. J. Busschau (1961), *Gold and International Liquidity*, South African Institute of International Affairs, Johannesburg, 1961.

—— (1967), " Future Trends in Gold Production," *Kyklos*, 1967.

F. Cassell (1965), *Gold or Credit?*, Pall Mall Press, London, 1965.

E. Claassen and P. Salin (1972), eds., *Stabilization Policies in Interdependent Economies*, N. Holland, Amsterdam, 1972.

P. B. Clark (1970a) " Optimum International Reserves and the Speed of Adjustment," *Journal of Political Economy*, March 1970.

—— (1970b), " The Demand for International Reserves: A Cross-Country Analysis," *Canadian Journal of Economics*, November 1970.

—— (1973), " Interest Payments and the Rate of Return on an International Fiat Currency," *Weltwirtschaftliches Archiv*, 1973.

M. O. Clement (1963), " A Functional Approach to the Concept of International Reserves," *Kyklos*, 1963.

R. W. Clower and R. G. Lipsey (1968), " The Present State of International Liquidity Theory," *American Economic Review*, May 1968.

B. J. Cohen (1966), *Adjustment Costs and the Distribution of New Reserves*, Princeton Studies in International Finance No. 18, Princeton 1966.

—— (1971a), *The Future of Sterling as an International Currency*, Macmillan, London, 1971.

—— (1971b), " The Seigniorage Gains of an International Currency," *Quarterly Journal of Economics*, August 1971.

S. D. Cohen (1970), *International Monetary Reform 1964–69: the Political Dimension*, Praeger, London, 1970.

Cmd 6437 (1943), *Proposals for an International Clearing Union* (Keynes Plan), H.M.S.O., London, 1943.

Cmnd 827 (1959), *Committee on the Working of the Monetary System: Report* (Radcliffe Report), H.M.S.O., London, 1959.

R. N. Cooper (1968), " The Relevance of International Liquidity to Developed Countries," *American Economic Review*, May 1968.

T. J. Courchene and G. M. Youssef (1967), " The Demand for International Reserves," *Journal of Political Economy*, August 1967.

A. C. L. Day (1954), *The Future of Sterling*, Clarendon Press, Oxford, 1954.

—— (1960), " The World Liquidity Problem and the British Monetary System," in *Principal Memoranda of Evidence Submitted to the Committee on the Working of the Monetary System*, Vol. 3, H.M.S.O., London, 1960.

E. Despres, C. P. Kindleberger, W. S. Salant (1966), " The Dollar and World Liquidity—A Minority View," *The Economist*, 5 February 1966.

W. A. Eltis, M. Fg. Scott, J. N. Wolfe (1970), eds., *Induction, Growth and Trade*, Clarendon Press, Oxford, 1970.

H. Ezekiel (1966), " The Present System of Reserve Creation in the Fund," *I.M.F. Staff Papers*, November 1966.

P. D. Fells (1972), *Gold 1972*, Consolidated Gold Fields Ltd., London, 1972.

M. J. Flanders (1969), " International Liquidity is Always Inadequate," *Kyklos*, 1969.

—— (1971), *The Demand for International Reserves*, Princeton Studies in International Finance No. 27, Princeton, 1971.

J. M. Fleming (1961), " International Liquidity: Ends and Means," *I.M.F. Staff Papers*, December 1961, reprinted in Fleming (1971b).

—— (1967), *Towards Assessing the Need for International Reserves*, Princeton Essays in International Finance No. 58, Princeton, 1967, reprinted in Fleming (1971b).

—— (1971a), " The SDR: Some Problems and Possibilities," *I.M.F. Staff Papers*, March 1971.

—— (1971b), *Essays in International Economics*, Allen and Unwin, London, 1971.

Sir O. Franks (1958), Statement by the Chairman of Lloyd's Bank Ltd., *Report and Accounts of Lloyd's Bank Ltd.*, January 1958, reprinted in *The Times*, 23 January 1958.

J. A. Frenkel (1974), " The Demand for Reserves by Developed and Less Developed Countries," *Economica*, February 1974.

E. R. Fried (1969), " International Liquidity and Foreign Aid," *Foreign Affairs*, October 1969.

M. Friedman (1951), " Commodity-Reserve Currency," *Journal of Political Economy*, June 1951, reprinted in Friedman, *Essays in Positive Economics*, University of Chicago Press, Chicago, 1953.

M. Gilbert (1968), *The Gold-Dollar System: Conditions of Equilibrium and the Price of Gold*, Princeton Essays in International Finance No. 70, Princeton, 1968.

V. Giscard d'Estaing (1965), *Les Problèmes Monétaires Internationaux*, Institut d'études bancaires et financières, Paris, 1965.

H. N. Goldstein (1965), " Does it Necessarily Cost Anything to be World Banker? " *National Banking Review*, March 1965.

—— (1969), " Gresham's Law and the Demand for NRUs and SDRs," *Quarterly Journal of Economics*, February 1969.

J. K. Green (1969), " The International Role of the Pound Sterling: its Benefits and Costs to the UK," University of Virginia Ph.D., 1969.

Group of Ten (1964), *Ministerial Statement*, 1 August 1964, reprinted in Roosa (1965).

—— (1965), *Report of the Study Group on the Creation of Reserve Assets* (Ossola Report), 1965.

H. G. Grubel (1963), ed., *World Monetary Reform*, Stanford University Press, Stanford, 1963.

—— (1964), " The Benefits and Costs of Being the World Banker," *National Banking Review*, December 1964.

—— (1965), " The Case Against an International Commodity Reserve Currency," *Oxford Economic Papers*, March 1965.

—— (1971a), " The Demand for International Reserves: a Critical Review of the Literature," *Journal of Economic Literature*, December 1971.

—— (1971b), " Interest Payments and the Efficiency of the International Monetary System," unpublished, 1971.

H. G. Grubel (1972), " Basic Methods for Distributing SDRs and the Problem of International Aid," *Journal of Finance*, December 1972.

R. L. Haan (1971), *Special Drawing Rights and Development*, Stenfert Kroese NV, Leyden, 1971.

G. Haberler (1971), " The Case Against the Link," *Banca Nazionale del Lavoro Quarterly Review*, March 1971.

H. A. Hagemann (1969), " Reserve Policies of Central Banks and their Implications for U.S. Balance of Payments Policy," *American Economic Review*, March 1969.

G. N. Halm (1965), " Gold-Value Guarantees," *Weltwirtschaftliches Archiv*, 1965.

E. M. Harmon (1959), *Commodity Reserve Currency*, Columbia University Press, New York, 1959.

S. E. Harris (1961), ed., *The Dollar in Crisis*, Harcourt, Brace and World Inc., New York, 1961.

Sir Roy Harrod (1953), " Imbalance of International Payments," I.M.F. *Staff Papers*, April 1953.

—— (1958), " The Role of Gold Today," *South African Journal of Economics*, March 1958.

—— (1961), *Alternative Methods for Increasing International Liquidity*, European League for Economic Co-operation, Brussels, 1961.

—— (1966), *Reforming the World's Money*, Macmillan, London, 1966.

A. G. Hart (1966), " The Case for and Against an International Commodity Reserve Currency," *Oxford Economic Papers*, July 1966.

A. G. Hart, N. Kaldor, J. Tinbergen (1964), " The Case for an International Commodity Reserve Currency," in *Proceedings of the UN Conference on Trade and Development* (Vol. III), United Nations, 1964.

Sir Ralph Hawtrey (1962), " Too Little Liquidity—or Too Much ?," *The Banker*, November 1962.

M. A. Heilperin (1962), " The Case for Going Back to Gold," *Fortune*, September 1962.

H. R. Heller (1966), " Optimal International Reserves," ECONOMIC JOURNAL, June 1966.

—— (1968), " The Transactions Demand for International Means of Payment," *Journal of Political Economy*, January 1968.

Sir Hubert Henderson (1932), " A Monetary Proposal for Lausanne," reprinted in H. D. Henderson, *The Inter-war Years*, Clarendon Press, Oxford, 1955.

F. Hirsch (1968), " Influences on Gold Production," I.M.F. *Staff Papers*, November 1968.

—— (1969), " The Future of Gold: Comment," *American Economic Review*, May 1969.

—— (1971), " SDRs and the Working of the Gold Exchange Standard," I.M.F. *Staff Papers*, July 1971.

—— (1974), " Control of International Liquidity and the Euro-dollar Market," in H. G. Johnson and A. R. Nobay, eds., *Issues in Monetary Economics*, Oxford University Press, Oxford, 1974.

J. K. Horsefield (1969), ed., *The IMF 1945–65*, I.M.F., Washington, D.C., 1969.

P. Høst-Madsen (1964), " Gold Outflows from the US 1956–63," I.M.F. *Staff Papers*, July 1964.

E. S. Howle (1974), " Real Reserves, Nominal Reserves, and Balance-of-Payments Adjustment," *Journal of International Economics*, February 1974.

I.M.F. (1953), " The Adequacy of Monetary Reserves," I.M.F. *Staff Papers*, October 1953.

—— (1958), *International Reserves and Liquidity*, I.M.F., Washington, D.C., 1958.

—— (1961), *Summary Proceedings of the Sixteenth Annual Meeting of the Board of Governors*, I.M.F., Washington, D.C., 1961.

—— (1962), *Summary Proceedings of the Seventeenth Annual Meeting of the Board of Governors*, I.M.F., Washington, D.C., 1962.

—— (1964), *Annual Report, 1964*, I.M.F., Washington, D.C., 1964.

—— (1965), *Annual Report, 1965*, I.M.F., Washington, D.C., 1965.

—— (1966), *Annual Report, 1966*, I.M.F., Washington, D.C., 1966.

—— (1968), *Summary Proceedings of the Twenty-third Annual Meeting of the Board of Governors*, I.M.F., Washington, D.C., 1968.

—— (1970), *International Reserves: Needs and Availiability*, I.M.F., Washington, D.C., 1970.

M. A. Iyoha (1973), " The Optimal Balance-of-Payments Strategy of a Less Developed Country," *Economic Record*, June 1973.

W. S. Jevons (1875), *Money and the Mechanism of Exchange*, 1875.

H. G. Johnson (1958), *International Trade and Economic Growth*, Unwin, London, 1958.

—— (1964), " The International Competitive Position of the United States and the Balance of Payments Prospect for 1968," *Review of Economics and Statistics*, February 1964.

—— (1966), " International Monetary Reform and the Less Developed Countries," *Malayan Economic Review*, April 1966.

H. G. Johnson (1967), " Theoretical Problems of the International Monetary System," *Pakistan Development Review*, Spring 1967.

—— (1969), *The International Monetary Problem: Gold, Dollars, SDRs, Wider Bands and Crawling Pegs*, University of Calgary, Calgary, 1969.

—— (1972a), *Inflation and the Monetarist Controversy*, N. Holland, Amsterdam, 1972.

—— (1972b), " The Link that Chains," *Foreign Policy*, Fall 1972.

H. G. Johnson and A. K. Swoboda (1973), eds., *The Economics of Common Currencies*, Macmillan, London, 1973.

Joint Economic Committee (1961), *International Payments Imbalances and the Need for Strengthening International Financial Arrangements*, Hearings, Subcommittee on International Exchange and Payments, Joint Economic Committee, U.S. Congress, Washington, D.C., 1961.

—— (1968), *Next Steps in International Monetary Reform*, Hearings, Subcommittee on International Exchange and Payments, Joint Economic Committee, U.S. Congress, Washington, D.C., September 1968.

N. Kaldor (1971), " Bretton Woods and After," *The Times*, September 6, 7, 8, 1971.

M. Kalecki and E. F. Schumacher (1943), " International Clearing and Long-term Lending," *Oxford University Institute of Statistics Bulletin*, August 7, 1943.

E. J. Kane (1965), " International Liquidity: a Probabilistic Approach," *Kyklos*, 1965.

J. H. Kareken (1965), " How Much Does Being World Banker Cost?," *National Banking Review*, September 1965.

J. R. Karlik (1969), *On Linking Reserve Creation and Development Assistance*, a staff study prepared for the Subcommittee on International Exchange and Payments of the Joint Economic Committee, U.S. Congress, Washington, D.C., 1969.

M. G. Kelly (1970), " The Demand for International Reserves," *American Economic Review*, September 1970.

P. B. Kenen (1960), " International Liquidity and the Balance of Payments of a Reserve-Currency Country," *Quarterly Journal of Economics*, November 1960.

—— (1963a), *Reserve-Asset Preferences of Central Banks and Stability of the Gold Exchange Standard*, Princeton Studies in International Finance No. 10, Princeton, 1963.

—— (1963b), " International Liquidity: the Next Steps," *American Economic Review*, May 1963.

P. B. Kenen and R. Lawrence (1968), eds., *The Open Economy*, Columbia University Press, New York, 1968.

P. B. Kenen and E. Yudin (1965), " The Demand for International Reserves," *Review of Economics and Statistics*, August 1965, reprinted in Kenen and Lawrence (1968).

J. M. Keynes (1913), *Indian Currency and Finance*, Macmillan, London, 1913.

—— (1930), *A Treatise on Money*, Vol. II, Macmillan, London, 1930.

—— (1933), " The Means to Prosperity," *The Times*, London, 1933.

C. P. Kindleberger (1965), *Balance-of-Payments Deficits and the International Market for Liquidity*, Princeton Essays in International Finance No. 46, Princeton, 1965.

A. P. Kirman and W. E. Schmidt (1965), " Key Currency Burdens: the UK Case," *National Banking Review*, September 1965.

S. C. Kolm (1970), " Les états-unis bénéficient-ils du ' droit de seigneur '?," *Kyklos*, 1970.

L. B. Krause (1970), " A Passive Balance-of-Payments Strategy for the United States," *Brookings Papers on Economic Activity*, 1970.

—— (1971), *Sequel to Bretton Woods*, Brookings Institution, Washington, D.C., 1971.

D. Laidler (1969), " The Case for Raising the Price of Gold: a Comment," *Journal of Money, Credit and Banking*, August 1969.

A. Lamfalussy (1968), " Pour une augmentation de la liquidité internationale," *Recherches Économiques de Louvain*, December 1968.

—— (1969), *The Role of Monetary Gold over the Next Ten Years*, I.M.F., Washington, D.C., 1969.

J. R. La Pittus (1970), " The Demand for Official Reserves to Finance International Trade under a System of Fixed Exchange Rates," Yale University Ph.D., 1970.

F. A. Lutz (1962), *The Problem of International Economic Equilibrium*, N. Holland, Amsterdam, 1962.

—— (1963), *The Problem of International Liquidity and the Multiple-Currency Standard*, Princeton Essays in International Finance No. 41, Princeton, 1963, reprinted in Grubel (1963).

—— (1965), " World Inflation and Domestic Monetary Stability," *Banca Nazionale del Lavoro Quarterly Review*, June 1965.

F. Machlup (1962), in *Outlook for U.S. Balance of Payments*, Hearings, Subcommittee on International Exchange and Payments, Joint Economic Committee, U.S. Congress, Washington D.C., December 1962, reprinted in Grubel (1963).

—— (1964), *Plans for Reform of the International Monetary System*, Princeton Special Papers in International Economics No. 3, Princeton, 1963, revised edition 1964.

—— (1965), " The Cloakroom Rule of International Reserves: Reserve Creation and Resource Transfer," *Quarterly Journal of Economics*, August 1965.

—— (1966), " The Need for Monetary Reserves," *Banca Nazionale del Lavoro Quarterly Review*, September 1966.

—— (1968a), *Remaking the International Monetary System: the Rio Agreement and Beyond*, Johns Hopkins, Baltimore, 1968.

—— (1968b), " The Transfer Gap of the United States," *Banca Nazionale del Lavoro Quarterly Review*, September 1968.

—— (1969), " Speculation on Gold Speculation," *American Economic Review*, May 1969.

F. Machlup and B. G. Malkiel (1964), eds., *International Monetary Arrangements: The Problem of Choice*, International Finance Section, Princeton University, Princeton, 1964.

J. H. Makin (1971a), " The Composition of International Reserve Holdings: A Problem of Choice Involving Risk," *American Economic Review*, December 1971.

—— (1971b), " Swaps and Roosa Bonds as an Index of the Cost of Cooperation in the ' Crisis Zone '," *Quarterly Journal of Economics*, May 1971.

S. N. Marris (1970), *The Bürgenstock Communiqué: A Critical Examination of the Case for Limited Flexibility of Exchange Rates*, Princeton Essays in International Finance No. 80, Princeton, 1970.

H. M. Mayer (1970), *Some Theoretical Problems Relating to the Euro-Dollar Market*, Princeton Essays in International Finance No. 79, Princeton, 1970.

G. W. Maynard (1972), *Special Drawing Rights and Development Aid*, Overseas Development Council, Washington, D.C., 1972.

G. D. A. MacDougall (1957), *The World Dollar Problem*, Macmillan, London, 1957.

R. I. McKinnon (1969), *Private and Official International Money: The Case for the Dollar*, Princeton Essays in International Finance No. 74, Princeton, 1969.

M. Michaely (1970), *The Responsiveness of Demand Policies to Balance of Payments: Postwar Patterns*, National Bureau of Economic Research, New York, 1970.

F. Modigliani and P. B. Kenen (1966), " A Suggestion for Solving the International Liquidity Problem," *Banca Nazionale del Lavoro Quarterly Review*, March 1966.

S. Mookerjee (1966), " Policies on the Use of Fund Resources," *I.M.F. Staff Papers*, November 1966.

R. A. Mundell (1965), *The International Monetary System: Conflict and Reform*, Private Planning Association of Canada, Montreal, 1965.

—— (1968), *International Economics*, Macmillan, London, 1968.

—— (1969), " Real Gold, Dollars, and Paper Gold," *American Economic Review*, May 1969.

—— (1971), *Monetary Theory: Inflation, Interest and Growth in the World Economy*, Goodyear, Pacific Palisades, 1971.

R. A. Mundell and A. K. Swoboda (1969), eds., *Monetary Problems of the International Economy*, University of Chicago Press, Chicago, 1969.

J. C. Murphy (1964), ed., *Money in the International Order*, Southern Methodist University Press, Dallas, 1964.

R. Nurkse (1944), *International Currency Experience*, League of Nations, Geneva, 1944.

L. H. Officer and T. D. Willett (1969), " Reserve-Asset Preferences and the Confidence Problem in the Crisis Zone," *Quarterly Journal of Economics*, November 1969.

—— (1970), " The Interaction of Adjustment and Gold-Conversion Policies in a Reserve-Currency System," *Western Economic Journal*, March 1970.

J. H. G. Olivera (1969), " A Note on the Optimal Rate of Growth of International Reserves," *Journal of Political Economy*, March 1969.

P. M. Oppenheimer (1969), " The Case for Raising the Price of Gold," *Journal of Money, Credit and Banking*, August 1969.

—— (1973), " The Nature of the World Monetary Problem," paper presented at a Royal Economic Society conference at Ditchley Park, January 1973.

J. J. Polak (1971), *Some Reflections on the Nature of Special Drawing Rights*, I.M.F., Washington, D.C., 1971.

S. Posthuma (1963), " The International Monetary System," *Banca Nazionale del Lavoro Quarterly Review*, September 1963.

W. B. Reddaway *et al.* (1968), *Effects of UK Direct Investment Overseas: Final Report*, Cambridge University Press, Cambridge, 1968.

R. R. Rhomberg (1966), " Trends in Payments Imbalances, 1952–64," I.M.F. *Staff Papers*, November 1966.

R. V. Roosa (1961), " Assuring the Free World's Liquidity," *Business Review Supplement*, Federal Reserve Bank of Philadelphia, September 1962, reprinted in Grubel (1963).

—— (1965), *Monetary Reform for the World Economy*, Harper and Row, New York, 1965.

D. E. Roper (1972), " On the Theory of the Devaluation Bias," *Kyklos*, 1972.

J. Rueff (1961), " The West is Risking a Credit Collapse," *Fortune*, July 1961.

W. S. Salant (1969), " International Reserves and Payments Adjustment," *Banca Nazionale del Lavoro Quarterly Review*, September 1969.

W. A. Salant (1964), " The Reserve Currency Role of the Dollar: Blessing or Burden to the US?," *Review of Economics and Statistics*, May 1964.

P. A. Samuelson (1969), ed., *International Economic Relations*, Macmillan, London, 1969.

J. A. Schumpeter (1954), *History of Economic Analysis*, Allen and Unwin, London, 1954.

T. Scitovsky (1958), *Economic Theory and Western European Integration*, Allen and Unwin, London, 1958.

—— (1965), *Requirements of an International Reserve System*, Princeton Essays in International Finance No. 49, Princeton, 1965.

—— (1966), " A New Approach to International Liquidity," *American Economic Review*, December 1966.

M. Stamp (1958), " The Fund and the Future," *Lloyd's Bank Review*, October 1958.

—— (1962), " The Stamp Plan—1962 Version," *Moorgate and Wall Street*, October 1962, reprinted in Grubel (1963).

—— (1965), " The Reform of the International Monetary System," *Moorgate and Wall Street*, Summer 1965.

L. Stekler and R. Piekarz (1970), " Reserve-Asset Composition for Major Central Banks," *Oxford Economic Papers*, July 1970.

L. E. Streeter (1970), " Optimal International Reserve Holdings: an Inventory Model and Empirical Tests," Illinois (Urbana) Ph.D., 1970.

E. Streissler (1969), " A Stochastic Model of International Reserve Requirements During Growth of World Trade," *Zeitschrift für Nationalökonomie*, December 1969.

R. S. Thorn (1967), " The Demand for International Reserves: a Note on Behalf of the Rejected Hypothesis," *Review of Economics and Statistics*, November 1967.

H. Thornton (1802), *An Enquiry into the Nature and Effects of the Paper Credit of Great Britain*, ed. by F. A. von Hayek, 3rd edition, Frank Cass, London, 1962.

J. Tobin (1963), " The Problem of International Liquidity," Statement to the Joint Economic Committee, U.S. Congress, Washington, D.C., November 15, 1963.

E. Tower and T. D. Willett (1972), " More on Official Versus Market Financing of Payments Deficits and the Optimal Pricing of International Reserves," *Kyklos*, 1972.

R. Triffin (1947), " National Central Banking and the International Economy," *Review of Economic Studies*, February 1947.

—— (1959), " The Return to Convertibility . . ."; " Tomorrow's Convertibility . . .," *Banca Nazionale del Lavoro Quarterly Review*, March, June 1969.

—— (1960), *Gold and the Dollar Crisis*, Yale University Press, New Haven, 1960.

—— (1961), " After the Gold Exchange Standard?," *Weltwirtschaftliches Archiv*, 1961, reprinted in Grubel (1963).

—— (1967), " The Coexistence of Three Types of Reserve Asset," *Banca Nazionale del Lavoro Quarterly Review*, June 1967.

—— (1968), *Our International Monetary System: Yesterday, Today and Tomorrow*, Random House, New York, 1968.

—— (1971), " The Use of SDR Finance for Collectively-Agreed Purposes," *Banca Nazionale del Lavoro Quarterly Review*, March 1971.

UNCTAD (1965), *International Monetary Issues and the Developing Countries*, United Nations (Sales No.: 66.II.D.2), 1965.

—— (1969), " International Monetary Reform and Cooperation for Development," United Nations, TD/B/285, October 13, 1969.

UN (1952), *Measures for International Economic Stability*, Economic and Social Council, United Nations, 1952.

C. R. Whittlesey (1964), " Liquidity, International Liquidity, and the Dollar Problem," *Weltwirtschaftliches Archiv*, 1964.

J.H. Williamson (1963), " Liquidity and the Multiple Key Currency Proposal," *American Economic Review*, June 1963.

—— (1971), *The Choice of a Pivot for Parities*, Princeton Essays in International Finance No. 90, Princeton, 1971.

—— (1972), " SDRs, Interest, and the Aid Link," *Banca Nazionale del Lavoro Quarterly Review*, June 1972.

P. Wonnacott (1963), " A Suggestion for the Revaluation of Gold," *Journal of Finance*, March 1963.

W.J. Woodfine (1958), " The Adequacy of International Monetary Reserves," M.I.T. Ph.D., 1958.

L. B. Yeager (1959), " The Misconceived Problem of International Liquidity," *Journal of Finance*, September 1959.

—— (1961), " The Triffin Plan: Diagnosis, Remedy, and Alternatives," *Kyklos*, 1961.

X. Zolotas (1961), *Towards a Reinforced Gold Exchange Standard*, Bank of Greece, Athens, 1961.

ADDENDUM

1. *Introduction*

The period since this survey was completed has witnessed the collapse of the adjustable peg and the move to generalised managed floating; the unsuccessful attempt by the Committee of Twenty (C-20) to reconstruct the international monetary system according to an agreed blueprint; a fundamental change in the basis of valuation of the SDR; a global inflation without precedent in time of peace; the largest international redistribution of income in history, with consequent massive current-account imbalances; and increasing demands for a " new international economic order " that would distribute the fruits of economic activity more equitably between nations. While some of the literature in international monetary economics during this period has represented an evolution from what went before, the greater part has reflected these new developments. There has, in particular, been much analytical (as opposed to predominantly advocatory) work on flexible exchange rates, one aspect of which has concerned the impact of floating on the demand for reserves. This addendum is designed to cover such of this new work as falls within the scope of the original survey.

The addendum, like the survey itself, is confined to the subject of official reserves. It should, however, be acknowledged that there is a growing tendency to question the propriety of drawing a sharp distinction between official and private holdings of internationally-liquid assets. For example, Cooper (1972) argued that the role of the dollar as private international money, which he argued was based on deep-rooted efficiency considerations,[1] would make it extremely difficult to diminish the official role of the dollar as required by the concern of the Committee of 20 to establish legal symmetry between currencies, and hence that any reform that was to succeed in eliminating the asymmetries would also need to replace the dollar in its private international role. A second example is provided in I.M.F. (1974b) p. 44 where the Fund's annual survey of the adequacy of international liquidity included note of developments in private international liquidity, on the implicit ground that private holdings of liquid foreign assets by a country's residents are to some undetermined extent a substitute for official reserves. Perhaps the most explicit endorsement of this position is by Chrystal (1975), who argues that the efficient conduct of international trade requires that some agent hold stocks of internationally-acceptable media of exchange, and that there may be economies of scale in the central holding of such balances which lead to a part of them being concentrated in official reserve holdings, but that it is more appropriate to consider the aggregate of official and private balances than it is to analyse them

---

[1] But see Grassman (1973), who questions the empirical basis for this assertion.

individually. The question is an interesting and important one, but this is not the place to pursue it.

II.1. *The Demand for Reserves*

Cohen (forthcoming), in another survey of international liquidity with a scope broadly comparable to that of the one reprinted above, placed particular emphasis on the need for more systematic exploration of the interrelationship between the demand for reserves and the adjustment techniques employed. Most of the recent work on the demand for reserves goes some way, though perhaps not very far, to answering this call. In particular, the approach pioneered by Iyoha (1973)—and also by Williamson in Clayton *et al* (1971)—has been further explored by such writers as Korkman (1973) and Nybery and Viotti (1974), but without any outstanding new results.

Both Claassen (1974) (1975) and Hipple (1974) have offered developments of the Clark–Kelly model characterised by distinctive treatment of adjustment responses. Claassen argued that adjustment is not in fact varied continuously in response to deviations of reserves from their target level, but is better characterised as occurring discontinuously when reserves hit critical upper and lower levels. He showed that such a discontinuity implied an asymmetry between the reactions in surplus and deficit situations, with the reaction to reserve stringency being quicker but smaller than that to a surfeit of reserves. (He also discussed the problem of optimal choice of adjustment policies, but without integrating this analysis into the formal model.) Hipple developed an elegant synthesis of previous models[1] that is notable particularly for its combination of the Clark–Kelly assumption of a regular response of adjustment policy to discrepancies of reserves from their target level, and of the Heller assumption that reserve depletion compels precipitate adjustment and therefore a loss of income. He is thus able to deduce the optimal depletion probability as a part of the optimising process rather than having to assume an arbitrary acceptable depletion probability. Nevertheless, one may wonder (despite Claassen) whether—to develop a thought of Lesser (1974)—it can really be rational to pursue a discontinuous strategy of this character; the optimum adjustment policy should surely involve the adoption of adjustment responses of progressively increasing intensity as the threat of reserve depletion grows. (This seems a clear enough corollary of, for example, Nybery and Viotti (1974).)

A particular aspect of the interrelationship between reserve demand and adjustment techniques that emerged into the limelight following the move to generalised floating in March 1973 concerns the impact of floating exchange rates on the demand for reserves. Since the new regime was one

[1] Incidentally, Hipple brought to light the first stochastic model of optimal reserve-holding policy, constructed by Nagabhushanam and Sastry (1962), but subsequently overlooked by other workers in this field, the author included. Another oversight in the main survey, brought to my attention by Makin (1974), was the pioneering use of the reserves/imports ratio in League of Nations (1930).

of managed rather than free floating, the move could hardly be expected to eliminate the demand for reserves, but it had always been taken as axiomatic that there was an inverse relationship between the demand for reserves and the degree of flexibility. (See, for example, the unqualified remark [on p. 10] above: " . . . the need for reserves will decline as exchange rate flexibility increases.") Makin (1974) provided the most explicit model justifying this traditional presupposition, and used Canadian experience to estimate the impact of a widening of the band on the demand for reserves. He concluded that a doubling of the band width would reduce the demand for reserves by between one third and one half (p. 238).[1] This conclusion is, however, critically dependent on Makin's assumption that the demand and supply curves for foreign exchange are independent of the exchange-rate regime and of the previous history of the exchange rates itself. It is precisely these assumptions which Williamson (1976a) challenged, after noting that the use of reserves had in fact increased in the year following the move to floating, and had remained high in the subsequent year. He constructed a model which demonstrated the possibility that greater flexibility would actually increase reserve use (and therefore presumably the demand for reserves). One may perhaps judge this possibility empirically remote, but the point is not conclusively established and, while the qualitative effect of exchange-rate flexibility on the demand for reserves remains open to doubt, one cannot place much faith in Makin's quantitative estimate.

Even if one sees little reason to doubt the traditional assumption that floating reduces the demand for reserves by the country that floats, it has been argued—see, for example, Kafka (1975)—that floating between third currencies will increase the level of reserves needed to insure against reserve depletion by a country that continues to peg to one of the floating currencies. The reason is that flexibility between the third currencies adds to the instability of the pegging country's payments balance. While qualitatively correct, it has been shown that the effect is quantitatively negligible (Williamson (1975)). Another extension of reserve-demand analysis of particular applicability to developing countries was the attempt of Pereira-Leite (1974) to model the effect of increased reserves in increasing confidence and thereby permitting increased borrowing; any such effect naturally tends to increase the optimal level of reserves.

Two further empirical estimates of reserve demand have appeared, by Hipple (1974) and Iyoha (1974). Hipple's estimate was based on a cross-section study of 61 nations over the period 1960–65. It sought to explain average reserve holdings in terms of a measure of payments variability, a proxy for the marginal efficiency of investment, a proxy for the cost of

[1] Makin's analysis included an interesting adaptation of the analysis of optimal precautionary balances by Whalen (1966), who derived a cube-root rule for the relationship between reserves and transactions analogous to the square-root rule of Olivera (1969) noted in the main paper; after allowing for a proportionate dependence of the cost of depletion on the size of the reserve shortfall, Makin concluded that a square-root rule was in fact the appropriate form.

expenditure-switching policies, G.N.P., per capita income, the average propensity to import, a dummy variable representing willingness to change the exchange rate, and the growth rate. The results were consistent with those reported in the main survey. Payments variability proved highly significant, as did G.N.P. (which was being treated as a proxy for wealth, but may simply have acted as a scale variable analogous to the level of imports in previous studies). The import propensity was sometimes significant, and had a positive coefficient. The exchange-rate flexibility proxy was sometimes significant (with the traditionally expected negative sign) for the developed countries, although one can conceive of this being due to a simultaneity problem. Per capita income and the proxy for the cost of expenditure-switching policies gave some significant results for L.D.C.s. The other variables, including the " marginal efficiency of investment " (the inverse of the gross marginal capital–output ratio), were insignificant. The results of Iyoha's study, which was based on 29 L.D.C.s and embodied a distributed-lag specification, were for the most part consistent. Payments variability and the average import propensity were again significant, with the same signs. The domestic interest rate also proved significant, with a positive sign. Iyoha interpreted this as a measure of the return on reserve holding, and therefore concluded that he had succeeded in establishing the predicted relationship between reserve-holding and its opportunity cost. The interpretation is not convincing, however, since the return a country earns on its reserves is quite independent of its own interest rate. Indeed, it would be more persuasive to treat the interest rate as a measure of the productivity of investment, in which case the empirical result is the opposite of that predicted. It is, however, possible that a simultaneity problem is present: high interest rates attract a capital inflow and cause large reserves. The striking failure to confirm the expected inverse association between the quantity of reserves demanded and the opportunity cost of reserve holding therefore remains.

II.2. *The Composition of Reserves*

The two principal recent contributions in this area had both been empirical. Chrystal (1975) provided fairly convincing evidence that total (private plus official) foreign holdings of dollars, pounds, deutschemarks, and French francs were interest-sensitive. Officer (1974) developed an empirical test of the Officer–Willett conjecture that reserve-management policy is largely guided by strategic reasoning rather than portfolio management. He sought to explain the proportion of reserves held in foreign exchange of up to 76 countries in each year from 1958 to 1967, on the basis of proxies of the country's own power (its military expenditure or level of economic development) and its dependence on the reserve centres (proportion of trade with the U.S. and U.K., and the ratio of aid from the U.S. to G.N.P.). He found that the former variables had significant negative, and the latter had significant positive, co-efficients, as the theory would predict. He also found that restraint in converting dollars into gold, as measured by the absolute size of the co-efficients, reached a peak in 1964 and thereafter declined, and offered a tentative explanation of this in terms of the international monetary negotiations of the period.[1] Now that the gold-exchange standard has collapsed, we know that it was rather less unstable than it was argued to be at the time, on the basis of portfolio-management theory. This must, however, be scant comfort for Makin (1972), who offered an analysis of the gold exchange standard based on portfolio theory in which he deduced from the correspondence principle that its co-efficients must be such as to render it stable, but had the misfortune to have his paper published after the system had in fact collapsed.

II.3. *The Supply of Reserves*

It can be argued that, since central banks have been extremely reluctant to use gold when in deficit since August 1971 because of their unwillingness to sell to another central bank at the official price when that was far below the market price and to sell on the market because of the fear of depressing the market price, gold has ceased to function as an effective reserve asset (Williamson (1976b), Chapter 7). It is nonetheless still treated as a reserve asset in official statistics, and may again start to function as one when the agreement reached in September 1975 is brought into effect. In either event, there are major undiscussed and unresolved problems of correctly valuing gold in reserve statistics.

The last three years have seen no further S.D.R. creation, but significant innovations in the provision of conditional liquidity in the form of the oil facility and the extended Fund facility in the I.M.F., and the O.E.C.D. " safety net ". Barattieri and Batzella (1974) provided a careful analysis of the impact of the operations of the I.M.F.'s General Account on international liquidity.

Laffer in Machlup *et al* (1972) attempted to test the " international financial intermediation " hypothesis which is closely related to the demand-determined theory of the U.S. deficit. He interpreted his results as being consistent with the theory, but it is far from clear that this was justified; the " supply-side " variables of U.S. monetary policy and real growth carry significant co-efficients. Although there has still been no systematic study of the episode, the experience of 1971–73 seems blatantly inconsistent with the demand-determined theory. It is, however, widely agreed that, whatever the advent of floating may have done to the demand for reserves, it must have made the supply of reserves more responsive to demand (I.M.F.

---

[1] Specifically, he suggested that restraint declined when the United States indicated that she would veto any threat to the pre-eminent role of the dollar. This is a questionable interpretation of history—it was not until 1965 that the United States gave any support to the creation of a fiduciary reserve asset.

(1975) p. 39), and therefore have increased the element of truth in the supply-determined theory.

II.4. *Reserves and Adjustment*

A specific attempt to test the international quantity theory was made by Parkin (1975). He examined each of the links in the hypothesised causal chain from international reserves to high-powered money to total money supplies to inflation (for the Group of Ten, 1961–71), and concluded that the evidence for the first link was very weak indeed.

A simple but interesting example of " world-macro " model building was undertaken by Roper (1973), who contrasted the adjustment impli-cations of the gold standard with those of the gold-exchange standard. He argued that there were two key differences between these two systems. The first is that the use of the dollar as the intervention currency shifted the exchange rate instrument away from the United States, thus explaining why the overvaluation of the dollar was perpetuated long after the initial need for it provided by the reserve shortage in the rest of the world had disappeared. The second difference is that, by holding dollars in their reserves, the rest of the world automatically sterilised reserve losses for the United States, despite the fact that this was bound to shift the burden of adjustment on to themselves. He argued that this occurred because of an externality problem: each non-reserve centre individually weighed the benefit of holding an interest-yielding asset in its reserves against the cost of having to accept a greater adjustment burden, but because the latter was dispersed among many countries it was of negligible importance in their calculations. Hence, he argued, the " implicit bargain " being sought in the reform negotiations was one that would suppress both the asymmetries in the gold-exchange standard: the United States would accept more discipline in its balance of payments policies in return for greater control over its exchange rate.

III.1. *Alternative Proposals for Increasing Liquidity*

The supply of proposals for new reserve assets is evidently demand-determined, for it has dried up.[1] The equivalent demand during the period under review was for proposals for a new international monetary system to replace that devised at Bretton Woods, and these were supplied liberally. Rather than attempt to review the issues here, however, I shall be pre-sumptuous enough to refer the reader to my forthcoming book on the reform negotiations (Williamson (1976b)).

[1] However, Vaubel (1974) has developed interesting proposals on the related issue of the possible creation of a European parallel currency.

III.2. Desirable Characteristics of Reserve Assets

One important characteristic of the S.D.R. that provoked no discussion when the S.D.R. was being created, and that went unremarked in the preceding survey, concerns the question as to how its value should be defined. In the 1960s it seemed natural enough to define the S.D.R. in terms of gold, which was still regarded as the basic reserve asset, but this became unsatisfactory with the divorce between the official and monetary price of gold, the widespread floating of currencies, and the consequent *de facto* denomination of the S.D.R. in terms of the U.S. dollar. The solution adopted in 1974 (initially for a 2-year period) was to base the value of the S.D.R. on that of a " basket " of the 16 most important currencies in world trade, on the theory that this would insulate the purchasing power of the S.D.R. from the effects of exchange-rate changes. This proposal was anticipated by Helliwell (1973), while the international discussions on the subject have been described by Polak (1974) and Williamson (1976b) Chapter 7.

It has also been suggested at times (*e.g.* Fellner (1972)) that the real problem with the dollar standard, from the non-United States standpoint, was not the asymmetrical assignment of the responsibility for initiating adjustment (*cf.* Roper's analysis noted in II.4 above), but rather the absence of a purchasing-power guarantee on foreign official holdings of dollars. Not everyone would agree with the implicit premise that the rest of the world's vulnerability to imposition of the inflation tax by the United States was the only, or even the major, ground for legitimate complaint.

Girton (1974) has drawn attention to the danger that certain rules for international reserve creation (such as Keynes' proposals for increasing banc- or quotas automatically in proportion to the increase in the value of trade) might result in instability, of a similar character to that which would result from domestic application of the real-bills doctrine. He also examined whether this threat would exist under a dollar standard, and concluded that it would not provided that the monetary policy of the reserve centre was not guided by the " real-bills doctrine," either in its domestic guise or in the form of a monetary policy which was guided by helping the rest of the world achieve " adequate " reserves.

Williamson (1974) offered a somewhat tedious analysis of the impact on the distribution of the social saving of the alternative reserve-supply arrangements discussed in the negotiations on international monetary reform.

III.3. The Aid Link

The literature on the link has continued to proliferate, at both official (I.M.F. (1974a) pp. 95–110) and academic levels, to the point where the subject has started to generate surveys either wholly (Park (1973)) or partially (Maynard and Bird (1975)) devoted to the subject. The increased volume of literature has not, however, been accompanied by any very novel proposals or analyses, except perhaps for the suggestion—see, for example,

Isard and Truman (1974) p. 93—that payment of a competitive interest rate on S.D.R.s could be reconciled with maintenance of the income-redistributive impact of the link through continuing to base the responsibility for servicing S.D.R.s on I.M.F. quotas even if the distribution of S.D.R.s was modified in favour of the L.D.C.s. Proponents of the link, such as Maynard (1972) and Economides (1973), have continued to emphasise what they consider to be its value in reconciling payments objectives, while opponents, such as Bauer (1973) and Stek (1974), have stressed what they consider to be its inflationary implications. These stem in large part from the fact that link aid, not being included in the budget, will be less likely than other aid to generate offsetting deflationary fiscal action; to which Kahn (1973) has replied that the impact of link aid on demand will be no less perceptible than a rise in any other form of exports. Stek also queried whether the link could be expected to reconcile current-account targets, since he viewed these as being rationally determined by liquidity needs rather than exogenously given, and hence argued that targeted surpluses would rise under the link by the sum of S.D.R.s not being allocated to the developed countries, plus a safety margin.

III.4. *The Normative Theory of Reserve Supply*

A semantic point that received no attention in the survey concerns the relationship between the need for reserves, the demand for reserves, the adequacy of reserves, and optimum reserves. Claassen (1974) has offered a useful definition of the relationship between the latter three concepts. The demand for reserves is conceived as the target reserve level that a country is pursuing. Reserves are adequate if the aggregate demand for reserves is equal to the supply of reserves. They are optimum if demand is equated to supply at the level where adjustment costs are minimised (which the optimum-quantity-of-money theory assents will occur when the interest rate on reserves is equal to the marginal product of capital). "Need," as Machlup (1966) long ago emphasised, always needs to be supplemented by a description of the specific purpose that a reserve level is needed to achieve or avoid.

III.5. *The Adequacy of Reserves*

Makin (1974) claimed that the increase in reserve supply over the period 1960–71 had been approximately equal to the increase in the demand for reserves, where he calculated the latter by assuming that the square root law applied for volume increases in trade while proportionate increases were required for price rises. Although the square root law is far from firmly established, this does seem consistent with the evidence that the explosion in reserves after mid-1971 produced an excess of liquidity which contributed to the inflation of 1973 (I.M.F. (1974) p. 42). Because of the widespread view that liquidity was excessive,[1] no further S.D.R. allocations were authorised after the first " basic period " covering 1970–72. After 1973 the widespread adoption of floating exchange rates made it far more difficult to interpret the adequacy of reserves. The most recent Annual Report of the I.M.F. (1975) did not attempt the customary analysis of symptoms of reserve ease and stringency, but contented itself with remarks on the impact of floating on the demand for and supply of reserves, and on the policy conclusion that there was a need for additional conditional liquidity.

[1] This view gained ground so rapidly that Johnson's contention that it was not a liquidity shortage, but rather a surfeit, that constituted the real problem with the dollar standard, has never been seriously challenged.

REFERENCES

V. Barattieri and F. Batzella (1974), " Fund Transactions and Reserve Creation, 1951–73," IM *Staff Papers*, March 1974.

P. Bauer (1973), " Inflation, SDRs and Aid," *Lloyd's Bank Review*, July 1973.

K. A. Chrystal (1975), " Demand for International Media of Exchange," University of Essex Ph.D., 1975.

E. M. Claassen (1974), " The Optimizing Approach to the Demand for International Reserves," *Weltwirtschaftliches Archiv*, 1974(3).

—— (1975), " Demand for International Reserves and the Optimum Mix and Speed of Adjustment Policies," *American Economic Review*, June 1975.

G. Clayton, J. C. Gilbert, R. Sedgwick (1971), eds., *Monetary Theory and Monetary Policy in the 1970s*, Oxford University Press, 1971.

B. J. Cohen (forthcoming), " International Reserves and Liquidity: A Survey," in P. B. Kenen, ed., *International Trade and Finance: Frontiers for Research*, Cambridge University Press, Cambridge.

R. N. Cooper (1972), " Eurodollars, Reserve Dollars, and Asymmetries in the International Monetary System," *Journal of International Economics*, September 1972.

C. Economides (1973), " Earned International Reserve Units," *World Development*, March/April 1973.

W. Fellner (1972), " The Dollar's Place in the International System: Suggested Criteria for the Appraisal of Emerging Views," *Journal of Economic Literature*, September 1972.

L. Girton (1974), " SDR Creation and the Real-Bills Doctrine," *Southern Economic Journal*, July 1974.

S. Grassman (1973), " A Fundamental Symmetry in International Payments Patterns," *Journal of International Economics*, 1973(3).

J. Helliwell (1973), " Dollars as Reserve Assets: What Next? " *American Economic Review*, May 1973.

F. S. Hipple (1974), *The Disturbances Approach to the Demand for International Reserves*, Princeton Studies in International Finance No. 35, 1974.

I.M.F. (1974a), *International Monetary Reform: Documents of the Committee of Twenty*, I.M.F., Washington D.C., 1974.

—— (1974b), *Annual Report, 1974*, I.M.F., Washington D.C., 1974.

—— (1975), *Annual Report, 1975*, I.M.F., Washington D.C., 1975.

P. Isard and E. M. Truman (1974), " SDRs, Interest and the Aid Link: Further Analysis," *Banca Nazionale del Lavoro Quarterly Review*, March 1974.

M. A. Iyoha (1974), " Demand for International Reserves in Less Developed Countries: A Distributed Lag Specification," Department of Economics, State University of New York at Buffalo, Discussion Paper No. 309, July 1974.

A. Kafka (1975), " The Payments Adjustment Process and the Exchange Rate Regime: What Have We Learned?—Discussion," *American Economic Review*, May 1975.

R. K. Kahn (1973), " SDRs and Aid," *Lloyd's Bank Review*, October 1973.

S. Korkman (1973), " Foreign Exchange Reserves and the Adjustment Mechanism," Institute for International Economic Studies, Stockholm, Seminar Paper No. 31, 1973.

League of Nations (1930), *Interim Report of the Gold Delegation to the Financial Committee*, 1930.

B. Lesser (1974), " A Note on Balance of Payments Deficits, Adjustment Costs and Optimal Reserves," *Weltwirtschaftliches Archiv*, 1974(3).

F. Machlup, W. S. Salant, L. Tarshis (1972), eds., *International Mobility and Movement of Capital*, National Bureau of Economic Research, Columbia University Press, New York, 1972.

J. H. Makin (1972), " On the Success of the Reserve Currency System in the Crisis Zone," *Journal of International Economics*, 1972(1).

—— (1974), " Exchange Rate Flexibility and the Demand for International Reserves," *Weltwirtschaftliches Archiv*, 1974(2).

G. W. Maynard (1972), *Special Drawing Rights and Development Aid*, Overseas Development Council, Washington D.C., 1972.

G. Maynard and G. Bird (1975), " International Monetary Issues and the Developing Countries," *World Development*, September 1975.

K. Nagabhushanam and M. Perayya Sastry (1962), " A Stochastic Model for Foreign-Exchange Reserves," *Journal of Economic Behaviour*, April 1962.

L. Nybery and S. Viotti (1974), " Optimal Reserves and Adjustment Policies," *Swedish Journal of Economics*, December 1974.

L. H. Officer (1974), " Reserve Asset Preferences in the Crisis Zone, 1958–67," *Journal of Money, Credit, and Banking*, May 1974.

Y. S. Park (1973), *The Link Between Special Drawing Rights and Development Finance*, Princeton Essays in International Finance No. 100, 1973.

J. M. Parkin (1975), " International Liquidity and World Inflation in the 1960s," mimeo, 1975.

S. Pereira-Leite (1974), " Optimal Monetary Reserves for Developing Countries: A Note," *Weltwirtschaftliches Archiv*, 1974(2).

J. J. Polak (1974), *Valuation and Rate of Interest of the SDR*, I.M.F., Washington D.C., 1974.

D. E. Roper (1973), " Implications of the Gold Exchange Standard for Adjustment," *Economia Internazionale*, August/November 1973.

P. Stek (1974), " SDR Creation, Development Aid and the Adjustment Process," *De Economist*, 1974(5).

R. Vaubel (1974), " Plans for a European Parallel Currency and SDR Reform," *Weltwirtschaftliches Archiv*, 1974(2).

E. L. Whalen (1966), " A Rationalization of the Precautionary Demand for Cash," *Quarterly Journal of Economics*, May 1966.

J. Williamson (1974), " The Financial Implications of Reserve Supply Arrangements," I.M.F. *Staff Papers*, November 1974.

—— (1975), " Generalized Floating and the Reserve Needs of Developing Countries," Conference organised by the Agency for International Development, Washington D.C., June 1975.

—— (1976a), " Exchange Rate Flexibility and Reserve Use," *Scandinavian Journal of Economics*, 1976(2).

—— (1976b), *The Failure of World Monetary Reform, 1971–74*, Thomas Nelson, London, 1976.

II

FLOW OF FUNDS ANALYSIS[1]

A. D. Bain

I. Introduction and Origins

I.1. *Introduction*

Flow of funds *analysis* does not have any generally accepted meaning in economics.   The flow of funds *account* is now well known; it is one component of the national accounts system, which shows the financial transactions between broad sectors of the economy, thus linking the saving and investment aggregates in other components of the national accounts with their associated lending and borrowing activities.   Like these other components the flow of funds account is designed to provide a framework which gives a systematic, comprehensive and consistent description and analysis of the facts.   It brings the various financial activities of an economy into explicit statistical relationship with one another and with data on the non-financial activities that generate income and production (Goldsmith, 1965; Board of Governors, 1970).

Flow of funds accounts are essential raw material for any comprehensive analysis of capital market behaviour, because they help to identify both the role of finance in the generation of income, savings and expenditure, and the influence of economic activity on financial markets (Bank of England, 1972). But the identities which are implicit in a flow of funds account are not in themselves sufficient to provide any real knowledge of financial processes; they must be supplemented by a set of behaviour equations which account for the expenditure, production and portfolio choices of the various actors in the system (Duesenberry, 1962).   Thus the accounts are in no sense a substitute for analysis.

In this article the term " flow of funds analysis " will be taken to refer to a set of techniques which have been developed for the study of financial processes and to the applications of these techniques in the fields of prediction and planning.   The distinctive features of the methods adopted for flow of funds analysis are their explicit emphasis on financial transactions, sometimes at the expense of allotting a subsidiary role to the influence of balance

[1] This is the sixth of a series sponsored jointly by the Social Science Research Council and the Royal Economic Society.

sheet positions, and their insistence on a comprehensive coverage of the
system, thus ensuring overall consistency and eliminating the risk that
implications for the behaviour of some parts of the financial system will be
overlooked. The survey will be confined to work which exhibits these
characteristics or which has a direct bearing on the role of flows in capital
market behaviour. Most of the discussion concerns work in the United
Kingdom and the United States, with reference being made to other countries only for the purpose of illustration.

I.2. *History of Flow of Funds Analysis*

Morris Copeland's classic N.B.E.R. volume *A Study of Moneyflows in the
United States* (1952) is usually regarded as the first significant contribution
to flow of funds analysis. In this work Copeland not only presented for the
United States a set of moneyflows accounts—which he conceived as an
alternative to national income accounts—but also showed how these accounts
might be employed to interpret events in the U.S. economy. Its origins
have been described by Lintner (1972) in a survey of the N.B.E.R.'s programme of research in finance and capital markets. The compilation of a
new body of statistics was a major achievement; but Cohen (1972), reviewing developments since the study of moneyflows was published, claims that
Copeland's greatest contributions were his interpretation of the accounts,
his attempt to carry out an analysis of economic behaviour in terms of the
extent to which sectors exercised their discretion to spend amounts which
differed from their incomes, and his study of the mechanism through which
they were able to do so.

After the completion of Copeland's study responsibility for preparing
flow of funds accounts in the United States was taken on by the Federal
Reserve System. The broad objective of providing a statistical description
of financial behaviour remained the same, but a number of major changes
were made, the general drift being to link the accounts more closely with the
main components of the national accounts system and to focus on transactions in particular financial markets irrespective of the financing of any
associated monetary payments (Board of Governors, 1955; 1963; 1970).
This trend to consistency has been echoed in many other countries which
now prepare flow of funds (or financial transactions) statistics. While
differences exist in the amount of detail included in income flows, in the
extent to which sectors are subdivided, and in the use of gross as opposed
to net flows, the objective of consistency with the national accounts statistics
seems to be universally accepted. This process has been fostered by discussions held under the aegis of the U.N. Department of Economic and Social
Affairs culminating in the proposed revised system of national accounts
(U.N., 1968).

Progress on the analytical front has been slower. While Keynesian
analysis has looked to certain components of expenditure as the driving force

causing fluctuations in national income, this model is scarcely adequate if savings and investment are interdependent (Polak, 1959). Attempts have therefore been made to develop an alternative financing approach in which the sector balance—the balance of saving over investment—is crucial. While some difficulties remain, developments of this approach have proved valuable (*e.g.*, Holtrop, 1957; Segré, 1958; Bank of Israel, 1970).

Less formal approaches to analysis have been adopted by many writers (*e.g.*, Hood, 1958 and Goldsmith, 1958; 1965), and attempts have also been made to develop models based upon stability in the pattern of flows (*e.g.*, Stone, 1967). These and other models will be discussed later. Flow of funds data have also been employed in the estimation of most recent financial econometric models, though these models seldom focus explicitly on financial flows. Indeed, some of the leading practitioners in the flow of funds field emphasise that the accounts should be regarded primarily as a data source which is needed for a wide variety of purposes, in the same way as other components of the national accounts can be employed in many ways, and while seeing merit in employing a constrained and comprehensive system they do not regard the flows themselves as of special importance (*e.g.*, Board of Governors, 1970).

Flow of funds has been the subject of a number of conferences and earlier surveys. Reference may be made to the Conference on the Flow of Funds Approach to Social Accounting (N.B.E.R., 1962, and surveys by Dorrance, 1966; Wallich, 1969; and Cohen, 1972). In addition the conceptual and statistical problems connected with the compilation and presentation of financial accounting data have been discussed at a number of conferences, but this article will not attempt to survey these questions in detail.

I.3. *Outline*

The next section gives an introduction to the flow of funds system, and examines its relationship with other components of the national accounts. The conceptual and statistical problems are also discussed briefly. Section three outlines the approaches which have been adopted for flow of funds analysis: descriptive analysis, the sector balance and liquidity approaches, fixed technical coefficient models, interest-rate forecasting models, models for short-term macro-economic prediction and econometric models of the financial system. Finally, the deficiencies, possibilities and prospects for flow of funds analysis are considered in a short concluding section.

II. THE FLOW OF FUNDS SYSTEM

II.1. *Flow of Funds in the National Accounts System*

Elementary descriptions of the flow of funds system are now widely available so only a brief introduction will be given here (see, *e.g.*, Ritter, 1968; Bank of England, 1972). The flow of funds account is one component of a comprehensive and inter-connected system of national accounts: part is simply a disaggregation by sectors of the saving and investment flows in the capital account.   In this section the " financial surplus " of each sector— the net amount of funds available for or arising from capital and credit market transactions—is derived from statistics of the sector's gross saving and capital expenditure.   The other part shows each sector's transactions in capital and credit market instruments; it has its closest connections with the national balance sheet, because the transactions in financial assets form an important component of changes in balance sheet values (Goldsmith, 1965; Stone, 1966; United Nations, 1968).

For any sector the financial surplus can be computed as the excess of saving (current income less current spending) plus capital transfers over capital expenditure (net of disposals).   National income accounting identities ensure that in principle the financial surpluses of all the sectors together must add to zero: taking the economy as a whole, transfers net out and the sum of factor incomes is equal to the sum of current and capital expenditures. The financial surplus (or deficit if it is negative) of any sector can also be derived directly from a combined source and uses of funds statement for its constituents.   An illustrative example is shown in Table II.1 for a hypothetical " non-financial companies " sector.   The sources and uses of funds associated with net changes in financial assets or liabilities (" financial transactions ") are separated from other sources and uses reflecting income and expenditure flows (" non-financial transactions ").   The upper half of Table II.1 displays the sector's current and capital receipts and payments, which give rise to its financial deficit (a net use of funds), while the lower half shows the increases in the sector's financial liabilities (sources of funds) which have allowed it to finance this deficit and acquire additional financial assets (uses of funds).   Since total sources and total uses of funds must be the same, the sector's financial deficit is necessarily equal to the net increase in its financial liabilities.

The sources and uses of funds statement, in the form of Table II.1, comprises the flow of funds account for one sector.   For the economy as a whole the flow of funds account is simply a matrix in which sector statements of this kind are set alongside one another. The economy can be divided into as many or as few sectors as is convenient or practicable.   To ensure that the rows are the same for every sector a common classification of financial instruments must be employed, but again there is a choice over the degree of disaggregation.   Thus within the matrix the pairs of columns for each sector show the sector's non-financial and financial transactions in all the instruments, and the rows show for each financial instrument the transactions by every sector in that market.   In the upper half of the account the sum of the entries in any row (adopting the convention that sources will be treated as negative uses) must add to the corresponding national income accounting magnitude; as already indicated the sum of the financial surpluses must be zero.   Since any financial instrument is at the same time both an asset to the holder and a liability to the issuer, the sum of entries in every row in the lower half of the account must be zero.

The transactions in financial and real capital assets which are the substance of the flow of funds account form the most important means by which economic agents alter the level and composition of their balance sheets;

TABLE II.1

Hypothetical Sources and Uses of Funds Statement, Non-financial Companies

(£ millions)

	Uses.	Sources.
I. NON-FINANCIAL TRANSACTIONS		
Current transactions		
Current receipts and expenditures . . .	4,800	6,000
Current transfers	500	
Gross savings		700
Capital transactions		
Capital transfers		150
Fixed assets	1,100	50
Change in stocks.	250	
Financial (surplus or) deficit	450	
II. FINANCIAL TRANSACTIONS		
Money	50	
Other liquid assets	70	
Bank loans.		500
Capital issues		150
Trade credit	350	300
Foreign investment	30	
Net increase in financial (assets or) liabilities . .		450

acquisitions of real assets are shown in the upper part of the account and net purchases or sales of financial instruments in the lower.   But changes in the value of asset holding from one period to the next reflect not only actual transactions but also revaluations resulting from changes in the market value of existing assets and liabilities.   Thus for complete consistency with the sector balance sheets for successive accounting dates the flow of funds account must be supplemented by an account showing revaluations of existing holdings (see, *e.g.*, Stone and Roe, 1971).

In a comprehensive system of national accounts the flow of funds account must also be linked with the accounts for the rest of the world.   The normal procedure is to treat the rest of the world as an additional sector, whose financial surplus is equal to the balance of payments deficit on current account.   Foreign assets, both financial and tangible, held by domestic sectors are treated as financial assets of those sectors; domestic financial assets held by foreign residents are shown as assets in the rest of the world account and as corresponding liabilities of the relevant domestic sector's account; and investment by foreigners in domestic tangible assets, which is included in the capital formation figures for the domestic sector, gives rise to a corresponding financial liability of that sector to the rest of the world matched by a financial asset in the rest of the world account. This treatment corresponds with national income accounting practice.

The constraints on row and column totals discussed above, which are formal properties of a flow of funds account, are frequently violated in practice because of deficiencies in the coverage and inaccuracies in the data collected. For the United Kingdom these matters have been fully discussed by Berman (1965).

In the United Kingdom the convention of treating sources as negative uses of funds is carried to the point of offsetting all sources against the corresponding uses, so that instead of having two columns for each sector there is only one. This simplifies the presentation of the table at the cost of some loss of information. An example of the United Kingdom flow of funds accounts is shown as Table II.2 opposite.

II.2. *Conceptual and Statistical Problems*

The conceptual and statistical problems which arise in compiling flow of funds statistics have been the subject of extended discussion among national income accountants and capital market analysts (see, *e.g.*, Tice, 1967). According to Goldsmith (1965) the six basic questions which must be settled in setting up a comprehensive system of accounts are:

    (i) the scope of flows and stocks
    (ii) the classification of assets
    (iii) valuation
    (iv) the coverage of economic units
    (v) sectoring
    (vi) the degree of netness

As already indicated, Copeland's (1952) pioneering study was concerned with moneyflows, pure and simple. The early U.S. flow of funds statistics concentrated on the capital and credit markets, omitted much of the detail contained in Copeland's work, but still covered a range of activities which was narrower than those included in the national income account. Thus, imputed items of income, such as income in kind and barter transactions, were excluded (Board of Governors, 1955; Young 1957). Subsequent work has moved in the direction of ensuring that coverage consistent with other components of the national accounts statistics is achieved, and the non-financial transactions now include imputed items in most countries (*e.g.*, Read, 1957; Board of Governors, 1970). However, there are still some differences in the treatment of particular items, and in the United States, for example, purchases of consumer durables are treated as a current

TABLE II.2

Flow of Funds in the United Kingdom, 1970

(£ millions)

Line		Public Sector	Overseas sector	Personal sector	Industrial and commercial companies	Banking sector	Other financial institutions
	Capital Formation (Financial surplus +/deficit −)						
1	Saving	+5023		+2890	+2703	+335	
2	Taxes on capital and capital transfers	−64		−358	+486	−64	
	less:						
3	Gross fixed capital formation at home	−4004		−1089	−3197	−596	
4	Increase in value of stocks and work in progress	−99		−205	−1126		
5	Financial surplus +/deficit −	+856	−579	+1238	−1134	−325	
	Changes in financial assets and liabilities (Assets increase +/decrease −; Liabilities increase −/decrease +)						
6	Net indebtedness of Government to Bank of England, Banking Department.	−276				+276	
7	Life assurance and pension funds			+1755	−26		−1755
8	Loans by U.K. Government	+110	−83	−2			+1
9.1	Total external currency flow	+1287	−1287				
9.2	Other central government external transactions	+59	−59				
10	Banks' net external transactions	+115	+789			−789	
11	Miscellaneous investment overseas (net)	−231	+72		−146		−41
12	Notes and coins	+44		+115	+206	−90	+220
13	Bank deposits of domestic sectors		+51	+822	+179	−1265	−1700
14	Deposits with other financial institutions			+1659	−10	−21	+8
15.1	National savings	+51		−51			
15.2	Tax reserve certificates	+18		+1	−6		
15.3	Import deposits	+257			−225		
16	Bank lending to domestic sectors	−126	−32	−59	−1125	+1391	−81
17	Hire purchase debt	−1		−49	+3		+47
18	Loans for house purchase	+46		−1210		+40	+1124
19	Other loans and accruals	+32		−51	−276	−1	+296
	Marketable government debt:						
20	Treasury bills ⎱ held by domestic sectors	−553			+9	+550	−6
21	Stocks ⎰	+313		−225		−410	+322
22	Local authority debt	−547	−38	−73	−119	+483	+294
	U.K. company and overseas securities:						
23	Capital issues	+6	+12		−193	−27	−56
24	Other transactions		−97	−880	+351	+94	+790
25	Unit trust units.			+89			−89
26	Identified financial transactions	+604	−672	+1841	−1378	+231	−626
27	Unidentified	+252	+93	−603	+244	+70	
28	TOTAL (Financial surplus +/deficit −)	+856	−579	+1238	−1134	−325	

(The +70 and −325 in lines 27 and 28 are bracketed together across the Banking sector and Other financial institutions columns.)

Source: Bank of England (1972), table 4(1).

expenditure in the income and product accounts but as a capital expenditure in the flow of funds accounts, because of the close behavioural links between transactions in certain financial assets and purchases of these items. The practice of restricting the coverage of moneyflows mainly to those affecting the capital and credit markets has received widespread support. In principle the coverage of transactions in financial assets in the flow of funds statistics should be complete, though in practice lack of data may lead perforce to the omission of some items, such as the bulk of trade credit in the United Kingdom.

Assets are generally classified according to two criteria—their homogeneity and their importance. Homogeneity may refer to the sector of issue, the nature of the financial instrument—*e.g.*, whether it is a claim or an equity—to its maturity, or to the object of financing. For analytical purposes a classification by liquidity, as suggested by Dorrance (1963), would also be helpful, but within the framework of the flow of funds account such a classification cannot be complete because instruments such as ordinary stocks would be placed higher in the liquidity arrays of the sectors which held them as assets than of the sectors of which they were liabilities. Nevertheless, the ordering of the financial instruments in most flow of funds tables does contain a liquidity element. It is not always practicable to subdivide assets as far as is desired; for example, there is no classification by maturity in the United Kingdom (Berman, 1965). Financial instruments which play only a small part in the credit market may be aggregated with others which are similar in character or put in a single group: an example of such a catch-all category is " other loans and accruals " in the U.K. statistics (see Table II.2, line 19).

In the flow of funds account the values recorded should be the values at which transactions actually took place or the best possible approximations to them. Statistically this may raise considerable problems, especially where the estimates of transactions are derived from changes in balance sheet value, since these may be at book, nominal or market value, and some revaluation of existing assets may be required. An allowance must also be made for any taxes or brokerage costs. Nevertheless, the conceptual basis of valuation for the transactions in financial assets is clear. There has been more argument about the appropriate valuation basis for the stocks shown in the national balance sheet, though the general opinion is that these should be shown at market value or replacement cost throughout. Detailed discussions of many of the statistical problems can be found in Berman, 1965; Dorrance, 1963; 1966; and Revell, 1966.

The coverage of economic units and sectoring are closely related questions. In principle all independent decision-taking units should be included within the statistics and allocated to one and only one sector, but in practice this gives rise to conflicts. The criterion by which sectors are distinguished in the national accounts is that of homogeneity, but this principle leads to a different classification scheme for the production accounts and for the financial accounts (Høst-Madsen, 1960; Ruggles and Ruggles, 1970). Within the production account sectoring is on an industrial basis and may go into considerable detail in distinguishing between industries whereas the sectoring appropriate for the financial account is concerned much more with institutional differences in the financial markets. This means that the integration of the detailed sectoring of the flow of funds data and the income and product data is not complete. Nevertheless, at the broad sector level a consistent classification is desirable. Within the financial system it is usual to distinguish the monetary system from other financial institutions, and in most countries (though regrettably not the United Kingdom) a sub-sectoring of these financial institutions is provided. The minimum division within the non-financial domestic sector is between the public sector and the private sector, on the grounds that government is affected by different constraints from the private sector (Dorrance, 1959). Since households (consumers) behave differently from business (producers) these are allocated to different sectors whenever practicable. The question of subdividing the government sector has been debated. A justification for treating the public sector as a single unit in the United Kingdom is provided by Beales and Berman (1966).

The principle that assets or transactions which are under common control should not be divided between two or more sectors, causes considerable complications. It has implications for the treatment of certain types of economic unit, particularly unincorporated businesses and farms, where the criterion of homogeneity dictates that production and consumption activities should be distinguished. Since transactions in financial assets of a single decision-taking unit can seldom be allocated to specific functions, it is necessary to fall back on conventions. In the United States farm business is treated as a separate sector, and the income of unincorporated farms is transferred to the household sector; a similar procedure is adopted for non-farm non-corporate business (Board of Governors, 1970). In the United Kingdom it has not yet proved possible to separate out these business transactions from the transactions of households, and the " personal " sector consequently displays very considerable heterogeneity. Similar problems of allocation also arise in some countries with government life assurance and pension schemes which, although controlled by the public sector, often have many of the characteristics of financial institutions carrying out similar business in the private sector.

The optimal degree of disaggregation in the upper and lower parts of the account is another problem. It has been argued that a considerably greater degree of disaggregation by sector is desirable for financial transactions than in the non-financial transactions part of the account (Høst-Madsen, 1960). For analytical purposes it is much more important to have a detailed knowledge of financial institutions' transactions in financial assets than about their profitability or their expenditure on real assets.   In the United Kingdom the practice is adopted of distinguishing the banking sector and other financial institutions in the lower parts of the account, but of aggregating them together in the upper part (see Table II.2).   .

The final problem is the degree of netness in the statistics.   Copeland (1952) attempted to measure gross moneyflows, showing receipts or payments between economic units classified by sector without any offsetting either within sectors or between sectors.   This kind of data has been variously described as " to-whom-from-whom " (Mendelson, 1962; Cohen, e.g., 1972) and as the " identified form " (Goldsmith, 1965).   Concern with compactness and with displaying the information in a form suitable for analysis of particular segments of the credit market has led subsequently to a considerable degree of netting.   For example, the purchases of one particular category of security by a company are netted against the sales of that security by the same company, and within any sector the net purchases of the security by some companies are netted against the net sales by others.   Furthermore no attempt is made to distinguish the other party to the transactions, and the statistics are presented in the " unidentified form " in which a sector's net transactions in a security with all other sectors together are shown [1] (Goldsmith, 1965).   Where sources and uses of funds are shown separately, as in Table II.1, it is still possible to show gross figures if these are available; but in some cases—e.g., changes in bank deposits or bank loans—they are not. The single column presentation of the United Kingdom statistics goes to the extreme limit of netness.

While statistical practice varies, it is clear that the optimum degree of netting in the flow of funds accounts cannot be settled without reference to the question which the analyst has in mind.   For example, gross extensions of credit are likely to be important in studies of the demand for consumer durables or real estate (Mendelson, 1962).   However, there is much to be said for adopting a consistent approach to netting throughout the flow of funds accounts, and providing details of gross flows where these are thought to be relevant in supplementary tables (Denison, 1962).

II.3. *Data availability*

A comprehensive survey of the availability of flow of funds data in different countries is contained in Heth (1970).   There is a wide variation in the degree of disaggregation both of sectors and financial instruments, with the United States at the upper end of the range showing 20 sectors and 48 financial categories.   In the United States annual data are now available since 1945 and quarterly data in both unadjusted and seasonally adjusted forms since 1962.   In the United Kingdom the most recent comprehensive publication contains annual data from 1952 to 1970, and quarterly un-

---

[1] Presumably, in the absence of market imperfections involving the identities of particular transactors, the unidentified form is sufficient for analysis.

adjusted and seasonally adjusted data from 1963 on (Bank of England, 1972). Current data are published regularly in the Bank of England Quarterly Bulletin and in Financial Statistics, and detailed discussions of the conceptual and statistical problems connected with the U.K. data can be found in Berman (1965), Maurice (1968) and Bank of England (1972).

III. APPROACHES TO FLOW OF FUNDS ANALYSIS

III.1. *Flow of Funds as a Data Source*

Many practitioners in the field have regarded the main function of the flow of funds account as the provision of data on transactions in financial markets in as neutral a form as possible, from which commentators and analysts can select the particular information which is relevant for the purpose in hand and employ it in conjunction with data from other sources. Principal applications include problems of inter-relationships between financial and non-financial conditions in the economy, such as studies in the incidence of monetary policy and short-run projections of financial markets (Taylor, 1958). Some of the techniques which have been devised to assist in these applications will be discussed in later sections; but first some examples will be given of specific applications of flow of funds data in interpreting and explaining financial and economic behaviour.

As already noted, Copeland (1952) and his reviewers (*e.g.*, Mendelson, 1955) used moneyflows data to survey the general development of the U.S. economy during the period 1936–42. In Canada, Hood (1958) employed the national transactions accounts data to carry out a major study of the financing of economic activity, which is noteworthy for its comprehensive treatment of financing and for the detailed discussion given to structural factors as regulators of the flow of funds. Hood sets out three broad categories of regulators—government influence, namely central bank operations of all kinds, taxation and legislative restrictions on investment practices; the price system, through its effects both on relative yields within financial markets and on the ability of economic units to finance expenditures out of internal funds; and other regulators, such as custom, tradition and the need to make provision for retirement. His extensive treatment of structural factors is in sharp contrast to many more recent studies of financial behaviour which emphasise relative yields to the comparative neglect of other important influences.

In a similar vein the key study of flows of funds in the United States in the postwar period is Goldsmith's (1965) volume in the N.B.E.R. series on the U.S. capital market. Goldsmith sets out his framework for capital market analysis, and then proceeds to examine the size of the financing task arising from capital spending during the period considered, the volumes of internal and external financing, and the distribution of sources and uses of funds among sectors. The emphasis of the study then moves to markets, and the five main components of the U.S. capital market are discussed—U.S. Government securities, state and local government securities, corporate bonds, corporate stock and residential mortgages. For each of these markets in turn Goldsmith considers the characteristics of the financial instruments and technical nature of the market, the sources of supply and demand, and the role played by the instrument in the liabilities of the borrowing and the assets of the lending sectors. The analysis is illuminated by its historical perspective and by the depth of institutional knowledge. There is no comparable study of financial flows in the U.K. capital market.

Flow of funds statistics also provide a basis for comment upon the behaviour of financial markets in the recent past. For example, an " analysis of financial statistics " is published regularly in the Bank of England Quarterly Bulletin, in which the recent behaviour of capital and credit markets is interpreted in relation to the general development of the economy. A regular analysis of developments in the previous calendar year is published in the June issue of the *Quarterly Bulletin,* and an example of a similar kind of analysis is contained in Bank of England (1972). Some Central Banks find it convenient to employ the flow of funds system as the framework for the analysis of capital market behaviour published in their Annual Reports—examples are the Central Banks of Israel and Yugoslavia.

Another fruitful application of flow of funds data is the analysis of financial behaviour in particular conditions. Examples of this kind of study in the United States are Copeland (1962), which includes a study of war finance, studies of cyclical behaviour by Weiler (1962) and Atkinson (1965), and studies of the impact upon credit flows of particular monetary measures, such as Mitchell's (1967) study of the effects of Regulation Q ceilings. There are also a large number of studies of the behaviour of specific sectors or financial markets in an economy, showing how expenditures are financed and relating changes in the volume and cost of the funds flowing through particular channels to the behaviour of ultimate borrowers and lenders.

III.2. *Sector Balances and Liquidity Analysis*

From the outset analysts have attempted to employ flow of funds data to describe and analyse past macro-economic behaviour and to forecast developments in the future. Through flow of funds analysis they have sought to elaborate upon and correct some defects inherent both in simple Keynesian analysis, with its sharp contrast between autonomous investment and induced saving, and in the monetary survey approach, with its concentration on the behaviour of the banking sector. If a sector's investment is constrained by its saving in the same period, then an increase in investment cannot be taken as evidence of an expansionary influence emanating from that sector. " Business and other entrepreneurs who finance investment out of their own savings are neutral in their effect on expansion or contraction . . . the net expansionary pressures come from those who wish to borrow more than they lend and net contractionary pressures from those who wish to lend more than they borrow during the period " (Dorrance, 1966, p. 203). Attention is therefore directed to the sectors' financial surpluses and to their net borrowing.

The existence of persistent financial surpluses in some sectors combined with persistent deficits in others, which simply reflect the normal sector distribution of saving and investment, is in no way inconsistent with overall economic equilibrium. However, *changes* in sector surpluses may reflect autonomous disturbances to equilibrium, and even before his major work was complete Copeland (1947) had noted that these changes might be related to income generation. But there is a problem: *ex post* the sum of all the sector financial surpluses and deficits is equal to zero, an autonomous change in one sector inducing compensating changes in the same and other sectors. How then are the autonomous and induced effects to be distinguished? Copeland sought a solution by classifying transactors as " bulls, bears and sheep." Bulls were the sources of inflationary disturbances. Their spending on goods and services (current and capital) was rising faster than their receipts from factor incomes. Bears showed the reverse behaviour, and exerted a contractionary influence; and sheep spent less than the increase in their incomes when incomes were rising and correspondingly cut spending by less than any fall in income.

Copeland's classification scheme depended on the economic behaviour which led to a change in the financial surplus, rather than merely on the change itself. But the system is not watertight. For example, when money-flows are expanding, both bears and sheep will be increasing their expenditure more slowly than their incomes; and in a contraction, bulls and sheep could not be readily distinguished. Moreover, the difficulty of distinguishing different types of behaviour is not wholly statistical: as Baumol (1954) suggests, passiveness on the part of sheep may be an over-simple view, particularly if they react to bullishness or bearishness elsewhere in the economy.

In spite of the difficulties, changes in sector financial surpluses have formed a basis for analysis in a number of countries, with circumstantial evidence being employed to distinguish autonomous from accommodating flows. Taylor (1958) discusses experience in the United States, the Bank of England's regular financial analysis in the *Quarterly Bulletin* was for many years tightly knit around sector surpluses and deficits, and a study of sector " demand surpluses " forms one step in the analysis carried out by the Bank of Israel (Heth, 1970; Bank of Israel, 1972). Beales and Berman (1966) call attention to the financial surplus of the public sector in particular, because of its importance for the money supply—a point also taken by Holtrop (1957) who observes that in practice the government cannot be denied finance.

In evaluating this kind of analysis Wallich (1969) concluded that it was most likely to be useful in an open economy with strong domestic sectors. For in an open economy the sum of the financial surplus of the *domestic* sectors is not necessarily zero and sharp changes in *ex ante* surpluses in these sectors are likely to be reflected in a change in the surplus of the foreign sector, *i.e.*, in the balance of payments. Moreover, in the absence of strong and clearly distinguished domestic sectors, no sharp changes in financial surpluses will be identifiable. In both the United Kingdom and Israel the foreign sector has generally absorbed part of the effects of disturbances originating in domestic sectors, and in the former at least there have been sharp changes in the surplus of the government sector, which can justifiably be treated as autonomous.

A number of writers have referred to the *practical* impediments caused both by the absence of essential sector data, which make it impossible in some countries to separate the household from the business sector, and by discrepancies between estimates of the sector financial surpluses obtained by different means (see, *e.g.*, Heth, 1970, and Dorrance, 1966, who comments on the difficulties caused by large discrepancies in the U.K. sector estimates).

The counterpart of a financial surplus reflecting an excess of saving over investment is a net acquisition of financial assets. Expansionary behaviour can therefore be associated with borrowing (or a reduction in net lending), and contractionary behaviour with an increase in lending. The traditional monetary survey has analysed money creation in terms of the changes in bank lending to individual sectors of the economy, associating increases in lending with an inflationary impulse. But the diagnosis may be wrong: for example, an inflationary impulse would be attributed to the government sector in a monetary survey if bank lending to that sector increased; but, if the increased lending resulted from sales of liquid government debt by the private sector in order to finance an increase in its spending, rather than from a change in the government's own total borrowing, it can be argued that the inflationary impulse should properly be attributed to the private and not the government sector. The correct diagnosis would be made if attention was focused on the sectors' financial surpluses or the changes in their liquidity positions (Dorrance, 1969).

Liquidity analysis concentrates on the *financing* of sector surpluses or deficits rather than on their *size*, and was first adopted by the Netherlands. According to Holtrop (1957), ". . . the essence of monetary disturbances is to be found in the possibility . . . of exercising effective purchasing power in excess of, or in deficiency of, current contribution to production. This can be done only by financing expenditure out of the creation of new money or by drawing on available liquid reserves, or, reversely, by hoarding money or taking it out of circulation " (p. 306). Holtrop excluded the transfer of funds by way of the capital market because in his view it was part and parcel of the normal flow of funds and had little to do with actual or potential monetary disturbances. Baffi (1957) and Polak (1959) have also drawn attention to the inter-relations between flows of funds, liquid assets and the cyclical behaviour of the economy.

The validity of this approach to diagnosing the sources of disturbances seems to depend upon the existence of two institutional features in financial markets. The function of absorbing short-term imbalances between receipts and expenditures (the short-term store of value function) must be shared by other liquid assets as well as money. And there must be a clear-cut distinction between the financial instruments in which liquid reserves are held and those, such as bonds or ordinary shares, which are the domain of long-term savings.

The idea is that sectors which are reducing their liquidity—increasing their short-term borrowing or running down holdings of liquid assets—are providing an inflationary stimulus to the economy, whereas the reverse holds for those sectors which are increasing their net liquidity. However as it stands this is too strong: a distinction has to be drawn between *temporary* changes in liquidity, which are likely to be reversed, and *permanent* changes which may be associated with the growth of economic activity—a demand for liquid assets which corresponds to the transactions demand for money. Such changes in net liquidity are part of normal dispositions, and cannot be regarded as any more inflationary or deflationary than the persistent financial deficits and surpluses of the non-financial companies and household sectors respectively. A correction has therefore to be made for any change in the equilibrium holdings of net liquidity by each sector. In the Netherlands desired liquid asset holdings of the private sector are calculated by reference to a measure of aggregate expenditure, and in Israel, the " liquidity impulse " generated by each sector is calculated after allowing for the change in liquid assets required to maintain a constant ratio of liquid assets to total nominal purchases (Bank of Israel, 1972).

The failure to consider capital market flows explicitly has been criticised. As Segré (1958) points out, inflationary impluses may be wrongly attributed to sectors which engage in short-term borrowing or reductions in liquid asset holdings if there are compensating capital market flows. To take account of the domestic capital market and allow for autonomous external capital movements he therefore proposes the tabular analysis shown in Table III.1 overleaf (see also the similar table in Tinbergen and Schouten, 1955). The first part of this table shows the derivation of the sector financial surpluses and deficits. In the second part, financing is divided between long-term domestic finance, external capital movements, and the liquidity balance, which corresponds to Holtrop's change in net liquidity before adjustment for changes in transactions requirements. Finally the liquidity balance is divided between the increase in indebtedness (in liquid form) and the change in liquid asset holdings. In applying this scheme the relevant criterion for distinguishing between liquidity and capital market items is that the former have a more direct bearing on spending decisions and are more immediately affected by other sectors' spending decisions. The advantage of this tabular presentation is that it is comprehensive, so that the effect of any unusual capital market movement is immediately obvious and can be allowed for in interpreting liquidity changes. Again, it is desirable to make some adjustment for permanent changes in demand for liquid assets.

TABLE III.1

Sector Liquidity Financing

Sources and uses of funds.	Total. Domestic economy.	Sector. Government.	Business enterprises.	Households.
(1) Income	360	40	130	190
(2) Expenditure	366	49	167	150
(3) Finance Balance . . .	−6	−9	−37	40
(= 1 − 2 = 4 + 5 + 6) expressing an income expenditure disequilibrium financed by:				
(4) Recourse to Domestic Capital Market and Financial Institutions Other than Banks (net borrowing)	X *	−5	−10	15
(5) External Autonomous Capital Movements (net imports) . .	−8	−3	−10	5
(6) Liquidity Balance . . .	2	−1	−17	20
(= 3 − 4 − 5 = 7 + 8) expressing a change in liquidity resulting from:				
(7) Recourse to the Banking System and Issue of Secondary Liquid Assets (increase in indebtedness) .	−6	−1	−15	10
(8) Absorption (+) or Drawing Down (−) of Liquid Assets . . .	8	X †	−2	10

* Equals zero by definition.

† Equals zero by definition, inasmuch as any accumulation of liquid funds by the government is automatically used to decrease its short-term indebtedness.

Source: Segré (1958), p. 110.

This approach to financial analysis has not in fact been applied widely. Four reasons may be suggested. First, there is the practical reason that in most countries the relevant information is either not available at all or not available soon enough for policy purposes: it is much more demanding on information than simple monetary analysis. Secondly, there is much support for Wallich's (1969) view that because the monetary system supplies the residual funds, it is unnecessary to pay attention to the behaviour of the rest of the financial system. While this opinion does seem open to question in countries where a wide variety of liquid debt instruments is available, it clearly has considerable force in those countries in which the banks are dominant in the provision of short-term liquid assets and short-term credit. Thirdly, it may be difficult to define a boundary between liquid assets and long-term assets, and the disposition of asset portfolios may be highly sensitive to changes in the relative rates of return on different assets. This adds to the difficulty of isolating the temporary element in the change in net liquidity, and even the presentation in Table III.1 may be difficult to interpret. Finally, there has not yet been sufficient empirical work on the relationships between temporary liquidity surpluses or deficits in spending sectors and their subsequent expenditures on goods and services; it has therefore been difficult to integrate information about sector liquidity positions into economic forecasting procedures.

III.3. *The Fixed Technical Coefficients (input–output) Approach*

One approach to flow of funds analysis emphasises the possibility of linkages between particular uses and specified sources of funds. For example, non-financial companies might find finance for investment in tangible assets in relatively stable proportions from a number of sources, such as their own retentions, the issue of new long-term debt and bank loans. In some economies stable relationships of this kind may exist among the flows within the financial system and between financial institutions and the ultimate saving and spending sectors; this might be expected if the composition of desired balance sheets within each sector was stable and insensitive to changes in relative interest rates, or if regulations governed the patterns of asset acquisition. A financial structure with these characteristics would lend itself to analysis by input–output methods, with a particular source of finance being treated as a necessary input for a specified use of funds. The amount of each input (source of funds) required per unit of each output (use of funds), would be a fixed technical coefficient of the system.

Chipman (1950) carried out a major theoretical study of inter-sectoral moneyflows and income formation using these ideas. He assumed that the economy could be divided into a number of sectors and that each sector's disbursements to every other sector were a given linear function of its receipts, with changes in disbursements following changes in receipts after a specified time lag. The fixed technical coefficients of the system were the coefficients of these linear functions. Chipman noted that it might seem implausible to treat certain capital receipts, such as loans from financial institutions, as determinants of expenditures: on the contrary, it seemed more likely that the decision to borrow would be a consequence of a decision to spend on goods and services. This kind of difficulty could be overcome by treating certain receipts as negative disbursements. By introducing additional sectors, which simply acted as " collecting agencies " whose sole purpose was to delay moneyflows, it was also possible to allow for different time lags within the system. On these foundations Chipman constructed a theoretical matrix multiplier model of income formation and analysed its properties.

More recently Stone (1966) and Stone and Roe (1971) have developed models of the financial system based upon the social accounting matrix, and have attempted to apply one such model in the United Kingdom. The starting point of this model is the assumption that certain fixed relationships exist within the national balance sheet.

Let A_{jk} $(j = 1 \ldots n, \ k = 1 \ldots m)$ be an $(n \times m)$ matrix of the n sectors' holdings of the m financial instruments as assets and L_{kj} be the corresponding $(m \times n)$ matrix of liabilities. Then two coefficient matrices can be calculated, one showing the proportions in which each financial instrument held as an asset is distributed over the sectors, and the other showing the proportions in which the total liabilities of each sector are distributed over the set of financial instruments.

Thus define the $(n \times m)$ coefficient matrix A^*_{jk}

$$A^*_{jk} = A_{jk}\hat{a}_k^{-1} \qquad . \qquad . \qquad . \qquad . \quad (1)$$

where $\hat{a}_k$ is the $(m \times 1)$ vector of the total holdings as assets of the m financial instruments, expressed as an $(m \times m)$ diagonal matrix. The column sums of A^*_{jk} are one, and the elements of the matrix show the proportions of every asset total held by each sector. The corresponding matrix for liabilities is

$$L^*_{kj} = L_{kj}\hat{x}_j^{-1} \qquad . \qquad . \qquad . \qquad . \quad (2)$$

where $\hat{x}_j$ is the $(n \times 1)$ vector of the total liabilities (including net worth) of the n sectors, expressed as an $n \times n$ diagonal matrix. The elements of L^*_{kj} show the proportion of each financial liability in the sector's total liabilities, and the column sums are one minus the ratio of the sector's net worth to its total liabilities. Both of these coefficient matrices are assumed to be fixed.

Let w_j be the total assets (financial and tangible) of the j'th sector
$\quad e_j$ be the tangible asset holding of the j'th sector
$\quad l_k$ be the total holdings as a liability of the k'th financial instrument by all sectors

Then
$$w_j = A^*_{jk}a_k + e_j \qquad . \qquad . \qquad . \qquad . \quad (3)$$
$$l_k = L^*_{kj}x_j \qquad . \qquad . \qquad . \qquad . \quad (4)$$
$$w_j = x_j \qquad . \qquad . \qquad . \qquad . \quad (5)$$
$$a_k = l_k \qquad . \qquad . \qquad . \qquad . \quad (6)$$

Hence
$$w_j = A^*_{jk}L^*_{kl}w_l + e_j$$
$$= (I_{jl} - A^*_{jk}L^*_{kl})^{-1} e_l \qquad . \qquad . \qquad . \quad (7)$$

where I_{jl} is the unit matrix of order n

Similarly
$$l_k = L^*_{kj}(I_{jl} - A^*_{jk}L^*_{kl})^{-1} e_l \qquad . \qquad . \qquad . \quad (8)$$

The term $(I_{jl} - A^*_{jk}L^*_{kl})^{-1}$ in equation (7) is the matrix multiplier which converts the holdings of tangible assets of each sector into a vector of total assets holdings (tangible and financial) for each sector. Equation (8) shows the totals of the financial liabilities which correspond to the same tangible asset holdings.

As it stands this model refers to balance sheet values, but (ignoring revaluations) it can be transformed into a flow of funds model by substituting the change in tangible asset holdings of each sector for the level. The key assumptions in the model are that the marginal propensities to finance expenditure from different sources (*i.e.*, from self-financing or by issuing different types of liability) are constant and equal to the average propensities observed from the balance sheet statement and represented by the matrix L^*_{kj}; and that the total amounts of new financial liabilities issued are distributed in fixed proportions, represented by the matrix A^*_{jk}, among the asset portfolios of the various sectors.

Although for any vector of sector investments in tangible assets this model will produce a completely balanced flow table for the corresponding acquisitions of financial assets and liabilities, the marginal acquisitions of assets by the sectors will not, unless by accident, be in the same proportions as the existing balance sheet.[1] Thus a consequence of imposing a given pattern of liability financing in the model is that each sector's asset portfolio must be allowed to depart from its previous composition: in effect, the model gives infinite weight to preferences over liabilities and zero weight to preferences over assets. This implies further that, quite apart from the form which saving takes, the sector distribution of saving is likely to differ from that which accords with the sectors' saving preferences.

Stone draws attention to these difficulties, and suggests two ways by which internally consistent flow tables can be obtained without making such extreme assumptions. He points out that an alternative polar model can be formulated, which sets out the consequences of assuming a given vector of changes in sectors' net worths and a given pattern of asset acquisition. With such a formulation it would be the pattern of liability financing and the sectors' investment in tangible assets which would have to adjust. This too will give rise to a balanced flow table.

Stone also demonstrates that, using the RAS technique (Stone, 1963), a balanced flow table can usually be obtained which respects both the sectors' savings intentions and their investment programmes. Either the quantities of different financial claims issued by the various sectors or the preferred pattern of their asset holdings can also be imposed, but whichever of these is imposed the other has to give to balance the system. It is also possible to obtain a balanced flow by taking a weighted average of tables drawn up on different assumptions.

---

[1] The same proportional distribution would occur only if the pattern of new investment in tangible assets by the various sectors were the same as that of their existing tangible assets.

A fundamental difficulty with this kind of model is the question of how far it is legitimate to treat the coefficients in the system as stable. The structure of the financial system may be very flexible and its response to changes in relative yields may be large.

An empirical test of the stability of the coefficients in the United Kingdom was carried out by Stone and Roe. Using the model set out in equations (1) and (7) above they estimated the matrix multipliers for the United Kingdom in 1962 and 1966, employing five sectors and forty three types of financial instrument, and compared their results in the two years. They found that some coefficients had changed substantially, particularly in the rest of the world and government sectors, a consequence presumably of the rapid growth of international capital markets and changing practices in government financing. They also examined the stability of the coefficients reflecting the issue of liabilities (using equation (9)) and found that at this disaggregated level there was even greater variation. The conclusion must be that the fixed technical coefficient approach is not suited to a complex financial system such as the United Kingdom's.

This does not however mean that the approach is valueless. It may be applied to problems of medium-term financial planning in financial systems which have not reached a high state of development or in which regulations rather than market preferences govern the acquisition of assets and issue of liabilities. A major objective of medium-term financial planning in these conditions is to discover what changes in institutional structure are likely to be needed, and models which assume an unchanged structure can be employed fruitfully.

The techniques used to construct medium-term plans generally ensure that sufficient saving is available in aggregate to pay for whatever amount of net investment is envisaged. But saving and investment in individual sectors will not be equal: the problem therefore is to ensure that the patterns of saving and investment by sectors are consistent with any limits which there may be on their financial behaviour. The object of a financial projection is to discover whether, in the absence of structural changes, any shortages or surpluses of capital funds for particular sectors are likely to arise.

The methods adopted for medium-term financial planning in France and India have been described by Barthelemy (1969) and Bhatt (1971) respectively. In France the non-financial projection is taken as basic, and projections of sector financial surpluses and deficits are derived from it. Fixed technical coefficients, derived from empirical studies of financing and from existing regulations, are then applied to obtain the supply and demand for each category of financial instrument. These are unlikely to balance and the excess demands for particular financial instruments indicate where tensions are likely to arise in the capital and credit markets, thus suggesting where the authorities should take action to modify the supplies of funds to the different sectors by suitable institutional arrangements. The projection therefore gives advance warning of changes in financial practices or institutional structure which may be required.

Barthelemy draws attention to some limitations in the method. The assumption of fixed coefficients undoubtedly exaggerates the inflexibility of the financial system; even if the portfolio practices of the financial institutions are subject to regulation the behaviour of unregulated non-institutional sectors may be expected to adapt. Nevertheless, if the financial projection showed that the adjustment required to achieve balance would be very large in the absence of measures to induce changes in institutional investment practices, considerable doubt would be cast upon the feasibility of the plan as a whole, unless special measures were taken.

In India the real projection is again taken as basic, and the aggregate saving of each sector is derived. With flows of funds from abroad treated as autonomous, the total asset acquisition of households is calculated and allocated among the various financial instruments. This determines the funds available to banks and other financial institutions, and when the normal lending patterns of these institutions are imposed the supply of funds direct to each ultimate spending sector can be calculated. The assumptions and methods thus correspond to Stone's model in which the sector distribution of saving is given and the pattern of asset acquisition is governed by fixed technical coefficients of the system. The corresponding issues of liabilities and the distribution of investment by sector can then be derived.

The level of investment in each sector warranted by these funds is compared with the net capital formation implicit in the real projection. Any substantial disparities in the pattern of investment warranted by savings flows and the pattern implicit in the real projection can be interpreted as requiring a change in the institutional structure. Indeed, if a very large surplus of funds was available in the household sector it would imply that the forecasts of capital formation by other sectors were unrealistic, unless new institutions capable of attracting these funds and redistributing them to other sectors could be created.

In addition to these applications in the planning field the notion of fixed technical coefficients has been employed by Cohen (1957, 1961, 1963, 1968) both to construct circular flow models of economic behaviour and in empirical studies of the determinants of certain categories of expenditure. These studies are open to the objection that it may be illegitimate to assume even approximate fixity of the coefficients and the direction of causation is seldom clear. Cohen does not demonstrate conclusively that the flows of credit can be treated as exogenous variables, and that they are determinants of, rather than determined by, the levels of expenditures.

III.4. *Interest Rate Forecasts*

Capital market analysis, carried out with the intention of forecasting the behaviour of interest rates, is an important use of flow of funds data. Forecasts of this kind have been prepared at regular intervals for a number of years by private organisations in the United States, such as The Bankers Trust Company, The Life Insurance Association of America and Salamon Brothers, and by the Sun Life Assurance Company of Canada in that country. Although the techniques employed differ in detail the general approach has been described by Freund and Zinbarg (1963, 1970) and the analytical basis for an important aspect of the method—the emphasis upon " the residual "—has been discussed in detail by Ronk (1965). The forecasts are compiled within a loanable funds framework: thus, while monetary expansion is an important influence, supplies of capital funds and demands for credit are also considered explicitly.

The object is to compile a prospective sources and uses of funds statement for the economy as a whole, showing the net new funds supplied through the capital and credit markets. This involves the preparation of a systematic forecast which takes account of the factors determining the demands for credit by final users and the supply of credit to these users both through the intermediation of financial institutions and directly from the ultimate sources of funds; to avoid duplication, funds placed with financial intermediaries must be excluded. Since borrowing by financial intermediaries does not appear in this statement, it is not strictly necessary to forecast the entire flow of funds matrix, but in practice it is convenient to do so in order to ensure that there is overall consistency. The individual elements of the forecast matrix depend upon assumptions made by the forecaster about the prospective conjunctural situation and about monetary policy: fixed coefficients are not assumed, and an iterative procedure enables the forecaster to adjust his initial estimates of flows in the light of the emerging financial conditions until a consistent picture appears.

The normal practice is to show the demand for credit classified by category of financial instrument and the supply of funds to be invested in these instruments classified by institutional or other source. The coverage of sources for which independent predictions can be made is not comprehensive, and the balance between the demand for credit and the net supply from identified sectors is allocated to a residual sector described as " Individual and Miscellaneous."

In the United States the size of the residual balance has been found to correlate well with the corporate bond rate, a high residual being associated with a high bond yield. A number of possible explanations for this correlation have been offered: individuals may be induced by rising interest rates to step up the volume of their savings, particularly in the form of marketable securities; in response to a rise in interest rates investors may alter the composition of their asset portfolios in favour of bonds and against money; and if the foreign sector acts as a residual source of funds, international capital movements may be stimulated by changes in domestic relative to foreign interest rates.

Some capital market forecasts provide a breakdown between the different categories of financial instruments, and this allows a corresponding breakdown of " the residual," but while the residual correlates well with the corporate bond yield, it is apparently much less significant in the equity market.   Homer (1968) attributes this difference to the relative importance of the " Individuals and Miscellaneous " group in the two markets and to the incidence of new issues in relation to the outstanding volume of securities.

In the corporate bond market net new issues are significant in relation to the volume of bonds outstanding, averaging about 10% per year.   About 75% of the total bonds outstanding are held by the non-bank investing institutions, who also have a substantial but variable demand for new issues each year.   In contrast " Individuals and Miscellaneous " still account for under 25% of outstanding bonds, although their holdings have become more important in recent years.   Since the new supply of corporate bonds is determined mainly by corporations' cash flow and liquidity positions, and appears to be relatively inelastic to interest rates in the short-run, and since demand for funds tends to be high at the same time as the resources available from the non-bank institutions are under pressure, the amount of funds demanded from the residual group fluctuates substantially from year to year and is significant relative to their total holdings.   Substantial fluctuations in corporate bond yields are necessary to persuade these relatively reluctant holders to absorb the marginal supply.   In contrast, until recently net new issues of corporate stocks in the United States have been very small, and the " Individuals and Miscellaneous " category of holder accounts for a much larger proportion (about 80%) of corporate stock outstanding.   The market is also strongly influenced by changes in expectations of future profitability, a factor which exerts much less influence in the corporate bond market.   The net transactions (usually net sales rather than net purchases) of the " Individuals and Miscellaneous " group appear therefore to be of much less consequence in determining yields.

Emphasis on the residual as a forecasting tool has the major disadvantage that the estimate incorporates all the statistical and estimating errors in the other components, and may therefore be particularly unreliable (Atkinson, 1963).   From an analytical point of view, it is also unsatisfactory because so little is known about its properties.   Nevertheless, analysts who employ this kind of approach do seem to have had some success, both in predicting changes in the general level of long-term interest rates and in identifying segments of the capital market in which the pressure of demand for funds is likely to be particularly intense.   The approach depends, however, on an ability to forecast correctly the behaviour of the monetary authorities.

III.5. *Short-term Flow of Funds Projections*

In many countries a flow of funds forecast is prepared in conjunction with other aspects of official short-term national income forecasts. Their object differs from that of the capital market forecasts already described, in that, while private forecasters aim to predict what financial conditions will actually emerge under the assumption of a specified official monetary policy, official forecasts are carried out with a view to guiding the authorities in the formulation of that and other aspects of macro-economic policy. In some countries, for example Britain and the United States, the financial forecast is derived from the main official economic forecast constructed in real terms, and while the financial forecast is consistent with the main forecast it is in no sense an independent prediction of financial developments. In others, for example Italy and Yugoslavia, financial forecasting is integrated to a greater extent with the real forecast and some aspects of the real forecast are contingent upon finance being available. The distinction is perhaps one of degree rather than of kind, and the end result of either approach ought to be a consistent picture of real and financial developments.

The procedures employed in Britain and America have been described by Berman and Cassell (1968) and Taylor (1963) respectively. In each country the main economic forecast is prepared in real terms. The first stage in constructing a flow of funds forecast is therefore to convert the real forecast to a current price basis, and to calculate the implied sector surpluses and deficits. Next, account has to be taken of assumptions about financial conditions generally or the supply of funds for particular activities. The nature of these assumptions may vary: foreign interest rates may be regarded as exogenous, consumer borrowing may be regulated, and official policy on gilt-edged yields or alternatively the expansion of the monetary base must be assumed. A first attempt is then made sector by sector to fill in the elements of the matrix, consistent with each sector's savings and investment flows and taking a view of the likely pattern of financial transactions in these credit market conditions.[1] This is done for the household, non-financial companies, government and overseas sectors, with the banks and other financial institutions following when the projected level of their liabilities is known.[2]

With this procedure it is assumed in every case that institutions have some notional preferred portfolio patterns (depending on the relative yields expected on their investments), which they will attempt to adhere to. An example illustrating how a highly condensed hypothetical table might appear at this stage is shown in Table III.2(a). While the construction of the

[1] This stage involves a large number of assumptions (usually implicit) about relative yields, which are additional to those assumptions made explicit in compiling the main forecast.

[2] Where the expansion of the monetary base is taken as given the change in bank deposits is not calculated as a residual.

table ensures that the column constraints are satisfied there is no reason to expect the row totals to be zero. Any value other than zero implies an excess demand or supply of that particular financial instrument. Table III.2(a) shows an excess supply of private sector securities amounting to £750m matched by an equivalent excess demand for public sector securities. There is also an excess supply of long-term liabilities (including new equity issues) amounting to £400m matched by an equal excess demand for short-term assets.

TABLE III.2(a)

Flow of Funds Projection—First Round

£ million.

	Public.	Over-seas.	House-hold.	Non-financial com-panies.	Banks.	OFI.	Total.
Financial surplus . .	+350	−650	+1850	−1050	+200	−700	0
Public sector:							
Short-term borrowing .	−150	—	+100	+200	+150	—	+300
Long-term borrowing .	−500	—	+50	−100	+300	+700	+450
Private sector:							
Short-term borrowing .	—	—	−100	−800	+850	+150	+100
Long-term borrowing .	+100	—	−2200	−600	+50	+1800	−850
Domestic bank deposits .	+50	—	+700	+250	−950	−50	0
OFI liabilities . .	—	—	+3300	—	—	−3300	0
External currency flow .	+850	−850	—	—	—	—	0
Banks' net external transactions . . .	—	+200	—	—	−200	—	0
	+350	−650	+1850	−1050	+200	−700	0

These discrepancies suggest that the initial assumptions about financial conditions are not consistent with equilibrium in financial markets. The rates of interest on private sector assets are likely to be higher than assumed initially, with financial institutions bidding actively for funds in order to accommodate demand. There is also likely to be a tendency for non-financial companies to borrow more at short-term if capital market conditions become less favourable for long-term borrowing. An iterative procedure is therefore employed, with the assumptions at each round being revised in the light of the discrepancies revealed in the previous round.

Table III.2(b) overleaf shows a new projection based upon this amended view of probable financial conditions. The sector surpluses and deficits have been left unchanged, since it has been assumed for this illustration that there is no feedback in the short run from financial conditions to real income and expenditure flows. The following adjustments have been made to achieve this balance: (i) in response to the higher level of domestic interest rates in the private sector banks have switched an extra £300m of overseas funds into sterling.   (ii) Persons have increased their acquisitions of OFI liabilities (*e.g.*, building society deposits) and reduce their net sales of private sector securities (included in the figure for long-term borrowing) in response to higher yields offered, and have also substantially reduced their net acquisitions of national savings securities and increased their net sales of government stocks.   (iii) Higher long-term borrowing rates have led non-financial companies to switch £500m of borrowing from the long-term to the short-term segment of the market, and to avoid a further £50m of long-term

Table III.2(*b*)

Flow of Funds Projection—After Adjustment

£ million.

	Public.	Over-seas.	House-hold.	Non-financial com-panies.	Banks.	OFI.	Total.
Financial surplus . .	+350	—650	+1850	—1050	+200	—700	0
Public sector:							
Short-term borrowing .	—750	—	+100	+200	+450	—	0
Long-term borrowing .	—200	—	—350	—100	+100	+550	0
Private sector:							
Short-term borrowing .	—	—	—100	—1300	+1250	+150	0
Long-term borrowing .	+100	—	—1900	—50	+50	+1800	0
Domestic bank deposits .	+50	—	+700	+200	—1150	+200	0
OFI liabilities . .	—	—	+3400	—	—	—3400	0
External currency flow .	+1150	—1150	—	—	—	—	0
Banks' net external transactions . . .	—	+500	—	—	—500	—	0
	+350	—650	+1850	—1050	+200	—700	0

borrowing by cutting back their net acquisitions of domestic bank deposits. (iv) Banks have bid for additional deposits (from other financial institutions) and switched additional funds into sterling.   They have used their additional funds mainly for lending to the private sector, but have also increased their net acquisitions of short-term public sector debt, in order to maintain their liquidity, partly at the expense of a reduction in their net acquisitions of government stocks.   (v) Other financial institutions have increased their liabilities slightly, invested less in long-term government stocks, and employed the additional funds in bank deposits.   Certain items are unchanged, either because they are treated as autonomous (*e.g.*, long-term lending by the public sector to the private sector) or because they are thought to be insensitive to changes in relative interest rates.

The configuration of flows illustrated in Table III.2(*b*) is not necessarily in all respects plausible; it is intended to illustrate how the matrix approach allows the individual parts of the forecast to be kept in touch with each other, and how, by a process of successive approximation, consistency in the flows can be obtained. " The merit of this system is that each element can be tested by the plausibility of its counterparts in other areas of the matrix. The whole is reasonable only if the parts are " (Bank of England, 1972, p. 13).

Within the official forecasting procedure in Britain an attempt is now made to incorporate some current feedback from the projected financial forecast to the real spending flows. Thus the influence of flows of funds through building societies on investment in dwellings is now recognised, and the probable behaviour of short-term interest rates may be allowed to influence the forecast of stock-building. Practice in regard to the choice between an interest rate or money supply assumption has varied. Formerly a level of Bank Rate was assumed for the forecasting exercise. An attempt was made for a time to use a monetary expansion datum for the forecast, with the level of short-term interest rates being treated as a dependent variable, but the recent poor performance of models of the demand for money in the United Kingdom has caused a reversion to interest rate assumptions.

The financial projection allows the authorities to assess the probable implications of the main forecast for monetary growth, for changes in net liquidity and for interest rates. Even if current financial conditions are thought to have only a slight immediate influence on the real behaviour of the economy there is general agreement that they have more substantial implications both for real expenditures and for prices in the future. A financial projection might thus have one or more of a number of consequences: it might cause the authorities to amend their forecast of the behaviour of the economy in later periods; or, if an interest rate target had been assumed, it might cause the authorities to revise it upwards (downwards) in order to prevent an undue expansion (squeeze) on liquidity; or finally, if a monetary base target had been assumed, the target might be modified to avoid undesired consequences for interest rates. In any event, the financial forecasting process enables the authorities to evaluate some of the probable consequences of alternative policies, and hence to choose among them.

There are still very considerable difficulties in assessing the plausibility of any projection. Some of these difficulties are statistical in character: the quality of some of the data is often very poor. But probably more important is ignorance of the sectors' portfolio behaviour and of their reaction to changes in financial conditions. As a result, no great weight can be given to the details of the financial forecast, and progress towards a fuller integration with the real forecast has inevitably been slow.

In Italy the financial forecast is more closely related to real spending. It is used to determine the level of government borrowing and expansion of the monetary base which are likely to be consistent with an assumed rate of growth of income (Cotula and Masera, 1971; Bank of Italy, 1971). The forecasting procedure starts with assumptions about the level of GDP at current prices, private investment and the balance of payment surplus. Using these assumptions, and with the aid of demand functions for the relevant assets, the Bank of Italy can predict the required rate of expansion of the monetary base. With the aid of further assumptions about private sector borrowing, the supply of finance from various sources to the government sector is determined as a residual.

In Yugoslavia a distinction is drawn between long-term finance and short-term finance, and policy rules do not permit long-term uses of funds such as investment to be financed to more than a very limited extent from short-term sources. This means that there are clear financial constraints upon the level of investment, and the forecasting procedure takes account of this (Dimitrijevic, 1969). A financial forecast is first built up independently for each individual sector, and these sectoral forecasts are put together so that imbalances can be identified. If the supply of long-term finance to any sector is substantially less than the amount required for its investment programme, the assumed level of investment is cut. Thus an iterative process is followed, involving adjustment both to the financial transactions and to the real income and expenditure flows which lie behind them. When a consistent overall projection, which satisfies the policy constraints, has been found the implications for monetary and credit policy can be derived.

These examples serve to show some of the ways in which flow of funds analysis can be adapted to fit into the short-term forecasting procedures utilised in different countries. Where the financial forecast is derived from the real forecast, without any current feedback from the former to the latter, the main function of the financial forecast is to provide some insight into the financial conditions which are likely to emerge if the authorities follow a particular monetary policy. This gives the authorities an opportunity to adjust their policy in good time, and so to avoid creating in the short run conditions thought likely to disturb the smooth development of the economy in the future. A more complete integration of the financial and real projections can be achieved by incorporating current feedback from financial to real variables, reflecting either policy constraints or known behavioural relationships. In principle, the integration of financial and real projections can be expected to improve the accuracy of both aspects of the forecasts.

III.6. *Financial Econometric Models* [1]

To qualify as a flow of funds model, a model must have the following characteristics: it must be comprehensive in its coverage, it must be disaggregated by sector and by financial instrument, and it must explain the transactions by each sector in every financial instrument or group of financial instruments specified. In a formal sense most existing financial econometric

---

[1] This is *not* a survey of financial econometric models, and reference will be made to particular models only where they illustrate some specific point.

models are comprehensive because, although behavioural relations are often not specified for each asset in every sector, the presence of balance sheet constraints ensures that relations are specified implicitly for any residual assets.   However, as Brainard and Tobin (1968) have noted, the implicit specification of the residual assets is often unsatisfactory.   Explicit treatment of all financial instruments must be a feature of a flow of funds model, with the balance sheet constraints imposing limitations on the form of the functions specified and upon the parameter values.

The second, perhaps obvious, requirement for a flow of funds model is that it must explain the *net transactions* in financial assets by each sector. Most models do not satisfy this requirement, because they concentrate on balance sheets and do not distinguish between changes in asset holdings which reflect transactions in financial assets and those which are a consequence of revaluations in existing asset holdings.   The distinction may be important.   Transactions involve costs and presumably reflect conscious decisions on the part of economic agents; whereas changes in balance sheet composition consequential upon a revaluation by the market are costless and may simply reflect a failure to keep portfolios under continuous review rather than a conscious decision to leave a holding of an asset or liability unchanged.

A third feature of a flow of funds model is that supply and demand functions must be formulated for each segment of the capital market which is separately distinguished.   There must be either a rate-setting equation or a market clearing condition for the yield on every financial instrument which is determined endogenously within the system.   This seems to rule out the use of mechanical models of the interest-rate structure, though it does not of course imply that interest rates in different parts of the market will not conform with relationships established in this way.   What it does mean is that if such relationships do exist at least one group of investors in the market—one sector in this context—must be prepared to vary the composition of its asset portfolio in an elastic way in response to any deviations from the normal rate-structure.

In recent years most econometric studies of financial markets have put more emphasis on the structure of the balance sheets of asset holders and the issuers of liabilities than on their transactions in financial assets.   The theoretical foundation has generally been some form of utility-maximising model, in which economic agents are supposed to maximise the utility they derive from their asset holdings, the sources of utility being the expected streams of income derived from the various assets, and diversification being explained in terms of transactions costs or other characteristics of the assets and liabilities such as their riskiness.   The demand functions derived from models of this kind specify the desired holdings of any particular asset or liability as a function of a vector of interest rates, with net wealth or some other asset aggregate acting as a constraint.

With the net wealth of each sector taken as given, the general practice has been to specify the main behavioural assumptions in the following way (*e.g.*, De Leeuw, 1965; Goldfeld, 1966). First, as already mentioned, economic agents have some desired relationship between their holdings of individual financial assets and some measure of their " wealth," this relationship being a function of the relative interest rates on the components of their assets and liability portfolios. Secondly, where the actual stock of any asset held in the portfolio does not equal the desired stock, adjustment to the desired level is not instantaneous but takes place gradually, with the change in any period depending in part on the discrepancy between the desired and actual stocks. Thirdly, changes in the composition of a sector's portfolio in any period depend also in part on the amount of readily available funds, which may act as a short run constraint. Since changes in the asset portfolio may have to be planned some time in advance, expected flows of funds may also influence behaviour, and this means that lagged as well as current values of the constraint variables may be important as indicators of these expected flows. Fourthly, it is usually assumed that all relationships are homogeneous of degree one in all money values, so that asset holdings can be expressed as a ratio of some measure of " wealth."

The adjustment mechanism and the role of constraint variables warrant further discussion. Most models specify a standard partial adjustment mechanism, whereby a proportion of the gap between the desired holding of any asset and the actual holding at the beginning of the period is closed within the period. The proportionate adjustment factor has not been the subject of detailed economic analysis, and has generally simply been treated as a constant parameter of the system which is estimated through statistical analysis. Thus the rate of adjustment does not depend upon the size of the gap, relative interest rates or the availability of liquid funds. Similarly, when other adjustment mechanisms, such as Almon lag distributions, have been employed no theory of the process of adjustment has been specified. The empirical evidence on rates of adjustment has been mixed, with earlier studies (*e.g.*, De Leeuw, 1965; Goldfeld, 1966) finding generally very low rates of adjustment—sometimes less than 10% per quarter—and some more recent studies (*e.g.*, Hendershott, 1971; Helliwell and others, 1971) reporting quite rapid adjustment.

The constraint variables have been introduced into the models because increases in net wealth or in particular assets or liabilities may not be distributed immediately in an equilibrium manner over the portfolio as a whole, but instead may be allocated in the first instance in a way which depends upon the source of the funds: an unexpected change in a company's cash flow is reflected first in its holdings of liquid financial assets or short-term borrowing, and only later in its operating assets; banks which receive a deposit inflow are likely initially to build up their holdings of liquid assets; and an increase in asset portfolios resulting from a revaluation of equity shares is likely to continue to be held in this form for some time. Again, the initial distribution of such accruals to the " wealth " portfolio is treated as a parameter of the system, which is independent of the arguments determining the equilibrium composition of the balance sheet—there is no interaction between interest rate variables and these constraint variables. The implication is that interest rates do not have a direct influence on the disposition of accruing funds between alternative investment opportunities, but influence transactions only indirectly through adjustments carried out to correct discrepancies between desired and actual stocks of particular assets. Many investigators have included flow-constraints in their models, and in some instances the statistical significance of the reported estimates suggests that these variables are important; indeed, they sometimes seem much more significant than the interest rates which enter into the theoretical model determining the equilibrium stocks of assets (see, e.g., Goldfeld, 1969; Silber, 1970; Hendershott, 1971).

Consistently with the emphasis in recent work upon balance sheet positions rather than transactions, a liquidity-preference approach to the determination of interest rates in capital markets has been adopted. Although attempts have often been made to explain a number of money-market and other short-term interest rates by specifying the supply and demand for particular financial instruments, there has been a widespread reliance on interest-rate structure relationships in the determination of long-term interest rates. In some markets rate-setting equations have been specified which reflect the behaviour of the relevant institutions—an example is the bank loan rate. Where an interest-rate structure relationship has been employed, the rate of interest in one market, such as the long-term bond market, has been modelled mechanically in terms of current and lagged values of other interest rates determined elsewhere in the structure of the system. Little attempt seems to have been made to specify the supply and demand for long-term bonds or for equities explicitly, and thereby to determine the yields ruling in these markets.

This treatment of interest rates represents a departure from earlier practice. In what was probably the first econometric study of the United States Tinbergen (1939) considered demand and supply in the money and capital markets explicitly. He specified demand and supply functions from firms, individuals and banks, in the markets for a variety of instruments including bonds, shares and short claims. The yields on these assets were determined by the condition that the market for each financial instrument should clear. Dawson (1958) constructed a model of financial markets in the United States, which explicitly adopted the flow of funds framework. His model had five sectors and four financial instruments—currency and deposits, federal obligations, corporate securities and bank loans. The sector financial surpluses and deficits were taken as given, and demand and supply functions were specified for these financial instruments, with the market clearing condition again determining the interest rates. Finally, Brown (1964) constructed a financial econometric model with 25 endogenous variables including several interest rates, most of which were determined through market clearing conditions.

Perhaps the nearest recent approach to a flow of funds model is that of Hendershott (1969), who formulated a model in the Tinbergen tradition of financial behaviour in the United States. The model is comprehensive and interest rates are to be determined explicitly; the economy is divided into five sectors and financial instruments are grouped into five broad categories; and the model is specified in general equilibrium terms, with the desired composition of balance sheets being determined by a vector of interest rates and by flow variables, such as contractual savings and the change in total financial assets in recent periods.

Hendershott (1971) has employed this model to study the behaviour of the non-bank finance sector in the United States. The weighting pattern applied to current and lagged values of the different interest rates was allowed to vary, but a common pattern was imposed on the lag distribution for each interest rate in every equation to ensure that balance sheet constraints were satisfied. Symmetry conditions on the responses of asset holdings to changes in interest rates were also specified and complementarity between any pair of assets was ruled out. With these restrictions Hendershott found that the adjustment to a change in interest rates was always completed within a year, and sometimes much faster, and that quite precise estimates of substitution elasticities could be obtained. However, his results also demonstrated the importance of flow-constraints—the volume of contractual savings and the change in total financial assets—as determinants of the changes in asset holdings of each kind.

Smith (1971) has also formulated a model of the disequilibrium behaviour of the financial sector of the United States, which satisfies most of the conditions for a flow of funds model. The theoretical foundation of the model is in the general equilibrium tradition, but care is taken to ensure that the model specifies the behaviour of all sectors and that all financial instruments are treated explicitly. Balance sheet constraints are satisfied and special attention is paid to the rates of adjustment towards equilibrium; these rates of adjustment are imposed rather than estimated. The predictive performance of an early version of this model was tested against alternatives, but it was not found to be particularly successful. Efforts to improve the model are continuing.

Neither Hendershott's nor Smith's model satisfies all the conditions for a flow of funds model. While they are comprehensive in their coverage of financial instruments and markets, and while they are consistent with balance sheet constraints and avoid the use of interest-rate structure equations, neither model distinguishes between transactions in financial assets and changes in holdings due to revaluations in the course of adjustment to disequilibrium.[1] The role of financial *transactions* in short-run behaviour is not considered explicitly.

IV. CONCLUSION

What has been the contribution of flow of funds in the last 30 years? First, in a substantial number of countries consistent bodies of data have been produced which integrate financial transactions with national income accounts, and now permit economists to incorporate financial behaviour in their description and analysis of economic affairs. The new material has been provided which enables greater insight to be gained into the working of the main sectors of economies, and which allows the connections between particular aspects of financing and income or expenditure flows to be investigated. Secondly, techniques for summarising financial transaction statistics have been developed which assist in presenting the data in a manner relevant to analysis of past economic behaviour, and which help to avoid some of the pitfalls inherent in the use of simpler techniques such as monetary surveys. Thirdly, the growing body of statistical data on financial markets has enabled analysts to develop techniques for integrating financial factors into the methods employed in forecasting national income and interest rates. Finally, analytical methods, which are normally associated with input–output, have been developed and applied in medium-term planning with a view to discovering any financial constraints which might impede economic development. This has all been worth while; but it does not add up to a coherent body of analysis.

Why has progress been so limited? There are two reasons. The first is in a sense subsidiary—lack of good data, particularly data on sector balance sheets. Before existing or new theories of portfolio behaviour can be tested adequately consistent sector balance sheet and transactions data for a run of years must be available; and at the present time only the United States provides this. The second, and more fundamental, reason is concerned with theory. The reader may have been struck by the lack of any common theoretical core running through this survey. Attempts have been made to develop and apply standard economic theory, in the form of the linear fixed-coefficient model and the general equilibrium model, to the analysis of financial markets; and the latter has been developed to take account explicitly of a variety of financial instruments and markets (Tobin, 1969; Pearson, 1971). But, although the sector balance approach was a move in this direction, no theory has been developed which stands comparison with the Keynesian model of income generation, emphasising

---

[1] Smith does allow for a differential *impact* effect of revaluations and changes in total assets for other reasons; but no distinction is drawn between the transactions of the individual and the consequences of changes in the market during the process of adjustment.

short-run income and spending flows rather than long-run equilibrium situations.

Yet there is a considerable body of evidence to suggest that actual flows, as opposed to desired stocks, are important in explaining short-run disequilibrium behaviour. The long-term corporate bond yield in the United States seemed to depend upon the flow of new issues in that market; the flow of new consumer credit has a substantial influence upon purchases of consumer durable goods, and the flow of mortgage finance influences residential construction—in these instances in the short run it is the flow of credit, reflecting perhaps credit rationing rather than its price, which is the important determinant of real spending; and econometric studies of financial markets and institutions provide further evidence of the significance of flow-constraints. It follows that flow-constraints need to be integrated more fully into theories of financial behaviour, and as Roe (1973) has argued, the influence of these constraints upon the behaviour of the economy in dynamic disequilibrium may be closely comparable to the role of income-constraints on spending which has been emphasised in the recent reinterpretations of Keynesian theory (Clower, 1967; Leijonhufvud, 1968).

During the last two decades great progress has been made in the development of economic theory bearing upon the equilibrium characteristics of financial markets. Flow of funds analysis, in contrast with the study of balance sheets, does not have any immediate application to this problem. Its importance lies rather in the processes of adjustment towards equilibrium and in the behaviour of the economic system when it is in disequilibrium. The need now is for theories of sector and market behaviour, which can explain the reactions in the short run of sectors to autonomous disturbances, which can permit the characteristics of their behaviour in disequilibrium to be traced out, and from which the implied behaviour of financial markets can be ascertained. In our present state of knowledge, if the economic system is stable, we can hope to predict the destination towards which it is heading; what we need now is a theory to tell us the speed and route by which it will travel towards its goal.

A. D. BAIN

University of Stirling.

BIBLIOGRAPHY

W. H. L. Anderson, *Corporate Finance and Fixed Investment: An Econometric Study*, Harvard University Graduate School of Business Administration, 1965.

S. N. Atkinson, " Financial Flows in Recent Business Cycles," *Journal of Finance*, Vol. 20, March 1965.

T. R. Atkinson, " The Flow-of-Funds Accounts: a New Approach to Financial Market Analysis," *Journal of Finance*, Vol. 18, May 1963.

P. Baffi, " Monetary Analysis in Italy," *International Monetary Fund Staff Papers*, Vol. 5, February 1957.

A. D. Bain, " Flow of Funds Analysis in the Formulation of Economic Policy," *Transactions of the Manchester Statistical Society*, Session 1972-3.

Banca D'Italia, *Report* for the year 1970, Rome, 1971.

Bank of England, " Personal Saving and Financial Investment: 1951-65," *Bank of England Quarterly Bulletin*, Vol. 6, September 1966.

Bank of England, " Company Finance: 1952-65," *Bank of England Quarterly Bulletin*, Vol. 7, March 1967.

Bank of England, *Statistical Abstract*, No. 1, 1970.

Bank of England, *An Introduction to Flow-of-Funds Accounting: 1952-70*. Bank of England, London, 1972.

Bank of England, " Analysis of Financial Statistics," *Bank of England Quarterly Bulletin* (Quarterly Article; Annual Review each June).

Bank of Israel, *Annual Report* 1970, Jerusalem, October 1971.

S. Barthelemy, "La Methode de Projection à Moyen Terme des Circuits Financiers Utilisée dans la Préparation du Ve Plan Français," *Review of Income & Wealth*, Series 15, March 1969.

W. J. Baumol, " Professor Copeland's Study of Moneyflows," *Review of Economics and Statistics*, Vol. 36, February 1954.

R. E. Beales and L. S. Berman, " National Accounts for Analysing Credit Market Conditions," *Review of Income & Wealth*, Series 12, September 1966.

L. S. Berman, " Flow of Funds in the United Kingdom," *Journal of the Royal Statistical Society*, 128, part 3, 1965.

L. S. Berman and F. Cassell, " Short-term Forecasts of Income, Expenditure and Saving," *Economic Trends*, 172, February 1968.

V. V. Bhatt, " Saving and Flow of Funds Analysis: a Tool for Financial Planning in India," *Review of Income & Wealth*, Series 17, March 1971.

Board of Governors of the Federal Reserve System. *Flow of Funds in the United States, 1939-53*, Washington, 1955.

Board of Governors of the Federal Reserve System, *Flow of Funds Accounts 1945-62*, 1963 Supplement.

Board of Governors of the Federal Reserve System, *Flow of Funds Accounts 1945-68*, Washington, 1970.

B. Bosworth and J. Duesenberry, " A Flow of Funds Model and its Implications," in *Issues in Federal Debt Management*, Federal Reserve Bank of Boston, 1973.

W. Brainard and J. Tobin, " Pitfalls in Financial Model Building," *American Economic Review*, Vol. 58, May 1968.

E. H. Brau, " The Variability of Velocity and Credit Ceilings," *International Monetary Fund Staff Papers*, Vol. 18, November 1971.

M. Brown, " An Econometric Model of the United States with Special Reference to the Financial Sector, Technical Appendix to I. Friend. The Effects of Monetary Policies on Nonmonetary Financial Institutions and Capital Markets," in *Commission on Money and Credit, Private Capital Markets, 1964*.

J. S. Chipman, *The Theory of Intersectoral Money Flows and Income Formation*, Johns Hopkins Press, 1951.

R. W. Clower, " A Reconsideration of the Microfoundations of Monetary Theory," *Western Economic Journal*, Vol. 6, December 1967.

J. Cohen, " A Moneyflows Approach to Consumer Behaviour," *Southern Economic Journal*, Vol. 23, January 1957.

J. Cohen, " Sector Investment and the Availability of Finance," *Southern Economic Journal*, Vol. 27, January 1961.

J. Cohen, " Circular Flow Models in the Flow of Funds," *International Economic Review*, Vol. 4, May 1963.

J. Cohen, " Integrating the Real and Financial, via the Linkage of Financial Flows," *Journal of Finance*, Vol. 23, March 1968.

J. Cohen, " Copeland's Moneyflows after Twentyfive Years: A survey," *Journal of Economic Literature*, Vol. 10, March 1972.

M. A. Copeland, " Tracing Money Flows through the United States Economy," *American Economic Review* (Supplement), Vol. 37, May 1947.

M. A. Copeland, *A Study of Moneyflows in the United States*, National Bureau of Economic Research, 1952.

M. A. Copeland, " Some Illustrative Analytical Uses of Flow of Funds Data," in National Bureau of Economic Research, Studies in Income and Wealth, Vol. 26—*The Flow of Funds Approach to Social Accounting* (Princeton University Press, 1962).

F. Cotula and F. Masera, " Targets, Instruments and Lags in the Economic Policy of Italy," *Demand Management Symposium* 1971 (ed. H. Giersch, Institut für Weltwirtschaft an der Universität Kiel).

W. E. Davies and P. J. Drake, " Flow-of-Funds Social Accounting: A Malayan Example," *Malayan Economic Review*, Vol. 9, October 1964.

J. C. Dawson, " A Cyclical Model for post war United States Financial Markets," *American Economic Review* (Supplement), Vol. 48, May 1958.

F. de Leeuw, " A Model of Financial Behaviour," in J. S. Duesenberry et al. (eds.), *The Brookings Quarterly Econometric Model of the United States*, Chicago, 1965.

E. F. Denison, Comment on Mendelson, " The Optimum of Grossness in Flow-of-Funds Accounts," in National Bureau of Economic Research, Studies in Income and Wealth, Vol. 26, *The Flow-of-Funds Approach to Social Accounting*, 1962.

D. Dimitrijevic, " The Use of Flow-of-Funds Accounts in Monetary Planning in Yugoslavia," *Review of Income & Wealth*, Series 15, March 1969.

G. S. Dorrance, " Financial Accounts in a System of Economic Accounts," *International Monetary Fund Staff Papers*, Vol. 4, February 1955.

G. S. Dorrance, " Survey of Monetary Analyses," *International Monetary Fund Staff Papers*, Vol. 5, February 1957.

G. S. Dorrance, " Balance Sheets in a System of Economic Accounts," *International Monetary Fund Staff Papers*, Vol. 7, October 1959.

G. S. Dorrance, " The Present Status of Financial Accounts: A Review of Recent Developments," in International Association for Research in Income and Wealth, *Studies in Social and Financial Accounting, Income and Wealth*: Series IX, Quadrangle Books, 1961.

G. S. Dorrance, " The Entries in Financial Transactions and Balance Sheet Accounts," *Journal of the Royal Statistical Society*, Vol. 126, part 3, 1963.

G. S. Dorrance, " Financial Accounting: its Present State and Prospects," *International Monetary Fund Staff Papers*, Vol. 13, July 1966.

G. S. Dorrance, " The Role of Financial Accounts," *Review of Income & Wealth*, Series 15, June 1969.

G. S. Dorrance, " A Framework for the Determination of Central Banking Policy," *International Monetary Fund Staff Papers*, Vol. 17, July 1970.

J. S. Duesenberry, " A Process Approach to Flow of Funds Analysis," in National Bureau of Economic Research, Studies in Income and Wealth, Vol. 26, *The Flow-of-Funds Approach to Social Accounting* (Princeton University Press, 1962).

W. C. Freund, " An Appraisal of the Sources and Uses of Funds: Approach to the Analysis of Financial Markets," *Journal of Finance*, Vol. 13, May 1958.

W. C. Freund and E. D. Zinbarg, " Application of Flow-of-Funds to Interest Rate Forecasting," *Journal of Finance*, Vol. 18, May 1963.

W. C. Freund and E. Zinbarg, " Sources and Uses of Funds Analysis," Chapter 23 in Murray E. Polakoff et al. *Financial Institutions and Markets*, (Houghton Miffin and Co., 1970).

E. L. Furness, " Income Flows and Financial Asset Holdings," *Oxford Economic Papers*, New Series, Vol. 21, March 1969.

G. Garvey, " Flow-of-Funds Accounts in Eastern Europe," *Review of Income & Wealth*, Series 17, September 1971.

S. M. Goldfeld, *Commercial Bank Behaviour and Economic Activity*, North-Holland Publishing Company, Amsterdam, 1966.

S. M. Goldfeld, " An Extension of the Monetary Sector," in J. Duesenberry (ed.), *The Brookings Model: Some further Results*, Rand McNally, 1969.

R. W. Goldsmith, " Financial Structure and Economic Growth in Advanced Countries," in National Bureau of Economic Research, *Capital Formation and Economic Growth*, Princeton University Press, 1955.

R. W. Goldsmith, *A Study of Saving in the United States*, Vol. III, Princeton University Press, 1956.

R. W. Goldsmith, *Financial Intermediaries in the American Economy, since 1900*, Princeton University Press for National Bureau of Economic Research, 1958.

R. W. Goldsmith, *The Flow of Capital Funds in the Postwar Economy*, Columbia University Press, 1965.

R. W. Goldsmith and R. E. Lipsey, *Studies in the National Balance Sheet of the United States*, Princeton University Press for National Bureau of Economic Research, 1963.

A. Greenspan, *et al.*, " Monetary Analysis and the Flow-of-Funds: discussion," *American Economic Review* (supplement), Vol. 48, May 1958.

J. F. Helliwell, *et al.*, *The Structure of RDX2*, Bank of Canada Staff Research Studies, No. 7, Bank of Canada, 1971.

P. H. Hendershott, *A Flow-of-Funds Model of Interest Rate Determination: Theoretical and Institutional Underpinnings*, Krannert School of Industrial Administration Institute Paper No. 259, October 1969.

P. H. Hendershott, " A Flow-of-Funds Model: Estimates for the Nonbank Financial Sector," *Journal of Money Credit and Banking*, Vol. 3, November 1971.

M. Heth, *The Flow of Funds in Israel*, Praeger, 1970.

E. Hicks, " Monetary Analyses," *International Monetary Fund Staff Papers*, Vol. 5, February 1957.

E. Hicks, " The Theory and Use of Financing Accounts," *International Monetary Fund Staff Papers*, Vol. 7, October 1959.

C. Hillinger, " Stock-Flow Adjustment and Distributed Lags," *Indian Economic Journal*, Vol. 15, No. 4, 1968.

A. Holmes, " Flow-of-Funds Accounts," *The Bankers' Magazine*, November 1963.

M. W. Holtrop, " Method of Monetary Analysis used by De Nederlandsche Bank," *International Monetary Fund Staff Papers*, Vol. 5, February 1957.

W. C. Hood, *Financing Economic Activity in Canada*, Ottawa: Queens Printer, 1959.

S. Homer, " Stocks versus Bonds: A comparison of Supply and Demand Factors," *The Institutional Investor*, August 1968.

P. Høst-Madsen, " The Integration of Sector Finance and National Income Accounts," *International Monetary Fund Staff Papers*, Vol. 7, April 1960.

S. Ishida, *Flow-of-Funds of the Japanese Economy in 1971*, The Bank of Japan, Special Paper No. 47, Tokyo, 1972.

D. R. Khatkhate, " Analytic Basis of the Working of Monetary Policy in Less Developed Countries," *International Monetary Fund Staff Papers*, Vol. 19, November 1972.

A. Leijonhufvud, *On Keynesian Economics and the Economics of Keynes*, Oxford University Press, London, 1968.

J. Lintner, " Finance and Capital Markets," New York, National Bureau Economic Research, 1972 in *Economics Research; Retrospect and Prospect. Finance and Capital Markets, Fiftieth Anniversary Colloquim II* (National Bureau of Economic Research, General Series, 96).

R. Mathews, " The Australian Flow-of-Funds Accounts," *Economic Record*, Vol. 38, March 1962.

R. Maurice (ed.) *National Accounts Statistics: Sources and Methods*, H.M.S.O., London, 1968.

D. Meiselman, Review of R. Goldsmith " Flow of Capital Funds in the Postwar Economy," *American Economic Review*, Vol. 57, No. 3, 1967.

M. Mendelson, " A Structure of Money Flows," *Journal of American Statistical Association*, Vol. 50, March 1955.

M. Mendelson, " The Flow-of-Funds through the Capital Market 1953-55," *Journal of Finance*, Vol. 12, May 1957.

M. Mendelson, " The Optimum of Grossness in Flow-of-Funds Accounts," in National Bureau of Economic Research, Studies in Income and Wealth, Vol. 26, *The Flow of Funds Approach to Social Accounting* (Princeton University Press, 1962).

A. Minocha, " Inter-sectoral Financial Flows in Indian Economy—Some implications for policy," *Economic Affairs*, Vol. 14, January 1969.

G. W. Mitchell, " Interest Rates Versus Interest Ceilings in the Allocation of Credit Flows," *Journal of Finance*, Vol. 22, May 1967.

National Bank of Yugoslavia, *Annual Report* 1971, Belgrade, 1972.

J. J. O'Leary, " Application of Flow-of-Funds data to Capital Market Analysis," in National Bureau of Economic Research, Studies in Income and Wealth, Vol. 26, *The Flow-of-Funds Approach to Social Accounting*, 1962.

G. Pearson, *A Framework for Analysis of the Financial Sector*, Harvard Institute of Economic Research, Discussion Paper No. 194, June 1971.

J. J. Polak, " Monetary Analysis of Income Formation and Payments Problems," *International Monetary Fund Staff Papers*, Vol. 6, November 1957.

J. J. Polak, " Financial Statistics and Financial Policy," *International Monetary Fund Staff Papers*, April 1959.

J. P. Powelson, *National Income Analysis and Flow-of-Funds Analysis*, New York, McGraw-Hill, 1960.

F. B. Rampersad, " An Integrated System of Real and Financial Accounts," *Social and Economic Studies*, Vol. 11, June 1962.

L. M. Read, " The Development of National Transactions Accounts: Canada's Version of or Substitute for Moneyflows Accounts," *Canadian Journal of Economics and Political Science*, Vol. 23, February 1957.

J. Revell, " The National Balance Sheet of the United Kingdom," *Review of Income & Wealth*, Series 12, December 1966.

J. Revell, *The Wealth of the Nation*, Cambridge University Press, 1967.

L. S. Ritter, " An Exposition of the Structure of the Flow-of-Funds Accounts," *Journal of Finance*, Vol. 18, May 1963.

L. S. Ritter, " The Flow of Funds Accounts: A Framework for Financial Analysis," New York University Graduate School of Business Administration, Institute of Finance, *The Bulletin*, No. 52, August 1968.

R. I. Robinson, " The Flow-of-Funds Accounts: A New Approach to Financial Market Analysis," *Journal of Finance*, Vol. 18, May 1963.

A. R. Roe, " The Case for Flow-of-Funds and National Balance Sheet Accounts," ECONOMIC JOURNAL, Vol. 83, June 1973.

S. S. Ronk, " The Flow-of-Funds Approach to Interest Rate Forecasting," Unpublished Ph.D. thesis, New York University, 1965.

W. Rosenberg, " Sources and Uses of Capital Funds: A Pilot Study of New Zealand 1955/56 to 1961/62," *New Zealand Economic Papers*, No. 1, 1966.

N. Ruggles and R. Ruggles, *The Design of Economic Accounts*, Economic Research General Series No. 89, New York, National Bureau of Economic Research (Columbia University Press, 1970).

T. Samukawa, " The Public Sector in Financial Flow Statements: Japan's Case," *Review of Income & Wealth*, Series 13, December 1967.

C. Segré, " Monetary Surveys and Monetary Analysis," *Quarterly Journal of Economics*, Vol. 72, February 1958.

F. Seton, " Money and the Social Accounts," *The Bankers' Magazine*, January 1965.

R. Shapiro, " Financial Intermediaries, Credit Availability and Aggregate Demand," *Journal of Finance*, Vol. 21, September 1966.

G. Shatto and L. Stern, " The Portfolio Adjustments by Corporations and the Role of Liquid Financial Assets," *Economic Business Bulletin*, Vol. 22, Spring/Summer 1970.

W. L. Silber, *Portfolio Behaviour of Financial Institutions* (Holt, Rinehart, Winston Inc.) New York, 1970.

G. Smith, " Estimating a General Disequilibrium Model of the Financial Sector," Unpublished Yale University Ph.D. Dissertation, 1971.

P. F. Smith, *Economics of Financial Institutions and Markets*, Irwin, 1971.

R. Stone, *A Programme for Growth (3): Input–Output Relationships 1954–1966*, Cambridge, 1963.

R. Stone, "Social Accounting Matrix Models—A Framework for Economic Decisions," in C. M. Berners-Lee (ed.) *Models for Discussion*, London, 1965.

R. Stone, " The Social Accounts from a Consumer's Point of View," *Review of Income & Wealth*, Series 12, March 1966.

R. Stone and A. Roe, *A Programme for Growth No. 11: The Financial Interdependence of the Economy, 1957–66*, (Chapman & Hall, 1971).

S. Taylor, " An Analytic Summary of the Flow-of-Funds Accounts," *American Economic Review* (supplement) Vol. 48, May 1958.

S. Taylor, " Uses of Flow-of-Funds Accounts in the Federal Reserve System," *Journal of Finance*, Vol. 18, May 1963.

H. S. Tice, " Report of a Conference on the Proposals for Revision of the United Nations System of National Accounts," *Review of Income & Wealth*, Series 13, March 1967.

J. Tinbergen, *Business Cycles in the United States of America, 1919–1932*, Geneva, League of Nations, 1939.

J. Tinbergen, " A Model for a Flow of Funds Analysis of an Open Country," *Rivista Internazionale di Scienze Economiche e Commerciali*, Vol. 12, March 1965.

J. Tinbergen and D. B. J. Schouten, " National Income Accounts as a Means of Currency Analysis," *International Economic Papers*, No. 5, 1955.

J. Tobin, Comment on J. S. Duesenberry, " A process approach to Flow-of-Funds Analysis," in National Bureau of Economic Research, Studies in Income and Wealth, Vol. 26, *The Flow-of-Funds Approach to Social Accounting* (Princeton University Press, 1962).

J. Tobin, " A general equilibrium approach to Monetary Theory," *Journal of Money, Credit and Banking*, Vol. 1, February 1969.

C. M. Torrance, " Gross Flows of Funds through Savings and Loan Associations," *Journal of Finance*, Vol. 15, May 1960.

United Nations, Department of Economics and Social Affairs, *A System of National Accounts*, Studies in Methods, series F, No. 2, United Nations, New York, 1968.

H. G. Wallich, " Uses of Financial Accounts in Monetary Analysis," *Review of Income & Wealth*, Series 15, December 1969.

E. T. Weiler, " The Impact of Severe Monetary Restraint on Money Flows," in National Bureau of Economic Research, Studies in Income and Wealth, Vol. 26, *The Flow-of-Funds Approach to Social Accounting*, 1962.

J. B. Willis, " Gross Flows of Funds through Mutual Savings Banks," *Journal of Finance*, Vol. 15, May 1960.

K. M. Wright, " Gross Flows of Funds through Life Insurance Companies," *Journal of Finance*, Vol. 15, May 1960.

R. A. Young, " Federal Reserve Flow-of-Funds Accounts," *International Monetary Fund Staff Papers*, Vol. 5, February 1957.

Postscript

In the last two years in the United Kingdom flow of funds analysis has attracted considerable public attention—a consequence of very large swings in the sector financial surpluses and deficits, notably the massive increase in the public sector deficit, and the sharp deterioration in the position of the company sector in 1974 followed by a recovery in 1975. Financial analysts are now accustomed to examine the implications of changes in *ex ante* surpluses and deficits of the domestic sectors for the balance of payments and for monetary expansion.

The so-called " New " Cambridge School have also proposed the hypothesis that changes in the public sector's financial deficit are reflected eventually in equal changes in the current account of the balance of payments. There is no published statement of a behavioural model underlying this hypothesis, which has been discussed mainly in newspaper articles, but one version can be found in Cripps, Godley and Fetherston (1974).

The authors assert that the financial surplus of the private sector is fairly small and predictable. This does not mean that it is constant in the short term but they assert that " if fixed investment rises (for whatever reason) in relation to post-tax profits currently being earned, then sooner or later dividends will be reduced and/or prices increased so that the flow of net borrowing (or capital raising) is not greatly affected," an example illustrating their general principle that changes in total expenditure will closely follow changes in private disposable income. There are exceptions. Bank advances to persons and consumer instalment lending stimulate additional spending, and stock appreciation is financed by borrowing. But taking account of these exceptional factors the New School assert that the private sector's net acquisition of financial assets can be predicted tolerably accurately in terms of the level and change in real disposable income.

This hypothesis ignores the influence of interest rates on the composition of the private sector's financial asset portfolio—except in so far as they may be reflected in the consumer lending variables. If, by raising rates of interest on government securities, more of the private sector's saving is lent to the government with correspondingly less being channelled back into private spending, the financial surplus of the private sector will be increased. The hypothesis must imply therefore either that private borrowers are wholly insensitive to interest rates—so that the funds channelled back to private spending are unaltered—or that, apart from self-cancelling short-run aberrations, the authorities on average keep the interest rate margins between public and private sector securities constant. It is difficult to find theoretical support for either contention.

The statistical evidence is also open to question. The authors found it necessary to use a constructed figure rather than the actual figures for bank advances in 1971 and 1972 to obtain their fit; and contrary to their contention for earlier years the exceptionally large figures for stock appreciation in 1973 and 1974 do not seem to have been reflected fully in borrowing by companies. Indeed, since the end of 1974 the United Kingdom's balance of payments deficit has, fortunately, not increased at all closely in line with the public sector deficit. However, while the rigid link proposed by the New Cambridge School does not seem valid, the experience of the last 20 years in the United Kingdom does support Wallich's (1969) assertion that in an open economy, sharp autonomous changes in the financial surpluses of domestic sectors are likely to find a partial reflection in the balance of payments (see p. 86 above).

Work on financial econometric models has continued, with the standard balance sheet equilibrium approach still dominant. But Bosworth and Duesenberry (1973), in their model of the United States economy, found that both conventional portfolio optimisation concepts and flow constraints made a significant contribution to explaining behaviour. In a study of the United Kingdom quoted companies Bain, Day and Wearing (1975) attempted to integrate flow constraints into the theoretical structure of the model, and showed that they accounted for about two-thirds of the explained variation in companies' capital issues and liquidity financing on an annual basis, with the remainder attributable to portfolio optimisation. The relative importance of flow constraints in this sector is not perhaps very surprising, since the standard portfolio optimisation model, complete with partial adjustment process, makes little allowance for the important buffer stock function of short-run financial assets and liabilities, or for the inflexibility of companies' fixed capital assets.

More subversive of the conventional model, because they are concerned with financial institutions for which that model might be expected to be appropriate, are studies by Cummins (1973) and Pesando (1974) of the United States life insurance sector. Both found it necessary to focus on the allocation of cash flows rather than the optimisation of existing portfolios to obtain statistically satisfactory explanations of the investment behaviour of United States life insurance companies. In a study of the United Kingdom life offices' behaviour Munro (1974) had a similar experience.

Where does this leave us? Flow of funds concepts have now entered the thinking of practical economists in government and financial institutions in the United Kingdom. The financial implications of policy measures are given active consideration, and attempts are now made outside official circles to present a coherent picture of probable developments in financial markets. On a theoretical plane, portfolio optimisation within a general equilibrium framework is still the dominant approach which has overwhelming support in the economics profession. But accumulating evidence indicates that this model abstracts from aspects of reality which are sometimes of great importance in determining short-run economic behaviour.

Although they may not determine the goal, cash flows do influence the process of adjustment; models of short-run financial behaviour which omit cash flows miss out a central feature of reality.

ADDITIONAL BIBLIOGRAPHY

A. D. Bain, C. L. Day and A. L. Wearing, *Company Financing in the United Kingdom: a Flow of Funds Model*, Martin Robertson, London, 1975.

F. Cripps, W. Godley and M. Fetherston, Public Expenditure and the Management of the Economy, Ninth Report from the Expenditure Committee, Minutes of Evidence, HC 328, H.M.S.O., London 1974.

J. D. Cummins, " An Econometric Model of the Life Insurance Sector of the U.S. Economy," *Journal of Risk and Insurance*, Vol. 40, December 1973.

A. Munro, " The Investment Behaviour of U.K. Life Offices," University of Stirling Discussion Paper No. 29, 1974.

J. E. Pesando, " The Interest Sensitivity of the Flow of Funds through Life Insurance Companies: an Econometric Analysis," *Journal of Finance*, Vol. 29, September 1974.

III

EMPLOYMENT IMPLICATIONS OF INDUSTRIALISATION IN DEVELOPING COUNTRIES: A SURVEY[1,2]

DAVID MORAWETZ

INTRODUCTION

THE expansion of industrial manufacturing alone cannot be expected to solve the unemployment and underemployment problem in most developing countries. A manufacturing sector employing 20 % of the labour force would need to increase employment by 15 % per year merely to absorb the increment in a total work force growing at an annual rate of 3 %. The required rate of increase of manufacturing output is even greater than 15 % if increases

[1] This is the seventh of a series sponsored jointly by the Social Science Research Council and the Royal Economic Society.

[2] I am deeply indebted to Helen Hughes, who suggested the subject of this study, and to the International Bank for Reconstruction and Development, which financed it; it was extremely helpful to do most of the basic work at the Bank's Office. For helpful discussions and comments on earlier versions, I wish to thank Montek Ahluwalia, Haim Barkai, Charles Blitzer, Michael Bruno, Nicholas Carter, Peter Clark, Carlos Díaz-Alejandro, Kathleen DiTullio, Edgar Edwards, Franklin Fisher, Ralph Hofmeister, Thomas Hutcheson, Timothy King, Ruth Klinov-Malul, Raj Krishna, Keith Marsden, Hal Mason, Dipak Mazumdar, Frank Meissner, Ricardo Moran, Vinod Prakash, Yung Rhee, Hugh Schwartz, Michael Sharpston, Lyn Squire, Ardy Stoutjesdijk, Francisco Thoumi, Raymond Vernon, David Wall, Gordon Winston, participants in the IBRD Industry Division seminar and, in particular, Bela Balassa, Helen Hughes, and Paul Streeten. After it was submitted for publication, the paper benefited significantly from the incisive and detailed comments of Professor W. B. Reddaway, an editor of this JOURNAL, and anonymous referees. I am indebted to Sam Akinsete, Orffa Montoya, and Narayana Poduval for helpful research assistance, and to Naimeh Hadjitarkhani and Vinod Prakash for permission to use their as yet unpublished data. I retain sole responsibility for all views expressed. [Footnotes in square brackets refer to papers received too late for inclusion in the body of the survey.]

TABLE 1

Industrialisation and Employment in Developing Countries

Region/countries	Persons engaged in manufacturing (annual growth rate 1963–69)* (1)	Employees in manufacturing (annual growth rate 1963–69)† (2)	Employees in manufacturing (annual growth rate 1960–69)† (3)	G.N.P. per capita (annual growth rate 1960–70) (4)	Manufacturing labour force as % of total labour force 1970 (5)	Gross value added in manufacturing as % of value added in commodity production, 1970 (6)	Gross value added in manufacturing (annual growth rate 1960–69) (7)	Manufactured exports as % of merchandise exports, 1969‡ (8)
East Africa								
Botswana	—	—	—	—	1·0	17·1 (q)	—	—
Ethiopia	4·3	6·4	—	2·8	—	15·4 (r)	12·8	2·39
Kenya	7·8 (d)	7·1 (b)	—	3·6	—	23·9	6·4	16·08
Malawi	1·2 (f)	1·4 (f)	—	2·1	—	19·4	—	2·96
Mauritius	—18·0 (f)	—18·0 (f)	—	—1·1	14·6	36·7	—	—
Somalia	—	—	—	1·0	5·0	—	—	5·33
Sudan	4·8	—	—	2·4	8·0	19·7	6·6	0·12
Uganda	13·9 (g)	14·0 (g)	—	3·6	—	12·1 (r)	11·8	0·82
United Republic of Tanzania	—	—	—	2·7	3·1	15·5	6·3 (w)	7·15
Zaire	—	15·3 (h)	—	7·1	2·6	10·1	—	0·50
Zambia	—	—	10·5 (m)	—	—	18·7 (q)	13·8 (m)	—
West Africa								
Gabon	8·1	—	—	—	1·9	19·8 (q)	—	28·84
Ghana	—	6·3 (i)	—	—0·4	8·6	35·9 (q)	10·6	16·90
Ivory Coast	—	—	—	4·5	0·8	18·3 (q)	—	0·28
Liberia	—	—	—	0·9	2·1	8·1 (q)	—	3·15
Niger	—	—	—	—2·0	0·1	8·5 (a)	—	1·49
Nigeria	5·3 (h)	5·7 (h)	—	0·1	—	13·7	14·1	0·03
Sierra Leone	—	—	—	4·7	4·4	9·7 (q)	—	—
Asia								
China, Republic of	12·7 (d)	13·3 (d)	—	7·1	7·0 (a)	50·5 (r)	16·8	79·26
Fiji Islands	—	—	—	—	—	26·8	—	—
Hong Kong	—	9·2	—	—	41·4	88·6	15·9	88·60
India	3·3 (j)	—	3·8 (v,n)	1·2	9·5	20·5 (r)	5·9	51·82
Indonesia	—	—	—	1·0	5·6	15·4	4·1	19·65

Country	(1)	(2)	(3)	(4)	(5)	(6)	(7)	(8)
Khmer, Republic of	—	—	—	0·1	2·7	—	—	—
Korea, Republic of	12·6	13·0	13·1 (v)	6·8	13·2	35·0	18·4	76·20
Malaysia (East Sabah)	15·1 (f)	12·3 (f)	—	—	—	—	—	—
Malaysia (West)	10·5 (i)	8·1 (d)	—	3·1	8·7	21·6 (r)	8·6	13·13
Nepal	—	—	—	0·5	1·9	13·9 (a)	12·3	56·35
Pakistan	4·9	2·6 (h)	5·3	2·4 (k)	9·5	21·0	6·1	—
Philippines	17·2	4·8	—	2·9	11·4	32·6	17·7 (d)	28·03
Singapore	—	17·4	—	—	13·9	79·5	5·4	1·99
Sri Lanka	18·0 (d)	—	—	1·5	9·1	26·1	10·7	11·68
Thailand	−12·0 (i)	−12·0 (i)	—	4·9	3·4	33·5	—	—
Europe, Middle East, North Africa								
Algeria	−17·0 (g)	−27·0 (d)	—	1·7	6·4	31·6	−0·5	18·32
Cyprus	0·2	8·3	—	—	13·7	30·3	−5·9	—
Egypt, Arab Republic of	0·7 (g)	0·7 (g)	1·3	1·7	12·9	40·0	11·2	28·10
Finland	1·8	1·9	6·0	3·9	24·4	62·4	6·6	91·13
Greece	0·7 (h)	1·3	—	6·6	16·4	45·3	8·0	49·79
Iceland	—	—	—	—	24·3	67·5	2·8	—
Iran	9·2 (h)	9·8 (h)	—	5·4	16·7	22·7	11·2	2·59
Iraq	—	7·7	—	2·5	9·5	14·5 (r)	5·2	44·67
Ireland	—	1·9 (h)	2·6 (m)	3·6	18·5	66·3 (r)	15·0	40·40
Israel	2·4	3·0	5·1	4·7	23·2	81·5	12·1	—
Jordan	6·4	3·9 (j)	—	2·9	8·4	39·8	—	21·97
Malta	13·4	13·9	—	1·0	21·6	54·1	—	79·55
Morocco	—	—	—	5·3	8·2	26·6	3·6	—
Portugal	4·2	4·5	3·9	7·7	20·3	65·4	8·4	62·29
Rumania	4·5	2·5	—	6·1	19·4	—	13·2 (m)	12·16
Spain	2·3	—	2·9	3·4	27·0	61·9	12·0	28·64
Syria	−2·5 (f)	7·8	—	0·5	7·4	50·2	9·2	12·28
Tunisia	7·4	8·3 (h)	—	3·9	9·5	37·4	4·1	—
Turkey	7·9 (h)	—	5·2 (m)	−5·0	7·1	31·9 (q)	14·5	74·41
Yemen, People's Democratic Rep.	—	—	—	—	25·3	—	—	—
Yugoslavia	2·1	—	3·3 (v)	4·3	11·9	58·0	8·5	21·81
Latin America and the Caribbean								
Argentina	—	—	—	2·5	25·1	65·1	4·6	—
Barbados	—	—	—	—	14·6	33·5 (q)	6·2	1·13
Bolivia	2·0 (g)	−17·0 (g)	1·1 (l)	2·5	10·3	26·0	—	19·38
Brazil	1·6	1·1	—	2·4	17·8 (b)	50·2 (p)	6·5	—
British Honduras	—	—	—	—	14·1	—	—	6·26
Chile	—	4·2 (i)	—	1·6	23·2	57·6 (r)	4·8	—

TABLE 1 (cont.)

Region/countries	Persons engaged in manufacturing (annual growth rate 1963–69)* (1)	Employees in manufacturing (annual growth rate 1963–69)† (2)	Employees in manufacturing (annual growth rate 1960–69)† (3)	G.N.P. per capita (annual growth rate 1960–70) (4)	Manufacturing labour force as % of total labour force 1970 (5)	Gross value added in manufacturing as % of value added in commodity production, 1970 (6)	Gross value added in manufacturing (annual growth rate 1960–69) (7)	Manufactured exports as % of merchandise exports, 1969‡ (8)
Latin America and the Caribbean (cont.)								
Colombia	0·4 (h)	2·8	3·0	1·7	12·8	33·4 (r)	5·9 (m)	—
Costa Rica	−3·0 (h)	2·8 (h)	—	3·2	11·5	37·4 (p)	8·9	20·11
Dominican Republic	—	−3·3 (h)	1·1 (m)	0·5	8·2	41·9	1·7 (m)	1·41
Ecuador	5·8	6·0	—	1·7	14·0	32·2 (r)	11·4	34·55
El Salvador	10·0	—	—	1·7	12·8	40·2	10·8	—
Guadaloupe	—	—	—	—	10·4	—	—	—
Guatemala	—	—	—	2·0	11·4	36·8 (r)	4·2	—
Guyana	—	—	—	—	15·1	22·6 (r)	8·4 (m)	—
Haiti	—	—	—	−0·9	4·9	18·3	0·3	—
Honduras	10·2 (h)	10·6 (h)	4·1 (v,m)	1·8	7·8	27·6 (q)	8·2	17·56
Jamaica	—	—	—	—	13·7	40·0 (r)	5·0	13·79
Martinique	—	—	—	—	8·8	—	—	—
Mexico	—	—	—	3·7	16·7 (b)	56·8	8·7	25·13
Netherlands Antilles	—	—	—	—	25·8	—	—	—
Nicaragua	—	—	—	2·8	12·0	32·2 (r)	5·9	14·83
Panama	7·2	7·4	11·1	4·2	7·6	37·2 (q)	12·9 (m)	2·61
Paraguay	—	—	—	1·3	15·1	32·8 (r)	4·8	7·18
Peru	3·2	—	—	1·4	13·2	39·4 (q)	6·9	—
Puerto Rico	—	—	—	—	17·2	74·4 (r)	8·8 (m)	—
Surinam	—	—	—	—	8·9	25·5 (o)	8·3 (m)	—
Trinidad and Tobago	—	20·0 (d)	—	1·9	14·7	30·9 (q)	10·1	4·74
Uruguay	—	—	—	−0·4	21·6	65·6 (r)	1·3	1·52
Venezuela	—	—	—	2·3	18·6	30·1 (r)	6·2	—
Developed market economies								
Australia	3·5	2·8 (h)	—	3·1	26·9	64·5 (r)	5·0	22·55
Austria	—	0·5	—	3·9	28·6	76·1 (r)	5·2	90·30
Belgium	neg	0·4	—	4·0	34·7	79·0 (r)	5·9	80·34 (x)

	1	2	3	4	5	6	7	8
Canada	2·6	2·7	3·1	3·6	21·0	67·8 (r)	6·8	69·96
Denmark	-0·6 (h)	-0·6 (h)	—	3·7	28·7	77·1 (r)	6·7	69·51
France	0·3	2·9	—	4·6	26·1 (c)	80·3 (r)	6·0	77·51
Germany, Federal Republic of	0·5	0·6	—	3·5	36·4	84·9 (r)	6·0	90·40
Italy	3·7 (f)	3·7 (f)	3·3	4·6	31·1 (c)	65·2 (r)	7·1	86·63
Japan	2·7	1·5	1·3	9·6	25·5	63·3 (r)	14·2	96·01
Luxembourg	1·5	1·5	—	—	33·7 (a)	81·1 (r)	2·7	—
Netherlands	0·1	-0·9	neg	3·9	29·9	85·6 (r)	6·5	65·96
New Zealand	2·7 (h)	2·8 (h)	—	2·1	26·6	62·4	6·6	10·65
Norway	1·7	1·5	1·1	4·1	25·5	72·0 (r)	5·2	75·64
Sweden	-0·4	-0·4	—	3·8	28·4	87·1	6·5	88·27
Switzerland	3·2	3·2	—	2·5	39·7	—	5·1	93·91
United Kingdom	—	—	—	2·2	34·8	80·5 (r)	3·2	88·04
United States	—	2·8	1·9	3·2	24·1	80·0 (r)	5·4	75·99

Notes to Headings

* The number of persons engaged is defined as the total number of persons who worked in or for the establishment during the reference year. The concept covers working proprietors, active business partners and unpaid family workers as well as regular employees. Homeworkers are excluded. The figures reported refer normally to the average number of persons engaged during the reference year, obtained as the sum of the "average number of employees" during the year and the total number of other persons measured for a single period of the year.

† The category "employees" is intended to include all persons engaged other than working proprietors, active business partners, unpaid family workers and homeworkers.

‡ UNCTAD Total A, basic data at current prices, f.o.b.

Notes

—, Not available.

(a) 1966	(g) 1966-68	(m) 1960-68	(s) Includes mining
(b) 1970	(h) 1963-68	(n) 1960-66	(t) Includes petroleum, but no other mining
(c) 1971	(i) 1963-67	(ø) 1965	(u) Excludes oil refining
(d) 1966-69	(j) 1963-66	(p) 1967	(v) Persons engaged in manufacturing
(e) 1968-69	(k) Includes Bangladesh	(q) 1968	(w) 1964-67
(f) 1967-69	(l) 1959-69	(r) 1969	(x) Includes Luxembourg

Sources

Columns 1, 2, and 3: United Nations, *The Growth of World Industry*, Vol. I, 1967 and 1970 editions.
Column 4: IBRD, *Trends in Developing Countries*, 1973, Table 1.4.
Column 5: IBRD, *General Characteristics of Human Resources*, Table 3.
Columns 6 and 7: IBRD, *General Characteristics of Industrial Development*, Table 1 B.
Column 8: IBRD, *Manufactured Exports as Percent of Merchandise Exports, 1960 and 1965-69*, Table 7.

in labour productivity are taken into account.[1] In the light of these orders of magnitude, the contribution of the industrial sector to employment growth over the last decade has been disappointing in many developing economies (see Table 1). In a number of countries in Latin America and Africa, despite significant investments in manufacturing, employment in the sector grew less rapidly than population, and in some cases even declined in absolute terms.

In recent years, a voluminous literature has emerged attempting to explain this poor performance, and to suggest ways in which it might be improved. Most of it is directed to three fundamental and interrelated questions: Is there necessarily a conflict between increasing employment and increasing output? Which goods should be produced (the output composition problem)? How should they be produced (the choice of techniques problem)? Sections I–III of this survey are organised around these three questions. Policies to increase labour use which have been proposed in the literature are discussed in each section.

In order to keep it to a reasonable length, this review is confined basically to literature which has appeared in the period—less than a decade—since the last survey article on the subject (Baer and Hervé, 1966). However, references to some earlier works have also been included where they seemed likely to be particularly helpful. I have no doubt failed to note some important papers, as any surveyor must, and apologise in advance to the authors concerned. I have often been forced, for space reasons, to present authors' conclusions without all the qualifications which properly surround them; again, I can but apologise.

The question might be asked: is there need for a survey on industrialisation and employment at this time? I think the answer is a clear yes. In their 1966 review, Baer and Hervé cite only a dozen references; a brief glance at the bibliography appended to this paper attests to the large quantity of work done since then, much of it in quite new directions. Turnham's (1971) useful review of the evidence on unemployment in developing countries devotes only six pages to the analytical relationship between industrialisation and employment, and only a dozen references are cited. Most of the works covered by the present survey appeared after Turnham's study was completed. The widely scattered places of publication of much recent work, and the significant proportion of it that is as yet unpublished (40 % of the 300 or so references cited), provide additional justification for a survey.

A major problem with much of the literature on industrialisation and employment is the loose way in which key terms have been used. In particular, the term "labour intensive" has been used in a number of different senses, sometimes by the same author in different parts of a single article.

---

[1] Turnham (1971). On labour productivity growth over time, see also Reynolds and Gregory (1965), Tidrick (1970), Pack (1971), Bacha et al. (1972) and Ranis (1973a).

Similarly, authors have been vague about what they regard as the constraining factors—capital, managerial capacity, skilled labour, foreign exchange, capacity to absorb investment, and so forth. In many cases, authors seem hardly to have thought about the latter problem, working implicitly with an oversimplified two factor model. Yet capital can hardly be thought to be the chief constraint on development in a number of natural-resource-rich developing countries, nor in those which receive large inflows of foreign funds.

The "correct" definition of labour intensity depends on the purpose for which the term is needed.[1] In the present context, we are concerned with the implications of industrialisation for the employment of unskilled labour.[2] Therefore we need a way of ranking industries and techniques of production according to their total (direct and indirect) use of such labour.[3]

In a simple world with two homogeneous factors of production—scarce capital (K) and abundant labour (L)—the reciprocal of the stock of physical capital per worker (L/K) is an acceptable measure of the degree of labour intensity of production. However, once labour and capital are allowed to be non-homogeneous, each unit of each factor (K_i, L_i) must be weighted to enable aggregation. The logical weights to use are the shadow or scarcity prices to the economy. Further, once capital is not homogeneous, it is no longer satisfactory to measure it as a stock, because different types of capital may have different lengths of life. Therefore K_i must now be redefined to represent capital *services* of type i, that is, the amount of such capital actually used up in the production process. Similarly labour (and, when introduced, all other factors) should be measured in terms of flows of services.

Define r_i as the shadow rate of return to the ith type of capital, and w_i as the shadow wage of the ith type of labour. The index of labour intensity (x_0) now becomes:

$$x_0 = (\sum_i L_i . w_i)/(\sum_i K_i . r_i) \qquad . \qquad . \qquad . \qquad (1)$$

In the two-factor case, the index of capital intensity is simply the reciprocal of the index of labour intensity.

Once more than two factors are introduced, simple extension of the above procedure suggests that factor intensity should be measured by the ratio of the costs of the factor being considered to the sum of all other factor costs. However, it would seem desirable to have a definition which treats all factors rather more symmetrically. This can be achieved quite simply by placing "total factor costs" in the denominator in place of "the costs of all other factors". Redefine L to refer now only to unskilled labour (the labour we are chiefly interested in when discussing labour intensity in a development context), and denote by q_i the shadow returns to the ith other scarce

---

[1] For an excellent discussion of some problems of defining labour intensity, see Reddaway (1962).

[2] The term unskilled labour is used to include both unskilled and semi-skilled workers throughout this survey.

[3] Throughout the following discussion, the symbols K, L, and M should be taken to refer to both direct and indirect use of the factor concerned.

factor (M_i). The index of labour intensity (or, more strictly, of intensity in unskilled labour) (x_1) now becomes:

$$x_1 = \frac{\sum_i L_i . w_i}{\sum_i L_i . w_i + \sum_i K_i . r_i + \sum_i M_i . q_i} \qquad . \qquad . \qquad (2)$$

Using equation (2) we can state:

> *Definition.* Measuring factor usage in terms of factor services, and valuing these services at shadow prices, an industry or technique is labour intensive if its ratio of unskilled labour costs to total factor costs is high relative to that of other industries or techniques. Similarly, an industry is capital (import, management) intensive if its ratio of capital (import, management) costs to total factor costs is high relative to that of other industries or techniques. Finally, an industry is "scarce factor intensive" if its ratio of total scarce factor costs to total factor costs is high relative to that of other industries or techniques. Assuming that unskilled labour is the only abundant factor, the index of scarce factor intensity is clearly equal to 1 minus the index of unskilled labour intensity $(1 - x_i)$.
>
> I have tried to stick to these definitions throughout the survey, but this was not always possible, because some authors have used the same terms to denote slightly different concepts. Note that once more than two factors are introduced, an industry may be relatively intensive in two or more factors—for example, unskilled labour and management (or land, or imported raw materials). However, it is not possible for an industry to be both labour intensive and scarce factor intensive, since the former ranking is exactly the inverse of the latter.

Even if there are only two factors of production, a labour intensive technique is not necessarily capital saving—that is, it does not necessarily have a high output–capital ratio.[1] For example, even ignoring problems of aggregation, it is not necessarily true that a large number of men, each working with simple tools, can produce a greater value of output (value added) than a smaller number of men using more sophisticated equipment of the same total value. On the contrary, it is quite possible for a labour-intensive technique to be more capital-using (have a lower output–capital ratio) than an alternative capital-intensive technique. This important point will be discussed in some detail in Section I.

Most recent analyses of the employment implications of industrialisation have concentrated on the demand for labour, and that will be the main focus of this survey. However, at least brief mention ought to be made of the work which has been done on the impact of industrialisation on urban labour supply. In the Harris–Todaro (1970) model, developed from African experience, it is hypothesised that migration to the towns proceeds in response

---

[1] Wherever output–capital or output–labour ratios are referred to in this survey, the term output refers to value added. A technique with a high (low) output–capital ratio is defined as capital-saving (capital-using).

to rural–urban differences in average expected earnings, allowing for the chance of being unemployed, with the employment rate acting as an equilibrating force.[1] Expected urban earnings, in turn, are an increasing function of the urban–rural wage differential, and of the probability of finding a job in town. Industrial development, by creating more jobs in urban areas, thereby induces an increase in available industrial labour supply. Paradoxically, an increase in urban job creation, or an urban wage subsidy, may lead to increased urban unemployment.

I. Conflicts Between Output and Employment[2]

In the two decades up to the mid-1960s, most development economists agreed that growth in aggregate output should be the over-riding economic objective in developing countries. The poor would be better off, the argument went, if they received a constant share of a rapidly growing pie than if they received a larger share of a slower growing one. Measures to actively redistribute income in favour of the poor were to be postponed until the G.N.P. was larger. These priorities have been reversed to some extent in recent years. Development economists have begun to emphasise equity as a primary goal, partly as a result of disillusionment with the apparently inequitable results of fast G.N.P. growth in countries such as Pakistan and Brazil.

Many writers have focused on employment creation as the means to achieving increased equity, advocating it rather than income redistribution for several reasons.[3] The political power balance is at least partly related to the pre-tax income distribution, so that, in many countries, established power groups oppose policies which would allow redistribution of increased output and income.[4] Even if there is a political will to use fiscal or other instruments to improve the income distribution, such action may not be administratively feasible. Finally, the sense of frustration and lack of human dignity associated with unemployment make employment creation worthy of special attention.

The introduction of employment as a major independent policy goal immediately raises the question of the extent to which there is a conflict

[1] The pioneering paper most often cited is Harris and Todaro (1970). See also Stiglitz (1969, 1973), Farooq (1971), Todaro (1971), Fields (1972), Hartley and Revankar (1972), Tidrick (1972), Mazumdar (1973), and, for surveys of the literature, Brigg (1973), and Todaro (1973). Evidence from Brazil, India, Jamaica, Kenya, Sierra Leone, Taiwan, and Tanzania appears to be consistent with the Harris-Todaro model's hypothesis that expected earnings is a critical variable in determining rural–urban migration flows (Todaro, 1973).

[2] The conflict between output and employment can best be discussed in general terms rather than in the context of industry alone. Therefore, this section is less specifically directed to industry than the rest of the paper. Much of the discussion in this section is based on the classic article by Stewart and Streeten (1971). The reader is referred to this article for a more detailed discussion of a number of issues which are presented baldly here.

[3] Stewart and Streeten (1971), Thorbecke (1973).

[4] It is not clear that policies to promote employment will necessarily be more acceptable to the power groups than policies to distribute the benefits of growth by other means.

between the employment objective and the output or growth objective.[1] If there exist two factors of production (abundant unskilled labour and scarce capital) a single neoclassical production function, and a single homogeneous product, there can be no conflict between current output and current employment. In this simple model, output is maximised when the productivity of the one scarce factor, capital, is maximised. But as long as the marginal productivity of labour is positive, every increase in employment increases the productivity of capital. Therefore, increasing employment always raises output.

However, even maintaining the assumption of two factors of production, if increasing labour use is associated with changing the technique of production, adding to employment may, but need not, decrease output. A number of cases have been found to support each of these two contradictory possibilities. For example, rice milling using labour-intensive pestle-and-mortar techniques requires only one hundredth as much capital per man, but yields only half as much output per unit of capital, as sheller machine milling.[2] Conversely, the output–capital ratio in Indian cotton weaving is highest for the most labour-intensive technique, the fly-shuttle handloom, and lowest, less than half as great, for the automatic power loom.[3] Although industry or process studies like these help to elucidate the output–employment conflict, most such studies done to date suffer from a number of important shortcomings. In particular, most authors assume that capital is the only scarce factor of production, use market rather than shadow prices, and ignore the possibility of conflicts over time. In order to ensure more meaningful results, future studies should incorporate other scarce factors (management, skilled labour, foreign exchange) examining total scarce-factor productivity rather than simply output–capital ratios. Factors and products should be evaluated at their social prices, and the implications for future as well as current employment and output should be taken into account.

Next, abandon the assumption that there is a single homogeneous form of output. Even if it is assumed that each output good has its own unique technique of production, it now becomes possible to increase employment with a given stock of scarce factors by changing the product mix.[4] For example, if shoes are produced in a more labour intensive manner than chemicals, it may be possible to produce more of the former and less of the

[1] The possibility of such a conflict has been noted from the mid-fifties onwards. See, for example, Galenson and Leibenstein (1955), ILO (1961), Lewis (1962), Baer and Hervé (1966), and Carter (1969). For a survey of mathematical modelling techniques designed to incorporate conflicts between two or more policy goals, see Loucks (1973).

[2] Bhalla (1965). Other cases in which labour intensive processes yield *lower* output–capital ratios than their less labour-intensive competitors include Ambar Charkha cotton spinning in India (Bhalla, 1965) pulp and paper, aluminium, and agglomerated wood in Peru (Tokman, 1972a).

[3] Sen (1968). Other examples in which labour-intensive processes yield *higher* output–capital ratios than their less labour-intensive competitors include traditional cotton spinning in India (Bhalla, 1964), textiles in Latin America (UN ECLA, 1966), beverages and tobacco in Peru (Tokman, 1972a), and metal and wood processing (Netherlands Economic Institute, 1957–59, Boon, 1964).

[4] The subject matter of this paragraph is examined in more detail in section II below.

latter, increasing aggregate employment. In a closed economy, the scope for such shifts is limited by the structure of domestic demand. However, once the possibility of engaging in foreign trade is taken into account, the potential scope increases significantly. A number of developing economies appear to have succeeded in increasing both employment and output in precisely this way, by concentrating on the production and export of labour intensive goods.[1]

Maximising output itself becomes a somewhat ambiguous concept once the assumption of a single homogeneous good is abandoned. If output is made up of a number of different goods, some system of weights or prices must be used to aggregate them. But, of course, the prices used are not independent of the income distribution. Similarly, factors of production are not homogeneous, and prices have to be used in order to aggregate them. If factor prices are distorted,[2] socially efficient techniques of production may appear to be inferior to techniques which are socially less efficient, but privately more profitable. In particular, if the wage-rental ratio is kept arbitrarily high, as it is in many developing countries, using more labour-intensive techniques of production may appear to conflict with increasing output, whereas it is possible that no such conflict would exist if goods and factors were priced at their social (no distortion, post income redistribution) values.

The conflicts discussed up to now have been mainly between current output and current employment. Just as important are conflicts over time.[3] In particular, situations may arise in which more production and less employment now lead to more employment later. This might occur if less labour-intensive techniques of production yield higher aggregate savings and investment, or are associated with more rapid technical progress, than more labour-intensive techniques.

Where s is the average propensity to save, and Y is total output, total savings (S) are:

$$S = s.Y.$$

Techniques of production using little labour could yield higher aggregate savings than labour-intensive methods if they yield higher ratios of output to usage of total scarce factors, if they are associated with higher propensities to save, or for a combination of the two reasons. The available evidence on

[1] Evidence for Taiwan, Korea and Colombia suggests that in the import substitution phase of development, which involved moving into sectors more and more alien to the countries' comparative advantage, there seemed to be a conflict between output growth and employment growth, whereas in the later "export substitution" stages, output and employment expansion went hand in hand. Fei and Ranis (1972a, b), Berry (1972a, b), Díaz-Alejandro (1973). See also Bruton (1967) and Nelson (1968).

[2] "Undistorted factor prices" is generally used to refer to the prices which would rule in a perfectly competitive economy with no government or other intervention. However, income distribution clearly affects factor prices as well as product prices. Therefore, in defining "undistorted factor prices", perhaps one should add the condition that the income distribution in the society is ethically "fair".

[3] On employment conflicts over time, see Sen (1968), and Stewart and Streeten (1971).

the former possibility, which concentrates on the scarce factor capital, has been examined and shown to be ambiguous. On the latter point, the possibility that less labour-intensive techniques tend to be associated with higher savings propensities has been mentioned a number of times.[1] However, I know of no attempt to test this hypothesis rigorously.

Similarly, it has been claimed that capital-intensive techniques of production are more likely to be associated with rapid technical progress than labour-intensive techniques. Once again, detailed supporting evidence is rarely forthcoming; this is an area in which more research is needed. Preliminary evidence from Kenya and China suggests that some disembodied technical progress may be possible in association with labour-intensive techniques.[2]

It is not enough for policy-makers to know the objective possibilities for trade-off between present and future output and employment; they must also have some basis for choosing between different time paths of the two variables. This means that they must know the discount rates that attach to employment and output. The main reason for arguing that future consumption (taking the implied consumption stream to represent output) should be discounted at a positive rate is that the marginal utility of consumption is lower for a richer society (Marglin, 1963). This argument does not apply in the same way to employment; the value of extra employment generated need not decline as its level increases. Nevertheless, the fact that increasing incomes per head may make employment less important as a means of income redistribution in the future, and the uncertainty which affects at least the more distant future, both indicate that current employment is likely to be preferred to future employment, at least to some extent. Whether the discount rate for employment should be greater or less than that for output is a question which has not yet been satisfactorily resolved.

In conclusion, the conflict between output and employment is rather more complex than has sometimes been supposed. Further theoretical and applied research is needed to elucidate the circumstances in which the two objectives do not conflict, to describe the exact parameters of the trade-off in cases in which they do conflict, and to suggest the relative weights that should be given to current and future output and employment.

II. Output Composition

The particular product mix to be manufactured, at both the inter-industry and the intra-industry levels, is clearly a critical determinant of the employment implications of any industrialisation strategy. Yet it is only in the past few years that economists have devoted a significant amount of systematic

---

[1] On choice of technique, income distribution, and the savings rate, see, for example, Lubell (1947), Kaldor (1960), Sen (1968, 1969), and Soligo and Land (1972).

[2] Pack (1972a), Dean (1972), Ishikawa (1972), Sigurdson (1972, 1973), Karcher (1973), Perkins (1973a, b).

attention to this subject. Baer and Hervé (1966) do not even mention it, concentrating almost solely on questions of factor proportions and technological choice.[1]

II.1. *Inter-Industry Choice*

The composition of output at the industry level is determined to a large extent by the structure of aggregate demand, that is, by the demands of domestic consumers, foreigners, the government, and private investors. These four components of demand will be examined in turn.

II.1.1. *Consumption Demand and Income Distribution*[2]

If persons in all income groups consume goods in the same proportions, *or* if all goods are produced with the same factor intensities, income redistribution will not change the over-all pattern of factor use. However, if rich people consume different goods from poor people (more consumer durables, less textiles), *and* if different goods are produced with differing factor intensities (textiles are more labour intensive than consumer durables) then redistributing income to the poor will lead to an increased demand for labour and increased employment with any given stock of scarce factors, assuming that the supply of labour has positive elasticity.

To take the second point first, despite the fact that there is scope for factor substitution in most activities, it seems clear that some goods can be regarded as unambiguously more labour intensive in production than others. For example, the direct and indirect labour intensity of leather footwear or clothing is almost always greater than that of petrochemicals. Similarly, most processes that are subcontracted internationally (assembly of electronic and photographic products, stitching of many kinds) must necessarily be labour intensive at almost any observed factor price ratio.[3] It seems clear also, from budget studies, that different income groups do consume somewhat different bundles of goods. However, it is less clear whether redistribution of income from richer to poorer people in any particular society will, in practice, have significant implications for the pattern of factor use, in particular for employment.

---

[1] Some early writers who at least touched on the importance of the demand side include Eckaus (1955), Reddaway (1962), Bhardwaj (1964), and Furtado (1967). On the contribution of the first three in this area see Currie (1971).

[2] Recent studies of income distribution in developing countries include Adelman and Morris (1971), Webb (1972, 1973), Adelman and Robinson (1973), Jain and Tiemann (1973), and Mamalakis (1973).

[3] This is not to deny that factor intensity reversals can occur for some pairs of products at some factor price ratios. On differences in direct factor intensity rankings between industries, and the employment implications of such differences see, for example, Lary (1968) Herman and Tinbergen (1969, 1973), and Herman (1973). Studies incorporating indirect as well as direct effects include Boon (1969), Hazari and Krishnamurty (1970), and Anand (1972) for Mexico, India, and Yugoslavia. On international sub-contracting see Watanabe (1972a), Helleiner (1973), and Sharpston (1973a).

Models designed to examine the impact of income redistribution on aggregate employment generally begin by assuming a specific pattern of income redistribution, based on targets for the lowest group, on social objectives, or on taxation possibilities.[1] The impact of the redistribution on savings and total investment is calculated from aggregate consumption functions for each group, plus assumptions as to external capital flows. The total consumption of each income group is then broken down into its component parts, using Engel curves or some other kind of demand function, and the new levels of total consumption for each commodity are fed into an input–output system in order to determine direct and indirect changes in production, imports, employment, and income distribution. Finally, on the basis of these changes, the more complete models iterate back through the system. Production, imports, and employment can now be compared to projections of their magnitudes assuming that there was no initial income redistribution.

Once estimates have been made of the impact of income redistribution on domestic savings, external capital flows, investment, and foreign exchange needs, the effect on total output can also be estimated. The welfare effects of income redistribution can then be divided into a growth effect (positive or negative), an income redistribution effect (positive), and an employment effect (hopefully positive.)[2]

Studies like these have a number of weaknesses. Generally, little attention is paid to the way in which the initial income redistribution is to be achieved; it must surely be significant for final factor use patterns whether it is by capital or income transfers, or by indirect taxation. In a number of cases, a simplistic two factor model is used. Aggregate consumption and savings data are notoriously unreliable in developing countries, not to speak of data on sectoral demand patterns and elasticities,[3] income distribution, and future

[1] The following description is based on Blitzer (1973). Demands for factor use can be derived from almost any macro model; the present discussion covers only those whose focus is explicitly on employment. This narrows down the field considerably, since until a few years ago most models concentrated on the foreign exchange and capital constraints, and intersectoral resource allocation, rather than job creation and income distribution. For surveys of theoretical and practical problems in the use of multi-sector models in development planning see Blitzer (1973), and Taylor (1973). Theoretical models exploring the relationship between income distribution, consumption patterns, and employment, which have not yet been empirically tested, include Land and Soligo (1971), Mellor and Lele (1971), and Soligo and Land (1972). See in addition Chenery et al. (1973), and Stoutjesdijk (1973). Other models whose results are not reported here include ILO (1971, appendix), Lopes (1972), and Sunman (1973). Studies which do not explicitly incorporate income distribution, but estimate the future demand for labour from projected future sectoral demand patterns, include Parnes (1962), Harbison and Myers 1965), Thorbecke and Stoutjesdijk (1971), Jolly and Colclough (1972), Thorbecke and Sengupta (1972), ILO (1973a, appendix), and Lluch and Powell (1973). For critiques of simple employment projection models, see Blaug (1967), Hollister (1968), Bowles (1969, 1970), and Dougherty (1972).

[2] Some models incorporate labour supply constraints—Adelman (1966), Adelman and Sparrow (1966), Bruno (1966), Blitzer (1972), Keesing and Manne (1973). Some divide labour into a number of skill categories, and project labour demand (and sometimes supply) for each. Adelman (1966) and Blitzer (1972) each use six skill categories; others have fewer.

[3] Musgrove (1974) claims that the conventional use of current rather than permanent income in demand studies in developing countries could cause estimated industry demand elasticities to be systematically upward-biased by up to 30%.

foreign capital flows. Government savings are not always treated explicitly. The use of fixed coefficient input–output tables involves assuming that technology does not change over time. (This is not a very realistic assumption where the period under discussion is ten or twenty years, and is particularly doubtful in countries where a stated aim of policy is the alteration of intra- and inter-industry production relationships.) Input–output data are frequently derived only from firms of a certain minimum size; firms smaller than this minimum may well use quite different technologies and may produce a significant and changing share of total output.[1] Moving from the functional to the size distribution of income involves a number of problematical assumptions, yet models which do not incorporate the final iteration cannot be said to be fully consistent. Finally, many of the studies ignore the implications of differing income distributions for total scarce factor productivity, employer incentives, the creation of an investible surplus, economic growth, and thus longer-term employment.

Yet even if they are highly imperfect, macro-economic studies provide the only currently available means of investigating the recently fashionable claim that redistribution of income in favour of the poor is likely to increase total employment. Countries for which empirical studies of the employment implications of income redistribution have been, or are being, undertaken include India and Chile (three studies each), Colombia, Mexico, Peru, and Venezuela (two each), Argentina, Brazil, Puerto Rico, and Pakistan.[2] Hypothetical redistributions which were experimented with include moving to a British income distribution in Brazil and Mexico (Cline, 1972); redistributing 6% of national income from richer to poorer groups in Peru (Figueroa, 1972); and raising average *per capita* consumption of the lowest 30% of income recipients by 60% over a five-year period in India (Indian Planning Commission, 1973). In the Indian study, average *per capita* consumption of the top 30% is lowered by 3%, instead of allowing it to increase by 16% as it would do without redistribution.

In most cases, investigators find that the consumption basket of the poor

---

[1] Thorbecke (1973) rationalises the use of fixed coefficient input–output tables in such studies by arguing that the resulting projections provide policy makers with a quantitative view of the consequences of essentially neutral technological policies. On other problems associated with the use of input–output tables in macro models, including aggregation, construction of price indices, and estimation of competitive imports, see United Nations (1968) and Taylor (1973).

[2] Fashions sweep the profession so quickly nowadays that a dozen investigators or teams began empirical work on the employment implications of income redistribution more or less independently at virtually the same time. All but one of the studies cited here are as yet unpublished (the exception is Cline, 1972), and in spite of their remarkable similarities in methodology and findings, most of their authors seem to have been unaware of most of the other projects. The studies are: Cline (1972) —Argentina, Brazil, Mexico, Venezuela; Figueroa (1972) and Tokman (1972a)—Peru; ILPES (1972)—Chile; Jimenez (1972) and Thorbecke and Sengupta (1972)—Colombia; Soligo (1972)— Pakistan; Tokman (1972b)—Venezuela; Bardhan (1973) and Indian Planning Commission (1973), described in Blitzer (1973)—India; Weisskoff (1973)—Puerto Rico. An ILPES study on Mexico is reported on by Tokman (1972b). Additional studies which were not yet fully completed in early 1974 are by Peter Clark and associates (Chile), Markos Mamalakis (Chile), and Raj Krishna (India).

is at least to some extent more labour intensive than that of the rich. However, Weisskoff (1973) comes to the reverse conclusion in Puerto Rico. Soligo (1972) finds that rural households consume a more labour-intensive basket of goods and services than urban households in Pakistan, and that within each group the consumption pattern of the poor is more labour intensive than that of the rich. However, if the labour required to produce capital goods (especially housing) is included, this ranking is reversed. Thus, in the short term, employment is maximised for income redistribution favouring the rich, because of their high marginal propensity to consume housing services, whereas in the longer run (ten years were used in the calculations), more employment is generated by redistributions favouring lower income groups. Jimenez (1972) obtains similar results in a study of the four main cities in Colombia.

Turning now to orders of magnitude, rather to the surprise of a number of the investigators, the almost unanimous conclusion is that even quite significant redistributions of income seem likely to have only marginal effects on growth and employment, usually increasing the latter by less than 5 %. One possible reason for this pessimistic finding, which is noted in several studies, is that whereas redistribution of income in favour of the poor appears to increase the demand for agricultural products, it apparently decreases the demand for services. In some countries agricultural products are relatively labour intensive, though where arable land is scarce this may not be the case. Most services do seem to be labour intensive. Whether in fact the poor do consume fewer services than the rich is a hypothesis worth further examination.

A second possible explanation is based on the aggregation problem. Almost all of the studies which have been done to date use data aggregated at the two-digit level.[1] This means that entire industries (food processing, chemicals, transport equipment) are treated as if they produced homogeneous goods. But of course, cars and bicycles are produced with quite different factor intensities, as are electronic calculators and simple transistor radios. *If* there is significant scope for moving to more labour-intensive goods (as defined in equation (2)) within two-digit industries, and *if* the poor spend a greater percentage of their income on such goods than the rich, there may yet be scope for income redistribution significantly to increase employment, scope which would not show up in more aggregative studies. Preliminary sketchy evidence, discussed in section III.2.4, indicates that the first condition may be satisfied. What needs to be done now is to test the second "if", by collecting more detailed, disaggregated household expenditure data. The two sets of evidence may then be put together to derive fresh empirical estimates of the employment impact of income redistribution. Naturally, even if the results of this exercise turn out to be equally pessimistic, the case

[1] Throughout this survey, the number of digits refers to the International Standard Industrial Classification (ISIC) of the United Nations.

for income redistribution as a good in itself still stands. Note, however, that the above arguments have completely ignored the impact of income redistribution (higher taxes, etc.) on employer incentives.

II.1.2. *Exports and Import Substitutes*[1]

A number of writers on the industrialisation process in developing countries fail to make sufficient allowance for the fact that developing economies are usually open economies. They therefore ignore the fact that introduction of the foreign trade sector greatly increases the development options available. It is no longer necessary that each country should make its own machines to make machines.

The standard Heckscher–Ohlin–Samuelson factor proportions theory of the determination of trade flows states that a country has a comparative advantage in (and is likely to export) goods in whose production the country's relatively abundant factor is used intensively.[2] If this theory is correct, a labour-abundant country with a limited supply of other factors of production is likely to create more short-term employment by following an outward-oriented policy (allocating resources according to comparative advantage) than by protecting its import substitutes against foreign competition (Stolper and Samuelson, 1941).[3] Before accepting this conclusion as valid, it is worth examining some of the assumptions on which the theory is based. In particular, the simplest version of the factor proportions theory assumes that there exist two homogeneous factors of production, that there are no international factor intensity reversals, that factor prices reflect real social costs, and that technological leads and lags, demand influences, and government intervention do not over-ride comparative advantage.

Once extra factors of production are introduced, including, for example, human capital, the simple factor proportions theory of trade needs to be modified. For it is no longer necessarily true that a labour-abundant country will have a comparative advantage in all industries which use a lot of unskilled labour. Rather, if the country is poor in both physical and human capital, say, it will have a comparative advantage only in those industries

---

[1] Surveys of theoretical and empirical work on international trade, especially as it relates to policy issues in economic development, include Chenery (1961), Bhagwati (1964), Baldwin (1971), and Magee (1973). For a recent, particularly thoughtful piece on trade strategies and employment, see Streeten (1973). Other papers which discuss the employment implications of trade policies, and which are not cited elsewhere in this section include Bruton (1970, 1972a, c), Little *et al.* (1970), Balassa *et al.* (1971), Fei and Ranis (1972a, b), Berry (1972a, b), Ranis (1973b), Economic Growth Center (1973), Helleiner (1973), Ho and Huddle (n.d.). [Stewart (1972b) is one of the few authors to examine in detail the direct relationship between international trade and choice of techniques.]

[2] *See*, for example, Bhagwati (1964).

[3] Exporting need not be synonymous with following "outward-looking" policies. For example, Kenyan export patterns and policies appear to reflect a variation on the import substitution theme, as exports move further and further from the products in which Kenya has comparative advantage (Porter, 1973).

which use relatively high inputs of unskilled labour *and* relatively low inputs of scarce factors (*i.e.* industries which are truly labour intensive as defined in equation (2)). Modifications to the factor proportions theory based on the inclusion of extra factors of production have been found to be of considerable empirical significance.[1]

Returning to the two-factor model for simplicity, factor intensity reversals occur if a good which is produced with relatively labour-intensive techniques in one country is produced with capital-intensive techniques in another. If such reversals are common, goods cannot be unambiguously defined in terms of their factor intensities, and the factor proportions theory of trade breaks down, as do its implications for employment creation. Fortunately for the theory, Lary (1968) has demonstrated that, at least for the two factor case, international factor reversals are probably not common in manufactured goods.

The third assumption, that factor prices reflect real scarcity values, is not fulfilled in many developing countries. In particular, wages paid by modern manufacturing industry are often higher than the marginal social cost of labour, while capital tends to be under-priced as a result of credit subsidisation and interest rate ceilings. These two distortions together tend to make the private profitability of capital-intensive projects exceed their social profitability. They also tend to increase the average capital intensity of exports, as reflected in evidence from Colombia (Díaz-Alejandro, 1973), Korea (Ranis, 1972a), Mexico (Sheahan, 1971), and Puerto Rico (Weisskoff, 1973). Other factors are often under- or over-priced as well. For example, overvalued exchange rates, highly differentiated tariff structures and customs drawback schemes tend to cause the private prices of imported materials to be below their social value. This, in turn, leads to an increase in the average import content of production and, in the case of export drawback schemes, of exports. Electricity, too, is often under-priced.

Fourth, trade in manufactures may be affected by technological leads and lags, and demand factors.[2] The first producer may dominate the market for a time until producers in other countries, which may have more appropriate factor endowments, are able to organise production. He may then be able to continue to undersell his new competitors by successively improving his techniques, using a persistently superior production function to outweigh disadvantages of factor endowment. With differentiated products, buyer preferences may be strong enough to enable established firms to continue producing longer than would have been possible if factor proportions were the dominant influence.

Finally, trade flows may be influenced by several types of government intervention. First, governments may use tariffs, quotas and licensing arrangements to protect infant industries, in which it is believed that "learning by doing" may enable a currently non-competitive industry to become

---

[1] See, for example, Leontief (1954), Bhagwati (1964).

[2] Vernon (1966); Linder (1961).

competitive in the future. Second, the same measures may be used to protect particular industries for political or other reasons. Both developed and developing countries have recently protected industries which employ large numbers of workers.[1] Third, labour-abundant countries which have a dominant non-industrial enclave export sector may give generalised protection to industry, perhaps by adopting a dual or multiple exchange rate system, to encourage industrialisation and employment growth. The case for such action is particularly strong in countries like Venezuela, where the export is based on a non-renewable rapidly depleting natural resource. With each type of government intervention, trade patterns are likely to be altered to some extent, and the factor proportions theory of trade is less likely to hold.

Despite the need to modify the simple factor proportions theory to the extent that its assumptions are not valid, most of the available empirical evidence is consistent with its chief conclusion: that labour abundant countries are likely to create more employment by following an outward-looking strategy than if they are inward-looking.[2] For example, Lary (1968) finds that although less than half of total 1965 imports of manufactured goods by developed from developing countries were intensive in unskilled labour, the growth rate of such goods from 1953 to 1965 was 13 % per year, nearly three times as fast as that of aggregate exports from developing to developed countries.

Some of the countries whose exports of manufactured products grew most rapidly over the past decade have also had high rates of growth of industrial employment. In Korea and Taiwan, exports of manufactured goods grew by 35 % *per annum* in the 1960s, while employment in manufacturing grew by 13 % per year. Other countries registering high growth rates in manufactured exports and industrial employment include Hong Kong and Singapore. It is interesting that these four countries are all "blessed" with a poor natural-resource endowment, having few minerals and a high ratio of population to arable land. After a certain stage of development had been reached, they were forced to adopt outward-looking policies if they were to continue to grow. Achieving self-sufficiency was seen clearly to be an impossible task, more so than in some Latin American countries, for example.[3]

[1] Perhaps the most significant contribution which the developed countries could make to increasing employment in developing countries is to reverse this trend in their own policies. The difficulties standing in the way of such action are partly political. Nevertheless, economists have a role to play in calculating and publicising the costs of protection to developed country consumers, and in working out detailed, realistic, and equitable schemes (adjustment assistance, retraining incentives) to compensate those who are likely to be hurt by increased competition. For some recent theoretical and empirical work on adjustment problems, see Balassa (1966), Little *et al.* (1970), Willmore (1972), Frank (1973), Hughes (1973d), Isard (1973), and Morawetz (1973b).

[2] In addition to the references cited in the following paragraphs, see Keesing (1966) and UNCTAD (1970). An exception to this general conclusion is Weisskoff (1973), who finds that a policy directed more towards encouraging import substitution would have increased the rate of growth of output in Puerto Rico in the 1960s, and implies that employment would have increased too. He does not present quantitative estimates of the employment effects.

[3] On the experience of Korea, Taiwan, and also Japan, see Balassa (1970), Ranis (1972a, b), Watanabe (1972b), Westphal and Kim (1973).

After a detailed study of industrial policies in Korea, Westphal and Kim (1973) conclude that total employment generated by export expansion during the 1960s was far greater than that which would have been generated by an equivalent amount of import substitution.[1] Unfortunately, in the preliminary version of their report, they do not calculate the difference in the number of jobs that would be involved. The percentage of the manufacturing labour force directly engaged in production for export rose from 3·0 in 1960 to 16·8 in 1968. Since exports had stronger backward linkages than import substitutes, the percentage directly and indirectly engaged in exporting rose even faster. Watanabe (1972b) estimates that about 30 % of total employment in Korean manufacturing in 1969 was attributable directly or indirectly to exports. At least half of the increase in manufacturing employment between 1963 and 1969 (about 300,000 jobs) appears to have been created by the rapid increase (70 % *per annum*) in exports of manufactures and semimanufactures.

Using standard input–output techniques for Mexico, Sheahan (1971) finds that the mix of industrial goods exported in the 1960s used about 16–20 % more labour per unit of output than industrial goods produced as import substitutes; general domestic industrial production was slightly more labour intensive than exports. Exports also saved on capital and foreign exchange; the capital and imported inputs needed to replace 1,000 pesos worth of imports could have yielded about 1,060 pesos worth of exports. Exports tended to be marginally more skill-intensive than import substitutes, and significantly more skill-intensive than general domestic industrial production. These estimates depend, of course, on the particular mix of exports and import substitutes which Mexico produced in the 1970s. Unlike in Korea, where industrial exports grew significantly more labour-intensive during the 1960s in response to improvements in government policies (Westphal and Kim, 1973), the ratio of labour to scarce factors in Mexican exports and import-substitutes remained relatively constant throughout the decade.

In a less comprehensive study in a similar spirit, Morawetz (1974) analyses a 100 million dollar investment in Colombian import-substituting petrochemicals, to be undertaken in the 1970s, largely by the Colombian government. Direct (direct and indirect) employment created by this investment is only 2,500 (3,500) persons, compared with over 50,000 (100,000–150,000) persons if the same sum were invested in labour-intensive export industries like clothing, footwear, wooden furniture, textiles, glass products, and metal manufactures. Since total employment in firms of five or more persons in Colombian manufacturing industry is only about 350,000 persons, these are significant differences. Petrochemicals also performs worse than labour-intensive exports on net foreign exchange earned and saved, and on capital–output ratios. High tariffs on imported petrochemicals and the underpricing of capital help to explain why such investments continue to be

[1] Hong (1973) comes to the same conclusion.

undertaken despite their low social value. An additional reason is that the capital and know-how involved seem to be relatively sector-specific. The Colombian government-owned oil company derives a surplus from its refining operations. In the absence of some mechanism for siphoning it off into general government revenues, the company invests this surplus in lines with which its managers and engineers are familiar. Chemical engineers know more, and are more enthusiastic about, producing the latest petrochemicals, than about developing marketing outlets for, say, men's shoes in the United States.

The option of relying predominantly on an exporting strategy as the major means of increasing employment is probably open only to small and medium-sized countries which face fairly elastic international demands for most of their exports. Larger countries may have to rely more on producing for the domestic market. Nevertheless, even in large countries, producing according to comparative advantage is likely to yield employment pay-offs. In this connection, it will be interesting to study the Chinese experience when more data are available, for it seems to contradict this claim. There appears to have been a conscious decision in China to give up some of the benefits of scale economies and production according to comparative advantage, in order to foster local self-reliance and responsibility (Karcher, 1973). For instance, by 1971 half of China's counties had established a complete set of the "five small industries"—iron and steel, cement, chemical fertilisers, energy (coal, electricity) and machinery (Sigurdson, 1972). Yet according to "travellers' tales" Chinese employment creation has apparently been remarkably successful.[1]

II.1.3. *Government Demand*

Governments can influence the level of employment in the economy by directing their demands towards labour-intensive goods. In one of the few empirical studies on the subject, Morley and Williamson (1973) find that a hypothetical policy emphasising government employment expansion and favouring the urban service sector in Brazil during the 1950s would have slightly increased the growth rate of urban employment (4·8 % instead of 4·7) and total employment (4·0 % instead of 3·8), while reducing the growth

---

[1] A referee points out that up to 1958 China had the same employment problems as other developing countries, that no employment data are available for the period since 1958, and that the industrial growth rate fell from 18 % between 1952 and 1959 to 2 % between 1959 and 1970. Thus if post-1958 employment did increase significantly, it may have been at the expense of a large fall in the output growth rate (Howe, 1971; Field, 1972). The appeal of the Chinese experience has been well articulated by Haq (1971): "Is there not a practical illustration here of a selective attack on the problems of poverty, pursuit of a threshold income and minimum consumption standards, merger of production and distribution policies, and achievement of full employment with a meagre supply of capital? It is no use insisting that these results must have been achieved at tremendous social and political costs; people in the developing countries are often undergoing these costs without any visible economic results so that they look at the experience of China with great envy and praise. It is time, especially as China's isolation ends, that there be an objective and detailed study of its experience in place of the usual rhetoric to which we have been subjected so far."

rate of manufacturing employment (2·2 % instead of 3·5). Most studies of the
employment implications of the pattern of government spending concentrate
on public works or construction, which are probably extremely important,
but are beyond the scope of this survey. There has been some discussion of the
possibility of large-scale government purchase and distribution of mass consumption goods as one way of improving the effective income distribution,
(Bailey *et al.* 1973), but I know of no attempt at quantifying the employment
effects of such a programme.

II.1.4. *Investment Demand*

Investment goods as a group are by no means necessarily less labour
intensive in production than consumption goods. For example, some machine-
building operations use more labour-intensive techniques than consumption
goods like beverages, tobacco, and processed foods.[1] There may be scope,
then, for shifting investment demand towards those investment goods which
can be made effectively in the country and are relatively labour intensive in
production. A number of builders of large-scale models have added investment goods matrices to their input–output tables in order to derive better
estimates of the direct and indirect impact of different patterns of final
demand (*e.g.* Morley and Williamson, 1973). However, I know of no study
which has focused squarely on the employment implications of changing the
mix of purchases in investment goods. Such studies would only be of interest,
of course, in countries which have developed substantial productive capacity
in investment goods.

II.2. *Intra-Industry Product Mix*

In addition to the possibility that labour-intensive two-digit industries
may be encouraged at the expense of industries intensive in scarce factors
(clothing rather than chemicals) it may also be possible to encourage the
production of more appropriate goods within each industry (cotton shirts
rather than nylon). The newly emerging theory of intra-industry product
choice is based on the micro consumer theory of Lancaster (1966), and has
been developed and expounded in particular by Stewart (1972a, b, 1973).[2]
Products may be classified in at least three different ways. First, they may be
grouped according to cross-elasticities of demand, identical products having
infinite cross-elasticities. While this is the most satisfactory system of classification on theoretical grounds, it is rather difficult to measure cross-elasticities,
so that a second system of classification, grouping products by physical
attributes, is usually adopted in practice. Note that the existence of identical
physical attributes is neither a necessary (for those who *cannot* tell margarine

---

[1] Pack and Todaro (1969), Tokman (1972a, b).

[2] The following discussion is based on Stewart (1972a, 1973). See also Baranson (1969b) and
Hughes (1973a, b).

from butter) nor a sufficient (for those who *can* tell Gleem from Ultra-Brite) condition for commodities to be perfect substitutes. Once products are defined by physical attributes including some index of quality, the scope for choice of techniques in their production is usually quite narrow.

Third, products may be classified according to their "characteristics", that is, the needs that they fulfil (Lancaster, 1966). A single product may fulfil a variety of needs. A shirt may protect against cold or heat, may demonstrate by its cleanliness or smartness a certain status in society, may impress potential employers or lovers, may give pleasure by its colour and decoration to onlookers, and may avoid the need for ironing by being drip-dry. Similarly, a single need may be fulfilled by a variety of products. The need for accommodation may be fulfilled more or less well, by the sidewalks of Calcutta, caves, mud huts, multi-storey apartments, single family houses, or a palace.

This third classificatory scheme is enlightening in that it points to the scope for removing "excess" or "redundant" characteristics from existing products, and to the possibility of developing new products which are more "appropriate" to the needs of low-income consumers, and to the factor endowments of poor countries. Examples of excess standards might include a brick, strong enough to support a four-storey building, used for a single-storey house, or a drip-dry shirt produced in a low-income country, in which it would be socially more profitable to produce non-drip-dry shirts and iron them. Detergents produce a whiter wash than soap, and have other superior qualities, but they involve a less labour-intensive technology than some methods of producing soap. A low-income society may be better off with a poor-quality soap that everyone could afford than sophisticated detergents whose consumption must be confined to a rich minority. In medicine, many developing countries have adopted "high-income medicine" as their standard, involving capital-intensive drug production and long years of training. Unequal access to medicine for the poor and the rural parts of the population are the inevitable consequences. China, by contrast, with a much more equal income distribution, has made a determined attempt to develop a more appropriate pattern of medicine, making selective use of modern and traditional techniques, and introducing "barefoot doctors".[1]

In an approach which is similar, in many respects, to the appropriate goods strategy, several commentators have argued that industry in developing countries should concentrate on producing so-called mass consumption goods.[2] For instance, it is suggested that bicycle, bus and truck assembly should be given priority over the assembly of private cars. This approach overlaps also into the inter-industry output composition area, with proposals that particular sectors (low or medium income housing, public works)

[1] Rifkin (1972). A Ghanaian unequal-access case study is described by Sharpston (1972). Some of the above examples implicitly assume a closed economy. If the possibility of exporting is introduced, it may be precisely drip-dry shirts which are appropriate.

[2] See. for example, Currie (1971), Haq (1973b), and Hughes (1973b).

should be fostered to help provide an indigenous employment-creating engine of growth.[1]

Some writers on appropriate products are thinking of goods for which there would be high demand even with the current income-distribution pattern. However, others implicitly assume that income will be redistributed, after which there will arise mass demand for these goods. To the extent that such income redistribution does not in fact take place, the exhortation to produce such products is one to produce goods which will not be sold, at least in the domestic market.

It is often more or less explicitly assumed that goods which are appropriate in the sense that they just fulfil, and do not over-fulfil, their purchasers' needs, are also likely to be appropriate in that abundant factors are used intensively in their production. Several of the above examples are consistent with this hypothesis, but there is, of course, no *a priori* reason why it should be generally true. For example, plastic injection-moulded footwear may be more appropriate for consumers (cheaper, longer lasting), but leather shoes may be produced with more appropriate (labour-intensive) techniques, and may have more significant domestic backward linkages. Furthermore, even if some goods are more appropriate than others on both definitions, only empirical investigation can determine whether such differences are significant in terms of their aggregate employment implications.

Evidence from studies in Puerto Rico and Venezuela suggests that, with industry output totals held constant, an intra-industry move towards producing goods which use abundant factors intensively could have quite important macro employment implications.[2] However, in neither study is there any indication of whether goods which are appropriate in the factor-use sense are also appropriate in the consumption sense. Indeed, I know of no empirical estimates of the aggregate employment impact of increasing the production of goods which would be more appropriate on the need-fulfilling definition, and which would command an adequate market (or could be given one). Until such estimates are made, it is impossible to know whether it is worth devoting significant amounts of resources towards developing and producing such goods.

III. Choice of Techniques

After deciding which goods should be produced, or, more realistically, in conjunction with that decision, a decision still has to be made as to how they are to be produced, with what technology and factor proportions. So

[1] The low purchasing power of the average consumer in most developing countries means that corporations, domestic or international, have little incentive to experiment with and develop new products. Notable exceptions include the new Ford and General Motors low cost multipurpose cars, the Ford Developing Nation Tractor, and National Cash Register's simple machine in Argentina, tailored to the needs of the family business (Stewart, 1973).

[2] Tokman (1972b), Weisskoff (1973). The evidence is reviewed in section III.2.4 below.

much work has been done on the choice of techniques in recent years that this survey cannot hope to cover it all. The following discussion incorporates what it is hoped is a representative selection.[1]

III.1. *Econometric Estimates*

III.1.1. *Elasticity of Substitution*

One explanation of the existence of large-scale unemployment in developing countries is based on the assumption that the elasticity of factor substitution is about zero (Eckaus, 1955). According to the extreme version of this argument, technology alone determines the proportions in which factors are used; if labour is in over-abundant supply relative to capital with the available technology, unemployment will ensue. Conversely, attempts to increase the use of labour by lowering its price relative to that of other factors are based on the assumption that the elasticity of substitution is significantly greater than zero. The elasticity of substitution is relevant to a number of other problems as well, in both developed and developing countries. A high elasticity of substitution indicates that there exists flexibility in the face of external changes such as those which occur in international markets, and that prospects for output growth are relatively good, since the faster growing primary factor can be substituted relatively easily for the slower growing one. Under neoclassical assumptions, if the elasticity of substitution is less than one, decreasing the wage of one factor will increase its use but decrease its share in total output. Finally, the assumption that the elasticity of substitution is zero or close to zero underlies the use of many linear planning models.

Attempts which have been made to date to estimate elasticities of substitution using econometric methods suffer from a number of shortcomings.[2] Among the most important of these is the common assumption that in each industry only two factors, homogeneous labour and homogeneous capital, produce a single good, homogeneous output. No account is taken of other factors such as the quality of management, which may well play a key role in determining how much factor substitutability is possible. The existence of different grades of labour and different types of equipment is ignored. Nor is it recognised that a two-digit, or even a seven-digit, industry often comprises a variety of heterogeneous goods. Other shortcomings include the use of data which cover only technologies actually in operation; the assumptions, not necessarily realistic, that the elasticity of substitution is constant and that

---

[1] An annotated bibliography on the choice of techniques is currently being prepared by Gareth Jenkins and Frances Stewart at Oxford University. For earlier bibliographies, see Baranson (1967a) and Jackson (1972); also Ganière (1972), who includes a significant number of works in languages other than English. On defining technology, see Stewart (1973).

[2] For critiques, see for example, Arrow *et al.* (1961), Walters (1963), Nerlove (1967), Fisher (1969), Nadiri (1970), Johansen (1972), O'Herlihy (1972), Roemer (1972), Winston (1972) and Mundlak (1973a, b).

all firms are on their production frontiers; difficulties in incorporating technical change, working capital, and varying rates of capital utilisation over time; the assumption that capital is putty-putty, whereas in reality it seems more like putty-clay; identification—getting back to the initial production function equation from the form in which it is in practice estimated; distinguishing between long-run and short-run elasticities; simultaneous equations bias; multicollinearity; and the varying reliability and appropriateness of available data.

In the light of these theoretical and empirical problems, it is perhaps not surprising that attempts to estimate substitution elasticities econometrically have yielded unsatisfactory results. After a comprehensive examination of United States investigations, Nerlove (1967) concludes that "the major finding of this survey is the diversity of results: even slight variations in the period or concepts tend to produce drastically different estimates of the elasticity". A recent survey (Morawetz, 1973a) of sixteen econometric studies of elasticities of substitution in developing countries comes to the same pessimistic conclusion.[1] Not only do point estimates of the elasticity vary significantly from study to study; industry rankings, too, tend to be quite unstable. It is not possible to identify industries with consistently high or low elasticities in either the developing country or the United States estimates (Morawetz, 1973a).

In future, it may be worthwhile to shift emphasis away from attempts to estimate elasticities of substitution by econometric means on highly unrealistic assumptions (two homogeneous factors, etc.), concentrating instead on microeconomic studies of particular industries or processes, and especially on the social profitability of different techniques at various realistic factor price ratios.

III.1.2. *The Impact of Wages*

Attempts to estimate econometrically the impact of wage changes on employment run into many of the same problems as estimates of elasticities of substitution, and face an especially severe simultaneous equations problem. In most such studies the equation estimated incorporates the hypothesis that employment or the capital–labour ratio is some function of the wage rate or the wage–rental ratio. But the causation should not be uni-directional, since a higher capital–labour ratio is likely to increase labour productivity, and hence lead to higher wages.[2] A second equation is clearly needed to take this effect into account; without it, estimation of the first one is likely to yield biased coefficient estimates. I know of no wage-employment study in developing countries that uses a simultaneous equation approach.

[1] The studies are: Reynolds and Gregory (1965), Diwan and Gujarati (1968), Clague (1969)—two sets of estimates, Daniels (1969), Eriksson (1969), Harris and Todaro (1969), Katz (1969)—two sets, Tidrick (1970), Williamson (1971), Behrman (1972), Bruton (1972b)—two sets, Pack (1972b) and Roemer (1972).

[2] Harris and Todaro (1969), Reynolds (1965), Tidrick (1970). In such circumstances, wage restraint may simply lead to increased quasi-rents on existing capital.

Single equation wage–employment studies which have been carried out with comparable methodologies include Reynolds and Gregory (1965) for Puerto Rico, Bacha *et al.* (1972) for Brazil, and Roemer (1972) for Ghana.[1] A hypothesised 10 % fall in wages is found to lead to a rise in employment of 10, 4 and 12 % respectively in the three countries. In the light of the above theoretical problems (existence of more than two factors, etc.), these estimates should be treated with great caution.

A number of economists (*e.g.* Wells, 1974) have conjectured that stiff anti-firing legislation and the high severance payments required in many developing countries may be at least as important as high wages in holding back the growth of industrial employment. The reasoning here is that employers are unlikely to hire extra workers when they see an uncertain new sales opportunity if they know that they will not be able to release them if it does not turn out to be permanent. While this problem may well be important, I know of no attempt to quantify its magnitude.

III.2. *Appropriate Technology*

Appropriate technology may be defined as the set of techniques which makes optimum use of available resources in a given environment. For each process or project, it is the technology which maximises social welfare if factors and products are shadow priced. Other terms which have been used to describe more or less the same concept include optimal, progressive, intermediate, and middle level technology.[2]

In general, technologies which are appropriate in labour surplus developing countries will use more unskilled labour than those appropriate in developed countries. However, since capital is not the only scarce factor, this will not always be the case. For example, capital-intensive machine-paced or process-oriented operations, which may save on scarce management, may be appropriate in some cases (Hirschman, 1958). Modern factory methods of making shoes and wooden furniture use more capital per employee than cottage methods, but save on skilled labour, since each operative needs a narrower range of skills than the compleat shoemaker or carpenter. Thus, if skilled labour is a constraint, more modern methods may be appropriate.

Unfortunately, much of the literature on appropriate technologies implicitly uses a two-factor model. Not only does it therefore ignore the role of management, imported materials, power, etc., it also assumes that "a worker is a worker", whereas in terms of literacy, work habits and so on, workers

---

[1] Non-econometric discussion of wages policies and employment include Reynolds (1965), Frank (1968), and Gregory (1968).

[2] Baranson (1969b), Marsden (1970), Jackson (1972). Works discussing appropriate technology which are not cited elsewhere in this section include Reddaway (1962), Salter (1966), Myint (1964), Singer (1964), UNIDO (1964), Cohen and Leff (1967), Fei and Ranis (1970), Vaitsos (1970, 1971), Berry (1972c), Poats (1972), Roberts (1972), US AID (1972a), Dagnino-Pastore (1973), Leibenstein (1973).

may differ significantly from country to country. An appropriate technology in a developing country should be regarded as one which is suitable for particular workers producing particular products. Furthermore, as long as factor prices are distorted, it is unlikely that appropriate technologies will be implemented in a market economy, even if their nature can be established. For producers respond to prices that exist, rather than those which ought to exist. The extent to which the literature ignores these problems can be judged from the following survey.

III.2.1. *Why Worry about Appropriate Technology?*

In a perfect neoclassical world with no distortions, a full range of available techniques, perfect information, flexible, perfectly rational entrepreneurs, and an ideal income distribution, there would be no need for studies of "appropriate technologies". Faced with a given set of factor prices, each producer would choose the technology and factor proportions that maximise his and society's welfare. The problem in developing countries is that the range of known techniques may be limited, there are price distortions, information is not perfect, entrepreneurs are not always flexible and rational, and income distribution is not ideal.[1]

The use of labour is made artificially expensive in many developing countries by minimum wage legislation, fringe benefits, and shift differentials which are set at developed country levels, penalties for or restrictions on firing, and premature union pressures. At the same time, capital and imported materials are subsidised by regimes of cheap interest rates, the joint effect of overvalued exchange rates and low tariffs on imports of intermediate and capital goods, and tax incentives for investment. These distortions in the prices of labour, capital, and imports tend to encourage producers to substitute capital and imported materials for labour. However, even with the right factor prices, it is possible that the available range of techniques is simply not wide enough to increase labour use significantly by substituting labour for capital (Eckaus, 1955). (The sketchy empirical evidence which will be discussed shortly suggests that this consideration may be less important than was once thought.)

Information on available techniques is far from perfect in most developing countries. In some industries, the technology that would be appropriate to developing economies today is that which was in use in the United States and Europe half a century ago, but the machinery is not currently produced. Even if the right machinery is available somewhere in the world, it takes a capable manager with time, persistence, ingenuity and financial resources to find it. The Japanese linoleum manufacturer who travelled to the United States in the 1920s, found an obsolete hand block printing outfit lying in

---

[1] For econometric evidence indicating that developing country technologies are generally too capital intensive for their factor endowments, see Mason and Sakong (1971).

pieces in the storeroom of a United States firm, and shipped it home illustrates the point.[1] Further, even if old models can be located, unless there exists a reasonably well-developed domestic capital-goods industry, the need for spare parts and minor modifications may cause difficulties.

Entrepreneurs may not always be rational in the strictly economic sense. For example, they may sometimes choose a less labour-intensive means of production, thereby foregoing some profits, if it embodies a recent and appealing technology. Furthermore, entrepreneurs can only choose from among the options with which engineers present them. Developed country engineers who designed relatively capital-intensive sugar and footwear plants in Ethiopia and Ghana restricted themselves to variants of developed country best-practice techniques. They ignored methods currently available in other countries, which would have been more profitable in both social and private terms, the latter even at existing distorted factor prices.[2] Similar stories have been told for a variety of industries in Indonesia (Timmer, 1974; Wells, 1974). Further, the rationality or irrationality of an economic decision may depend on one's point of view. For example, in choosing tube-well technology in what was then East Pakistan, the modern technology was considered to be more risky by the local farmers, since it was installed by outsiders, difficult to operate and repair, less adaptable to local conditions, and required a large initial investment. For the donating agency, the modern technology was considered to be less risky, since it was installed by a foreign contractor, with whom a legal contract could safely be entered, and involved concentrated, easily supervisable drilling locations (Thomas, 1974).

III.2.2. *The Scope for Factor Substitution*

Detailed product-by-product (or process-by-process) studies are the surest way of estimating the extent to which the adoption of more appropriate techniques can be expected to increase labour use. But there must be at least a billion products in the world. To avoid the need to study each one separately it would be useful if some generalisations could be established, indicating the areas in which there is likely to be greater or less scope for factor substitution and adoption of more appropriate techniques. Such generalisations are likely to emerge only from the accumulated evidence of a considerable number of individual studies.[3] Nevertheless, several tentative suggestions have been already offered.

---

[1] Ranis (1972c). The selective use of older equipment was a feature of early Japanese economic development (Ranis, 1972b), and seems to be occurring to some extent in Kenya, though in the latter case older equipment seems to use only slightly more labour than modern machinery (Pack, 1972a).

[2] Pickett *et al.* (1973). See also Yeoman (1968), summarised by Mason (1973).

[3] In addition to the studies cited in section I (see especially Boon, 1964) and elsewhere in III.2, studies of appropriate and inappropriate technologies include: Ranis (1957, 1972c, d)—cotton and silk spinning and weaving, linoleum, plywood, and other industries in Japan, Taiwan, Korea, India, Pakistan, Mexico, and Kenya; Boon (1960)—wood-working; Unksov (1960)—welding and machine-

First of all, the scope for factor substitution seems to be drastically narrowed once the product has been fully specified.[1] Labour-intensive methods in textiles, brick- and road-making, and iron and steel are sometimes excluded if modern high-quality products are to be produced (Stewart, 1973). The development of power tillers and jeepneys in the Philippines and a motor pump in Vietnam provide illustrations of the close relationship between modification of technology and modification of product specification (Khan, 1973). In the United States the main aim of the research programmes of some 90 % of manufacturing firms is the development of new products or the improvement of old ones (Gustafson, 1962).

Second, peripheral or ancillary activities (materials receiving and handling, packaging, and storage) seem to offer greater scope for varying factor proportions than core processes (material processing).[2] It is almost always possible to use people instead of fork lifts and conveyor belts. Note, however, that considerations of product quality may, in some cases, dictate the use of more mechanised materials handling. In Kenya, machine mixing was found greatly to increase the strength and uniformity of cement blocks, while mechanical unloading of fruit decreased the percentage that was damaged.[3]

Third, adapatation of existing technologies and/or alteration of the product mix may facilitate the utilisation of particular local raw materials or skills which would otherwise be wasted. Adaptation of existing technology in India enabled buffalo milk to be used instead of cow's milk as the basis for powdered baby food (Nayudamma, 1973). In Kenya, by contrast, imported corrugated iron sheets are used instead of local materials for roofing, bamboo has been ignored as a source of building material and furniture, and plastics, often imported, are used widely instead of local wood (Stewart, 1973).

III.2.3. *Transfer, Generation, and Adaptation*

Technical knowledge is more difficult to market than other goods or factors because it possesses a number of peculiar features—inappropriability, embodiment in other factors, uncertainty, indivisibility, and impossibility of knowing its full value until bought. Given that some scope exists for the use of more appropriate technologies, there remains the problem of finding and implementing them. There are basically three possibilities—transfer them

---

building in USSR; Baranson (1967b, 1968, 1969b, 1970, 1971)—diesel engines in India, automobiles, air transport carriers, modular boat hulls, small farm tractors, and others; Vietorisz (1969a, b)—chemicals, engineering; Marsden (1970)—footwear, bread-baking, ceramic tiles, sewing machines, tanning, fibreboard; Díaz-Alejandro (1971)—cement in Latin America; US AID (1972b); and Sharpston (1973b)—metal working.

[1] Baranson (1969b), Stewart (1971, 1972a, 1973), Sharpston (1973b).
[2] Lewis (1966), Pack and Todaro (1970), Stewart (1971), Pack (1972a), Ranis (1972b, c).
[3] Stewart (1971), Pack (1972a).

from other countries, generate them locally, or adapt inappropriate technologies available elsewhere to suit local needs. In each case, a necessary though not sufficient condition for success is likely to be the correction of distorted factor prices.

International technology *transfer* is made difficult by two major obstacles: a communications gap and a suitability gap (Streeten, 1972). The communications gap arises as a result of high costs of transfer, international restrictions, or the exercise of monopoly power. Once these problems have been overcome and transfer has been effected, the suitability gap reflects the fact that most techniques which are available were designed to suit developed country factor endowments—including the *types* of labour available, and not merely aggregates. Policies which operate to close only one gap at a time may be useless, or even worse. Closing the suitability gap without doing something about communications is unlikely to improve the situation greatly. Improving communications but doing nothing about suitability may well make the situation worse, as developing countries adopt new, more labour-saving techniques faster and faster. It may also make technology generation more difficult.

Technology *generation* may be attempted in two quite different ways. An attempt may be made to force local entrepreneurs and engineers to be inventive by cutting them off from the outside world—the Chinese example is often cited in this regard. This is only likely to lead to the generation of appropriate technologies if factor and product prices are about right, if special subsidies are provided, or if inventors can be encouraged to take up the challenge of developing techniques which save on scarce factors for nationalistic or idealistic reasons. In such a case, the country must pay the price of forgoing those internationally discovered advances in technology which would have been appropriate, or adapatable to its needs.

Alternatively, conscious efforts may be made to establish research organisations designed specifically to generate appropriate technology— Appropriate Technology Institutions, or ATIs, for short. The main problem with this course of action is that institutions like ATIs tend to be isolated from producers. This is a serious drawback. Industrial research is almost always best done in the context of the producing unit, by people (entrepreneurs, managers, production and design engineers, marketing specialists) who are familiar with the specific technological characteristics of their industry and the characteristics of the available labour.[1] Without close links with industry, the relevance of research is likely to suffer, and dissemination and practical implementation of findings are likely to be unsatisfactorily handled. A number of existing technology centres and institutions have published catalogues or offer services, but such ventures must remain a drop in the bucket compared with overall technology needs.[2] Indeed, it is

[1] Bruton (1972a), Westphal (1973).

[2] The share of poor countries in world R & D expenditure is only 2 % (Singer, 1973). Institutions and groups currently working on technology development, adaptation, and transfer include the London-based Intermediate Technology Development Group—ITDG (1967), Schumacher (1972);

important that developing-country government should not be persuaded that by participating in the creation of some new ATI, they will somehow solve their technology problems. A much more concerted set of policy measures is needed than that.

Nevertheless, it may still be useful to establish some general criteria for the success of ATIs. For example, ATIs may be successful in exploiting a developing country's specific natural resource base, and in forming and operating social overhead capital. In the former case, Western technological research may not have been directed to the use of these resources; in the latter, there is little incentive for private research, and the magnitude of public investment in social overhead capital implies a significant impact (Westphal, 1973). The success of the green revolution research sets a goal to strive for, though breakthroughs in industry are not likely to be as dramatic.

The third approach to the introduction of a more appropriate techno-logy, technological *adaptation*, seems likely to be the most promising, particu-larly in semi-industrialised countries with entrepreneurial and engineering skills, and at least some capital goods production capacity. Entrepreneurship and engineering abilities are needed to identify the potential for the adapta-tions; capital goods production capacity is necessary to carry them through.[1]

Little systematic information is available on the process of technological adaptation in developing countries; a high priority should be placed on discovering where and how it has occurred, and why it has not occurred elsewhere.[2] It has been suggested that the incentive to adapt may be related directly to the importance of production costs relative to total sales price, and indirectly to the importance of quality relative to price considerations in marketing (Yeoman, 1968). Other important conditions may be the

the University of Strathclyde Overseas Development Unit—Pickett *et al.* (1973); the ILO World Employment Program—ILO (1973b); Volunteers in Technical Assistance Village Technology Center—VITA (n.d.); the Science Policy Research Unit at the University of Sussex—Cooper (1972). Stewart (1973), outlines the work of these groups, and also briefly discusses the Indian government's recently established Appropriate Technology Development Group, the Korean Institute of Science and Technology, the OECD Development Enquiry Service, the UNIDO Clearing House for Industrial Information, ongoing MIT research on technology adaptation, and a number of institutions which have been proposed but not yet created. In an Appendix, Stewart (1973) lists and gives detailed examples of queries answered by the ITDG Industrial Liaison Unit. For case studies of government and university science policy institutions in a number of developing countries, see US AID (1972b), Cooper (1973), and Subbarao (1973). On requirements for techno-logy help services, see Stewart (1973), and Westphal (1973).

[1] Baranson (1969b), Pack and Todaro (1969), and Pack (1972a). Additional arguments which have been advanced in favour of developing domestic capital goods capacity are that such goods are sometimes quite labour intensive in production (Pack and Todaro, 1969), and that imported capital goods sometimes tend to be associated with more capital-intensive techniques (McCabe and Michalo-poulos, 1971). Note though that the labour used in capital goods production is often quite skilled.

[2] The same might be said of technical change in general. For a summary of the information that is available on the process of innovation and adaptation in developed countries, see Nelson *et al.* (1967), Gruber and Marquis (1969), Scherer (1970), Mansfield (1971), Kennedy and Thirlwall (1972), and Katz (1973). Studies of successful technology adaptation include Granick (1957) and Strassman (1968). [The Yale Economic Growth Center is currently undertaking a large-scale investigation of technology transfer and adaptation in developing countries. See Economic Growth Centre (1974).]

absence of distortions in factor and product prices, and the existence of competition. High rates of protection may induce satisficing entrepreneurs to settle for existing inappropriate techniques instead of making the effort to adapt them to suit local conditions. Scattered evidence from Japan, Korea, Taiwan and other countries suggests that export industries may have higher rates of adaptation than import-substituting industries, though counter-examples like the Philippines jeepney also exist.[1]

Little is known on the role of the multinational corporation (MNC) in technology adaptation. Some investigators find that MNCs tend to use the same technology in developing countries as they do at home, and tend to use less labour-intensive techniques, on average, than local firms. Others, by contrast, argue that because of superior, more flexible management, MNCs sometimes adapt better to local factor scarcities than their local counterparts, and use more labour than at home, particularly in ancillary activities.[2] More research is needed on this problem, and also on the relationship between economies of scale and appropriate technology.[3]

III.2.4. *Empirical Evidence*

Despite the recent veritable flood of work on appropriate technology, I know of only three studies which give even a glimpse of the potential macro employment implications of adopting particular technology policies. All of them suggest that the payoffs could be quite significant.[4]

Tokman's (1972b) study of Venezuela is currently available only in Spanish, so it may be useful to describe it in more than the usual detail. Using a two-factor model, Tokman sets out to examine the macro employment implications of halting or reversing the historical trend away from labour-intensive techniques in industry, insofar as this is possible. He divides the 20 Venezuelan two-digit manufacturing industries into two groups: five industries which use only capital-intensive or only labour-intensive techniques and which play no further part in the analysis (petroleum and coal products, shoes and clothing, wooden furniture, machinery, transport equipment), and 15 industries in which a range of techniques is currently in use.[5] Next, Tokman disaggregates the data on the latter 15 industries to the

[1] Ranis (1957, 1970, 1972c, d, 1973b), Wells (1974).

[2] For the first view, see Reynolds and Gregory (1965) on Puerto Rico, Hughes and Seng (1969) on Singapore, and Baranson (1972) on the automobile industry. For the second, see ILO (1972a) and Pack (1972a) on Kenya, and Strassman (1968) and Mason (1971, 1973) on Mexico and the Philippines. [See also Courtney and Leipziger, 1973.] On MNCs, technology, and the product mix, see also Stewart (1973) and Vaitsos (1973).

[3] For the state of current theoretical and empirical knowledge on economies of scale, see Silberston (1972). An IBRD financed study of mechanical engineering currently in progress is designed partly to examine the relationship between economies of scale and choice of technique. See Westphal and Rhee (1971) and KIST (1973).

[4] A more aggregative empirical investigation of Japanese historical experience suggests that technological adaptation and assimilation was of some significance (Ranis and Fei, 1969).

[5] Intermediate goods differ from final goods in the leather industry, and in wood; knitted goods differ from spinning and weaving in textiles; and so on.

three-digit level, and weeds out cases where the scope for factor substitution appears to be slight.[1] This leaves 16 three-digit sub-industries in which (a) more than 15 % of total production is currently produced by labour-intensive techniques, and (b) there appears to be scope for technological choice with a relatively stationary product mix.[2] It is now postulated that 100 % of the projected 1985 output of these 16 sub-industries could be produced using labour-intensive techniques, without this having any effect on the output of these industries. Tokman estimates that such a policy would increase 1985 industrial employment by about 26 % over what it would be if historical trends towards increasing capital intensity were to continue. The choice of more labour-intensive techniques leads to a rise in the output–capital ratio, and about one quarter of the total increase in employment is associated with the resultant saving on capital. A less extreme policy aimed at freezing technology at its current factor intensity would, on the assumptions made, lead to an 8 % increase in 1985 employment.

In a similar type of study, Weisskoff (1973) finds that a ten-year "techno-logy freeze" policy in Puerto Rico could have increased 1963 employment from the actual figure of 600,000 to 1 million jobs, if this had not affected the level of industrial output. About 150,000 of the "lost" jobs appeared to be due to changes in the inter-industry flows between 1953 and 1963, the rest to direct increases in productivity. If no growth had occurred from 1953 to 1963, end period employment would have been only 400,000.

Finally, Chenery and Raduchel (1971) use a general equilibrium four sector non-linear programming model in a first attempt to compare the scope for direct labour–capital substitution in the production process with that for indirect substitution through changing output composition. Using hypo-thetical data, they find that the scope for direct substitution in production is greater than that for indirect substitution through trade and through varying the output mix in general. As the authors note, these results depend strongly on the assumed parameter values, and they also depend on the legitimacy of using a two factor model.

Clearly, there are enormous problems with all three studies. Nevertheless, even taken with a shaker of salt, their findings are at least consistent with the hypothesis that there may be significant macro employment payoffs to encouraging the use of more appropriate techniques.

III.3. Small-Scale Industry

Clearly, what is small in Brazil may be large in Togo. Nevertheless, small-scale industry, which includes the "informal" or "unorganised"

---

[1] Milk products, beer, pulp and paper, cement, tin cans, etc.

[2] Meats, canned fish and seafoods, non-alcoholic beverages, spirits, spun woven textiles, paper products, pharmaceutical and toilet articles, cement products, clay products, glass, hardware items, metallic structures, metal articles for domestic use, electrical apparatus, photographic and optical equipment, and plastic material.

sector, is most commonly arbitrarily defined to include all firms with up to 20–50 workers each, and this is the definition used here. Small-scale industry therefore includes enterprises ranging from the local tailor using only his family's labour to quite sophisticated, modern sub-contractors who manufacture automobile parts for large automobile makers. Process, locational, and market influences help to determine the industries in which small-scale firms are found. Small firms are common where manufacturing operations can be easily separated and specialised (pistons and valves, jewellery, simple mixing or finishing operations); where raw materials are dispersed (timber, butter); where transport costs are high (bricks); where products are highly differentiated (clothing); and where close proximity to customers is important (job printing, auto repair).[1]

Small-scale industry employs well over half the industrial labour force in most developing countries, yet remarkably little is known about its composition and characteristics.[2] Some of the most important questions which need to be answered include the following. Do small firms use less capital and other scarce inputs (power, imported materials) to produce a given volume of output? Do they use more labour-intensive techniques of production? How do existing government regulations differentially affect small industry? What are the growth implications of small- versus large-scale industry—which of the two generates and adapts technology more effectively, promotes entrepreneurship better, and has a higher marginal saving and reinvestment rate?[3] What are the main causes of small business failures—entrepreneurship deficiencies, lack of capital, biased government policies? Why have small firms been able to pool their production successfully for exporting in some countries (Hong Kong, Japan), while in others (Colombia—Morawetz, 1973c) it has been far more difficult and less common? What factors enabled the growth of the subcontracting system (large firms sending out work to small ones to cover peaks, special orders, etc.) in some areas (Japan, East Asia), but not in others (India).[4] Do large-scale enterprises which started out small differ from large enterprises which started out big? A separate survey would be needed to examine all these questions thoroughly.[5] This section briefly examines the first three.

Most of the scattered evidence that is available suggests that small firms do tend to require less capital per unit of output, though some

---

[1] Staley and Morse (1965), Marsden (1966). Staley and Morse (1965) present a "shopping list" of small-scale industries typically found in developed countries.

[2] In Iran, Colombia and Malaysia respectively, firms with fewer than 50 employees employ 77, 71 and 40 % of the industrial labour force, and produce 59, 37 and 25 % of industrial value added. Small scale industry employs 70 % of the industrial labour force in Nigeria, 43 % in Japan and from 12 (Germany) to 34 (Switzerland) % in the industrialised countries (IBRD, 1973, Aluko, 1973). Studies on small-scale industry which are not cited elsewhere in this section include: Yamanaka (1953), Singer (1964), Ishikawa (1966), Davenport (1967), Rao (1967), UN ECLA (1967), Hoselitz (1968), OECD (1969), UNIDO (1970), Inaba (1971), UN ECAFE (1971), and Meissner (1973).

[3] On entrepreneurship, see Papanek (1969), Harris (1970), Derossi (1971), Patel (1973), and Stewart (1973).   [4] Dhar and Lydall (1961), Koga (1968), Watanabe (1972b), IBRD (1973).

[5] For the best recent coverage of the subject, see IBRD (1973).

contrary indications are also to be found.[1] More research is needed on small firms' demands on entrepreneurship, skilled labour and other scarce factors.

With regard to the second question, most investigators agree that small firms tend to use relatively more labour-intensive techniques of production than their larger competitors.[2] It is tempting to conclude from this that, from the short-term employment point of view at least, small firms should be given special encouragement at the expense of large enterprises. The reasoning here is that a given amount of capital will apparently create more employment if it is spread over a large number of small firms than if it is concentrated in a few large ones. However, several considerations suggest that, at least in the present state of knowledge, it is difficult to draw any such general conclusions. First of all, if small firms tend to produce lower-quality products, which are demanded mainly by poor local consumers, it may take radical redistribution of income before there would be sufficient demand for the output of many extra small firms. Second, estimates of labour intensity in small and large industry generally confine themselves only to direct factor employment, ignoring indirect effects altogether. But whereas the small shoe-maker tends to be producer, transporter, and sales distributor all in one, large shoe firms have separate departments for each function, each employing significant numbers of people. These indirect effects need closer examination.[3]

Perhaps most important of all, it is agreed by most observers that small firms tend to be confronted with factor prices which are much closer to scarcity prices than those facing large firms. Wage legislation is less effective, so wages are lower, and subsidised credit and other capital subsidies are available only to the larger firms, so capital costs are higher. It may well be, therefore, that small firms tend to use more labour-intensive techniques not because they operate on a small scale, but because they face less distorted factor prices. If this is the case, the appropriate policy prescription from the point of view of short-term employment is not the encouragement of small-ness *per se*, but rather promotion of the use of more labour-intensive techniques in firms of all sizes through readjustments of factor prices to reflect real scarcities. Indeed, providing small entrepreneurs with credit and imports at the same concessionary rates as those available to large firms may well worsen the situation by encouraging them to use more capital- and import-intensive techniques of production.[4]

---

[1] Evidence of low capital–output ratios is presented by Marsden (1969) for Chile, India, Japan, Taiwan, the United Arab Republic, and the United States, Mehta (1969) for India, Todd (1971), and Berry (1972d) for Colombia. Contrary evidence for India is presented by Dhar and Lydall (1961), and Sandesara (1966, 1969).

[2] On Colombia, Kenya, India, Pakistan, and other countries, see Dhar and Lydall (1961), Ranis (1961), Shetty (1963), Marsden (1966), Berry (1972d), DiTullio (1972), and ILO (1972a). Dhar and Lydall (1961) and Ranis (1961) find in India and Pakistan that although firms with up to 10 workers tend to use labour-intensive techniques, those with from 10 to 50 workers are not significantly more labour intensive than larger firms. For evidence that small-scale firms can also be relatively capital intensive, see Lewis (1969), Winston (1971a).

[3] I am indebted to Ardy Stoutjesdijk for this point.

[4] Reddaway (1962) makes a similar point. See also IBRD (1973).

Existing government regulations and modes of operation tend to hinder the development of small-scale industry in many developing countries. For example, large firms with skilled administrative and clerical staffs are more able than small entrepreneurs to take full advantage of duty exemptions, export subsidies, and drawback schemes, and are more likely to have the influence necessary to obtain import and production licenses, and rationed cheap credit. In addition, cascading sales taxes, which are sometimes used, favour the large vertically integrated firm over the small producer who has to pay the tax on each input. Policies which could help to correct this anti-small-industry bias include decentralising government bureaucracy, and correcting factor and product price distortions to enable the gradual dismantling of at least some of the administrative controls and licensing arrangements.

III.4. Capital Utilisation

A simple and potentially quite powerful way of increasing labour use, at the same time lowering the capital–output ratio, is to utilise the existing capital stock more intensively, for example, by working two or three shifts instead of one. Japan is known to have used this technique early in its development process, running machines longer hours and at higher speeds than was customary in the United States. The subsequent increased need for maintenance added further to total employment (Ranis, 1957). At present, few hard data are available on actual rates of capital utilisation in developing countries, though a number of writers have suggested that they seem to be relatively low.[1]

Where capital utilisation rates are low, there are at least four possible classes of explanation, each with its own quite distinct implications for corrective policy.[2] The low utilisation rate may be planned or unplanned, and it may be determined by supply or demand factors. Taking low planned utilisation first, on the supply side, an entrepreneur may plan to use his capital at less than its maximum potential (usually assumed to be 24 hours less maintenance time) because of factor price distortions, which make capital relatively cheap and labour relatively dear, or because of expected rhythmic variations in the prices of capital, labour, or other inputs (night and seasonal differentials, and the like). On the demand side, planned utilisation rates may be below maximum potential rates if demand is expected to grow rapidly in the near future (assuming that machines and equipment are not perfectly divisible); if seasonal demand fluctuations are expected (the peak

[1] While Korea and Pakistan may have had fairly low utilisation rates (Hogan, 1968; Kim and Kwon, 1973; Winston, 1971a), preliminary evidence for Colombia, Kenya, Israel, Malaysia, and the Philippines leaves the question open (Merhav, 1970; Baily, 1973; Thoumi, 1973, ongoing IBRD Study). See also Stewart and Streeten (1972, p. 77, no. 1). China seems to have followed the Japanese example (Howe, 1971).

[2] Recent theoretical work on capital utilisation in developing countries, which has helped to clarify the nature of the problem, includes Phillips (1969), Winston (1971a, b), Winston and McCoy (1972), Betancourt and Clague (1973) and Schydlowsky (1973).

load problem); of if each firm faces a Chamberlinian (1958) downward-sloping demand curve.

Actual capital utilisation may be lower than the planned rate if there is an unexpected shortage of factors or inputs (skilled labour, imported inputs, working capital), an unanticipated change in costs, or unforeseen technological progress in the industry. Actual rates may also be lower than planned rates as a result of an unexpected shortfall of demand, which might be due to increased competition, new entry, recession, import liberalisation, or inaccurate demand forecasts.

The only quantitative evidence available, calculations based on as yet largely untested hypotheses (Millán and Schydlowsky, 1973), suggests that the employment payoff to increasing capital utilisation in developing countries could be quite significant. It is important then, that a clearer idea be gained of actual capital utilisation rates in developing countries, and of the causes of underutilisation where it appears, so that appropriate policies can be designed to deal with the problem.[1]

IV. CONCLUDING REMARKS

Policies to increase labour use have been discussed throughout the body of this survey. At the risk of oversimplifying and even caricaturing, three broad schools of thought, or strategies, may be distinguished. Most writers belong to at least one and half of these schools, and some belong to all three.[2] The three strategies have been proposed as ways of increasing labour use not only in industry but throughout the economy. Therefore, this section is pitched at a more general level than the rest of the paper.

The price-incentive school argues that getting factor, product, and foreign-exchange prices right, and "letting factor endowments speak" are the keys to increasing labour use. More equal treatment of exports and import substitutes will ensure that countries produce according to comparative advantage. Where income distribution is unequal, consumption taxes on luxury goods can be used to encourage the production of more appropriate products. The right factor prices will automatically induce firms to select appropriate (generally labour-intensive) techniques of production, and to utilise scarce factors as fully as possible. Abandoning import and investment licensing, credit subsidisation and rationing, and red tape in general, will ensure that small-scale firms are treated equivalently to their larger competitors.

---

[1] The International Bank for Reconstruction and Development and the Boston University Center for Latin American Development Studies are currently conducting systematic investigations into industrial capital utilisation in eight developing countries.

[2] Stewart (1973) uses a similar classification in the narrower context of technology policy. [After the revised version of this survey was completed, I received a copy of Acharya (1974), who reviews issues similar to those covered in this survey, but with different emphasis. References cited by Acharya which are not cited elsewhere in the present survey include Ahluwalia (1973), Baron (1973), Cooper and Kaplinsky (1973), Khan (1970), ILO (1972b), Lent (1972), Pack (1974), Peacock and Shaw (1971) and Young et al. (1974).]

Implicit in the argument that "getting prices right" will solve the employment problem is an assumption that markets are perfect. That is, the individual producer can sell as much as he wants at the ruling price, and hire as many skilled workers as he wants at the ruling wage. The assumption of perfect markets is sometimes made explicit in the treatment of export sales potential. But its relevance is much more general, and it becomes quite powerful when one recognises the problem of innumerable differentiated commodities, many specialised factors, and wide variations in quality. Furthermore, the price-incentive school implicitly assumes either that current prices (plus an assumption of a perfect market) are sufficient for making decisions concerning the future, or that accurate information on future demands, supplies and prices is easily available to private producers. As neither of these assumptions is likely to be correct, private producers do not have the information necessary to make logically based investment decisions, and government intervention may be advisable. For example, it may be necessary for the government to project future demand for electricity, steel, transport, or foreign exchange, and then to take action to ensure that these demands will be met in one way or another in the future. "Infant industry" and "infant industrial sector" arguments come under this general heading.

In addition to advocating government economic planning to cope with this type of problem, the second school, the interventionists, also suggests other forms of government action. Since income distribution is unequal, governments should buy up labour-intensive mass consumption goods and distribute them at subsidised prices to the poor. The existence of the communications and suitability gaps make it necessary for Appropriate Technology Institutes to be established. Trade negotiations are needed to remove developed country restrictions on exports from the developing world. Government decentralisation, special lending institutions, and training and technical assistance programmes are needed to help small entrepreneurs overcome their lack of education and business experience. Engineers should be taught more economics. At least in the short run, governments may have to legislate to cut down on rural–urban migration.

The third group, the radical reformists, claims that reform of the politico-economic system, or outright revolution, perhaps along Chinese lines, is a necessary precondition for increasing labour use; the rich, powerful minority is not about to legislate a partial or complete end to its monopoly on the reins of economic and political power. Without a radical redistribution of power, assets and income, output composition will continue to be biased towards inappropriate goods, and technological development will continue to be imitative and capital intensive rather than adaptive. Large powerful capital-intensive firms will continue to gain government favours and grow at the expense of small enterprises, and oligopolistic market structure will continue to cause capital to be under-utilised.

Clearly, the views appropriate for any one country depend on that country's particular circumstances. For small semi-industrialised countries with not too unequal income distribution and large reserves of entrepreneurial, managerial and engineering talent, simply getting factor, product, and foreign exchange prices more nearly right may be enough significantly to increase labour absorption. In small least-developed countries, which have inadequate stocks of human capital, some government intervention may be necessary. In societies where a small minority rules for its own benefit, there may be no alternative to revolution.

Finally, it is quite possible that changing one policy in isolation, apparently for the better, will actually worsen the overall employment situation.[1] During the last decade for example, stimulating the modern sector without removing factor price distortions led to little or no increase, or even an absolute decline, in industrial employment in many countries; the modern firms which grew were less labour intensive than the traditional enterprises whose place they took. The introduction of export subsidies helps to correct the bias in favour of import substitution which is imparted by the tariff system, but if something is not done about factor price distortions, the net result may simply be that the country increases exports of non-labour-intensive goods, helping neither employment nor growth. Even where the right policies are known or easily knowable, they are not always implemented. More research is needed, perhaps of an interdisciplinary nature, on the process of policy formulation, and the ways in which it may be influenced.

Perhaps the best way for this survey to end is the way it began. The growth of manufacturing industry alone cannot be expected to solve the employment problem in most developing countries – certainly not if the population continues to double every 25 years or so. It can however serve as an important element in a package of development measures, in particular, by helping to ease the balance of payments problem which otherwise appears when a policy of progressively expanding demand is followed. In this case, the additional employment may be largely in construction and services, but it would not have been created without an appropriate growth in the output of manufactures. Similarly, increased output of manufactures can help to provide directly local inputs for agriculture (spare parts, suitable implements) which cannot always be obtained so effectively by importation, even if foreign exchange is available. Further policy-oriented research on industrialisation is needed to assess its role as part of a comprehensive strategy.

DAVID MORAWETZ

Hebrew University, Jerusalem.

---

[1] This possibility follows from the well-known theory of the second best (Lancaster and Lipsey, 1956).

BIBLIOGRAPHY

Abbreviations

DP—Discussion Paper.
IBRD—International Bank for Reconstruction and Development, Washington D.C. (DRC, Development Research Center; DED, Development Economics Department; WP, Working Paper.)
Rice PDS—Rice University Program of Development Studies, Houston, Texas. (P—Paper.)
Williams CDE—Williams College Center for Development Economics, Williamstown, Mass. (RM—Research Memorandum).
Yale EGC—Yale University Economic Growth Center, New Haven, Conn.

Acharya, S. N. (1974). "Fiscal–Financial Intervention, Factor Prices, and Factor Proportions: A Review of Issues," mimeo, IBRD, DED.
Adelman, Irma (1966). "A Linear Programming Model of Educational Planning; A Case Study of Argentina," in I. Adelman and E. Thorbecke (1966)
—— and Taft Morris, Cynthia (1971). "An Anatomy of Patterns of Income Distribution in Developing Nations," IBRD, WP-116.
—— and Robinson, Sherman (1973). "A Micro-Economic Model of Korea: Factors Affecting the Distribution of Income in the Short Run," mimeo, IBRD, DRC.
—— and Sparrow, Frederick T. (1966). "Experiments with Linear and Piece-wise Linear Dynamic Programming Models," in I. Adelman and E. Thorbecke (1966).
—— and Thorbecke, Erik (eds.) (1966). *The Theory and Design of Economic Development*, Baltimore, Johns Hopkins University Press.
Ahluwalia, Montek (1973). "Taxes, Subsidies and Employment," *Quarterly Journal of Economics*, Vol. 87, 3, August, pp. 393–409.
Aluko, S. A. (1973). "Employment in Nigerian Small-Scale Industrial Sector," presented at Ford Foundation Conference on Technology and Employment, Delhi.
Ambannavar, J. P. (1970). "Changes in the Employment Pattern of the Indian Working Force, 1911–1961," *The Developing Economies*, Vol. 8, 1, March, pp. 128–46.
Anand, Sudhir (1972). "Input–Output Analysis Applied to Employment: A Case Study of Yugoslavia," mimeo, IBRD, DED.
Arrow, K., Chenery, H., Minhas, B. and Solow, R. (1961). "Capital–Labor Substitution and Economic Efficiency," *Review of Economics and Statistics*, Vol. 43, 3, August, pp. 225–50.
Bacha, E. L., de Mata, M. and Modenesi, R. L. (1972). *Encargos Trabalhistas a Absorção de Mão-de-obra, una Interpretação do Problema e Seu Debate*, Rio de Janeiro, IPEA-INPES, Coleção Relatorios de Pesquisa, No. 12.
Baer, Werner and Hervé, Michel (1966). "Employment and Industrialization in Developing Countries," *Quarterly Journal of Economics*, Vol. 80, 1, February, pp. 88–107.
Bailey, Charles, Dahl, Norman and Stewart, Frances (1973). "Summary of the [Ford Foundation] Seminar on Technology and Employment in Developing Countries," mimeo, Delhi.
Baily, Mary Ann (1973). "Capital Utilization in Kenya Manufacturing Industry," Cambridge, Mass., Unpublished Doctoral Dissertation, Massachusetts Institute of Technology.
Balassa, Bela (1966). "Tariff Reduction and Trade in Manufactures Among the Industrial Countries," *American Economic Review*, Vol. 56, 2, June, pp. 466–73.
—— (1970). "Industrial Policies in Taiwan and Korea," IBRD, WP-86.
—— et al. (1971). *The Structure of Protection in Developing Countries*, Baltimore, Johns Hopkins Press.
Baldwin, Robert E. (1971). "Determinants of the Commodity Structure of U.S. Trade," *American Economic Review*, Vol. 61, 1, March, pp. 124–46.
Baranson, Jack (1967a). *Technology for Underdeveloped Areas: An Annotated Bibliography*, Oxford, England, Pergamon Press.
—— (1967b). *Manufacturing Problems in India: The Cummins Diesel Experience*, Syracuse, N.Y., Syracuse University Press.
—— (1968). "Automotive Industries in Developing Countries," mimeo, IBRD, DED.
—— (1969a). "Role of Science and Technology in Advancing Development of Newly Industrialized States," mimeo, Washington D.C., U.S. Department of State.
—— (1969b). *Industrial Technologies for Developing Economies*, New York, Praeger.
—— (1970). "Technology Transfer through the International Firm," *American Economic Review, Proceedings*, Vol. 50, 2; May, pp. 435–40.
—— (1971). "International Transfer of Automotive Technology to Developing Countries," mimeo, New York, U.N. Institute for Training and Research.

—— (1972). "Multinational Corporations and Developing Country Goals for Technological Self-Sufficiency," mimeo; cited in Stewart (1973).

Baron, C. G. (1973). "Sugar-Processing Techniques in India," mimeo, Geneva, ILO.

Bardhan, Pranab K. (1973). *Planning Models and Income Distribution with Special Reference to India*, New Delhi, Indian Statistical Institute.

Behrman, Jere (1972). "Sectoral Elasticities of Substitution Between Capital and Labor in a Developing Economy: Time Series Analysis in the Case of Post-War Chile," *Econometrica*, Vol. 40, 2, March, pp. 311–26.

Berry, R. Albert (1972a). "Some Determinants of Changing Income Distribution in Colombia: 1930–1970," Yale EGC, DP-137.

—— (1972b). "Unemployment as a Social Problem in Urban Colombia: Some Preliminary Hypotheses and Conclusions," Yale EGC, DP-145.

—— (1972c). "The Rate of Interest and the Demand for Labor", Yale EGC, DP-144.

—— (1972d). "The Relevance and Prospects of Small Scale Industry in Colombia," Yale EGC, DP-142.

Betancourt, Roger and Clague, Christopher (1973). "An Economic Analysis of Capital Utilization," mimeo, College Park, Md., University of Maryland.

Bhagwati, Jagdish (1964). "The Pure Theory of International Trade: A Survey," Economic Journal, Vol. 74, 1, March, pp. 1–84.

Bhalla, A. S. (1964). "Investment Allocation and Technological Choice—A Case of Cotton Spinning Techniques," Economic Journal, Vol. 74, 295, September, pp. 611–22.

—— (1965). "Choosing Techniques: Handpounding *v.* Machine Milling of Rice: An Indian Case," *Oxford Economic Papers*, Vol. 17, 1, March, pp. 147–57.

—— (1970). "Economic Efficiency, Capital Intensity, and Capital–Labor Substitution in Retail Trade," Yale EGC, DP-94.

Bhardwaj, R. C. (1964). "Factor Proportions and Full Employment," *Economia Internazionale*, Vol. 17, 2, May, pp. 250–67.

Blaug, Mark (1967). "Approaches to Educational Planning," Economic Journal, Vol. 77, 306, June, pp. 262–87.

Blaug, Mark (ed.) (1968). *Economics of Education*, Baltimore, Penguin Books.

Blitzer, Charles R. (1972). "A Perspective Planning Model For Turkey: 1969–1984," mimeo, IBRD, DRC.

—— (1973). "Employment, Human Capital, and Income Distribution," mimeo, IBRD, DRC.

Boon, Gerard K. (1960). "Choice of Industrial Technology: The Case of Wood-Working," Vienna, UNIDO, *Industrialization and Productivity Bulletin*, No. 3.

—— (1964). *Economic Choice of Human and Physical Factors in Production*, Amsterdam, North-Holland.

—— (1969). "Factor Intensities in Mexico with Special Reference to Manufacturing," in H. C. Bos (ed.), *Towards Balanced International Growth*, Amsterdam, North-Holland.

Bowles, Samuel (1969). *Planning Educational Systems for Economic Growth*, Cambridge, Mass. Harvard University Press.

——(1970). "Aggregation of Labor Inputs in the Economics of Growth and Planning: Experiments with a Two-Level CES Function," *Journal of Political Economy*, Vol. 78, 1, January–February, pp. 68–71.

Brigg, Pamela (1973). "Some Economic Interpretations of Case Studies of Urban Migration in Developing Countries," IBRD, WP-151.

Bruno, Michael (1966), "A Programming Model for Israel," in I. Adelman and E. Thorbecke (1966).

Bruton, Henry J. (1967). "Productivity Growth in Latin America," *American Economic Review*, Vol. 57, 5, December, pp. 1099–1116.

—— (1970). "The Import Substitution Strategy of Economic Development: A Survey," Williams CDE, RM-27; *Pakistan Development Review*, Vol. 10, 2, Summer, pp. 123–46.

—— (1972a). "Economic Development and Labor Use," presented at Ford Foundation Seminar on the Employment Process, Bogota; Williams CDE.

—— (1972b). "The Elasticity of Substitution in Developing Countries," Williams CDE, RM-45.

—— (1972c). "Employment, Productivity and Import Substitution," Williams CDE, RM-44.

Carter, Nicholas G. (1969). "A Linear Programming Model of the Output and Employment Possibilities of the Economy of Jamaica 1965–1975: Preliminary Results," IBRD, WP-8.

Chamberlin, E. H. (1958). *The Theory of Monopolistic Competition*, 7th edition, Cambridge, Mass. Harvard University Press.

Chenery, Hollis B. (1953). "Process and Production Functions from Engineering Data," in W. Leontief (ed.), *Studies in the Structure of the American Economy*, New York, Oxford University Press.

—— (1961). "Comparative Advantage and Development Policy," *American Economic Review*, Vol. 2, 6, March, pp. 125–55.

—— Duloy, John and Jolly, Richard (eds.) (1973). "Redistribution with Growth: An Approach to Policy," mimeo, IBRD, DRC.

—— and Raduchel, William J. (1971). "Substitution in Planning Models," in H. Chenery (ed.), *Studies in Development Planning*, Cambridge, Mass. Harvard University Press.

Clague, C. K. (1969). "Capital–Labor Substitution in Manufacturing in Underdeveloped Countries," *Econometrica*, Vol. 37, 3, July, pp. 528–37.

Cline, William R. (1972). *Potential Effects of Income Redistribution on Economic Growth: Latin American Cases*, New York, Praeger.

Cohen, Benjamin I. and Leff, Nathaniel H. (1967). "Employment and Industrialization: Comment," *Quarterly Journal of Economics*, Vol. 81, February, pp. 162–64.

Cooper, Charles (1972). "Science, Technology and Production in the Underdeveloped Countries: An Introduction," *Journal of Development Studies*, Vol. 9, 1, October, pp. 1–18.

—— (1973). "Science Policy and Technological Change in Underdeveloped Economics," presented at Ford Foundation Seminar on Technology and Employment, Delhi.

—— and Kaplinsky, R. (1973). "Second-hand Equipment in a Developing Country—A Study of Jute Processing in Kenya," mimeo, Geneva, ILO.

Courtney, William H. and Leipziger, Danny M. (1973). "Multinational Corporations in LDCs: The Choice of Technology," mimeo, Washington D.C., US AID.

Currie, Lauchlin (1971). "The Exchange Constraint on Development—a Partial Solution to the Problem," ECONOMIC JOURNAL, Vol. 81, 324, December, pp. 886–903.

Dagnino-Pastore, José-María (1973). "A Policy for the Purchase of Technology by Latin American Countries," presented at Rehovot Conference on Economic Growth in Developing Countries, Israel.

Daniels, Mark R. (1969). "Differences in Efficiency Among Industries in Developing Countries," *American Economic Review*, Vol. 59, 1, March, pp. 159–71.

Davenport, R. W. (1967). *Financing the Small Manufacturer in Developing Countries*, New York, McGraw-Hill.

Dean, Genevieve (1972). "A Note on the Sources of Technological Innovation in the People's Republic of China," *Journal of Development Studies*, Vol. 9, 1, October, pp. 187–99.

Derossi, Flavia (1971). *The Mexican Entrepreneur*, Paris, OECD.

Dervis, Kemal (1973). "Substitution, Employment, and Intertemporal Equilibrium in a Non-Linear Multi-Sector Planning Model for Turkey," New Jersey, Unpublished Doctoral Dissertation, Princeton University.

Dhar, E. N. and Lydall, H. F. (1961). *The Role of Small Enterprises in Indian Economic Development*, Delhi, Asia Publishing House.

Díaz-Alejandro, Carlos F. (1971). "Labor Productivity and Other Characteristics of Cement Plants: An International Comparison," Yale EGC, DP-117.

—— (1973). "Turning from Import Substitution to Export-Promotion in Colombia," mimeo, Yale, EGC.

Di Tullio, Kathleen Ann (1972). "The Role of Small Industries in the Political Economy of Pakistan," Syracuse, N.Y., Unpublished Doctoral Dissertation, Political Science Department, Syracuse University.

Diwan, R. K. and Gujarati, D. N. (1968). "Employment and Productivity in Indian Industries—Some Questions of Theory and Policy," *Artha Vijnana*, 10, 1, March, pp. 29–67; cited in O'Herlihy, 1972.

Dougherty, C. R. S. (1972). "Substitution and the Structure of the Labour Force," ECONOMIC JOURNAL, Vol. 82, 325, March, pp. 170–82.

Eckaus, R. S. (1955). "The Factor Proportions Problem in Underdeveloped Countries," *American Economic Review*, Vol. 45, 4, September, pp. 539–65.

—— and Parikh, Kirit S. (1968). *Planning for Growth: Multisectoral, Intertemporal Models Applied to India*, Cambridge, Mass., MIT Press.

Economic Growth Center (1973). "Summary of Recent Research Results Relevant to Employment in Developing Countries," mimeo, Yale EGC.

Economic Growth Center (1974). "The Micro Analysis of Technology Choice and Employment," mimeo, Agenda for Workshop, Yale EGC.

Edwards, Edgar O. (1973). "Employment in Developing Countries," mimeo, New York, Ford Foundation.

Eriksson, John R. (1969). "Wage Policy and Economic Development in Latin American Countries." *Tijdschrift voor Sociale Welenschappen*, Vol. 14, 4, Special issue, pp. 82–99.

—— (1970). "Wage Change and Employment Growth in Latin American Industry," Williams CDE, RM-36.

Farooq, Ghazi M. (1971). "An Aggregative Model of Labor Force Participation in Pakistan," Yale EGC, DP-133.

Fei, J. C. H. and Ranis, Gustav (1970). "LDC Innovation Analysis and the Technology Gap," Yale EGC, DP-98.

—— (1972a). "Growth and Employment in South Korea and Taiwan," mimeo, Yale EGC.

—— (1972b). "A Model of Growth and Employment in the Open Dualistic Economy: The Cases of Korea and Taiwan," mimeo, Yale EGC.

Field, R. M. (1972). "Chinese Industrial Development: 1949-1970," in, Joint Economic Committee, *The People's Republic of China: An Economic Assessment*.

Fields, Gary S. (1972)."Rural–Urban Migration, Urban Unemployment and Under-Employment, and Job Search Activity in LDCs," Yale EGC, DP-168.

Figueroa, Adolfo (1972). "Income Distribution, Employment, and Development: The Case of Peru," Nashville, Tenn., Unpublished Doctoral Dissertation, Vanderbilt University.

Fisher, Franklin M. (1969). "The Existence of Aggregate Production Functions," *Econometrica*, Vol. 37, 4, October, pp. 553–77.

Frank, Charles R. Jr. (1968). "Urban Unemployment and Economic Growth in Africa," *Oxford Economic Papers*, Vol. 20, 2, July, pp. 250–74.

—— (1973). *Adjustment Assistance: American Jobs and Trade With the Developing Countries*, Washington D.C., Overseas Development Council, Occasional Paper.

Furtado, Celso (1967). *Development and Underdevelopment*, Berkeley, California University Press.

Galenson, Walter and Leibenstein, Harvey (1955). "Investment Criteria, Productivity, and Economic Development," *Quarterly Journal of Economics*, Vol. 69, 3, August, pp. 343–70.

Ganière, Nicole (c. 1972). *Transfer of Technology and Appropriate Techniques: A Bibliography*, Paris, OECD.

Granick, David (1957). "Economic Development and Productivity Analysis: The Case of Soviet Metal-Working," *Quarterly Journal of Economics*, Vol. 71, 2, May, pp. 205–33.

Gregory, Peter (1968). "Evolution of Industrial Wages and Wage Policy in Brazil 1959–1967," mimeo, Washington D.C., United States Agency for International Development.

Griliches, Zvi (1967). "Production Functions in Manufacturing: Some Preliminary Results," in M. Brown (ed.), *The Theory and Empirical Analysis of Production*, New York, NBER, Studies in Income and Wealth, Vol. 31, Colombia University Press.

Gruber, William H. and Marquis, Donald G. (1969). "Research on the Human Factor in the Transfer of Technology." in Gruber and Marquis (eds.), *Factors in the Transfer of Technology*, Cambridge, Mass., MIT Press.

Gustafson, W. E. (1962). "Research and Development, New Products, and Productivity Change," *American Economic Review Proceedings*, Vol. 52, 2, May, pp. 177–85.

Haq, Mahbub Ul. (1971). "Employment in the 1970s: A New Perspective," *International Development Review*, Vol. 13, 4, December, pp. 9–13.

—— (1973a). "Crisis in Development Strategies," *World Development*, Vol. 1, 7, July, pp. 29–31.

—— (1973b). "Developing Country Alternatives," in H. Hughes (ed.), *Prospects for Partnership: Industrialization and Trade Policies in the 1970s*, Baltimore, Johns Hopkins University Press.

Harbison, F. H. and Myers, C. A. (1965). *Manpower and Education*, New York, McGraw-Hill.

Harris, John R. (1970). "Some Problems in Identifying the Role of Entrepreneurship in Economic Development: The Nigerian Case," *Explorations in Economic History*, Vol. 7, 3, Spring, pp. 347–69.

—— and Todaro, Michael P. (1969). "Wages, Industrial Employment and Labor Productivity: the Kenyan Experience," *Eastern Africa Economic Review*, Vol. 1, 1, June, pp. 29–46.

—— (1970). "Migration, Unemployment, and Development: A Two-Sector Analysis," *American Economic Review*, Vol. 60, 1, March, pp. 126–42.

Hartley, Michael J. and Revankar, Nagesh (1972). "Labour Supply Under Uncertainty and the Rate of Unemployment," State University of New York at Buffalo, Economic Research Group, DP-228.

Hazari, Bharat and Krishnamurty, J. (1970). "Employment Implications of India's Industrialization: Analysis in an Input-Output Framework," *Review of Economics and Statistics*, Vol. 52, 2, May, pp. 181–86.

Helleiner, G. K. (1973). "Manufactured Exports from Less Developed Countries and Multinational Firms," ECONOMIC JOURNAL, Vol. 83, 329, March, pp. 21–37.

Herman, B. (1973). "On the Choice of the Optimal Industry: A Check of a Controversy," Rotterdam, Center for Development Planning, Erasmus Universiteit, Reprint Series No. 16.

—— and Tinbergen, J. (1969). "The International Division of Labor: A Quantitative Illustration," mimeo, Rotterdam, Netherlands Economic Institute.

—— and Tinbergen, J. (1973). "Planning of International Development," Rotterdam, Center for Development Planning, Erasmus Universiteit, Reprint Series No. 15.

Hirschman, Albert O. (1958). *The Strategy of Economic Development*, New Haven, Conn., Yale University Press.

Ho, Yhi Min and Huddle, Donald L. (n.d.). "The Contribution of Traditional and Small Scale Culture Goods in International Trade and in Employment," mimeo, Rice PDS.

Hogan, Warren (1968). "Capacity Creation and Utilization in Pakistan Manufacturing Industry," *Australian Economic Papers*, 7, June, pp. 28–53.

Hollister, R. G. (1968). "An Evaluation of a Manpower-Forecasting Exercise," in M. Blaug (1968).

Hong, Wontak (1973). "Factor Supply and Factor Intensity of Trade: The Case of Korea," mimeo, Seoul, Korea Development Institute, Interim Report 7304.

Hoselitz, Bert F. (ed.) (1968). *The Role of Small Industry in the Process of Economic Growth*, The Hague, Mouton.

Howe, Christopher (1971). *Employment and Economic Growth in Urban China*. London, Cambridge University Press.

Hughes, Helen (1973a). "The Scope for Labor Capital Substitution in the Developing Economies of Southeast and East Asia: A Sectoral Approach," IBRD, WP-140.

—— (1973b). "Trade and Industrialisation Policies: the Political Economy of the Second Best," IBRD, WP-143.

—— (1973c). "Import Substitution, Protection, and Development," presented at the Rehovot Conference on Economic Growth in Developing Countries, Israel.

—— (ed.) (1973d). *Prospects for Partnership: Industrialization and Trade Policies in the 1970s*, Baltimore, Md., Johns Hopkins University Press.

—— and You Poh Seng (1969). *Foreign Investment and Industrialization in Singapore*, Madison, Wisconsin Press.

Inaba, N. (1971). *The Economic Theory of Medium and Small Industries in Japan*, Kobe, Japan, Kobe University.

Indian Planning Commission (1973). *Technical Papers for Approach to Fifth Five-Year Plan*, New Delhi, cited in Blitzer (1973).

Instituto Latinoamericano de Planificación Economica y Social (ILPES) (1969). "Consideraciones Sobre Ocupación Industrial," Anticipos de investigación, Serie II, No. 8, Santiago, Chile; cited in Tokman (1927b).

Instituto Latinoamericano de Planificación Economica y Social (ILPES) (1972). "Ocupación y Estructura del Consumo: Ejercício con Incremento del 40 Porciento en el Consumo Familiar," Documento de trabajo, Santiago, Chile; cited in Tokman (1972a).

Intermediate Technology Development Group (ITDG) (1967). *Tools for Progress 1967–1968: Guide to Equipment and Materials for Small-Scale Development*, London, Allen and Unwin.

International Bank for Reconstruction and Development (IBRD) (1973). "Small Enterprises in Manufacturing: The Emerging Issues," mimeo, IBRD, DED.

International Labor Office (ILO) (1961). *Employment Objectives in Economic Development*, Report of a Meeting of Experts, Geneva.

—— (1970). *Towards Full Employment. A Programme for Colombia*, Geneva.

—— (1971). *Matching Employment Opportunities and Expectations: A Programme of Action for Ceylon*, Geneva.

—— (1972a). *Employment, Incomes, and Equality: A Strategy for Increasing Productive Employment in Kenya*, Geneva.

—— (1972b). *Fiscal Measures for Employment Promotion in Developing Countries*, Geneva, ILO.

—— (1973a). *Employment and Income Policies for Iran*, with mimeographed appendices, Geneva.

—— (1973b). "Scope, Approach, and Content of Research-Oriented Activities of the World Employment Programme," mimeo, Geneva.

Isard, Peter (1973). "Employment Impacts of Textile Imports and Investment: A Vintage-Capital Model," *American Economic Review*, Vol. 63, 3, June, pp. 402–16.

Ishikawa, Shigeru (1966). "Choice of Techniques and Choice of Industries," *Hitotsubashi Journal of Economics*, Vol. 6, 2, February, pp. 13–44.

—— (1972). "A Note on the Choice of Technology in China," *Journal of Development Studies*, Vol. 9, 1, October pp. 161–86.

Jackson, Sarah (1972). "Economically Appropriate Technologies for Developing Countries: A Survey," Washington D.C., Overseas Development Council, Occasional Paper.

Jain, S. and Tiemann, A. (1973). "The Size Distribution of Income: A Compilation of Data," mimeo, IBRD, DRC.

Jimenez, Gustavo (1972). "The Capital, Labor, and Import Content of Urban Consumption Patterns in Colombia," Houston, Texas, Unpublished Masters Thesis, Rice University.

Johansen, Leif (1972). *Production Functions*, Amsterdam, North-Holland.

Jolly, Richard and Colclough, Christopher (1972). "African Manpower Plans: An Evaluation," *International Labor Review*, Vol. 106, 2-3, August-September, pp. 207-64.

Kaldor, Nicholas (1960). *Essays on Value and Distribution*, London, Duckworth.

Karcher, Martin (1973). "Unemployment and Underemployment in the People's Republic of China," mimeo, Cambridge, Mass., Harvard University, Center for International Affairs.

Katz, J. M. (1969). *Production Functions, Foreign Investment and Growth*, Amsterdam, North-Holland.

—— (1973). "Industrial Growth, Royalty Payments, and Local Expenditure on Research and Development," in V. Urquidi and R. Thorp, *Latin America in the International Economy*, New York, Wiley, pp. 197-224.

Keesing, Donald (1966). "Labor Skills and Comparative Advantage," *American Economic Review Papers and Proceedings*, 56, May pp. 249-58.

—— and Manne, Alan S. (1973). "Manpower Projections," in L. M. Goreux and A. S. Manne (eds.), *Multi-Level Planning: Case Studies in Mexico*, Amsterdam, North-Holland.

Kennedy, Charles and Thirlwall, A. P. (1972). "Technical Progress: A Survey," ECONOMIC JOURNAL, Vol. 82, 325, March pp. 11-72.

Khan, A. R. (1970). "Capital Intensity and Efficiency of Factor Use," *Pakistan Development Review*, Vol. 10, No. 2, Summer, pp. 232-63.

Khan, Amir U. (1973). "Appropriate Technologies: Do We Transfer, Adapt or Develop?" presented at Ford Foundation seminar on Technology and Employment, Delhi; Laguna, Philippines, International Rice Research Institute.

Kim, Young Chin and Kwon, Jene K. (1973). "Capital Utilization in Korean Manufacturing, 1962-1971: Its Level, Trend and Structure," mimeo, De Kalb, Ill., Northern Illinois University.

Koga, M. (1968). "Traditional and Modern Industries in India," *The Developing Economies*, 6, 3, September, pp. 300-23.

Korean Institute of Science and Technology (KIST) (1973). *Final Report on a Study of the Scope for Capital-Labor Substitution in The Mechanical Engineering Sector*, IBRD, DRC.

Krishna, Raj (1972). "A Model of the Unemployment Trap with Policy Implications," in *Fiscal Measures for Employment Promotion in Developing Countries*, Geneva, ILO.

Kurz, Mordecai and Manne, Alan S. (1963). "Engineering Estimates of Capital-Labor Substitution in Metal Machining," *American Economic Review*, Vol. 53, 4, September, pp. 662-81.

Lancaster, Kelvin (1966). "New Approach to Consumer Theory," *Journal of Political Economy*, Vol. 74, 2, April, pp. 132-57.

—— and Lipsey, R. G. (1956). "The General Theory of Second Best," *Review of Economic Studies*, Vol. 24, 1, January, pp. 11-32.

Land, James W. and Soligo, Ronald (1971). "Income Distribution and Employment in Labor Redundant Economies," Rice PDS, P-9.

Lary, Hal, B. (1968). *Imports of Manufactures from Less Developed Countries*, New York, NBER.

Leibenstein, Harvey (1973). "The Transfer of Managerial and Technical Knowledge," presented at Rehovot Conference on Economic Growth in Developing Countries, Israel.

Lent, George E. (1972). "Tax Policy for the Utilization of Labor and Capital in Latin America," mimeo, Washington D.C., International Monetary Fund.

Leontief, Wassily (1954). "Domestic Production and Foreign Trade: The American Capital Position Re-examined," *Economia Internazionale*, Vol. 7, 1, February, pp. 9-38.

Lewis, Arthur (1966). *Development Planning*, London, Allen and Unwin.

Lewis, John P. (1962). *Quiet Crisis in India*, Washington D.C., The Brookings Institution.

Lewis, Stephen R. Jr. (1969). *Economic Policy and Industrial Growth in Pakistan*, Cambridge, Mass., MIT. Press.

Linder, S. B. (1961). *An Essay on Trade and Transformation*, New York, John Wiley.

Little, I. M. D. and Mirrlees, J. A. (1969). *Social Cost-Benefit Analysis, Manual of Industrial Project Analysis in Developing Countries: Vol. II*, Paris, OECD.

—— Tibor Scitovsky and Scott, Maurice (1970). *Industry and Trade in Some Developing Countries: A Comparative Study*, Paris, OECD.

Lluch, Constantino and Powell, Alan (1973). "International Comparisons of Expenditure and Saving Patterns," IBRD, DRC DP-2.

Lopes, F. L. (1972). "Inequality Planning in the Developing Economy," Cambridge, Mass., Unpublished Doctoral Dissertation, Harvard University.

Loucks, Daniel P. (1973). "Conflict and Choice: Planning for Multiple Goals," mimeo, IBRD, DRC.

Lubell, Harold (1947). "Effects of Redistribution of Income on Consumers' Expenditures," *American Economic Review*, Vol. 37, 1, March, pp. 157-70.

MacEwan, Arthur (1971). *Development Alternatives in Pakistan: A Multisectoral and Regional Analysis of Planning Problems*, Cambridge, Mass., Harvard University Press.

Magee, Stephen (1973). "Factor Market Distortions, Production, and Trade: A Survey," *Oxford Economic Papers*, Vol. 25, 1, March, pp. 1-44.

McCabe, James and Michalopoulos, Constantine (1971). "Investment Composition and Employment in Turkey," Washington, D.C., Agency for International Development, DP-22.

Mamalakis, Markos (1973). "Income Redistribution in Chile Under Salvador Allende," mimeo, Milwaukee, Wisc., University of Wisconsin-Milwaukee, Department of Economics.

Mansfield, Edwin (1971). "The Contribution of Research and Development to Economic Growth in the United States," in *A Review of the Relationship Between Research and Development and Economic Growth/Productivity*, Washington D.C., National Science Foundation, Office of Economic and Manpower Studies.

Marglin, Stephen (1963). The Social Rate of Discount and the Optimal Rate of Investment," *Quarterly Journal of Economics*, Vol. 77, 1, February, pp. 95-111.

Mardsen, Keith (1966). "The Role of Small Enterprises in the Industrialization of the Developing Countries," mimeo, Geneva, ILO.

—— (1969). "Towards a Synthesis of Economic Growth and Social Justice," *International Labor Review*, Vol. 100, 5, November, pp. 389-418.

—— (1970). "Progressive Technologies for Developing Countries," *International Labor Review*, Vol. 101, 5, May, pp. 475-502.

Mason, R. Hal (1971). "The Transfer of Technology and the Factor Proportions Problem: The Philippines and Mexico," New York, United Nations Institute for Training and Research, Research Report No. 10.

—— (1973). "Some Observations on the Choice of Technology by Multinational Firms in Developing Countries," *Review of Economics and Statistics*, Vol. 55, 3, August, pp. 349-55.

—— and Sakong, Il (1971). "Level of Economic Development and Capital-Labor Ratios in Manufacturing," *Review of Economics and Statistics*, Vol. 53, 2, May, pp. 176-78.

Mazumdar, Dipak (1973). "The Theory of Urban Underemployment in Less Developed Countries," mimeo, IBRD, DED.

Mehta, B. V. (1969). "Size and Capital-Intensity in Indian Industry," *Bulletin of Oxford University Institute of Economics and Statistics*, Vol. 31, 3, August, pp. 189-204.

Meissner, Frank (1973), "Capital and Technical Assistance Programs to Agricultural Marketing and Agroindustries in Developing Countries," mimeo, Washington D.C., Inter-American Development Bank.

Mellor, J. and Lele, U. (1971). "A Labor Supply Theory of Economic Development," Ithaca, N.Y., Cornell University Department of Agricultural Economics, Occasional Paper No. 43.

Merhav, Meir (1970). "Excess Capacity—Measurements, Causes and Uses: A Case Study of Industry in Israel," Vienna, UNIDO, *Industrialization and Productivity Bulletin*, No. 15.

Millan, Patricio and Schydlowksy, Daniel M. (1973). "Macroeconomic Consequences of Multiple Shifting: An Input–Output Approach," mimeo, Boston University, Center for Latin American Development Studies.

Morawetz, David (1973a). "Elasticities of Substitution in Industry: What Do We Learn from Econometric Estimates?", Jerusalem, Hebrew University, Economics Department, Research Report No. 51.

—— (1973b). "Optimal Commercial Policies in the Presence of Adjustment Costs," mimeo, Jerusalem, Hebrew University, Economics Department.

—— (1973c). "Extra-Union Exports from Customs Unions Among Developing Countries," Jerusalem, Hebrew University, Economics Department, Research Report No. 49.

—— (1974). "Output Composition, Technology, and Employment: Petrochemicals in Colombia," in Morawetz *et al.* (1974).

—— Thomas, John, Timmer, C. Peter and Wells, Louis (1974). *Studies of Inappropriate Technologies for Development*, Cambridge, Mass., Harvard University, Center for International Affairs, Monograph.

Morley, S. A. and Williamson, J. G. (1973). "The Impact of Demand on Labor Absorption and the Distribution of Earnings: The Case of Brazil," Rice PDS, P-39.

Mundlak, Yair (1973a). "Functional Forms of Production Functions: A Survey," mimeo, IBRD, DRC.

—— (1973b). "Estimation of Production Functions: A Survey," mimeo, IBRD, DRC.

Musgrove, Philip (1974). "The Estimation of Household Permanent Income from Cross Section Data: Colombia," Cambridge, Mass., Unpublished Doctoral Dissertation, Massachusetts Institute of Technology, forthcoming; to be available also from the Brookings Institution, Washington D.C.

Myint, Hla (1964). *The Economics of Developing Countries*, London, Hutchinson.

Nadiri, M. I. (1970). "Some Approaches to the Theory and Measurement of Total Factor Productivity," *Journal of Economic Literature*, Vol. 8, 4, December, pp. 1157–77.

Nayudamma, Y. (1973). "Patterns and Prospects for Technology Utilization in India," mimeo, University of Baroda, India.

Nelson, Richard R. (1968). "A 'Diffusion' Model of International Productivity Differences in Manufacturing Industry," *American Economic Review*, Vol. 58, 5, December, pp. 1219–48.

—— (1971). "Less Developed Countries, Technology Transfer and Adaptation, and the Role of the National Science Community," Yale EGC, DP-104.

—— Peck, Merton J. and Kalacheck, Edward D. (1967). *Technology, Economic Growth, and Public Policy*, Washington D.C., The Brookings Institution.

Nerlove, Marc (1967). "Recent Empirical Studies of the CES and Related Production Functions," in Murray Brown (ed.), *The Theory and Empirical Analysis of Production*, New York, NBER, Studies in Income and Wealth, Vol. 31, Columbia University Press.

Netherlands Economic Institute (1957–59). "Alternative Techniques of Production," Progress Reports No. 1, 2, 3 and 4 on filling and grinding, tuning, furniture, and wooden window frame production; cited in Tokman (1972b).

O'Herlihy, C. St. J. (1972). "Capital–Labor Substitution and the Developing Countries: A Problem of Measurement," *Bulletin of the Oxford University Institute of Economics and Statistics*, Vol. 34, 3, August, pp. 269–80.

Organization for Economic Cooperation and Development (OECD) (1969). *Promotion of Small and Medium-Sized Firms in Developing Countries Through Collective Actions*, Paris, OECD.

Pack, Howard (1971). "Employment and Industrial Growth—Some Cross-Section Results," mimeo, Yale EGC.

—— (1972a). "Employment and Productivity in Kenyan Manufacturing," *Eastern Africa Economic Review* Vol. 4, 2, December, pp. 29–52.

—— (1972b). "The Employment–Output Trade-off in Less Developed Countries: A Microeconomic Approach," mimeo, Swarthmore, Penn., Swarthmore College.

—— (1974). "Capital–Labour Substitution Possibilities in the Textile Industries," mimeo, Geneva, ILO (forthcoming).

—— and Todaro, Michael P. (1969). "Technological Transfer, Labor Absorption, and Economic Development," *Oxford Economic Papers*, Vol. 21, 3, November, pp. 395–403.

—— (1970). "Industrialization, Employment and the Choice of Alternative Vintage Equipment in Less Developed Countries," Yale EGC, DP-95.

Papanek, Gustav (1969). "The Industrial Entrepreneurs: Education, Occupational Background, and Finance," Cambridge, Mass., Harvard University, Development Research Group, Economic Development Report No. 128.

—— (1973). "Distribution of Income, Wealth, and Power," presented at Rehovot Conference on Economic Growth in Developing Countries, Israel.

Parnes, H. S. (1962). *Forecasting Educational Needs for Economic and Social Development*, Paris, OECD, Mediterranean Regional Project.

Patel, V. G. (1973). "Entrepreneurship Development: A Technology for Employment and Growth," presented at Ford Foundation Seminar on Technology and Employment, Delhi.

Peacock, Alan and Shaw, G. K. (1971). *Fiscal Policy and the Employment Problem*, Paris, OECD.

Perkins, Dwight, H. (1973a). "Plans and Their Implementation in the People's Republic of China" mimeo, IBRD, Economic Development Institute.

—— (1973b). "Growth and Distribution in the People's Republic of China," mimeo, IBRD, Economic Development Institute.

Phillips, Almarin (1969). "Measuring Industrial Capacity in Less Developed Countries," Philadelphia, Pa., University of Pennsylvania, Economics Department, Discussion Paper No. 110.

Pickett, James, Forsyth, D. J. C. and McBain, N. S. (1973). "The Choice of Technology, Economic Efficiency and Employment in Developing Countries," mimeo, Scotland, University of Strathclyde, Overseas Development Unit.

Poats, R. M. (1972). *Technology for Developing Nations*, Washington D.C., The Brookings Institution.

Porter, Richard C. (1973). "Some Doubts About Kenya's Future as an Exporter of Manufactures," Ann Arbor, Michigan, Center for Research on Economic Development, DP-31.

Ranis, Gustav (1957). "Factor Proportions in Japanese Economic Development," *American Economic Review*, Vol. 47, 5, September, pp. 594–607.

—— (1961). *Industrial Efficiency and Economic Growth: A Case Study of Karachi*, Karachi, Inter Services Press.

—— (1970). "Technology Choice, Employment and Growth," Yale EGC, DP-97.

—— (1972a). "The Role of the Industrial Sector in Korea's Transition to Economic Maturity," in Sung Huan Jo and Seong-Young Park (eds.), *Basic Documents and Selected Papers of Korea's Third Five-Year Economic Development Plan 1972-1976*, Seoul, Korea, Sogang University.

—— (1972b). "Technology, Employment and Growth: the Japanese experience," in ILO, *Automation in Developing Countries*, Geneva.

—— (1972c). "Some Observations on the Economic Framework for Optimum LDC Utilization of Technology," Yale EGC, DP-152.

—— (1972d). "Relative Prices in Planning for Economic Development," in D. J. Daly (ed.), *International Comparisons of Prices and Outputs*, New York, NBER, Columbia University Press.

—— (1973a). "Industrial Sector Labor Absorption," *Economic Development and Cultural Change*, Vol. 21, 3, April, pp. 387–408.

—— (1973b). "Employment and Labor Absorption in Development," presented at Rehovot Conference on Economic Growth in Developing Countries, Israel.

—— and Fei, J. C. H. (1969). "Technological Transfer, Employment, and Development," Yale EGC, DP-71.

Rao, R. V. (1967). *Cottage and Small Scale Industries and Planned Economy*, Delhi, Sterling Publishers.

Reddaway, W. B. (1962). *The Development of the Indian Economy*, London, Allen and Unwin.

Reynolds, L. G. (1965). "Wages and Employment in a Labor Surplus Economy," *American Economic Review*, Vol. 55, 1, March, pp. 19–39.

—— and Gregory, P. (1965). *Wages, Productivity and Industrialization in Puerto Rico*, Homewood, Illinois, Richard D. Irwin.

Rifkin, S. B. (1972). "Health Services in China," *Bulletin of Institute of Development Studies*, Sussex, Vol. 4, 2–3 June, pp. 32–8; cited in Stewart (1973).

Roberts, John (1972). "Engineering Consultancy, Industrialization, and Development," *Journal of Development Studies*, Vol. 9, 1, October, pp. 39–62.

Roemer, Michael (1972). "The Neoclassical Employment Model Applied to Ghanaian Manufacturing," Cambridge, Mass., Harvard University Development Research Group, Economic Development Report No. 225.

Salter, W. E. G. (1966). *Productivity and Technical Change*, 2nd edition, London, Cambridge University Press.

Sandesara, J. C. (1966). "Scale and Technology in Indian Industry," *Bulletin of Oxford University Institute of Economics and Statistics*, Vol. 28, 3, August, pp. 181–98.

—— (1969). "Size and Capital-Intensity in Indian Industry: Some Comments," *Bulletin of Oxford University Institute of Economics and Statistics*, Vol. 31, 4, November, pp. 331–34.

Scherer, F. M. (1970). *Industrial Market Structure and Economic Performance*, Chicago, Rand McNally.

Schumacher, E. F. (1972). "The Work of the Intermediate Technology Development Group in Africa, *International Labor Review*, Vol. 106, 1, July–December, pp. 75–92.

Schydlowsky, Daniel M. (1973). "Price and Scale Obstacles to Export Expansion in LDCs," presented at Rehovot Conference on Economic Growth in Developing Countries, Israel.

Sen, Amartya K. (1968). *Choice of Techniques*, 3rd edition, Oxford, Basil Blackwell.

—— (1969). "Choice of Technology: A Critical Survey of a Class of Debates," in *Planning for Advanced Skills and Technologies*, New York, Vienna, UNIDO, Industrial Planning and Programming Series No. 3.

—— (1973). "Employment Policy and Technological Choice," mimeo, London School of Economics.

Sharpston, Michael J. (1972). "Uneven Geographical Distribution of Medical Care: A Ghanaian Case Study," *Journal of Development Studies*, Vol. 8, 2, January, pp. 205–22.

—— (1973a). "International Sub-Contracting," mimeo, IBRD, DED.

—— (1973b). "Capital–Labor Substitution Possibilities: An Empirical Approach," mimeo, IBRD, DED.

Sheahan, John (1971). "Trade and Employment: Industrial Exports Compared to Import Substitution in Mexico," Williams CDE, RM-43.

—— (1972). "Import Substitution and Economic Policy: A Second Review," Williams CDE, RM-50.

Shetty, M. C. (1963). *Small-Scale and Household Industries in a Developing Economy*, Delhi, Asia Publishing House.

Sigurdson, Jon (1972), "Rural Industry—A Traveller's View," *The China Quarterly*, Vol. 50, April–June, pp. 315–32.

—— (1973). "Technology and Employment in China," presented at Ford Foundation Seminar on Technology and Employment, Delhi.

Silberston, Aubrey (1972). "Economies of Scale in Theory and Practice," ECONOMIC JOURNAL, Vol. 82, 285 (Supplement), March, pp. 369–91.

Singer, Hans W. (1964). *International Development: Growth and Change*, New York, McGraw-Hill.

—— (1973). "The Development Outlook for Poor Countries: Technology is the Key," *Challenge*, Vol. 16, 2, May–June, pp. 42–8.

Soligo, Ronald (1972). "Factor Intensity of Consumption Patterns, Income Distribution, and Employment Growth in West Pakistan," mimeo, Rice PDS.

—— and Land, James W. (1972). "Models of Development Incorporating Distribution Aspects," Rice PDS, P-22.

Staley, E. and Morse, R. (1965). *Modern Small Industry for Developing Countries*, New York, McGraw-Hill.

Stewart, Frances (1971). "The Choice of Techniques: A Case Study of the Manufacture of Cement Blocks in Kenya," mimeo, Oxford, Queen Elizabeth House; cited in Stewart (1972).

—— (1972a). "Choice of Technique in Developing Countries," *Journal of Development Studies*, Vol. 9, 1, October, pp. 99–121.

—— (1972b). "Trade and Technology," presented at Cambridge Conference on Development, Cambridge, England.

—— (1973). "Technology and Employment in Less Developed Countries," presented at Ford Foundation Conference on Technology and Employment, Delhi; Oxford, England, Queen Elizabeth House.

—— and Streeten, Paul (1971). "Conflicts Between Output and Employment Objectives in Developing Countries," *Oxford Economic Papers*, Vol. 23, 2, July, pp. 145–68.

—— (1972). "Little-Mirrlees Methods and Project Appraisal," *Bulletin of the Oxford University Institute of Economics and Statistics*, Vol. 34, 1, February, pp. 75–91.

Stiglitz, Joseph E. (1969). "Rural–Urban Migration, Surplus Labor, and the Relationship Between Urban and Rural Wages," *Eastern Africa Economic Review*, Vol. 1, 2, December, pp. 1–27.

—— (1973). "Alternative Theories of Wage Determination and Unemployment in LDCs: The Labor Turn-Over Model," Yale University, Cowles Foundation DP-335R.

Stolper, Wolfgang and Samuelson, Paul (1941). "Protection and Real Wages," *Review of Economic Studies*, Vol. 9, 1, November, pp. 58–73.

Stoutjesdijk, Ardy (1973). "Employment and Income Distribution in Peru," mimeo, IBRD, DRC.

Strassman, W. P. (1968). *Technological Choice and Economic Development: The Manufacturing Experience of Mexico and Puerto Rico*, Ithaca, Cornell University Press.

Streeten, Paul (1972). "Technology Gaps Between Rich and Poor Countries," *Scottish Journal of Political Economy*, Vol. 19, 3, November, pp. 213–30.

—— (1973). "Trade Strategies for Development: Some Themes for the Seventies," in P. Streeten (ed.), *Trade Strategies for Development*, London, Macmillan.

Subbarao, E. C. (1973). "Employment, Technology, and Universities," presented at Ford Foundation Seminar on Technology and Employment, Delhi.

Sunman, T. (1973). "Short-term Effects of Income Distribution on Some Macroeconomic Variables," Houston, Texas, Unpublished Dissertation, Rice University; cited by Soligo and Land (1972).

Taylor, Lance (1973). "Multisectoral Models in Development Planning: A Survey," mimeo, IBRD, DRC.

Thomas, John W. (1974). "The Choice of Technology for Irrigation Tubewells in East Pakistan: An Analysis of a Development Policy Decision," in Morawetz *et al.* (1974).

Thorbecke, Erik (1973). "The Employment Problem: A Critical Evaluation of Four ILO Comprehensive Country Reports," *International Labor Review*, Vol. 107, 5, May, pp. 393–423.

—— and Sengupta, J. K. (1972). "A Consistency Framework for Employment, Output, and Income Distribution Projections Applied to Colombia," mimeo, IBRD, DRC.

—— and Stoutjesdijk, Ardy (1971). *Employment and Output: A Methodology Applied to Peru and Guatemala*, Paris, OECD.

Thoumi, Francisco (1973). "The Utilization of Fixed Industrial Capital in Colombia: Some Empirical Findings," mimeo, IBRD, DED.

Tidrick, Gene M. (1970). "Wages, Output, and the Employment Lag in Jamaica," Williams CDE, RM-40.

—— (1972). "Wage Spillover and Unemployment in a Wage Gap Economy: The Jamaican Case," Williams, CDE, RM-47.

Timmer, C. Peter (1974). "Choice of Technique in Indonesia," in Morawetz *et al.* (1974).

Todaro, Michael P. (1971). "Income Expectations, Rural–Urban Migration, and Employment in Africa." *International Labour Review*, Vol. 104, 5, November, pp. 387–413.

—— (1973). "Rural–Urban Migration, Unemployment, and Job Probabilities: Recent Theoretical and Empirical Research," mimeo, New York, Rockefeller Foundation.

—— (n.d.). "The Case for Establishing an International or Regional Institute to Develop Needed Modern Labor Intensive Technologies for LDCs," mimeo, New York, Rockefeller Foundation.

Todd, John E. (1971). "Size of Firm and Efficiency in Colombian Manufacturing," Williams CDE, RM-41.

Tokman, Victor E. (1972a). "Technologia y Empleo en el Sector Industrial del Perú," mimeo, I-507-72-D, OEA-ILPES, Santiago, Chile.

—— (1972b). "Distribución del Ingreso, Tecnología y Empleo en el Sector Industrial de Venezuela," mimeo, I-620-72-S, OEA-ILPES, Santiago, Chile.

Turnham, David, assisted by Jaeger, Ingelies (1971). *The Employment Problem in Less Developed Countries: A Review of Evidence*, Paris, OECD.

United Nations (1968). *A System of National Accounts*, ST/STAT/SER.F/2/REV.3, New York.

United Nations Conference on Trade and Development (UNCTAD) (1970). *Trade in Manufactures of Developing Countries, 1969 Review*, New York, United Nations.

United Nations, Economic Commission for Asia and the Far East (UN ECAFE) (1971). *Small Industry Bulletin for Asia and the Far East*, New York, United Nations.

United Nations, Economic Commission for Latin America (UN ECLA) (1966). "Seleccion de alternativas tecnológicas en la industria textil latinoamericana," mimeo, Santiago, Chile.

United Nations, Economic Commission for Latin America (UN ECLA) (1967). "Small Scale Industry in the Development of Latin America," *Economic Bulletin for Latin America*, Vol. 12, 1, May, pp, 63–104.

United Nations Industrial Development Organisation (UNIDO) (1964). "Choice of Capital Intensity in Industrial Planning," Vienna, UNIDO, *Industrialization and Productivity Bulletin*, No. 7.

United Nations Industrial Development Organization (UNIDO) (1970). *Small-Scale Industries in Arab Countries of the Middle East*, New York, United Nations.

United States, Agency for International Development (US AID) (1972a). *Technology and Economics in International Development*, Washington D.C.

United States, Agency for International Development (US AID) (1972b). "Appropriate Technologies for International Development," Washington D.C., AID, Office of Science and Technology.

Unksov, Evgeny (1960). "Use of Welding in Machine Building," Vienna, UNIDO *Industrialization and Productivity Bulletin*, No. 3.

Vaitsos, Constantine (1970). "Transfer of Resources and the Preservation of Monopoly Rents," presented at Harvard Development Advisory Service Conference, Dubrovnik.

—— (1971). "Patents Revisited: Their Functions in Developing Countries," *Journal of Development Studies*, Vol. 9, 1, October, pp. 71–98.

Vaitsos, Constantine V. (1973). "Employment Effects of Foreign Direct Investments in Developing Countries," revised version, presented at Ford Foundation Conference on Technology and Employment, Delhi.

Vernon, Raymond (1966). "International Investment and International Trade in the Product Cycle," *Quarterly Journal of Economics*, Vol. 80, 2, May, pp. 190–207.

—— (1972). "U.S. Enterprise in Less Developed Countries," in G. Ranis (ed.), *The Gap Between Rich and Poor Countries*, London, Macmillan.

Vietorisz, Thomas (1969a). *Engineering Industry*, New York, United Nations.

—— (1969b). *Chemical Industry*, New York, United Nations.

Volunteers in Technical Assistance (VITA) (n.d.). *Village Technology Center Catalog: Tools for Development*, Schenectady, New York, Vita Inc., College Campus.

Walters, A. A. (1963). "Production and Cost Functions: An Econometric Survey," *Econometrica*, Vol. 31, 1–2, January–April, pp. 1–66.

Watanabe, Susumu (1972a). "International Sub-Contracting, Employment, and Skill Promotion," *International Labor Review*, Vol. 105, 5, May, pp. 425–50.

—— (1972b). "Exports and Employment: the Case of the Republic of Korea," *International Labor Review*, Vol. 106, 6, December, pp. 495–526.

Webb, Richard (1972). "The Distribution of Income in Peru," Princeton, N.J., Princeton University, Woodrow Wilson School, DP-26.

—— (1973). "Government Policy and the Distribution of Income in Peru, 1963–1973," Princeton, N.J., Princeton University, Woodrow Wilson School, DP-39.

Weisskoff, Richard, with Levy, R., Nisonoff, L. and Wolff, E. (1973). "A Multi-Sector Simulation Model of Employment, Growth and Income Distribution in Puerto Rico: A Re-evaluation of 'Successful' Development Strategy," mimeo, Yale EGC.

Wells, Louis T. (1974). "Economic Man and Engineering Man: Choice of Technology in a Low Wage Country," in Morawetz *et al.* (1974).

Westphal, Larry E. (1973). "Research on 'Appropriate' Technology," presented at Conference on Technology, Employment and Development, sponsored by Council on Asian Manpower Studies, Penang.

—— and Kwang Suk Kim (1973). "Industrial Policy and Development in Korea," mimeo, IBRD, DRC.

—— and Yung Whee Rhee (1971). "A Model for Evaluating Projects in the Mechanical Engineering Sector," mimeo, IBRD, DRC.

Williamson, Jeffrey G. (1971). "Capital Accumulation, Labor Saving, and Labor Absorption Once More," *Quarterly Journal of Economics*, Vol. 85, 1, February, pp. 40–65.

Willmore, L. N. (1972). "Free Trade in Manufactures Among Developing Countries: The Central American Experience," *Economic Development and Cultural Change*, Vol. 20, 4, July, pp. 659–68.

Winston, Gordon C. (1971a). "Capital Utilisation in Economic Development," Economic Journal, Vol. 81, 321, March, pp. 36–60.

——(1971b). "The Four Reasons for Idle Capital," Williams CDE.; revised and expanded as "The Theory of Capital Utilization and Idleness," *Journal of Economic Literature*, 1974 (forthcoming).

—— (1972). "On the Inevitability of Factor Substitution," Williams CDE, RM-46; *Journal of Development Economics*.

—— and McCoy, Thomas O. (1972). "Investment and the Optimal Idleness of Capital," mimeo, Williams CDE; *Review of Economics Studies*, 1974 (forthcoming).

Yamanaka, T. (1953). "The Nature of Small Industries: A Survey of the Economic Interpretation in Japan," *Annals of the Hitotsubashi Academy*, 4, October.

Yeoman, W. A. (1968). "Selection of Production Processes for the Manufacturing Subsidiaries of U.S. Based Multi-National Companies," Cambridge, Mass., Unpublished D.B.A. thesis, Harvard Business School; cited in Vernon (1972).

Young, N. G., Valenzuela, G. and Montes, P. (1974). "The Capacity of the Engineering Industry in Colombia: A Study of Equipment Development and Design in a Developing Country," mimeo, Geneva, ILO (forthcoming).

POSTSCRIPT

In the two years since the first draft of this survey was written one trend stands out in work on industrialisation and economic development: the increasing emphasis placed on equity as opposed to growth as a fundamental goal of development. Not just a privileged few but the mass of the people ought to take part in the development process.[1] A significant contribution to the recent literature has been made by the World Employment Program (W.E.P.) of the the International Labor Organization which, incidentally, was rather short-changed in the original survey; I was unaware of much of its work.[2]

If I were rewriting the survey from scratch today, I would place much greater emphasis on small-scale industries, both rural and urban. Take a typical less developed country with pressure on the land in the poor rural areas, and large urban centres full of backyard and frontyard workshops. Industrialisation in its standard form—building large, relatively modern factories in the cities—displaces smaller, often more labour-intensive workshops, and encourages in-migration by the rural poor who hope to get some of the newly created jobs. The net effect is that a few people find their standard of living improved, a few are made worse off, and most of the people of the country are untouched.

In most developing countries, if any dent is to be made in the economic problems of all the people, it must surely be by encouraging the two mass groups—the urban informal sector and the rural poor—to work together, to pull each other up by the bootstraps. Conditions of life in the villages might be improved by bringing electricity to them, extending the area under irrigation (digging more channels, using simple pumps), and building stronger houses. The supply of drinking water might be improved, better access roads to the fields constructed, and the development of small local industries encouraged (repair of simple implements, processing of agricultural products, furniture-making). Many of these are employment-creating, relatively labour-intensive activities. Not only would they help to stem the rural–urban migration flow by improving life in the villages, they could also enable the urban small-scale producers to be integrated into the development process. For example, governments could try to ensure that simple implements, pumps and the like are produced in small urban work-

[1] See for example Chenery et al. (1974), the I.L.O.'s draft document for its 1976 World Employment Conference (I.L.O. 1975), and the forthcoming book by Thorbecke and Pyatt (1976). For an important recent exploration of the micro-analytic underpinnings of many of the articles and theories discussed in the original survey, see Hawrylyshyn (1975).

[2] W.E.P. programs of research cover the connection between employment on the one hand and the urban informal sector (see e.g. Lubell 1975), technology (e.g. Bhalla 1975), income distribution (e.g. Maton, Paukert and Skolka 1975), trade expansion (e.g. Lydall 1975), population, and education on the other. For a summary of W.E.P. activities see I.L.O. (1974).

shops, and not by larger factories at home or abroad. They could do so either by ordering the goods from small producers directly, or by stipulating that each supplier have a minimum number of subcontractors. Small-scale urban producers could also be encouraged by other means (see section III.3 of the original survey), instead of regarded as a necessary evil as is often the case at present.

The upper and middle classes would presumably oppose such a radical change in strategy, and some way would have to be found to bring them into the industrialisation and development process without letting them dominate it. The challenge facing development economists today is to work out in full detail the economic and political implications of the increasingly heard slogan: "development for all the people".

REFERENCES

A. S. Bhalla (ed.) (1975), *Technology and Employment in Industry*, Geneva, I.L.O.
H. Chenery, M. Ahluwalia, C. Bell, J. Duloy, and R. Jolly (1974), *Redistribution With Growth*, London, Oxford University Press.
O. Hawrylyshyn (1975), "The Causes of Underemployment in Developing Economies: Some Micro-Analytic Clarifications," mimeo, Kingston, Ontario, Queens University, Institute for Economic Research.
International Labor Organization (1974), "World Employment Programme: A Progress Report on its Research-oriented Activities," mimeo, Geneva, I.L.O.
International Labor Organization (1975), "Employment, Growth and Basic Needs: Development Strategies in Three Worlds," mimeo, Geneva, I.L.O.
H. Lubell (1975), "The urban informal sector," mimeo, Geneva, I.L.O.
H. F. Lydall (1975), *Trade and Employment*, Geneva, I.L.O.
J. Maton, F. Paukert, and J. Skolka (1975), "Redistribution of Income, Patterns of Consumption and Employment: A Case Study for the Philippines," mimeo, Geneva, I.L.O.
E. Thorbecke, and G. Pyatt (1976), *Planning for Redistribution, Growth and Employment*, mimeo, Geneva, I.L.O.

IV

INFLATION: A SURVEY[1,2]

D. E. W. LAIDLER and J. M. PARKIN

I. INTRODUCTION

Inflation is a process of continuously rising prices, or equivalently, of a continuously falling value of money. Its importance stems from the pervasive role played by money in a modern economy. A continuously falling value of pins, or of refrigerators, or of potatoes would not be regarded as a major social problem, important though it might be for the people directly engaged in the production and sale of those goods. The case of money is different precisely because the role that it plays in co-ordinating economic activity ensures that changes in its value over time impinge upon the well-being of everyone.

Money is a means of exchange, a store of value, and a unit of account. The ability of an asset to act as a store of value is a necessary precondition to its fulfilling the role of a means of exchange. Hence, a falling value of money detracts from its desirability as a store of value and begins to affect for the worse the efficiency of the mechanism of exchange in a market economy. Money's role as a unit of account stems from its use as a means of exchange, and in this role too it is undermined by inflation. In particular its usefulness as a unit of account in transactions involving deferred payments is vitiated. Inflation thus has a potentially serious effect on credit markets.[3]

Inflation is, then, fundamentally a monetary phenomenon. Some would go further and agree with Friedman that "*Inflation is always and everywhere a monetary phenomenon*...and can be produced only by a more rapid increase in the quantity of money than in output" (Friedman, 1970, p. 24). Whilst few would deny that inflation is a monetary phenomenon in the sense that we have described, or in the sense that it is *accompanied* by a rise in the quantity of money, many would deny that its origins are monetary. Rather they would agree with Hicks that "our present troubles are not of a monetary character and are not

[1] This is the eighth of a series sponsored jointly by the Social Science Research Council and the Royal Economic Society.

[2] This survey has been prepared as part of the University of Manchester–S.S.R.C. research programme "Inflation: Its Causes, Consequences and Cures". Earlier drafts of the paper were presented at meetings of the Manchester Inflation Workshop and generated helpful comments from our colleagues, especially John Foster, Malcolm Gray, Jack Johnston, Alvin Marty, Graham Smith, Michael Sumner and George Zis. We have also received valuable comments from George Borts, David Champernowne, Brian Reddaway, Tony Thirlwall and from anonymous referees. We are grateful to all these and to Geoffrey Hilliard, Andrew Horsman, Linda Ward and Robert Ward for bibliographic assistance. The errors, omissions, misrepresentations and biases are our joint responsibility.

[3] Accounts of the social role of money were at one time a commonplace in the textbook literature. Developments in the so-called "new micro economics" which deal with behaviour in conditions of imperfect information have led to a revival of interest in this branch of analysis (cf., for example, Brunner and Meltzer, 1971; Feldman, 1973; Ostroy, 1973; Starr, 1972; Niehans, 1969; Laidler, 1974). Note that Alchian & Klein (1973) regard the effect of inflation on asset prices as sufficiently important for them to propose that conventional price indices in which asset prices are relatively unrepresented are inappropriate as bases for measuring inflation.

to be cured by monetary means", and that whilst "it was true in the old days that inflation was a monetary matter; prices rose because the supply of money was greater than the demand for it...money is now a mere counter, which is supplied by the banking system (or by the government through the banking system) just as it is required" (Hicks, 1975, p. 17). Some would go even further and agree with Harrod that the "new wage–price explosion is altogether unprecedented...the causes are sociological [and] first cousins to the causes of such things as student unrest" (Harrod, 1972, p. 44). It is virtually impossible in surveying a problem area as important as that of inflation, and one which generates such divergent views as those just cited, to be entirely fair to all positions. We have tried to be fair, but we are conscious that many will feel that we have not succeeded. We should declare at the outset, therefore, that, in terms of the alternative views cited above, we find ourselves in broad agreement with Friedman.

Since a large element in the debate on inflation centres on the direction of causation between money and prices it may seem natural to organise a survey of the literature around the traditional cost-push versus demand-pull distinction. The distinction is central to much of the literature surveyed here, but we have not, for several reasons, used it as a basis for our exposition. We find the distinction to be, first, imprecise – this imprecision being all too evident from the quotation with which Bronfenbrenner and Holzman (1963) began an earlier survey on this topic:[1] "The economic stalactite of inflated demand has met a sociological stalagmite of up-thrusting claims; when the stalactite and stalagmite meet and fuse in an icy kiss – I hope there is no geologist present to tell me that I am talking through my hat – nobody on earth can be quite sure where the one ends and the other begins" (Robertson, 1961). Secondly, the distinction implies that inflation can be analysed by examining separately the supply and demand sides of product and factor markets and investigating the forces making for shifts in functional relationships in all four areas. We do not believe that this way of looking at things accords well with the structure of much modern analysis of inflation. The role of excess demand as a proximate determinant of rising wages or prices lies at the centre of such analysis, but much of the analysis of the process of rising wages and prices is quite independent of whether the *source* of excess demand is a supply side or a demand side shift. Another major ingredient of modern theory is inflationary expectations and such expectations can influence both the supply and demand sides of both factor and product markets. It is helpful to distinguish between supply-side and demand-side factors when analysing a single micro-market, but the interdependence of aggregate demand and supply is a central feature of modern macro-economics. Since inflation is a phenomenon affecting the whole economy, we find the cost-push/demand-pull distinction analytically unhelpful as a device for classifying those developments in inflation theory that are grounded in macro-economics.

[1] A further earlier survey of inflation is Johnson (1963). Books which contain a large element of survey material but which also stand as major contributions to the subject at the time of their publication are Brown (1955) and Wilson (1961) as well as the I.E.A. conference proceedings edited by Hague (1962).

We have found the distinction between equilibrium, or perfectly anticipated inflation, and disequilibrium, or imperfectly anticipated inflation, more useful. Much recent work, particularly of a theoretical nature, on monetary explanations of inflation concentrates on the former, but clearly all the interesting and important practical questions concern macro-economic disequilibrium in which inflation is imperfectly anticipated: inflation can only be perfectly anticipated in any actual economy if all economic agents hold the same expectations, over each relevant time horizon, and are in a position to adapt their behaviour to them. The interaction of prices and wages with excess demand, unemployment, inventory changes and the like, when expectations and realisations are different, is an important element in the subject-matter of modern short-run macro-economics. Analysis of such problems goes back through the work of Keynes (1936) and Hayek (1933) to Fisher (1911) and Wicksell (1898). When expectations are not fulfilled the burden of adjustment falls partly on quantities of employment, output, and inventories, and partly on prices. Study of the behaviour of wage and price setters and their role in the transmission process of monetary and fiscal impulses to price and quantity decisions provides a necessary micro-foundation for macro-analysis and has attracted much attention recently. Discussion of the relevant literature takes up a large part of this survey. In surveying this literature, we also examine theories and evidence on the role of sociological or cost-push influences on inflation.

Much modern literature has returned to an older tradition in monetary theory in recognising that inflation is not, except in particular circumstances, a purely national phenomenon. Fixed exchange rates link countries together in a monetary union within which each country shares a common inflationary experience. The analysis of inflation in such a world has to be conducted at the level of the monetary union and not at the level of the individual nation state. As we shall see, the analysis of inflation as an international phenomenon is well developed for a world of fixed exchange rate countries but is still in its infancy as regards the behaviour of economies linked by temporarily rigid (or "jumping") exchange rates or by "dirty floating" rates.

These then are the main themes of our survey. We begin with an account of recent developments in the mainly theoretical analysis of fully anticipated inflation. Then we go on to deal with wage and price setting behaviour in situations of less than fully anticipated inflation, showing how such microanalysis may be incorporated into a "complete" macro-model of disequilibrium inflation. We next turn attention to inflation as an international phenomenon, after which, in the final substantive section of our survey, we deal with the consequences of inflation.

The reader will notice certain omissions from the list of topics that might have found a place in a survey such as this. First, we have hardly touched upon the extensive literature on inflation in less developed countries. Many of the issues involved in that literature are, of course, the same as those that arise in the context of the British or American economies, whence most of the applied work we discuss is drawn, but the interaction of inflation with the process of economic development provides an extra theme in literature on developing countries that requires expertise in development economics if justice is to be done to it. This expertise is possessed by neither of us, and since a survey article specifically on inflation in less developed countries by Kirkpatrick & Nixon (1975) already exists, we consciously chose to avoid dealing with this literature.

Our other major omission concerns explicit discussion of policy towards inflation as a separate topic. A good deal of policy discussion is, of course, implicit in the work that follows, and our omission is not as blatant as it might seem at first sight. Even so, policy aspects of the literature are relatively down-played in what follows, and for two reasons. First, a good deal of literature on anti-inflation policy, particularly in the context of the British economy, has been concerned with so-called "prices and incomes" policies, and one of us has only recently been involved in the preparation of a survey of that literature.[1] Secondly, and more important, in the process of preparing this survey we became painfully aware of an important gap in the literature in the area of what we might term the "political economy" of inflation; although, of course, much policy discussion in the post-war years did centre on political aspects of choice, which was sometimes considered to be constrained by a stable inflation–employment trade-off. The literature that we survey has a great deal to say about, and much light to shed upon, the behaviour of price and wage setters. It also has a great deal to say about how monetary and fiscal policy affects that behaviour. It does not have a great deal to say about why the particular policies which so often lead to inflation are pursued. A survey of the political economy of inflation will have to await the generation of literature to be surveyed, but it is within the context of this, as yet unwritten, literature, that we would ex-pect to find the fundamental issues involved in the design of policy towards inflation being clearly defined. As yet, in our judgment, they have not been.

2. THE QUANTITY THEORY AND PERFECTLY ANTICIPATED INFLATION

Though it has been under persistent challenge, the quantity theory of money has, in one form or another, dominated the literature on inflation for the greater part of the last three hundred years.[2] We therefore begin with an account of the post-war developments of this tradition as they impinge on the economics of inflation. The phrase "quantity theory of money" has two distinct meanings, and we use it here in its traditional sense to refer to a body of doctrine about the relationship between the money supply and the general price level, rather than in its more recent and narrow sense, to refer to a theory of the demand for money; although we shall see in due course that it is only in this latter sense that the quantity theory survives as a useful component of inflation theory.

The most attractive feature of the quantity theory as a theory of the price level is the simplicity that arises from its being a particular application of the

---

[1] Cf. Parkin, Sumner and Jones (1972).

[2] The first explanation of inflation in terms of monetary expansion seems to have been due to Jean Bodin, the seventeenth-century French philosopher, but it was the work of David Hume that estab-lished the dominance of the quantity theory in British economics. Viner (1937), particularly chapter VI, is still an excellent source on the development of the quantity theory tradition.

tools of supply and demand to the problem of determining a particular price, in this case the price of money in terms of goods, or to use the more familiar inverse concept, the general price level of goods in terms of money.[1] Certain preconditions must be met if supply and demand analysis is to be useful. First, the factors affecting the demand curve must be independent of those affecting the supply curve. Secondly, if price variations are to be attributed to supply curve shifts, as indeed they are in this particular application, the demand for money must be a stable function of rather few factors which in turn must remain relatively constant over time.

In the classical and neo-classical economic analyses with which the history of the quantity theory is inextricably bound, these conditions were assumed to be met. The demand for money was viewed as being proportional to the general price level or, equivalently, as being a demand for real money balances. With the determinants of the demand for real balances held constant and the demand for nominal money required to be equal to its nominal supply, the general price level was uniquely determined and proportional to the nominal money supply; in turn the percentage rate of inflation was equal to the percentage rate of change of the nominal money supply.[2] The determinants of the demand for real balances in neo-classical economics were the volume of real transactions, or the level of real income or even perhaps wealth – there is considerable ambiguity here – and occasionally, but not with any central importance being accorded to it, some measure of the opportunity cost of holding money.[3] The values of these variables were, according to neo-classical theory, determined by real factors such as population growth, technical change, productivity and thrift. Not only were these arguments few in number and independent of the money supply; they were also assumed to change so slowly over time that they could be regarded as constant for the purpose of analysing movements in the price level. In short, there was a completely real theory of allocation and distribution and a completely monetary theory of the price level – neutral money and the classical dichotomy.

The depressions of the 1920s and 1930s and concurrent developments in economic theory thoroughly undermined this view of the world. The central problem for monetary economics ceased to be the determination of the level or rate of change of prices and became instead the determination of the level of real income and employment. Variations in the money supply were accorded a role in influencing those variables, the classical dichotomy was given up, and the independence of the demand for real balances and the money supply, essential to the usefulness of the quantity theory, as a theory of the price level, was destroyed. Nevertheless, Keynes accorded the quantity theory validity as a special case of his "General Theory" applicable to a situation of pure inflation

[1] Pigou (1917) provides the most accessible account of the quantity theory cast in these terms.

[2] We implicitly assume zero real growth here. In a growing economy it is necessary to allow for the effect of growing real income on the demand for real balances. Also one should distinguish between the effects of growing *per capita* income on the one hand and growing population, *per capita* real income held constant, on the other. There is no reason why the aggregate demand for real balances should respond in the same fashion to aggregate growth coming from these two sources.

[3] On the importance (or lack thereof) of the opportunity cost of holding money in the demand for money function in pre-Keynesian monetary theory, see Patinkin (1974).

and full employment.[1] It is perhaps not surprising, therefore, that when the behaviour of the price level again became a central concern for policy after the second world war, there should be a revival of interest in the quantity theory.

This revival began in 1956 with the publication of *Studies in the Quantity Theory of Money*. In his introductory essay Friedman set out a theory of the demand for money and not a theory of the determination of prices, but work inspired by that essay was concerned with the role of money in generating inflation. However, the new quantity theory led to a more sophisticated theory of inflation than the pre-*General Theory* version. Though the opportunity cost of holding money played a role in pre-Keynesian discussions of the demand for money, that role was peripheral. Friedman's theoretical essay, however (in contrast to some of his later empirical work), laid stress on this matter, so much so that some writers have argued that this essay, far from reviving an earlier approach, represents a major contribution to the Keynesian tradition in monetary theory.[2] Specifically, he pointed out that a positive rate of inflation represented a negative yield on money balances and hence had a role to play in determining the demand for money. He thus predicted an inverse relationship between the demand for real money balances and the inflation rate.

Since a decision to hold money must be taken with respect to the future, it is the expected rate of inflation over some time-horizon that is relevant here rather than the actual rate that prevails at a particular instant. Even if we assume the constancy of other variables in the demand for money function, such as real income and the real interest rate, it is only permissible, in terms of the quantity theory as modified by Friedman, to predict that the rate of inflation will vary in proportion to the rate of monetary expansion if the expected rate of inflation is constant. It is hardly reasonable to suppose that the expected rate of inflation can be independent of the actual rate, so that the independence of the supply and demand sides of the market for money balances, essential to the traditional monetary analysis of inflation, begins to break down.

This problem would not undermine our ability to analyse inflation in terms of the supply and demand for money if the expected inflation rate remained constant over time, and it is usual to take it that this would be the case if the realised rate were to turn out to be equal to the expected rate.[3] If we did have such a state of affairs and if variations in the other arguments in the demand for

---

[1] See Keynes (1936), pp. 304–6.

[2] On this matter see Patinkin (1969). For Friedman's views on the same issue see Friedman (1972). In his famous empirical paper on the demand for money (1959) Friedman appeared to play down the importance of the opportunity cost of holding money in the empirical demand function. However, subsequent work by Friedman (1966) and Laidler (1966) showed Friedman's (1959) results to be misleading and established the empirical importance of the opportunity cost of holding money for the behaviour of velocity.

[3] This is not a point that can be taken for granted. It is not necessarily reasonable to suppose that, if individuals have made a correct forecast of a variable, they have no incentive to change that forecast in the future. They may well have other information apart from the value of the variable itself that would affect their expectations about it. Nevertheless so much of the literature on the influence of inflationary expectations on the demand for money rests on the assumption that equality of the actual and expected inflation rates implies no incentive to revise expectations as time passes that we maintain this assumption in the discussion that follows. We also follow the literature in assuming that economic agents behave as if they held their expectations with complete certainty and that they hold the same expectation about the inflation rate regardless of the time horizon considered.

money function – for example, real income and the real interest rate – could be ignored, we would predict proportionality between a given rate of monetary expansion and the rate of inflation. If the rate of monetary expansion then increased, we could also predict that, were the rate of inflation to increase by the same amount, and were this higher rate of inflation to be correctly anticipated, then there would be no forces in the system to cause the inflation rate to vary further. The inflation rate would have attained a new equilibrium value.

However, it is logically impossible that such a new equilibrium inflation rate could be established instantaneously when the rate of monetary expansion increases. The expected inflation rate affects the demand for money: if it rises, the demand for real balances falls. The higher is the *rate of change* of the nominal money supply, the higher will be the equilibrium *rate of inflation*. Hence for a given *level* of the nominal money supply the higher must be the equilibrium *price level*. Thus, if a new equilibrium inflation rate is to be established when the rate of monetary expansion is increased, inflation must proceed for some time at a greater than equilibrium rate.[1] But is the dynamic process which governs the behaviour of the inflation rate when it is out of equilibrium such as to ensure that the new equilibrium is reached? The predictions of the quantity theory about the proportionality of the equilibrium inflation rate to the rate of monetary expansion (given no change in real output, etc.) are of little practical interest if the equilibrium inflation rate in question is an unstable one. To put the same issue in another way, implicit in the interrelationship between the actual and expected inflation rates and the demand for money is the logical possibility of a "flight from money" leading to a self-generating and explosive inflationary process.

Though formulated in a different way, this problem was investigated by Keynes (1923) and by Bresciani-Turroni (1937), both of whom concluded that an explosive flight from money had not *in and of itself* been responsible for any of the particular inflations that they studied. The more recent literature has strengthened this conclusion. Friedman's analysis of the expected inflation rate as an argument in the demand for money function showed how this potential property of the inflationary process related to the general theory of the demand for money. Cagan formulated a specific version of the demand for money function and a specific hypothesis about the formation of inflationary expectations in terms of which econometric techniques could be brought to bear on the matter. Not that less formal analysis was superseded by Cagan's work: his results are heavily dependent upon the particular way in which he relates the expected to the actual inflation rate, while econometric techniques are particularly exacting in their data requirements. To give but two examples: Lerner (1956) in his study of the Confederacy and Patinkin (1972b) in his study of Israel

[1] Note that the above analysis is carried out on the assumption that the only monetary change at work here is an increase in the rate of expansion of the nominal money stock. The problem of the transition to a new equilibrium can in principle be avoided by cutting the *level* of the money stock to its new equilibrium value by a partial demonetisation of existing money at the same time as its rate of change is increased. Such a conceptual experiment is useful when analysing certain problems concerned with the role of money in growth models. It is a device used, for example, by Foley and Sidrauski (1971).

both took a more traditional approach in discovering that the inflations in question had not been self-generating.

Nevertheless, Cagan's paper posed and dealt with questions about the role of money in generating inflation with altogether more rigour than had previously been applied and produced results that have had applications far beyond the bounds of an exclusively monetary approach to inflation. Cagan confined his study to hyper-inflations where, he argued, fluctuations in the price level and the inflation rate swamped those in real income or the rate of return on capital goods. Hence he formulated a demand for real balances function in which the only argument was the expected inflation rate. Further, he postulated that the expected inflation rate adapted to the actual rate by being revised in proportion to the ratio of the actual to the expected inflation rate. Cagan chose a semi-logarithmic form for his demand for money function and his model can there-fore be written as

$$m - p = -\alpha \dot{p}^e, \quad d\dot{p}^e/dt = \beta(\dot{p} - \dot{p}^e)$$

where m is the logarithm of nominal money balances, and p is the logarithm of the price level, $\dot{p}$ the percentage inflation rate and the superscript e refers to the expected value of the inflation rate. Cagan shows that a self-generating inflation is impossible if the product of the parameters α and β is less than unity.[1] Thus econometric estimates of these two parameters provide vital evidence on the stability of the inflationary process.

Cagan estimated his model using data on seven hyper-inflations and was not able to reject the hypothesis that the stability conditions were satisfied. Thus he strengthened the conclusions reached less formally by Keynes and Bresciani-Turroni. A large number of subsequent studies of "rapid" in-flationary episodes have produced results broadly consistent with Cagan's. For example, studies of Argentina (Diz, 1970), Chile (Deaver, 1970), China (Hu, 1971), Brazil (Silveira, 1973a), Brazil and South Korea (Campbell, 1970), Turkey (Akyuz, 1973) all confirm that the sensitivity of the demand for money to the expected rate of inflation and the sensitivity of the expected inflation rate to the actual rate are both small enough to rule out a self-generated flight from money. Moreover, the sensitivity of the demand for money to the expected inflation rate in these countries seems to be of the same order of magnitude as that observed in other countries, such as the United States and Britain, when other measures of the opportunity cost of holding money, such as bond and bill rates, are used. This fact lends further strength to these con-clusions about the stability of the inflationary process.[2]

---

[1] Cagan's model produces a first order differential equation. Dutton (1971b) and Akyuz (1973) set out a difference equation version of Cagan's model that is second order and converges on a new equilibrium inflation rate with a time path that may, with plausible parameter values, be cyclical. One difficulty with Cagan's model is that it simultaneously has the money market always in equili-brium and real income given at full employment. Nevertheless, the actual inflation rate can depart from the expected rate. One might have thought that excess demand would be required for the latter effect, but none appears in the model (cf. Section 5 below). Note that Goldman (1972) modifies Cagan's model by dropping the assumption that the money market is always in equilibrium and finds its dynamic properties considerably altered by this modification. This problem might better be treated in terms of a "complete" model of inflation. Cf. pp. 774–81 below.

[2] Note that this is rather a broad generalisation drawn from a wide variety of empirical tests which

Now the foregoing analysis tells us that the rate of inflation has a stable equilibrium value if the rate of monetary expansion is constant. Further, if real income were constant, then that equilibrium value would be the rate of monetary expansion. We have the old quantity theory result then, but it was not obtained by the old quantity theory methods. It has proved impossible to maintain the assumption that one factor at least underlying the demand for money function – the expected rate of inflation – can be treated as independent of supply side factors. The key contribution of the revived quantity theory is to show that analysis which treats the demand function for real balances as independent of the behaviour of the money supply is both theoretically and empirically inadequate. In the long run the demand for real balances varies with the rate of change of the nominal money stock because that rate of change affects the actual and hence the expected rate of inflation. The question immediately arises as to whether the opportunity cost of holding real balances is the only variable on the demand side of the money market affected by the behaviour of the nominal money supply. Could the level of real income also be affected?

The work which we have considered so far has treated the behaviour of real income as exogenous. This assumption has been repeatedly questioned by work within the quantity theory tradition. In particular, it came in for a great deal of attention in the post-war literature on the integration of monetary and value theory. Such well-known contributions as those of Brunner (1951), Patinkin (1956), Archibald and Lipsey (1958), Clower and Burstein (1960) and Modigliani (1963) all dealt with the circumstances in which a change in the level of the money stock would change only the price level leaving the values of real variables unaltered. An important insight of this literature was highlighted by Marty (1964). He argued that the existence of monetary disequilibrium must imply the existence of disequilibrium *vis-à-vis* all assets and *vis-à-vis* consumption plans as well; that the demand for real money balances must be looked upon as interdependent with all other aspects of economic agents' utility-maximising choices and in particular with those involving the allocation of consumption over time. Now if different rates of inflation (expected and actual) imply different rates of return to real balances and hence provide economic agents with incentives to rearrange their portfolios, it follows immediately that, even if all real variables have equilibrium values that are independent of the *level* of the nominal money supply, there is no reason to suppose that those equilibrium values are independent of its *rate of change*.

A voluminous literature has dealt with this problem. To survey it fully would take us deeply into the fields of monetary theory and the theory of economic growth, but it will suffice to sketch its salient features.[1] First, virtually

---

on the whole did not attempt simply to replicate Cagan's results with other data. A tabular summary of much of the evidence on the interest elasticity of demand for money is to be found in the Bank of England (1970). The elasticity of demand for real balances with respect to the expected inflation rate, or with respect to short term nominal interest rates, seems almost universally to lie between 0 and −0·5.

[1] This literature whose major features are surveyed by Dornbusch & Frenkel (1973) has close links to that on the so-called "optimum quantity of money" problem (cf. Friedman (1969) and Feige and

all the analysis has been carried out in the framework of the neo-classical growth model initially developed by Swan (1956) and Solow (1956), despite the fact that, formally speaking, such models deal with a single output economy with continuous full employment in which it is hard to conceive of money having any role to play. In such a model, if technical change is ignored, the long-run rate of growth of real income is determined uniquely by the rate of growth of the labour force, this being fixed exogenously. Thus, the equilibrium inflation rate in such a model is still given by the quantity theory formula of the rate of monetary expansion minus the product of the income elasticity of demand for real balances and the rate of growth of real income.

However, in a neo-classical model the equilibrium level of the capital–output ratio, and hence the equilibrium level of real income, are determined by savings behaviour, and are susceptible to influence by the inflation rate along lines already sketched out above. The particular results generated here depend critically upon the assumptions made about savings behaviour. Tobin (1965), for example, assumes *per capita* real savings to be a function of *per capita* real disposable income. When money is included in the model its real rate of expansion adds to disposable income in a form that cannot be consumed but must be saved. Hence Tobin argues that an economy with money in it will grow at a lower capital–output ratio and a lower level of real income than a non-money economy. Johnson (1967a) argues that the utility yield on real balances should be included in disposable income as an item that must be consumed, and hence that the effect of introducing money (and of varying the rate of monetary expansion in a money economy) is ambiguous. There are virtually as many theoretical results in this literature as there are *a priori* plausible assumptions about the determinants of savings behaviour, but the almost universal result is that money is non-neutral. Variations in the inflation rate and hence in the rate of nominal monetary expansion do influence real variables.[1]

The lesson of the literature on money in growth models for those approaching the problem of inflation by way of the quantity theory of money is straight-forward. It is not just that behaviour on the supply and demand sides of the money market is interdependent; rather an analysis of that interdependence, even when only situations of long-run equilibrium are being considered, requires the construction and investigation of a complete general equilibrium model of the economy (albeit perhaps a highly aggregated one). Thus the most appealing feature of the old quantity theory tradition, namely that it enabled

Parkin (1971) for key contributions here). It is also closely related to the work on the "inflationary tax" on cash balances with which we deal in Section 6 below. See Burmeister and Phelps (1971) for a paper that explicitly recognises and exploits the interrelatedness of these problems.

[1] An exception arises in models of the type pioneered by Sidrauski (1967) in which the behaviour of the real side of the economy is kept independent of that of the money stock by making the marginal product of capital independent of the stock of real balances, and by maintaining it equal to an exogenously given rate of time preference. It is easy to be misled into believing that non-neutrality is introduced by explicit consideration of real growth. This is not the case. The key factor is that variations in the rate of monetary expansion affect the rate of inflation and that the latter variable is one of the relative prices affecting the allocative decisions of economic agents. Money can easily be shown to be potentially non-neutral in the special case of an economy with a zero growth rate (cf. Laidler, 1969b).

inflation to be treated as a problem susceptible to analysis with the tools of partial equilibrium supply and demand analysis, is totally undermined.

The one central feature of the quantity theory approach which is not undermined by the above analysis is the one insisted on by Friedman, that the quantity theory be formulated not as a theory of the price level but as a theory of the demand for money. It is crucial therefore to examine this feature of the quantity theory and ask whether its basic assumptions concerning the demand for money are supported or rejected by the empirical evidence. Those assumptions, as we have already noted, are that the demand for money is a demand for real balances and depends in a stable and predictable manner on the level of real income (or wealth) and on one or more opportunity cost (interest rate or expected inflation rate) variables. If such a demand function is a feature of actual economies then, although the price level cannot be determined simply by analysing the supply of and demand for money, the money market will, nevertheless, play a crucial part in a more complete and general analysis.

We have already cited evidence above about the stability of the demand for money function in conditions of rapid inflation, but Cagan's (1956) results are of little relevance to economies in which output fluctuations cannot be ignored. Although the other studies cited above (p. 748) do take output variations into account in generating their results, that evidence is drawn, by and large, from economies having relatively simple financial systems. It has been argued, notably by the Radcliffe Committee (1959) that for economies with sophisticated financial systems in which there exists a wide spectrum of assets of varying degrees of liquidity, the demand for money function will be much less stable.

There is, however, an overwhelming body of evidence against this general proposition, which has already been surveyed elsewhere (e.g. Laidler, 1969a; Bank of England, 1970). Even, indeed particularly, for economies as sophisticated as the United States or Britain, the aggregate demand for real money balances can be thought of as depending upon some measure of aggregate real income, and, with a rather low elasticity, upon the level of nominal interest rates, variations in which are thought of as capturing variations in both real interest rates and in inflationary expectations. More detailed and specific studies of the degree of substitutability between those assets usually classified as money – say the deposit liabilities of the commercial banking system – and other financial assets have consistently found the extent of such substitutability to be rather low. This matter has been extensively studied for the United States, and Feige (1974) provides a survey of the relevant literature. For the United Kingdom, less work has been done, but the study by Barrett Gray and Parkin (1975) suggests that the United Kingdom is no different from the United States in this respect.

It has been suggested by Kaldor (1970) that the apparent empirical stability of the demand for money relationship and the low degree of substitutability between money and other assets is the result of the supply of money being a passive variable in the economic system that simply adjusts to demand. He argues that if the monetary authorities were to pursue a policy of actively controlling the money supply, then the potential for an unstable demand for money function implicit in the structure of the financial system would soon manifest itself. As far as the United States is concerned, the evidence is strongly against this view. The studies of Friedman and Schwartz (1963) and Cagan (1965) carefully investigate the determination of the money supply in the United States using the techniques of the historian as much as those of the econometrician. They show that, although in certain episodes the supply of money did respond passively to demand, in most cases the direction of causation was clearly from supply side factors to demand side factors. Moreover, the same stable demand for money function can be shown to have existed under both types of monetary policy regime.

For Britain we have less evidence, but the institution of a new approach to monetary control in 1971 that lays greater emphasis on controlling monetary aggregates than did earlier methods promises to provide us with an important body of evidence on this question. So far we are aware of only one study on this question that exploits this new evidence (Artis and Lewis, 1975) and it produces results consistent with the proposition that the stability of the demand for money function in Britain survived the change in monetary policy regimes. Artis and Lewis do, however, argue that different econometric means must be adopted to measure the parameters of the demand for money function after 1971.

In short, there is every reason to believe that the stable demand for money function on which the quantity theory literature relies so heavily does exist over a wide variety of economies and financial systems. Thus, this literature is of considerable practical relevance. Changes in the quantity of money must, given the existence of a stable demand for money function, lead to changes in the values of some or all the arguments of the demand function. The form of those changes, and in particular the relative effects in the short-run adjustment process on real income (and hence employment) on the one hand and prices on the other cannot be predicted by the quantity theory.

The literature on such short-run problems has revolved around the so-called "Phillips Curve". As that literature has developed it has become increasingly apparent that the Phillips curve is no more capable of providing, by itself, a complete analysis of inflation than is the modern quantity theory of money. It provides a theory of labour market behaviour (and if extended to deal with price inflation, of goods market behaviour) but it is by now clear that in order to understand the short-run characteristics of the inflationary process it is necessary to analyse the interaction of markets, including labour, goods and money markets, in the context of a complete general equilibrium, or rather disequilibrium, system. Before we can go on to discuss the problems involved in achieving such a synthesis, however, we must first discuss the salient features of the literature on wage and price behaviour, and it is to that task that we now turn.

3. WAGE AND PRICE SETTING BEHAVIOUR AND EXPECTATIONS

The original stimulus, in the 1950s, for work on wage and price setting behaviour was the need to extend in an important direction the then widely accepted post-Keynesian framework for dealing with macro-economic issues.

That framework, enshrined in the Hicks (1937)–Hansen (1953) IS–LM model, treated the money wage rate (and in some versions the price level) as exogenous. It seemed natural and important, therefore, to extend that framework by explaining wage and price behaviour. How useful the framework might remain would, of course, depend crucially on the nature of the extension. Such an extension could take several forms, only one of which would leave the framework completely intact. This would be when wages and prices were completely independent of the state of aggregate demand, the central variable determined by the IS–LM model. In this case, inflation being determined by non-economic, institutional social and political factors, monetary and fiscal policy could, according to the model be used to achieve any desired level of aggregate demand and real income. At the opposite extreme, if wage and price inflation could be shown to depend *only* on excess demand, then only by analysing the interaction of the determinants of aggregate demand and of wage and price change could the rate of inflation and the level of real income (and employment) be understood. This would still be so even if, in addition to excess demand, inflation expectations also influenced wage and price change, provided such expectations themselves depended only on the previous history of inflation. In such a case, an explicit dynamic model of the evolution of real income and prices would be required to analyse inflation. Inflation and real income at any moment would depend not just on current demand creation policies, but also on their previous history. Of course, it was possible that an intermediate, more eclectic, position, would be a better representation of the facts than either of the two extremes just postulated with demand, inflation expectations, as well as socio-political and institutional factors proximately affecting the rate of wage and price change.

In the light of the above remarks it will be clear that the literature surveyed in this section is central to the problem of discriminating amongst competing hypotheses about the inflationary process around which much of the current policy debate revolves. First, we survey the literature on wage determination, then price determination and finally, since it features centrally in both of those areas, the determinants of inflation expectations.

The seminal contributions to the literature on wage inflation were empirical.[1] Brown (1955), Parkinson (1958), Phillips (1958), Klein and Ball (1959), Dicks-Mireaux and Dow (1959), Lipsey (1960), Dicks-Mireaux (1961) and Ball (1962) for the United Kingdom, and Bowen (1960a), Samuelson and Solow (1960), Bhatia (1961), Bodkin (1966) and Perry (1964) for the United States all found an inverse relationship between the rate of wage change and the unemployment rate.[2] Phillips, whose name more than the others has been

---

[1] Although Brown (1955) was the first to draw a scatter diagram showing the relation between wage change and unemployment, Irving Fisher (1926) seems to have been the first to discover and empirically investigate the basic idea. Also, it featured in the early econometric models of Tinbergen (1951) and Klein and Goldberger (1955).

[2] Similar findings for other countries are to be found in Kaliski (1964) and Reuber (1964) for Canada; Watanabe (1966) for Japan; Hancock (1966), Higgins (1973), Jonson et al. (1975), Nevile (1970), Parkin (1973b) and Pitchford (1968) for Australia; Gallaway, Koshall and Chapin (1970) for South Africa; Koshal and Gallaway (1971) for Germany; Modigliani and Tarantelli (1973) for Italy.

attached to that relation, made a particularly impressive contribution. He found that an inverse relation between wage change and unemployment derived from data for the United Kingdom for the period 1861–1913 could predict almost exactly the relationship between those two variables for the period between 1951 and 1957. However, as Knowles and Winsten (1959), Routh (1959) and Griffin (1962) were quick to point out, this gave a somewhat misleading impression of the nature of the stylised facts about the relation between wage change and unemployment. Those stylised facts for the United Kingdom[1] had four features, to which recent experience has added a fifth. First, there is a weak inverse correlation between wage change and unemployment.[2] Secondly, for the 19th century there are well-defined anti-clockwise loops in the relationship. (For any given level of unemployment, the rate of wage change was higher if unemployment was falling and lower if unemployment was rising.) Thirdly, in the post-second world war period the loops are still present but are clockwise. Fourthly, for the inter-war years the relation between wage change and unemployment is so weak as to be barely discernible. Fifthly, in the late 1960s and 1970s there has been a tendency for wage inflation and unemployment either to rise together or for wage inflation to rise independently of the unemployment rate. It is this latest development which has led many to search for an explanation for a "new inflation".

Theoretical work on wage inflation up to the middle 1960s focused on the negative correlation between wage change and unemployment and on the anti-clockwise loops. The first attempt was that of Lipsey (1960),[3] whose central idea was that the Phillips curve derives from two behavioural relations: first, a positive relation between wage change and excess demand for labour and second an inverse (and non-linear) relation between excess demand and unemployment as well as the rate of change of unemployment. The existence of a wage reaction function was justified by appeal to Walrasian *tâtonnement* but the hypothesis about the relation between excess demand and unemployment was novel and, therefore, given a fuller explanation.

Any change in the unemployment rate is equal to the difference between the quit rate and the hiring rate. Lipsey assumed the quit rate to be constant and hiring to respond positively both to the number of people looking for jobs (unemployment) and the number of jobs available (vacancies). Since excess demand for labour is by definition equal to the difference between vacancies and unemployment, the hiring rate depends positively on the unemployment rate and the level of excess demand. The rate of change of unemployment will thus vary inversely with both the unemployment rate and excess demand, from which the existence of an inverse relation between excess demand, unemployment and its rate of change immediately follows. Combining this with the

---

[1] The stylised facts for the United States and the other major countries are broadly the same as for the United Kingdom in the post-war period but, with the exception of the United States, little is known about other countries' wage and unemployment behaviour for earlier periods.

[2] Lipsey reports the simple correlation between wage change and the best fitting non-linear form of unemployment as 0·64 for the period 1862–1913.

[3] Alternative theories of the Phillips curve may be found in Sargan (1964), Kuska (1966), Corry and Laidler (1967), Kuh (1967) and Hansen (1970). Also an attack on the conventional theory has been presented by Holmes and Smyth (1970).

wage reaction function yields the proposition that the rate of wage change will be an inverse function of both the unemployment rate and its rate of change, thus generating an (on average) downward sloping relation between wage change and unemployment and an anti-clockwise loop configuration as unemployment moves through a cycle.[1] Phelps (1968) derived the same basic relation in a more general way and one which has a more appealing microeconomic foundation. In his analysis each firm sets its wage offer. so as to achieve a wage relative to its expectation of the market average wage which depends upon the average unemployment and vacancy rates and the firm's own vacancy rate. Vacancies are in turn shown to depend on the level and rate of change of unemployment.

Lipsey's theory of the Phillips curve cannot explain the large fluctuations in wage change relative to unemployment during the inter-war years or the tendency for there to be an upward sloping relation with clockwise loops in the post-war years. These facts raise questions about the stability of the inflation unemployment trade off and about whether it is more than a short-run phenomenon. Phelps's (1968) approach, as well as that of Friedman (1968), suggests that there is one systematic factor giving rise to shifts in the short-run wage change – unemployment trade off which not only ensures that in the long run the trade-off disappears but which also gives rise to the possibility of clockwise loops about an inverse relationship in the short run. The central idea of both Friedman and Phelps is the same. Both argue in effect that Lipsey's basic money-wage reaction function is an incomplete specification of the forces that make for money-wage change. They suggest (with different underlying stories) that the rate of money-wage change will be equal to the expected rate of inflation plus some adjustment for excess demand.

Friedman's argument is that it is *real* wages and not money wages which respond to excess demand. If that is so then *money* wages will respond both to excess demand and to expected changes in prices, in the latter case with a coefficient of unity. Phelps's analysis, briefly described above, leads firms to change their wage offers by the amount they expect other firms to change theirs, provided they are happy with their relative market positions. However, if a firm has an excess demand for labour (excessive vacancies) it will raise its wages by more than it expects others to be raising theirs and conversely for an excess supply. Thus, if all firms taken together have an excess demand for labour, wages will be raised on average by more than each firm is expecting the others to raise theirs. Thus, averaging over all firms, the rate of wage change will equal the expected rate of wage change plus an adjustment for

---

[1] It is interesting to note that Lipsey (1960) did not present the above analysis as an explanation for the loops. All the analysis is there in an extended footnote (footnote 1, p. 15) but its implications for the loops were not drawn out by Lipsey. Instead he used an aggregation argument starting from the proposition that the national labour market was made up of a number of micro labour markets each with its own "Phillips curve". As unemployment rose from a boom to a slump, Lipsey postulated that there would be a decrease in the dispersion of unemployment across the micro labour markets, whilst when the economy was moving from a slump to a boom, there would be an increase in dispersion. It follows from the non-linearity of the micro Phillips relation that the larger is the dispersion, the higher is the average rate of wage change. Hence with Lipsey's assumption anti-clockwise loops would be generated as an aggregation phenomenon.

excess demand. Both Phelps's and Friedman's explanations are identical in a world of zero productivity growth and easy to reconcile provided one recognises that in the Friedman formulation the time path of the real wage will depend on productivity growth. Both hypotheses are capable of generating clockwise loops in a wage change–unemployment space, and can thus account for periods of positive correlation between the two variables, so long as inflation expectations are generated by some simple distributed lag function of previous inflation. A full analysis of these matters is provided by Brechling (1968).

More rigorous choice-theoretic analyses of the Phillips relation have been provided by Lucas and Rapping (1969), Alchian (1960), Mortensen (1970), Gordon and Hynes (1970) and Gronau (1971). Each of these studies views the short-run Phillips curve as a short-run labour supply function and ignores involuntary unemployment arising from lay-offs. They also reverse the direction of causation between the variables postulated by Lipsey and Phelps, and return to Fisher's (1926) original interpretation, under which the causation is viewed as running from inflation to unemployment. However, in agreement with Friedman and Phelps, the analyses predict instability in the short-run relation between the variables and the absence of a long-run inflation–employment trade off. Lucas and Rapping develop a two-period analysis of a utility maximising household which supplies labour as a function of the actual and expected level of both money wages and prices. Unemployment is the difference between the supply of labour and the amount demanded by profit maximising firms. They show that these two propositions taken together imply a short-run inverse relation between inflation and unemployment.

Alchian provides a general theoretical analysis of the causes of resource (human and non-human) unemployment which, in broad terms, is similar to Mortensen's specific labour market analysis. The latter studies household job search under conditions of uncertainty. There are three types of households: those who are unemployed, those who are employed and deciding whether or not to quit their jobs in order to become unemployed searchers, and, third, those who are employed and deciding whether or not to quit their present job to take up a new job immediately. The household has in mind a wage which it believes with certainty it could obtain after a certain period of search. It also faces a concrete wage offer (or existing wage), and has to decide whether or not to accept the offer (or retain the job which provides the existing wage in the case of an employed person) or to remain (become) unemployed in order to seek a better wage. The household compares the present value of the income that it would obtain by accepting a job at a low wage with that of waiting (for a presumed known period) in order to obtain a job with a higher wage. The model predicts that the higher is the actual rate of wage change relative to the expected rate of wage change the fewer people will be unemployed and searching for a job. In addition, with a minimum of contrivance, Mortensen shows that the resulting relation between wage change and unemployment (for a given level of expected wage change) will not only be inverse but will also display anti-clockwise loops. He further shows that the equilibrium unemployment rate is independent of the rate of inflation.

Wages are determined in both the Lucas and Rapping and Mortensen models as a result of the interaction of the supply (Phillips curve) and demand sides of the labour market. Lucas and Rapping have a neo-classical demand for labour function. Mortensen has firms who choose a time path for wages to maximise their present values subject to an assumed Phillips curve labour supply constraint. Both models are incomplete in the sense that they hold expectations constant, but they do emphasise that the relevant expectations in the Phillips relation are those of workers and not those of firms.

The great difficulty with all this analysis in that it treats *all* unemployment as voluntary. Workers always voluntarily quit to search for better jobs and choose to remain unemployed until they have found their expected wealth (or utility) maximising offer. Lay-offs are ignored and their satisfactory explanation is clearly an important problem area for further research. Whether the qualitative conclusions of these models concerning the relationships between the actual and expected rates of wage change and unemployment will survive an adequate incorporation of involuntary lay-offs is, at this stage, an open question.

The theoretical arguments outlined above all deal with atomistically competitive markets. Theoretical work has also been done on monopolistic markets in which trade unions and monopolistic firms set wages. Much of this literature has been surveyed by De Menil (1971). He points out that whilst a variety of different bargaining models could be applied to the wage determination process their varying assumptions all lead to certain common results. The fixed threat game models of Nash (1950, 1953), Raiffa (1953) and Bishop (1963) and the non-game theoretic approaches of Zeuthen (1930), Harsanyi (1966), Hicks (1932), Foldes (1964), Cross (1965, 1966) and Coddington (1966, 1968) have in common the prediction of maximisation of the gains from trade and a sharing of those gains in proportion to the relative marginal disutility that each party could and would, but never does, inflict upon the other. In addition these models all predict that the rate of wage change thus determined will be homogeneous of degree one in all money prices which are assumed to be relevant. Which other prices are deemed relevant depends upon the detail of the analysis in question but could include product price and the price of labour in the competitive sector as well as taxes. The homogeneity prediction is also found in Johnston's (1972) model. Here only the firm takes an active part in the wage setting process.

None of these monopolistic models leads directly to the same detailed predictions as the competitive models, but there is no obvious conflict between them. The rate of unemployment is a natural variable to use as an indicator of the relative bargaining strengths of the two parties and expected inflation variables have an identical role to play in both competitive and monopolistic markets. A theoretical basis for the relation between wage change and unemployment may thus be derived either from competitive or monopolistic analysis but in either case the prediction is that the relationship will be crucially influenced by some expected rate of inflation.[1] Furthermore, both approaches predict that

---

[1] The expected rate of inflation of wages in the case of Phelps, of prices in the case of Friedman and of a variety of non-union wage variables and product prices in the case of monopolistic models.

the coefficient on the expected rate of inflation in the wage inflation equation will be unity. This implies that equilibrium situations in which the actual and expected rates of inflation are equal will all have the same unemployment rate regardless of the rate of inflation. How dependent these conclusions are on the – often unstated – assumptions that all economic agents hold the same expectations, and act as if they did so with perfect certainty, remains to be seen. They do, however, imply that, if inflation expectations are formed solely on the basis of past values of the actual rate of inflation, there will be a long-run trade off between *not the level of but the rate of change of the rate of inflation* and the *level of unemployment*.

The unemployment rate at which these models generate a stationary rate of inflation may be called an equilibrium rate in the sense that it is the rate which rules when expectations are fulfilled and therefore (on the model's assumptions) unchanging. This equilibrium unemployment rate is independent of the steady state inflation rate and often called the "natural" unemployment rate. However, it will not in general be constant. Its level depends upon a number of factors that might well vary. This is brought out very clearly for example by Mortensen's analysis in which the "natural" rate depends positively upon the degree of dispersion of wage offers, the rate at which new workers enter the labour force and the frequency with which employed workers consider quitting to search for a better job, negatively upon the frequency with which an employed worker receives an offer and ambiguously on the frequency with which an unemployed worker receives an offer.[1] Tobin (1972) has suggested that it is misleading to regard the natural unemployment rate as involving only a voluntary search unemployment. Dispersion across labour markets with asymmetric wage responses will mean that when there is no inflationary pressure on wages there is still an excess of unemployment over vacancies. There is a substantial literature on the role of dispersion in affecting the position of the short-run inflation–unemployment trade off and hence, by implication, the "natural" unemployment rate, and this subject is taken up below in more detail.

Phelps's (1972) discussion of the determination of the natural unemployment rate suggests that inflation may be non-neutral, that it may affect real rates of interest and real after-tax wages, by substituting the inflation tax for income tax, and thereby affect the equilibrium amount of consumption, leisure and search unemployment. He also suggests that the relationship in question may display "hysteresis", the equilibrium unemployment rate at any time depending on the previous path of inflation and unemployment. Akerlof (1969) and Stephens (1974) go even further and show that, in models where wages and prices are changed at fixed intervals, the "natural" unemployment rate might (on their assumptions) depend *positively* on the rate of inflation. It is clear from these pieces of analysis that it cannot be taken for granted on theoretical grounds that the size of the steady inflation unemployment rate is a constant or that no

---

[1] The reason for this counter-intuitive result is that an increase in the frequency of job offers to unemployed workers is assumed to (a) raise the job acceptance rate which lowers the "natural" unemployment rate and (b) lower the cost of search unemployment which raises the "natural" rate. The net effect cannot be assigned *a priori*.

long-run unemployment–inflation trade off exists. The factors which determine the natural unemployment rate as well as the nature of the long-run trade off between inflation and unemployment require further theoretical and particularly empirical investigation.

Empirical studies which have tested some form of the expectation–excess demand model of wage inflation abound. Broadly speaking, they show that the basic model is consistent with data taken from the United States (Brechling, 1968; Lucas and Rapping, 1969; Gordon, 1971; Nordhaus, 1972 b; Turnovsky and Wachter, 1972), Canada (Kaliski, 1972; Vanderkamp, 1972; Turnovsky, 1972), the United Kingdom (Parkin, Sumner & Ward, 1975; McCallum, 1975), Australia, (Parkin, 1973 b), and the aggregate "Group of Ten" countries (Duck et al., 1975). The size of the coefficient on the expected rate of inflation is not always unity as predicted by so many theoretical models but there are grounds for questioning many of the estimates in question. These grounds are discussed in detail below where we consider inflation expectations.

Most empirical studies of wage inflation have examined the effects on wages of factors other than excess demand and inflation expectations. In some studies these factors are seen as merely modifying the wage inflation–unemployment trade off, but in others the very existence and usefulness of the concept of an unemployment-wage inflation trade off is denied. First, we will deal with work which is entirely within the spirit of the expectations–excess demand model already discussed and then go on to examine work critical of that approach.

Recent empirically oriented studies by Gordon (1973) and Parkin et al. (1975) have suggested that a fully developed expectations hypothesis would have the rate of wage change depend upon the expected rates of change of all variables that affect the excess demand for labour. Phelps's "expected rate of wage change" is of course a variable which subsumes all such factors. However, it is possible to be more explicit and recognise that the expected rate of wage change will depend upon expected changes in such variables as payroll taxes, income taxes, foreign and domestic wholesale prices as well as domestic retail prices. Foreign price changes would be especially important in a fixed exchange rate open economy where they would have a direct and immediate effect upon the value of the marginal product of domestic labour and therefore on money wages. Such a line of argument does, however, imply that many difficult problems associated with measuring such expectations would be encountered in empirical work.

An important branch of the literature on wage inflation (still within the excess demand–expectations framework) deals with the effects of aggregation on observed relationships between variables. This issue was raised by Lipsey in his discussion of the Phillips curve loops. Data on industrial and regional unemployment make it possible to investigate the effects on average wage change of the structure of unemployment. These matters have been investigated by examining regional Phillips curves (Cowling and Metcalf (1967); Thirlwall (1969, 1970); Metcalf (1971); MacKay and Hart (1974) for the United Kingdom and Albrecht (1966), Kaun (1965); Kaun and Spiro (1970) for the United States) and by explicit aggregation over regional data (Archibald

(1969), Thomas and Stoney[1] (1971), Archibald, Kemmiss and Perkins (1974) for the United Kingdom, and Brechling (1973) for the United States). The central idea which emerges from Archibald's 1969 work is that the variance of the distribution of unemployment either between regions or industries should appear systematically to influence national average wage inflation.

Although Archibald's 1969 paper seemed to find evidence of this effect and expressed some optimism concerning the possibility of improving the overall short-run inflation–unemployment trade off by policies designed to reduce regional dispersion in unemployment rates his optimism may have been premature. First, at the empirical level, both Hines (1972) and in a subsequent paper Archibald et al. (1974) conclude that "for the post-war period at least, the aggregation or 'structuralist' hypothesis is poorly supported".[2] Secondly, even if it could be shown that the aggregate trade off depended on the structure of unemployment, it would be wrong to conclude that dispersion minimisation was the way to achieve the best possible trade off. Burns (1972) has shown that it is micro Phillips curve slope equalisation and not dispersion minimisation which is required to achieve the best possible trade off. In the light of the estimates of the slopes of regional Phillips curves in the cases cited above (provided those slopes could be projected outside the sample range (see Leslie, (1973)), dispersion minimisation would actually worsen the United Kingdom aggregate short-run trade off. A recent paper by Thomas (1974) on an industry cross-section study shows there to be important slope differences between industries thereby giving potential additional weight to Burns's point.

In addition to dealing with explicit aggregation, Brechling (1973) Thomas and Stoney (1971) and Mulvey and Trevithick (1974) have considered the possibility of transmission of wage change from "leading sectors" through to the rest of the economy. This hypothesis seems to work well. Using American data, Brechling found evidence for a transmission from leading sectors to the rest of the economy where the leading sector was defined as the high wage sector. Working with the United Kingdom data, Stoney and Thomas found a similar effect, but they defined the leading sector as that with the lowest unemployment rate.[3] Using data for Ireland, Mulvey and Trevithick find transmission from a "key" occupational sector.

A variety of other labour-market structural hypotheses have been advanced, most comprehensively perhaps, by Holt (1970b). In empirical work using United States data, Perry (1970) suggests that changes in the sex and age composition of the labour force have affected the Phillips curve during the 1960s; Gordon (1971) casts some doubt on the importance of those considerations and suggests instead that unemployment dispersion and hidden unemployment are better indicators of changing labour market tightness; Packer and Park (1973) use a variable which is designed to measure distortion in the relative wage structure and find a significant role for that and Flanagan (1973) investigates the role of the duration of unemployment.

[1] See also the exchange between Sharot (1973) and Thomas (1973).

[2] Archibald et al. (1974), p. 156.

[3] There is probably no difference between these two since for the United Kingdom the lowest unemployment region, London and the South East, is also the highest wage region.

A related problem concerns the selection of the most appropriate labour-market excess demand pressure variable. All the early studies, with the exception of Dicks-Mireaux (1961), and most of the more recent studies used the recorded unemployment rate. Dicks-Mireaux used an index of excess demand (cf. Dow and Dicks-Mireaux, 1958) based on unemployment and vacancies. Taylor (1970) calculated, and used in earnings equations, a measure of unemployment which included estimates of hoarded labour. Simler and Tella (1968) used a "labour reserves" variable based on variations in participation rates. For most of the time, the relationship between the alternative measures is sufficiently stable for a choice between them not to be too crucial. However, recently there have been some shifts in the relationship between unemployment and vacancies and there is room for some debate about alternative proxies for excess demand.[1]

None of the work surveyed so far challenges the basic notion of a short-run trade off between inflation and unemployment with inflation expectations removing or at least weakening the trade off in the long run. Several investigators have taken the view, however, that the short-run trade off is at best not a very useful concept and at worst totally misleading. The most influential of these have argued instead that trade union pushfulness is a crucial independent force in the determination of the rate of wage change. Early work on this problem (Morton, 1950; Bronfenbrenner, 1950; Lapkin, 1950; Slichter, 1954; Christenson, 1954; Gallaway, 1958) was mainly concerned with establishing the conditions under which wage push could lead to a sustained inflation and offering guesses as to whether it was or was not a major source of inflation.

The most systematic early study of the role of wage push via union strength is Hines (1964). He postulated that the rate of wage change depends directly upon union pushfulness and that union pushfulness itself can be measured (proxied) by the rate of change of the percentage of the labour force which is unionised (union density). The proxying of pushfulness with density change is justified on the assumption that militancy manifests itself simultaneously in wage negotiations and in union recruiting. If this is true, even though no direct causal link is postulated between the rate of change of density and the rate of wage change, we should observe a positive correlation between the two and might interpret that evidence as indicating the independent effects of trade union militancy on the rate of wage change. In studies for the United Kingdom by Hines (1964, 1968, 1969, 1971) and in a United States study by Ashenfelter, Johnson and Pencavel (1972) such a correlation was found.

However, Stoney and Thomas (1970) pointed out that Hines's 1964 model is dynamically unstable, while the legitimacy of using density change as a proxy for militancy has been attacked on several fronts. Purdy and Zis (1974) argue, on the basis of an analysis of the objectives of and constraints on union behaviour, that the change in density cannot be regarded as a useful proxy for militancy. They point out (1973) that there is at least one other plausible explanation for

[1] See Bowers, Cheshire and Webb (1970), Foster (1973, 1974), Gujarati (1972a, b), MacKay (1972), MacKay and Reid (1972), Taylor (1970, 1972, 1974).

any positive correlation between union density change and wage change – an explanation for which they find a good deal of empirical support. Purdy and Zis note that there are two sources of density change: that assumed by Hines resulting from a step up in recruiting effort, but also passive changes resulting from reallocation of the labour force away from sectors of the economy with low union densities towards those with high ones. In the extreme case there could be a reallocation from those with no unionisation to those with closed-shop union structures. If the highly unionised sectors are the high-wage sectors then there will be a correlation between the rate of change of average earnings (but not of the wage-rate index) and the rate of change of union density for reasons completely independent of union strength or militancy.

The Purdy and Zis view is in line with the analysis of Holt (1970a), who develops a theoretical model of wage determination for the union sector and the non-union sector and then aggregates the two. For Holt union behaviour simply determines an equilibrium union wage relative to the non-union wage. Aggregation over union and non-union workers brings in the rate of change in union density as one of the variables in the aggregate wage inflation relation but purely as a result of aggregation. This is also the view taken by Thomas (1974). Further, despite Hines's assertions to the contrary, the change in union density is correlated with the level of economic activity and hence may to some extent be working as a proxy variable for labour market demand pressure (see Purdy and Zis, 1973).

An alternative and in some respects superior method of investigating the role of trade unions, but a method which is more applicable to the United States than to the United Kingdom, is to divide the economy into unionised and non-unionised sectors and separately study the determinants of wage inflation in each sector. This has been done by Pierson (1968), Throop (1968) and Hamermesh (1970). Broadly speaking, these studies conclude that the wage change–unemployment trade off is present in both sectors but is steeper and therefore less important in the union sector. Hamermesh (1972a) goes even further and disaggregates the economy on the basis both of degree of unionisation and degree of concentration in product markets.[1] This work strengthens the conclusion that monopolised sectors are less responsive to market pressures, as measured by the unemployment rate, than are competitive sectors. However, these authors do not attempt to study whether changes in militancy play a role: the presence of monopoly is simply assumed to affect the position of the short-run trade off between wage inflation and unemployment and this leads to the prediction that the equilibrium unemployment rate will depend (in a way that has not been investigated) on the degree of monopoly power that is present in the economy as a whole.

An alternative measure of union pushfulness suggested by Taylor (1972), Knight (1972), Godfrey (1971) and Godfrey and Taylor (1973) is the volume of strike activity. They report a positive correlation between strikes and wage change. In contrast, Johnston and Timbrell (1973) and Ward and Zis (1974) report that they can find no robust correlation here. The problem of interpreting

[1] See also Eagly (1965), Gustman (1972) and Hamermesh (1972b).

such correlation (or lack of it) is even greater than in the case of changes in union density. First, the models of wage determination which incorporate strike activity (see, for example, Johnston, 1972) do not offer predictions about the sign of the relationship between the two variables. Secondly, like the Hines variable, strikes are well correlated with the level of economic activity (and hence inversely correlated with unemployment) (Ashenfelter and Johnson, 1969; Pencavel, 1970). Hence it may be the case that strikes are another possible proxy variable for labour-market demand pressure. Thirdly, it might be argued that strikes are the outcome of mismatched expectations about inflation rates held by employers and workers. It is entirely plausible that such mismatching increases as the rate of inflation increases and hence produces a positive correlation between strikes and wage change entirely independently of push or militancy. Fourthly, there is a tendency for wage changes and strikes to be seasonal in character; hence a correlation which ignores the seasonal nature of these relationships is likely to overstate the correlation between the two. Those studies which find a strong correlation are quarterly (Godfrey) or semi-annual (Taylor), whilst those which find little or no correlation are annual (Johnston and Timbrell and Ward and Zis). Fifthly, there are three alternative measures of strike activity not always closely correlated with each other (see Ward and Zis, 1974) and the investigator thus has scope to indulge in data mining in order to choose that definition which best suits his purpose.

A third possible way of measuring union militancy arises from the postulate that unions become more militant when profits are high and therefore push for higher money wages the higher the rate of profit. This matter has been investigated by Lipsey and Steuer (1961), who found little cross-section correlation between wage change and profits in the United Kingdom. In contrast, Bhatia (1961) and Perry (1964) in time-series studies of the United States do find a role for a profit variable. The correlation between profits and demand pressure is strong enough however to make it impossible definitely to interpret this result as showing effects of militancy as opposed to those of excess demand.

A further proposition about wage determination which challenges the universality of the short-run relationship between inflation and unemployment is that direct controls on wages either shift or flatten the relationship. The evidence on this for the United Kingdom is fairly clear. It suggests that whilst the short-run relation between wage change and unemployment appears to be less stable when wages controls are operating, the average wage inflation rate over the control period is not significantly different from what would be predicted in the absence of controls (see Parkin and Sumner, 1972). Evidence from the United States is less clear but seems best interpreted as indicating at most only a slight effect from controls (see Perry, 1967, 1969, 1970, 1972; Alexander, 1971; Anderson, 1969; Wachter, 1969; Throop, 1969; Ackley, 1972; Bosworth, 1972; Fiedler, 1972; Gordon, 1972; Weidenbaum, 1972; Parkin, 1973b). Furthermore, no study of wage controls in the United States has suggested anything other than a modification of an otherwise well-determined wage inflation–

unemployment relation. There is no suggestion that the relationship disappears in their presence.[1]

The view that the rate of wage change is largely independent of the state of excess demand but nevertheless the crucial central determinant of the overall rate of price inflation is widely held. It follows from the proposition that wage change depends upon the degree of "frustration" of wage negotiators and those whom they represent. This idea is closely related to the concept of "relative deprivation" introduced by Runciman (1966). It is argued that people come to feel "relatively deprived" when the rate of growth of their own real incomes is low relative to expectations, these being based on their own earlier experience and on observations of other peoples' real incomes. Attempts to improve their position will involve members of the labour force in trying to increase their money wages at a rate which they judge will put them in the desired real position. However, the economy's capacity to provide real income is limited by available resources and technology and may, from time to time, lag behind the desired rate of growth of real wages. It should be apparent that this hypothesis either requires that people suffer from money illusion or is in all essentials equivalent to the expectations hypothesis already discussed.

Models based on the notion of income claims adding up to more than the real output of the economy, but not relying explicitly on "frustration", can be found in the work of Turvey (1951) and Pitchford (1957, 1961, 1963). These authors simply assume a rigid structure of relative income claims which over-exhaust output. A related set of hypotheses concerning wage inflation is put forward by Balogh (1970), Harrod (1972), Jones (1972), Wiles (1973), Marris (1972), Baxter (1973) and Turner and Jackson (1970) and Hicks (1974), all of whom advance versions of the idea that the rate of wage change is an essentially sociological matter. Detailed propositions vary between authors and take in such matters as a rigid link between wage change and productivity growth in the faster-growing sector of the economy spreading to the rest of the economy (Turner and Jackson, 1970; Jones, 1972), the general moral climate (Wiles, 1973; Harrod, 1972; Marris, 1972) or inconsistent notions about the fairness of the structure of relative wages (Hicks, 1974). A related idea first advanced by Reddaway[2] (1965, 1966) and later by Phelps-Brown (1971) is that confidence in the government's capacity and willingness to maintain full employment leads organised labour to behave as if there was a highly inelastic demand for labour over a range of wage variation which has been progressively widening and hence to an institutionally generated inflation rate.

Testing all these competing hypotheses about the determination of wage inflation and discriminating amongst them is, as we have seen above, no easy matter. However, the weight of the available evidence leads us tentatively to accept some variant of the expectations excess demand view of wage inflation and to reject the sociological and other push hypotheses. The econometric studies cited above using post-war data up to the middle of the 1960s all agree that

[1] For a non-quantitative survey of the evidence on a large number of countries see Ulman and Flanagan (1971).

[2] Written in 1957 at the request of the then newly established Council on Prices, Productivity and Incomes.

during that period there was an inverse relation between the rate of wage change and unemployment.[1] Those studies that use data coming up to the early 1970s and which allow for the role of inflationary expectations continue to find a negative relation between the rate of wage change and unemployment.[2] Differences in the measure of unemployment used as an indicator of labour market demand pressure appear on the basis of the studies cited to be of secondary importance as far as their results are concerned. The role of inflationary expectations is clear and significant and in the studies by Vanderkamp (1972), Parkin (1973a), Duck et al. (1975), Parkin et al. (1975) and MacCallum (1975) the estimated coefficient of the effect of a change in inflation expectations on the actual rate of wage change is not significantly different from unity, thereby implying no long-run trade off between inflation and unemployment.[3] The roles of the rate of change of and dispersion of unemployment in generating wage inflation have, as we have seen, been harder to pin down.[4]

As to direct taxes, the work of Gordon (1972) and (with a bargaining theoretical justification) Johnston and Timbrell (1973) suggests that they play an important role. The rate of wage change is positively correlated with some definitions of the volume of strike activity but not others.[5] It is also correlated with changes in union density.[6] However, the interpretation of those correlations is at best ambiguous. As we have seen, some theoretical analyses imply either a causation that runs from wages to density and not vice versa or that the correlation is an aggregation phenomenon. Tests of the "frustration"[7] version of the sociological explanation of variations in the rate of wage inflation and of the power of incomes policies[8] have produced negative results. It has proved difficult to formulate testable versions of the other sociological explanations and they remain untested. Wage leadership models perform[9] well but they leave open the question as to what determines the rate of wage change in the leading sector.[10] Such models may well be interpreted as complementary to excess demand and inflation expectations models, telling us about the details of the transmission of wage inflation through the economy, rather than being alternatives to them.

[1] Especially Phillips (1958), Klein and Ball (1958), Lipsey (1960), Dicks-Mireaux (1961), Samuelson and Solow (1960), Bhatia (1961), Perry (1964), Brechling (1968), Cowling and Metcalf (1967), Taylor (1970), Simler and Tello (1968), Purdy and Zis (1973), as well as the literature on the "income policy debate" surveyed in Parkin, Sumner and Jones (1972).

[2] These (cited above) are Brechling (1968), Lucas and Rapping (1969), Gordon (1972), Nordhaus (1972b), Turnovsky and Wachter (1972), Vanderkamp (1972), Turnovsky (1972), Parkin (1973b), Parkin et al. (1975), Duck et al. (1975), McCallum (1975).

[3] In the Vanderkamp (1972), Parkin (1973b) and Duck et al. (1975) studies, inflation expectations were proxied by a distributed lag on past inflation; Parkin et al. (1975) used estimates based on surveys and McCallum used the future actual rate of inflation as a proxy for a "rational" expectation. The problems and methods of proxying and measuring inflation expectations are discussed on pages 770-3 below.

[4] See especially Archibald et al. (1974).

[5] See Taylor (1972), Knight (1972), Godfrey (1971), Johnston and Timbrell (1973), Ward and Zis (1974).

[6] See Hines (1964, 1968, 1969, 1971), Ashenfelter, Johnson and Pencavel (1972), Purdy and Zis (1973).

[7] The only test available appears to be that by Nordhaus (1972b) and is entirely negative.

[8] See Parkin and Sumner (eds.) (1972).

[9] Brechling (1973), Thomas and Stoney (1971) and also Eatwell, Llewellyn and Tarling (1974).

[10] Brechling and Thomas and Stoney embed their models in an excess demand framework whilst Eatwell et al. leave the question open of what determines the inflation rate in the leading sector.

So much for studies of wage inflation. We now turn to discuss work on the proximate determinants of price inflation. Two questions have dominated the literature on this matter. First: does excess demand exert an independent upward pressure on prices, particularly of manufactures, or does its influence come entirely through its effect upon factor prices, particularly wages, and hence upon costs? Second: inasmuch as prices respond to cost changes, do they respond to changes in actual costs or to changes in some normalised or expected cost measure?[1]

Walrasian price-level dynamics postulates a *tâtonnement* process in which an "as if" auctioneer calls a random set of prices, contemplates the excess demands and supplies that these generate and adjusts prices in proportion to excess demands until the market clearing set of prices has been found. At that point, but not before, trading takes place. In such a world we would never observe excess demands and equilibrium product prices would adjust in proportion to changes in marginal cost. At the other extreme, some recent Keynesian work (Clower 1965; Barro and Grossman 1971) drops the fiction of the auctioneer and introduces the "as if" assumption that prices are completely rigid so that all disequilibrium adjustments involve quantities only. In this world, we would observe excess demands, but price changes would not occur, let alone be related to excess demand.

The modern theory of price-setting behaviour (part of which is usefully surveyed by Nordhaus (1972 a)) owes much to a basic insight of Arrow (1959). Since in a perfectly competitive equilibrium all firms are price takers, a theory of price *setting* must be based on an analysis of monopolistic or quasi-monopolistic behaviour; in disequilibrium *all* firms must be quasi-monopolistic even if in equilibrium they would be operating in competitive markets. Following Arrow's lead, Phelps and Winter (1970) and Barro (1972 a) have developed explicit dynamic models of price setting. Phelps and Winter's analysis is similar to that employed by Mortensen in analysing wage setting. The key assumptions are that the firm is an expected-present-value maximiser facing a dynamic demand function which determines the rate of change of its sales as a function of its own product price relative to the market average price for the product. In equilibrium, when the firm's own price is equal to the market average, it maintains a constant level of sales. Barro deals with an expected present value maximising monopolist who faces a stochastic demand function and introduces an explicit cost of price adjustment. His firm trades off this cost against the expected profits lost through maintaining a disequilibrium price. In the Phelps–Winter model there is no explicit cost of price change, but, because the rate of flow of consumers from the rest of the market to the firm in question is a function of its price relative to the market average (or for operational purposes the firm's expectation of that average), there is an implicit cost to price adjustment. The present value-maximising time path for the firm's price gradually approaches the market average price, thereby stabilising its market share. The rate of price adjustment is a function of *both* the difference between actual and

[1] A third question which has been raised but not answered is: do monopolistic firms exert an independent push on prices in a similar manner to that in which it is suggested that trade unions affect wages?

expected average price and the actual and expected equilibrium quantity. This Phelps–Winter model also predicts homogeneity of degree one of the rate of price adjustment with respect to the expected rate of inflation.

Barro specifies the demand for a firm's output as depending only on its own price. In his model aggregation over individual firms yields the proposition that the rate of price change will be a positive function of market excess demand. Clearly if he made demand depend on own price relative to the general price level, then the expected rate of change of the general price level would also appear as a determinant of actual price change and with a coefficient of unity satisfying the usual homogeneity conditions.

These recent theoretical developments in price dynamics have not yet had an impact on empirical work. Most estimated price equations are based on some variant of a mark-up model sometimes allowing the mark-up to vary with excess demand, sometimes making the mark-up relate to actual costs and sometimes to "normal" costs.

The earliest United Kingdom empirical studies assumed no role for excess demand in price equations. Work by Dow (1956), Klein and Ball (1959), Dicks-Mireaux (1961), Neild (1963) and Godley and Rowe (1964) all postulated that price changes were determined by changes in labour costs and some measure of import prices. In addition, Dicks-Mireaux used a productivity variable, Klein and Ball indirect tax changes, while Neild and Godley and Rowe added a lagged dependent variable to the equation.[1] Subsequent work has however included excess demand, as well as factor price changes, amongst the explanatory variables and has found that it played a role in explaining price change. Papers by Rushdy and Lund (1967), McCallum (1970, 1974), Solow (1969) and Brechling (1972) all find positive and statistically significant coefficients on a variety of alternative excess demand variables. The studies by Rushdy and Lund and McCallum used the Dow-Dicks-Mireaux (1958) index, Solow used an index of capacity utilisation calculated by Paish (1962) while Brechling used the difference between real national product and a quadratic trend. In addition to excess demand, Rushdy and Lund used wage and import price changes; McCallum the lagged dependent variable; Solow, unit labour cost changes and the expected rate of inflation, and Brechling import price changes only.

In the light of these studies, it seemed to be well established that excess demand exerted an upward pressure on prices independently of changes in factor prices and hence costs, but Godley and Nordhaus (1972) presented results which challenged that consensus. They advanced the "normal" cost hypothesis, according to which prices respond to changes in "normal" costs and are independent of excess demand. By de-cycling factor price and productivity changes they computed a time series for "normal costs" and then, using that series along with ten alternative measures of excess demand in ten alternatively specified price equations (i.e. 100 equations in all) found only *one* significant

---

[1] Price equations used in studies, forming part of the "incomes policy" debate, by Lipsey and Parkin (1970) and Burrows and Hitiris (1972), were based essentially on the Dicks-Mireaux model, and hence did not examine the effects of excess demand.

positive coefficient on excess demand. They thus concluded in favour of the normal cost hypothesis that excess demand has no independent role to play in determining price behaviour.

This conclusion appears to be mistaken[1] for a variety of reasons, of which we mention three. First, in ninety of their regressions, Godley and Nordhaus specified the rate of price change as depending on *changes* in excess demand. This is an incorrect specification: it is at odds both with the usual theory of price setting and with earlier empirical work which had found the *level* of excess demand to be important. Secondly, of the remaining equations, only three use a goods market variable to measure excess demand, and all of those yield positive coefficients with *t*-statistics greater than one (though under 1·4). Thirdly, even in their "preferred" equation, the coefficient on price changes predicted from normal cost changes, which should be unity if the normal cost hypothesis is to be accepted, is 0·6 and significantly less than unity. This constitutes a refutation of the normal cost hypotheses.

Also relevant to the interpretation of all the empirical work on price determination is the fact that actual unit cost changes fall during booms and rise in recessions. Prices move pro-cyclically but with less amplitude. There is a fundamental difficulty here in identifying the separate effects of actual cost changes, "normal" cost changes and excess demand. When actual costs are combined with excess demand both variables are significant; the use of "normal" costs necessarily leaves a smaller role for excess demand to play.

Price equations for the United States by Kuh (1959), Schultze and Tryon (1965), Fromm and Taubman (1968), Perry (1966), Klein and Evans (1967), Solow (1968), Eckstein and Fromm (1968), Gordon (1972) and Andersen and Carlson (1970) are extensively surveyed by Nordhaus (1972 a) and a duplicate discussion is not required here. It is sufficient to note that with the exception of Kuh's equation for the corporate output deflator and Schultze and Tryon's durable manufacturing wholesale price index equation, all United States price equations display significant excess demand effects. Moreover, in a review of the role of demand in generating price changes, De Menil (1974) confirms this conclusion as does a recent disaggregated study by Ripley and Segal (1973). It is worth noting that the United States literature abounds with arbitrarily mis-specified price equations in which *levels* of price rather than rates of change of prices are regressed on the level of excess demand. In such cases, the excess demand coefficient, as would be expected, is often insignificant (see especially Schultze and Tryon, 1965). Finally, studies by the OECD (1970) and Ball and Duffy (1972) covering, with some duplication, twelve major countries also find the role of excess demand to be significant along with unit labour costs and import prices in all cases except France.

Whether or not prices respond to excess demand independently of cost changes is not relevant to the overall existence of a short-run trade off between the rate of inflation and excess demand. This trade off will exist if either product prices or factor prices or both are responsive to excess demand since no one disputes that cost (factor price) changes affect product prices. It is an almost

---

[1] We are grateful to Graham Smith for illuminating discussions on this point.

universal finding that prices respond to cost changes, a major element of which is wage change. Wages in turn, as we have seen, are usually found to be responsive to excess demand as well as to other variables, sometimes including current or expected price changes. By taking the wage and price equations together, it is possible to obtain quasi-reduced form relations which make both price and wage changes functions of excess demand and expected inflation, as well as of other exogenous variables which might appear in either structural equation.

Whether or not the quasi-reduced form price setting equation displays a partial long-run trade off between inflation and excess demand depends on the combined effects of inflation expectations on wage change and of wage changes on price changes. Most models for which such a quasi-reduced form relationship has been explored (mainly for the large-scale econometric models evaluated and compared by Hymans in Eckstein (ed.) (1972)) suggest that, even in the long run, there is a trade off between inflation and unemployment. The models in question invariably use a distributed lag relationship in actual inflation rates to generate the expected rate of inflation with weights restricted to sum to unity and declining geometrically. The estimated coefficient of the expected rate of inflation (as so defined) on the actual inflation rate is less than unity.

In the small-scale United States model constructed by the Federal Reserve Bank at St Louis (Andersen and Carlson 1972) no long-run inflation-unemployment trade off is present but the model imposes rather than estimates that result. In the case of the Canadian RDX2 model (Helliwell et al. 1971), no long-run trade off is present, while in a study which directly estimates a quasi-reduced form price equation for twenty countries, Cross and Laidler (1975) find a statistically significant role for excess demand in thirteen individual cases and no evidence of a long-run trade off in any country. The key reason advanced by Cross and Laidler for the failure of so many earlier studies to generate a no-long-run trade off (or "natural rate") result is their inadequate allowance for the influence of foreign inflation on expectations of domestic inflation. In six of the seven cases for which the excess demand variable did not take a coefficient significantly different from zero, the coefficient was nevertheless positive. Moreover, all seven cases were small very open economies (e.g. Ireland, Belgium, Norway) and Cross and Laidler argued that, in these cases, imported inflation was swamping any purely domestic influence on the inflation rate.

The "natural rate" hypothesis is further strengthened by the results of ingenious tests devised by Lucas (1973) (see also Lucas (1972a)). He shows that if there exists a long-run trade off then there should be a (cross-section) relationship between the variance of inflation rates and variance of real output about its trend. If no long-run trade off exists, no such relationship should be found. Using data for a cross-section of eighteen countries he shows the "natural rate" hypothesis to perform better than the alternative stable trade off view. Cagan (1968) attempts to test the "natural rate" hypothesis for the United States and United Kingdom using long-run average time series data and again concludes that the long-run trade off hypothesis is rejected by the data.

The *expected* rate of inflation plays a crucial role in many of the models of the proximate determinants of the *actual* rate of inflation of both wages and prices

198   SURVEYS OF APPLIED ECONOMICS: 2

outlined above.[1] It also influences the opportunity cost of holding (non-interest-bearing) money and therefore features centrally in the quantity theory analysis of perfectly anticipated inflation. In view of the central importance of inflation expectations, it is not surprising that this topic has generated a large literature in its own right. Three questions arise in connection with expectations. First, what precisely is the expected rate of inflation, is this a unique variable or may several measures of it coexist? And if they do, what consequences flow from differences between expectations? Secondly, how may expectations be measured (or proxied)? Third, how are expectations formed?

The first question has only received passing treatment in the literature. Expectations can vary over at least three important dimensions. First, different individuals and other agents will, in general, form different expectations of the same variable over the same future time horizon: this means that some expectations are bound to prove wrong, which is contrary to the assumptions made in analysing fully anticipated inflation. Second, different price indices will be relevant to different decisions and to different individuals: and expectations about, say, consumer prices and capital goods prices may differ significantly. Third, the time horizon over which an expectation is formed will depend on the problem for whose solution it is necessary to form the expectation, and the same person may easily have very different expectations about the course of prices over, for example, the next year and the next decade. In addition to these differences concerning individuals, indices and time horizons, expectations are seldom held with complete certainty and there will be variability concerning the degree of confidence with which any expectation is held. Except *en passant* none of these problems appear to have been addressed and it seems to us that their exploration will be a fruitful area for future work.[2] Until this work is done, one cannot know how far the conclusions which have been reached in much of the literature depend on the (usually unstated) assumptions that expectations are held with complete certainty and that a single inflation expectation is adequate for all purposes.

Much of the early empirical literature which made use of inflation expectations treated the other two questions as if they were one by making an untested assumption about how expectations are formed and then used that assumption as an auxiliary hypothesis in wage or price equations. The most common such assumption, first introduced by Cagan (1956), and followed in empirical work by many others,[3] is that inflation expectations adjust by a constant fraction of the difference between the most recently recorded actual inflation rate and the previously formed expectation.[4] This intuitively appealing idea of "error learning" or "adaptive expectations", as Cagan's hypothesis is

[1] We are grateful to Malcolm Gray for valuable discussions on the material on expectations which we now survey.

[2] A study which has considered multiple expectations is Parkin *et al.* (1975). One which has used as a central feature of its analysis the variability across individuals is Carlson and Parkin (1975) and one which has considered alternative forecast horizons is Rose (1972).

[3] See the works referred to on p. 765, above.

[4] In terms of a difference equation, $\Delta^2 p^e = \lambda(\Delta p - \Delta p^e_{-1})$, where p = log of price level, Δ = difference operator, λ constant fraction, superscript e = expectations, subscript $_{-1}$ = time lag. Cagan used a continuous time formulation, $d\dot{p}^e/dt = \lambda(\dot{p} - \dot{p}^e)$.

interchangeably called, was shown by Muth (1960) to provide an optimal fore-cast (in the sense of minimum mean square error) for a time series the first difference of which is a first order moving average process. Implicit here, and explicit in much literature in the field of mathematical statistics, popularised among economists by Box and Jenkins (1970), is the proposition that the optimal (minimum mean square error) forecast for a time series in general depends on the particular form of the stochastic process which characterises the series being forecast. Rose (1972) showed that provided the series being forecast could be described by an ARIMA (auto-regressive integrated moving average) process then there remains an "error learning" interpretation for the optimal forecast, but that in general the current period forecast would be revised by a weighted average of *all* previous errors, not just by a fraction of the last one.

A second approach to the problem of expectations, also started by Muth (1961), is that of "rational expectations". The idea here is that expectations are formed such that they "depend, in a proper way, on the same things that economic theory says actually determine that variable" (Sargent and Wallace, 1973, p. 328).[1] Such an approach is probably better suited to a characterisation of expectation formation in the very long run. In the short run, it seems more likely that expectations will be based on cruder forecasting procedures which, even if optimal (in a minimum mean square error sense) are capable of being systematically wrong. Moreover, if expectations are to be formed "rationally" it is important that those forming them be able to forecast government policy. This point poses a very serious problem for the advocates of "rational expectations". Lucas (1972a, b) shows, in papers that abstract from this type of problem, that even if expectations are formed rationally, because it is not possible for agents to distinguish absolute from relative price changes, a systematic deviation of output from its full equilibrium level would still follow a monetary disturbance.

A third approach to expectations is grounded in Bayesian statistics and the relationship between a Bayesian approach and "adaptive expectations" has been investigated by Turnovsky (1969).[2] He shows that, whilst a Bayesian fore-cast of a time series has an adaptive expectations interpretation, the speed with which expectations adapt to experience when a Bayesian approach to fore-casting is taken will not, in general, be constant and will depend on the nature of the time series being forecast.

Most empirical studies of wage and price determination using inflation expectations have made use of the simple error learning hypothesis. Models incorporating that hypothesis have typically performed well in the sense that they have provided an overall explanatory power of wage or price change that would be regarded as adequate. However, they often generate a coefficient on the expected rate of inflation, predicted by theory to be unity, which is signi-ficantly less than unity. About half of the recent studies that have used this expectations hypothesis, have generated a coefficient significantly different from

---

[1] In addition to Muth's seminal paper and Sargent and Wallace, see also Brock (1972) and, for a monetarist analysis of the essential ideas, Walters (1971).

[2] See also Aoki (1967) and Raiffa and Schlaifer (1961).

unity.[1] One possible reason for this is suggested by Sargent (1971). He shows that, if it is assumed that the rate of inflation is a stationary autoregressive process, then for expectations of inflation to be optimal forecasts, they should be formed as a weighted average of past inflation with the weights summing to less than unity.[2] The error learning hypothesis measures expectations as a weighted average of past inflation where the weights decline geometrically and sum to unity. Thus, if inflation is indeed a stationary autoregressive process, and if expectations are in fact formed optimally, to model expectations as being formed by an error learning process, this procedure will in general impart a downward bias of unknown magnitude to the estimate of the response of actual to expected inflation. If expectations are not formed optimally then nothing can be said *a priori* about the interpretation of such an estimate. This analysis would not, of course, apply to the formation of expectations about the level of the inflation rate if its rate was secularly increasing (but it might well apply to the formation of expectations about its rate of acceleration).

There is a general problem here, and it is simply stated: it is not possible to identify the coefficient relating actual to expected inflation without having an independent measure of inflation expectations.[3] One possible independent measure of the expected rate of inflation is the difference between *equilibrium* nominal and real rates of interest. However, in order to use that difference, which no one disputes would measure a unique expected rate of inflation for the economy if everyone dealt in the bond market and held identical expectations, it is necessary to observe both the equilibrium nominal and real rates. Setting aside the far from trivial question of our ability to identify equilibrium values of variables, nominal rates are market phenomena and therefore are observable but real rates are not usually observable. To overcome this problem an untested assumption about the real rate has to be made. The most common is that the real rate is a constant (which reflects real productivity and thrift) plus a random element uncorrelated with the expected rate of inflation. As Sargent (1972) points out, this assumption does not hold up in a simple Keynesian model and may well not hold in a wider class of models. In fact the real rate will move systematically with inflation and take a considerable length of time to return to its equilibrium level after a disturbance. Thus, using a nominal–real interest rate difference rather than some form of error learning to measure the expected inflation rate merely replaces one untested assumption with another, raises new problems in the process, and brings us no closer to being able to identify the relation between actual and expected inflation.

[1] Recent studies which in some forms examined obtained coefficients of unity are Nordhaus (1972*b*), Turnovsky (1972), Parkin (1973*b*), Vanderkamp (1972), Laidler (1973*a*), MacKay and Hart (1974). Those which obtain coefficients of less than unity are Parkin (1970), Nordhaus (1972*b*), Toyoda(1972) and Turnovsky (1972). Those listed twice found coefficients of unity in some cases but not in others. Solow (1969) found values of coefficients on expected inflation of less than unity but, on the sum of expected inflation and unit cost changes, the relevant sum not significantly less than unity.

[2] This conclusion has been generalised and shown to apply to any ARIMA process by Gray (1975).

[3] A special case of this is shown by Saunders and Nobay (1972). Using Parkin's (1970) United Kingdom wage equation they show that the replacement of the standard adaptive expectation model with an alternative but single parameter rational distributed lag function leads to the same reduced form parameter estimates but changes the interpretation of the coefficient relating expected to actual inflation.

The foregoing problems have led some investigators to attempt directly to estimate inflation expectations but such work is in its infancy.[1] Livingstone has obtained quantitative data on inflation expectations of United States business-men and business economists by using survey techniques. However, when his series is used in wage equations (Turnovsky, 1970; Turnovsky and Wachter, 1972) it performs little differently from the actual rate of inflation both in terms of its coefficient, which is less than unity, and its overall contribution to explana-tory power. Lack of success with this variable should perhaps not be too surprising in view of the highly specialised and hence potentially unrepresen-tative nature of the people whose expectations Livingstone was able to obtain by his survey. Carlson and Parkin (1975) have devised a method for deriving an estimate of the expected rate of inflation from a time series of *qualitative* survey data generated by asking people whether they believe certain prices will rise, fall or stay the same over some specific future period. If one knows what proportions of the population expect prices to rise, stay the same, or fall, and is willing to make sufficiently strong assumptions about the nature of the distribution of expectations across individuals, an estimate of the mean expected inflation rate can be derived for the population covered, though this estimate obviously depends on the nature of the assumptions made and on the accuracy of the respondents' statements as a reflection of their genuine expectations. Data drawn from Gallup Poll surveys of households and Confederation of British Industry surveys of business firms have been used to compute expected inflation rates for United Kingdom retail prices, domestic wholesale prices and export prices. When all three of these are used in an excess demand expectation wage inflation equation by Parkin *et al.* (1975) these series produce the predicted value of unity as the sum of the coefficients on the three expected rates of inflation variables and display significantly better explanatory power than the previous quarter's actual rate of inflation.

The availability of directly measured inflation expectations makes it possible to do more than discover the effects of expected on actual inflation. It also permits the investigation of hypotheses about the formation of expectations. Carlson and Parkin (1975) using the Gallup data described above find that a second-order error learning process (i.e. expectations adjust to the preceding two errors) with allowance for exchange-rate changes gave a plausible expla-nation of expectations formation in the British economy on a monthly basis from 1960 to 1973. They also found inflation expectations to be more strongly correlated with the previous expectation than with the most recently announced past actual inflation rate.

A common procedure in the literature on inflation (see especially Eckstein (ed.), 1972) is to combine the three relations which determine wages behaviour, price behaviour and expected price behaviour, in order to produce a quasi-reduced form which generates the short-run and long-run trade offs between inflation and unemployment, or more completely, the interrelated dynamic time paths of these variables. The drawback of this approach is that it treats excess

---

[1] Some of the earliest attempts to use survey techniques to discover how people learn about prices are those by Behrend (1964, 1966).

demand as if it were exogenous to the inflationary process. This is not the case; the full properties of the interactions between inflation and unemployment can only be analysed properly by broadening the framework to deal with models in which endogenous aggregate demand is influenced by fiscal and monetary policy. To the literature that deals with such models we now turn.

4. "COMPLETE" SHORT-RUN MODELS OF INFLATION, OUTPUT AND EMPLOYMENT

At the end of our survey of recent developments in the quantity theory approach to inflation we pointed out that, since changes in the rate of monetary expansion bring about changes in real income, a complete analysis of disequilibrium inflation requires an analysis of the interaction of the money market with markets for goods and services and labour. The work on wage and price setting behaviour and expectation formation which we have just surveyed is equally partial in that it examines wage and price setting behaviour and their inter-action, given some, as if exogenous, state of excess (or deficient) demand. We now need to bring these two elements in the analysis of inflation together into a "complete" macro-economic model of inflation, income and employment determination. In this section, however, we deal only with closed economies, and international problems are introduced in the next one.

The simplest post-Keynesian macro-economic models that dominate the pages of a generation of elementary and intermediate textbooks do not determine the price level at all but analyse the effects of monetary and fiscal policy changes on the levels of real output and employment. It would be wrong, however, to conclude that such fixed price-level models can shed no light on an inflationary economy. Developed from a well-specified choice–theoretic foundation, such models as those of Clower (1965) and Barro and Grossman (1971) give considerable insights into the working of an economy in which markets are characterised by excess demand but whose inflation is suppressed. For example, analysing such an economy, Barro and Grossman (1974) derive the interesting result that generalised excess demand combined with rigid wages and prices will, like deficient demand, lead to a less than full employment volume of economic activity. Furthermore, in their model either excess demand or supply can prevail even if the *real* wage is equal to its equilibrium value.

A more complex Keynesian model commonly advanced as an interpretation of the model implicit in the *General Theory* (Hicks, 1937; Modigliani, 1944; Patinkin, 1956), takes the money wage rate as given and then determines, along with output and employment, the price *level*. The latter variable, however, is of secondary interest. The effects of monetary and fiscal policy changes on real output and employment are still the focus of the model. Some work uses this model to examine the dynamics of the price level (e.g. Patinkin) but only analyses movements between two equilibrium price *levels*. It does not examine inflation as a continuing process.

Although mainstream post-Keynesian macro-economics represents a major advance in our understanding of fluctuations in real output and employment, as far as inflation analysis is concerned, it is a retrogression from the earlier Keynes of the *Tract* (1923) and from the Wicksellian tradition (Wicksell, 1898). This earlier tradition, presented in modern terms by Patinkin (1956) and Laidler (1972) had, as the focus of its attention, the determination of the price level and its rate of change. The Wicksellian economy never departed from full employment, however, and it is understandable that such analysis was widely regarded as having been discredited by the 1920s and 1930s. Nevertheless the influence of Wicksell on Scandinavian economists has been persistent; they have never lost the message that inflation needs to be analysed and explained in terms of a complete macro-economic model. They have not, however, achieved a convincing integration of the Wicksellian and Keynesian traditions in monetary theory for their analysis of inflation has always been for a fully employed economy (see, for example, Hansen, 1951, 1957; Paunio, 1961). Analysis of simultaneous inflation and unemployment in a macro-model has been achieved only relatively recently with the continuing development of large-scale econometric models (such as the FMP, Brookings, etc., models for the United States and the London Business School model for the United Kingdom)[1] and of small-scale, highly aggregative models (in some cases empirical and others analytical). The best-known examples are those of Andersen and Carlson (1970, 1972), Ball (1964), Black (1975), Brunner *et al.* (1973), Brunner and Meltzer (1972, 1973), Laidler (1973*a*), Lucas (1972*b*), McCallum (1973), Petersen, Lerner & Lusk (1971), Sargent (1972, 1973), Stein (1974), Vanderkamp (1975) and Williamson (1970). Such models are capable of analysing the simultaneous determination of both the inflation rate and the level of economic activity.

Although these models differ considerably among themselves in their degrees of aggregation and even in aspects of their basic specification, their essential structure can nevertheless be understood in terms of three sets of relationships which interact to determine the inflation rate, the expected inflation rate and the state of demand (or excess demand). First there is an equation, or group of equations which may be used to produce a single quasi-reduced form equation, which specifies the proximate determinants of the rate of inflation as being excess demand, inflation expectations and, possibly, other *exogenous* variables, i.e.

$$\Delta p = \alpha(L)\, x + \beta(L)\, \Delta p^e + \gamma(L)\, Z, \qquad (1)$$

where x is excess demand, Δp is the actual rate of inflation, Δp^e is the expected rate of inflation, Z is a vector of exogenous variables and where $\alpha(L)$, etc., indicate general distributed lag relationships. Second, there is a relationship which specifies how inflation expectations are generated. This may relate expectations purely to the past behaviour of prices or to other exogenous variables as well, i.e.

$$\Delta p^e = \lambda(L)\, \Delta p + \kappa(L)\, Z. \qquad (2)$$

Third, there is an equation (or again a number of equations reducible to one quasi-reduced form equation) which specifies the proximate determinants of excess demand as being the stock of real money balances, fiscal policy variables

---

[1] For a survey of large-scale models which is slanted towards the treatment of inflation see Eckstein (ed.) (1972).

and the expected rate of inflation, as well perhaps as other exogenous variables. Such an equation, with m the log. of the nominal money stock, p the log. of the price level and f as a vector of fiscal policy variables, may be thought of as the solution to a dynamic IS–LM type system combined with an aggregate supply analysis, i.e.

$$x = \delta(L)(m-p) + \phi(L)\Delta p^e + \mu(L)f + \psi(L)Z. \tag{3}$$

For an exogenously given time path of monetary expansion rates (Δm) and fiscal policy (f) and for given paths of the exogenous variables (Z), the above three equations will produce time paths for the actual and expected inflation rates and for excess demand. Models of the general class described by the above three equations can nevertheless differ in many details. The more important differences here are their long-run inflation–unemployment trade off properties, and the relative weights which they give to the effects of monetary and fiscal policy on excess demand. Whatever their differences in these respects, however, all the major models produce a response to monetary and/or fiscal policy changes which first affects real output and employment and only subsequently, and often with very long lags, affects the rate of inflation. The specific empirical estimates of some of the more important large-scale United States models and evaluations of time paths of inflation and output (or unemployment) on well defined policies have been extensively surveyed in Eckstein (ed.) (1972).

It is only in the context of a complete model such as that set out in highly aggregative form in (1), (2) and (3) that the full necessary and sufficient conditions for the non-existence or otherwise of the long-run inflation–unemployment trade off can be established. Essentially what is required for no long-run trade off is that equation (3) be a correct specification of the way in which money affects demand (i.e. that equation must be homogeneous of degree zero in money magnitudes); that the effects of inflation expectations on actual inflation in equation (1) be homogeneous of degree one; and that, in the long run, expectations be unbiased. These results, established in Gray and Parkin (1974) but intuitively obvious, are apparently different from those suggested by Turnovsky (1974). There is, however, no conflict here. Turnovsky shows with the aid of a complete macro model that the impact effect of an *exogenous* change in expectations on actual inflation will not in general be proportional. This proposition is true in terms of the model set out above and has nothing to do with the existence or otherwise of a long-run inflation–unemployment trade off.

An insight into the working of the class of models set out above can be obtained (though not of course a quantitatively accurate one) by considering the behaviour generated by a simple, special case of the general framework. Such a model, has been developed by Laidler (1973a) and may be set out as follows:[1]

$$\Delta p = \alpha x_{-1} + \Delta p^e_{-1}, \tag{4}$$
$$\Delta p^e = \lambda \Delta p + (1-\lambda)\Delta p^e_{-1}, \tag{5}$$
$$\Delta x = \delta(\Delta m - \Delta p). \tag{6}$$

In this model, Δp is the inflation rate over the current time period (Laidler suggests a year in his exposition), x_{-1} is the average level of excess demand

---

[1] See Laidler (1973a), pp. 371, equation (1)–(3).

(measured as the log. of the ratio of actual to trend output) over the previous year, Δp^e is the expectation of inflation held, as if with certainty, by all economic agents at the end of the previous period about the current period and Δm is the rate of change of the nominal money stock.

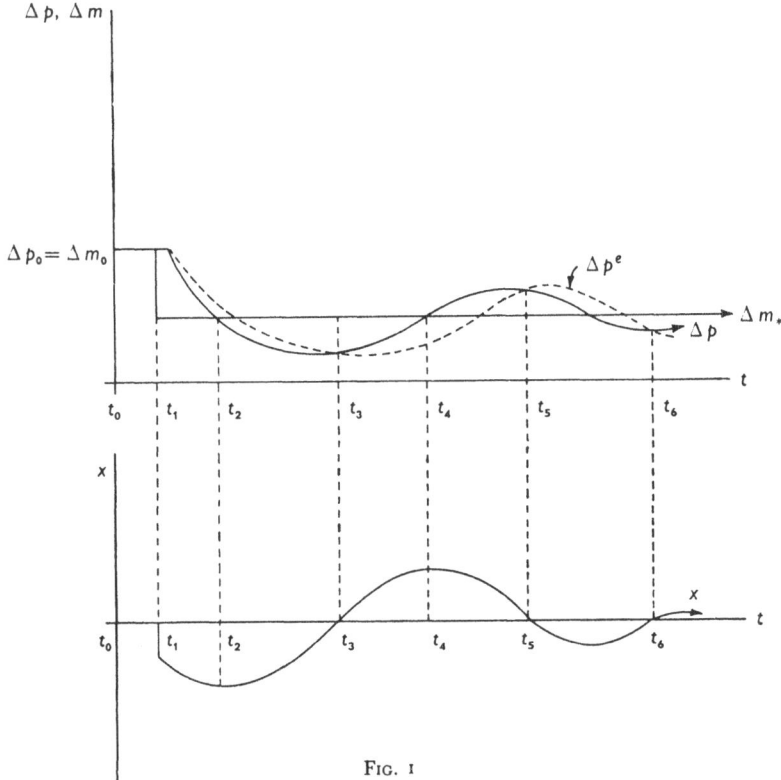

FIG. I

Although this very simple model ignores many features which would be present in an actual economy, it enables us to see how a model which is extremely "monetarist" in its assumptions about the influence of fiscal policy and in its long-run properties, nevertheless is capable of generating unemployment as well as inflation in response to a change in the rate of monetary expansion. One may get a feel for how this model behaves in general by considering the following experiment. Suppose the economy is initially in a full equilibrium with the actual and expected rates of inflation equal to each other and to the percentage rate of monetary expansion,[1] i.e. $\Delta p_0 = \Delta p_0^e = \Delta m_0$.

In this situation, of course, excess demand will be zero. This state of affairs is depicted as holding during the interval from t_0 to t_1 in Fig. I. At t_1 let the rate of monetary expansion fall but then maintain a new lower level for ever as shown by the steep drop in the line labelled Δm_*. At that instant there will be a fall in excess demand (that is the creation of excess supply) of an amount

---

[1] This formulation abstracts from real growth. It is, however, extremely simple to adapt the analysis to fluctuations of the economy about a rising trend and Laidler's paper contains such an analysis.

given by δ times the change in the rate of monetary expansion. After a delay of one time interval, the inflation rate will fall by $\alpha\delta$ times the change in the rate of monetary expansion. This change in the inflation rate will, for the purpose of the intuitive diagrammatic analysis, be presumed to be less than the change in the rate of the monetary expansion. Immediately after the point t_1 the inflation rate exceeds the rate of monetary expansion and hence real balances are falling. Falling real balances will generate additional excess supply through equation (6) so that by t_2 the inflation rate will have fallen via equation (4) to equal the rate of monetary expansion. At that point, via equation (6) excess demand will begin to turn around. Between t_2 and t_3 real balances are rising since the rate of inflation is below the rate of monetary expansion. However, inflationary expectations, which, by equation (5), are lagged behind the actual rate of inflation, will be above the actual rate and excess demand will continue to be negative although falling towards zero. At t_3 actual and expected inflation are equal to each other and excess demand is zero. However at t_3 the stock of real balances is increasing since both the actual and expected inflation rates are now below the rate of monetary expansion. This growth in real balances leads to positive excess demand and with excess demand increasing the actual and expected inflation rates continue to increase. Once more, as excess demand rises the actual rate of inflation eventually overtakes the rate of monetary expansion and real balances again begin to fall. Excess demand will also turn down again at this point and reaches zero at t_5 when the expected rate of inflation has caught up with the actual rate. The actual and expected inflation rates and excess demand will continue to cycle in a damped fashion towards a full equilibrium in which excess demand is zero and the actual and expected inflation rates are equal to the lower rate of monetary expansion.

It is worth emphasising that although the model just analysed embodies strong "monetarist" assumptions and although the change in the rate of inflation is, by hypothesis, caused by a change in the rate of monetary expansion, it predicts that there will be no close correlation between those two variables. Observations on the relationship between monetary expansion and inflation provide no test of such a model. Rather, the way to test such a model is to establish from an analysis of the behaviour of the monetary authorities whether or not the money supply has been controlled independently of inflation and excess demand, and to estimate equations of the type specified in general terms as (1), (2) and (3) above. If the equations "fit the facts" and if the money supply has been exogenous, then it may be inferred that inflation is caused by monetary expansion and transmitted via the price, wage and expectations adjustment process lying behind equations (1) and (2) [or (4) and (5)] and surveyed in the previous section of this paper.

Of course, the extreme assumptions embodied in equations (4), (5) and (6) are not offered by anyone as a complete characterisation of inflation. However, a series of empirical papers by Duck et al. (1975), Gray, Ward and Zis (1975) and Parkin et al. (1975) which apply components of the model to the aggregate economy of the "Group of Ten" countries (as an approximation to the closed world economy) show that they fit the broad facts of "Group of Ten" inflation very closely in the period from the mid 1950s to 1971, while Laidler's initial (1973) study showed the model to fit United States experience in the 1952–70 period rather well.

The main problem with the above analysis is, of course, the assumed exogeneity of the money supply. The work of Friedman and Schwartz (1963), Cagan (1965) and Sims (1972) suggests that this is a reasonable enough assumption to make about the United States economy, in the sense that causation has primarily run from money to income and prices rather than vice versa over most time periods, an important exception being in the post-second-world-war years when monetary policy was geared to supporting the price of government debt. However, for the United Kingdom, the work of Artis and Lewis (1975) suggests that only since 1971 has the money supply been exogenous in this sense. It is possible nevertheless to use the basic model to analyse an important alternative macro-economic policy regime, namely the pursuit of a target level of unemployment (or, in terms of the above model, excess demand) along with a money supply which is passively adjusted so as not to hamper measures to achieve that target.[1] In such a case, excess demand will be the exogenous variable, even though, in practice, temporary deviations from its target level would be inevitable, and the money supply and actual and expected inflation rates the endogenous variables. If the model displays a long-run trade off between inflation and unemployment, inflation and monetary expansion rates will eventually converge to the steady rate of inflation implied in the long run by the chosen unemployment (excess demand) rate. If there is no such long-run trade off then there will be no equilibrium rate of inflation; if unemployment is set below its equilibrium level there will be well-defined time paths for the rate of inflation and the rate of monetary expansion but the variables will eventually explode towards infinity. Whether or not one talks about inflation being "caused" by monetary expansion in this latter case seems to us to be semantic for, if the wage and price setting process does in fact respond only to the previous history of excess demand (as assumed in a strong form in equations (4) and (5)) then whether or not the money supply *has* been exogenous is irrelevant to the more important question of inferring what would happen *if* the money supply *were* made exogenous. "Exogenous" is used here not in the sense of the government being free to pick any rate of monetary expansion independently of its fiscal policy, exchange rate and interest rate policy or independently of the wider social and political implications of these policies, but in the narrow technical sense of conducting all its policies so as to ensure that the main line of causation stems from money to output and prices rather than vice versa. If policy is endogenous in the sense that the money supply and fiscal policy respond in part to output and prices then there are, of course, simultaneous equation problems in estimating the wage and price setting equations and the demand for money and policy response supply of money equation but these are not insuperable.[2]

[1] This appears to be a predominant view of the way U.K. monetary policy has been conducted, at least until recently, and a view with which we concur.

[2] There is already a growing empirical literature which has estimated monetary and fiscal policy response functions; see Reuber (1964), Fisher (1970), Nobay (1974), Pissarides (1972).

So far, in this review of complete short-run models of inflation, we have focused on a monetary "demand pull" view of the inflationary process to the neglect of the sociological "push" views. This focus and bias is in part a reflection of the weight of the literature and in part, perhaps, a reflection of our own views. For the most part, the literature has presented sociological forces as proximate determinants of wage and price setting behaviour and has not analysed them in the context of a complete macro-economic system. We have already referred to this work in the previous section. However, two important and influential analyses of sociologically generated inflation, those by Phelps-Brown (1971) and Hicks (1974), have been cast explicitly in the framework of a complete although informal macro-economic system. Both see the adoption of full employment demand management policies as a crucial factor in the inflation explosion of recent years. In this respect, there is a similarity between the Phelps-Brown and Hicks positions on the one hand and the alternative, exogenous excess demand interpretation of the monetarist model described and analysed above. However, there are differences of substance here, for both Phelps-Brown and Hicks not only argue that the money supply has been endogenous but also argue crucially that even if it could in fact be made exogenous, in the sense used above, it would fail to control inflation. This conclusion follows from their views that a removal of fear of unemployment (Phelps-Brown) and increasingly inconsistent ideas about equity (Hicks) have led money wages to rise almost independently of the state of excess demand for labour and without any systematic relationship to inflationary expectations.[1] Both view variations in the unemployment rate within politically feasible boundaries as being virtually without direct effect on the inflation, though they might have some influence on the outcome of political negotiations between trade unions and government. If they are correct then control of the money supply would moderate inflation only marginally and at the expense of totally unacceptable rises in the unemployment rate. Whether or not they are correct, however, is impossible to say. Their views derive from general observations of the course of events and not from any econometric or statistical analysis. However, an idea ought not to be dismissed because it has not been, and perhaps cannot be, subjected to *quantitative* testing. *Qualitative* evidence is still evidence. Nor should a line of thought be ignored because it is not yet sufficiently developed for its proponents to be able clearly to state what evidence, either qualitative or quantitative, would, if presented to them, cause them to change their views. At this stage, no final judgment can be passed on the views of Hicks and Phelps-Brown. All that we can do to evaluate their empirical relevance is to refer the reader back to the vast empirical literature on wage and price setting behaviour reviewed in the preceding section of this paper and to the conclusions which we drew from that literature and to note that, with Brunner *et al.* (1973) and Brunner (1974), we regard evidence of a systematic influence of excess demand on wage inflation in recent years as making it difficult to give

---

[1] As part of his analysis, Hicks makes use of what he terms the flexprice–fixprice distinction. It seems to us that the expectations augmented excess demand framework encompasses both of these. A flexprice market is one in which prices respond very quickly to excess demand whilst a fixprice market has a more sluggish response.

primary emphasis to sociological factors as proximate determinants of the inflation rate.

In the present state of the debate an eclectic position such as we described earlier (p. 753) appeals to many, with excess demand and inflationary expectations being combined with sociological and political factors into a multi-cause explanation of inflation. We would not adopt such a position ourselves if what is implied is that socio-political factors are important proximate determinants of wage and price inflation rates and hence that orthodox fiscal and monetary policies would not bring inflation under control without a permanent and large increase in the unemployment rate.

However socio-political factors do seem to us to be of crucial importance in understanding why governments pursue, either actively or passively, inflationary monetary and fiscal policies. The development of what may be termed a "political economy" of inflation is in its infancy. One possibility is that inflation is used as a tax, though it is hard to see why so many governments would have sought to gather extra revenue in this way at the end of the 1960s. It seems to us to be more plausible to look at events in terms of the use of demand management policies to raise the level of employment, and to maintain low real interest rates both on government debt and on certain politically sensitive private debt instruments, notably mortgages. Instability in inflation rates may be partly explicable in terms of the government's ability to extract a greater inflation tax with unanticipated inflation (Sjaastad, 1975) or, more plausibly in the context of the developed world, in terms of election frequency and the time horizon of Governments (Nordhaus, 1975). Literature on the social and political causes of inflationary monetary policy is however, in its infancy in comparison with that on its economic consequences.

Although we have characterised the models discussed in this section as "complete" an important sense in which they are "incomplete" is their neglect of international aspects of the generation and transmission of inflation. There is a long and important literature on this topic to which we now turn.

5. INTERNATIONAL ASPECTS OF INFLATION

Whether the generation of inflation is viewed as primarily a monetary phenomenon, or as primarily a sociological or socio-psychological one, the framework of the analysis applied to its explanation in individual countries has all too frequently been that of an economy operating in isolation. It is now widely recognised that this will not do and, on all sides of the debate about inflation, increasing attention has been given to placing the problem in an international setting.

The extension of the monetary analysis of inflation to an international setting is relatively easy precisely because the quantity theory of money was originally developed quite explicitly to deal with monetary phenomena in the context of a world made up of a number of open economies. The relative neglect of international factors in the monetary- and macro-economics in the 1940s and 1950s ran strongly counter to the quantity theory tradition. Bodin, after all, was concerned to explain a Europe-wide inflation in terms of the import of precious metals from the New World, while Hume developed the quantity theory not in isolation but as a vital component of his attack on mercantilist theories of the balance of trade. Thus, modern analysis of the monetary economics of an open economy pioneered in English language literature by Polak (e.g. 1957), who built on a long-standing tradition in Dutch monetary economics, and developed by Mundell, Johnson and their associates, represents not so much a new departure as a return to older ways of thinking.[1] The way in which money and prices interact on a world-wide basis depends critically upon the nature of international monetary institutions, and since the Bretton Woods system of fixed exchange rates between more or less convertible national currencies was in force until 1971, it is hardly surprising that the great majority of recent work has taken just such a framework as its starting point. In a world of fixed exchange rates the closed economy of the quantity theory models we have discussed earlier, in which the time path of prices is determined in the long run by the time path of the money supply, is not an individual country. Its appropriate empirical analogue is the aggregate of all those individual countries that are linked to one another by fixed exchange rates. Thus the relevant money supply, as far as the determination of prices is concerned, is the sum of the domestic money supplies of each national economy (converted to a common unit at the fixed exchange rates); its time path is determined as a result of the combined monetary policies of the individual countries. Thus, the monetary analysis of inflation described earlier becomes applicable at the level of the world economy.

Given this background the analysis of the relationship between money and the inflation rate in one particular country is viewed as having to do not with the causative mechanism of inflation in the economy as a whole but with the process whereby inflationary impulses are transmitted to a particular region of the economy. As far as long-run equilibrium is concerned, the predictions of the monetary approach are quite clear cut. If the world economy was always in full long-run equilibrium, any one country would be facing a level and structure of interest rates determined for it on world capital markets, and facing a price level and inflation rate (fully anticipated) also determined for it on world markets. It could operate at full employment only by conforming to these. Thus, domestic monetary policy would influence the domestic inflation rate in the long run only to the extent that domestic monetary expansion or contraction influenced the rate of change of the world money supply and hence the rate of change of world prices. Domestic monetary policy in any individual country would have its main long-run effects not on that country's inflation rate but on its balance of payments.

---

[1] De Jong (1973) gives a useful brief account of the development of monetary economics in the Netherlands. Mundell's contribution to this field is to be found in its most accessible form in (1968) and (1971). Johnson (1972) and (1973) contain much original material, but they are also extensive surveys to which the reader who is seeking a more comprehensive account of the literature on the monetary theory of the balance of payments than we have space for here should refer. In addition, volumes edited by Claassen and Salin (1972) and Connolly and Swoboda (1973) contain major contributions to this particular field.

A particular country's money supply is equal, by accounting identity, to the sum of its stock of foreign exchange reserves and the stock of credit extended by the banking system to domestic borrowers. The foreign-exchange reserves may be influenced to some extent by the floating of Government long-term loans abroad or by other types of intervention in the capital market, but the more important monetary policy variables potentially under the control of domestic authorities are the stock of domestic credit extended and its rate of change, the rate of domestic credit expansion. If the demand for nominal money is a stable function of real income, the price level, the level of real interest rates and the expected rate of inflation, then in the long run all its arguments are determined on world markets. If, in a particular country, the supply and demand for money are to be kept in equilibrium, it is the money supply that must adjust to accommodate demand and not the arguments in the demand for money that must adjust to accommodate supply. Thus, the rate of change of foreign exchange reserves must vary to eliminate any discrepancies between the rate of domestic credit expansion and the rate of change of the demand for money, but the rate of change of reserves is precisely the so-called "balance on official settlements" definition of the balance of payments.[1]

Now if we analyse the behaviour of a small open fixed exchange rate economy in this way, we can establish its long-run properties if the world economy stays in full long-run equilibrium but we leave many important questions about the short run unanswered. Morever, the correspondence of the predictions of this long-run analysis to the facts of the last decade or so is crude indeed. A step up in the rate of change of the world's money supply, mainly originating in the United States, in the mid-1960s did indeed accompany a world-wide acceleration of national inflation rates. Nevertheless major discrepancies between the inflation rates experienced by different countries persisted throughout the period in question and these divergences need explaining.

Changes in tariffs or in non-tariff barriers to trade could explain these divergences, but most recent work on these problems places at the centre of the analysis the awkward but apparently fruitful distinction between the determination of the prices of tradeable goods on the one hand and of non-tradeables on the other, a distinction which corresponds to that made in the "Nordic" literature between the output of the "exposed" and "sheltered" sectors of an economy. Non-tradeables are simply those items which, because they must be consumed at the point of production, have only a domestic market. The argument is that it is not the overall price level, but only the price level of tradeable goods that is determined on world markets. The behaviour of the non-tradeables is related to world-wide happenings, of course, but only indirectly. To the extent that the tradeable and non-tradeable sectors of an economy compete for labour, world price level trends will be transmitted through the labour market

---

[1] This is not to say that this definition of the balance of payments is in any way essentially more "correct" than any other, but only that it is the relevant one as far as the analysis of money and inflation in an open economy is concerned. The balance on official settlements does after all represent the net purchases of foreign currencies that a central bank has to make to maintain the parity of its own currency. Note that recent work by Brunner (1975) has adapted the well-known Brunner–Meltzer (1972) analytic schema to the level of the world economy.

to the non-tradeable sector, while to the extent that the division of domestic aggregate demand between tradeables and non-tradeables is related to their relative prices, there is another route whereby world-wide factors impinge upon the market for non-tradeables.

However, there is no reason to expect that the inflation rates in the two sectors will be the same even in the long run. If technical change in the two sectors is different in character then the possibility of the marginal productivity schedules of labour shifting at different rates arises. For given output mixes, and for a given rate of wage inflation, rates of price inflation will differ in such circumstances. They will also differ if, in a growing economy, the division of aggregate demand between the output of the two sectors changes over time. But if inflation rates differ between these two sectors, and if the overall domestic inflation rate is an average of the two then we have ample scope for any one country's inflation rate to differ from that ruling in the rest of the world, and to differ persistently.[1]

Even abstracting entirely from these matters, the process of transmitting changes in the world inflation rate through the labour market into changes in the inflation rate for non-tradeables is likely to be subject to time lags; the domestic inflation rate thus can differ from that ruling in the rest of the world while such adjustment is taking place. There is no reason to suppose that the lags in question will be sufficiently short as to be negligible. The time that must elapse for an economy fully to adjust to a new inflation rate is thought by some economists (notably Friedman; cf. 1968) to be more appropriately measured in decades than in years.[2]

We have so far said nothing about the interaction of inflation and unemployment in an international context. To the extent that the problem is to explain their interaction on a world-wide basis, there may be no particular difficulty. One of the more remarkable features of recent economic history has been the way in which employment fluctuations have been as closely synchronised across national boundaries as have fluctuations in the inflation rate. It may well be that the closed economy analysis of this problem dealt with earlier can fruitfully be applied at the level of the world economy.[3] However, as yet there is very little literature on the role played by fluctuations in income and employment in a particular economy in the transmission of world-wide variations in infla-

---

[1] The so-called Nordic model of inflation lays considerable stress on productivity growth differentials between sectors. Note that, although this model does not have anything to say about the monetary aspects of inflation in an open economy its structure is in no way inconsistent with that of a model that takes these factors into account. For one account of this Nordic model see Edgren, Faxen and Odhner (1969).

[2] Parkin (1974) explains discrepancies between the domestic inflation rate and that ruling elsewhere in the world solely in terms of lags of this sort, producing a model of a small open economy which in long-run equilibrium has the world inflation rate but in which the short-run inflation rate can deviate from its steady state value because the inflation rate in the non-tradeable sector takes time to catch up with that ruling in the tradeables sector. There is no necessary inconsistency between Parkin's model and the Nordic model because there is no reason why it could not be elaborated to deal with a situation in which productivity growth rates differed between sectors.

[3] The paper by Duck et al. (1975) presents results that suggest that an expectations augmented Phillips curve can successfully account for the interaction of unemployment and wage inflation rates for data aggregated over a number of countries, but a great deal more work is required before we can treat this result as anything more than tentative.

tion and unemployment rates into that particular economy. This surely is one of the more interesting problem areas currently in need of further research effort.[1]

Even more important, we need work on the operation of a system of flexible exchange rates in an inflationary environment. All the analysis discussed so far in this section has been cast against the background of a system of fixed exchange rates between convertible currencies. Such a system ceased to operate in 1971. Though there is a substantial historical literature on flexible exchange rates arising from the debates of the era of the Revolutionary and Napoleonic Wars, and from those of the 1930s, no systematic study of the operation of flexible exchange rates in an inflationary context is available in recently published literature.[2] This gap in knowledge at present detracts considerably from the confidence with which the monetary approach can be applied to contemporary policy problems. The usual approach taken is to argue that an open economy operating a flexible exchange rate may be analysed "as if" it were a closed economy. Even if this is correct, it is not clear what differences are made by the fact that we have a system, not of completely flexible rates, but rather of managed floating.

The last few pages have dealt with international aspects of inflation in terms of a predominantly monetary interpretation of the phenomenon. As we have already noted above, there exists a strong school of thought, particularly among British economists, that the roots of the current inflation are to be found in sociological and socio-psychological forces. It would be quite misleading to suppose that only monetary economists have noticed the international character of recent inflation. As long ago as 1970, for example, OECD drew attention to this aspect of the problem but offered an explanation of it that rested more on a growth in the importance of factors leading to social conflict than on a world-wide monetary expansion.[3] In terms of such an explanation one channel for the transmission of inflationary impulses across national boundaries is a "demonstration effect". Workers in one country become more "militant" in

---

[1] Papers by Laidler (1975b) and Scarfe (1973) are the only ones of which we are aware that attempt to deal with this problem on a theoretical level. Laidler builds upon Parkin's (1972) model and upon his own (1973) closed economy model (see above) by making fluctuations in income and employment an integral part of the mechanism whereby changes in the inflation rate in the world economy are transmitted through the tradeables sector to that for non-tradeables. Scarfe focuses on the inflation–unemployment trade off in an open economy and analyses the manner in which the adoption of flexible exchange rates enhances the domestic authorities' control over these variables.

[2] The early nineteenth-century literature did deal with the operation of flexible exchange rates in an inflationary environment and is dealt with by Viner (1937), chapters III, IV. More recent work was largely carried out against the background of deflation and its relevance in the context of inflation has not been fully developed in the literature. We do not have space to carry out this task here. Note, though, that there was a school of thought that regarded perverse speculation against the currencies in question as being an important cause of the post-first world war hyperinflations. Cagan's (1956) evidence that domestic monetary expansion was the key factor in these episodes has undermined this view and it is now usually accepted that the depreciation of these currencies was the consequence and not the cause of the domestic inflations that it accompanied.

[3] OECD (1970). See also Marris (1972). As we have already noted above, a sociological explanation of inflation is a natural partner to the view that so-called "prices and incomes policies" are required to deal with inflation. When combined with an hypothesis that sociological factors are at work on a world-wide scale, the policy application becomes one of internationally co-ordinated prices and incomes policies, an implication that was not altogether missed by OECD.

their wage demands; this is noticed by workers in other countries who also become more militant. Hence, the forces leading to cost inflation become world-wide in their operation. This is not the only channel of international transmission consistent with the sociological view. Some adherents of the sociological approach – for example, Hicks (1974) – regard goods-market as opposed to labour-market behaviour as being amenable to economic analysis. Thus they view pricing behaviour in world-wide goods markets, particularly for food and commodities, as being another channel whereby inflation spreads through the international economy. In this respect, their views do not significantly differ from those of the "monetarists".

Proponents of sociological explanations make much use of the "international demonstration effect". Though it is an intuitively appealing idea that relatively "docile" workers in one country might become more "militant" as a result of learning about the activities of a more "aggressive" labour force elsewhere, is it not equally plausible that "militant" workers might learn from the example of "docile" neighbours? It seems to us that demonstration effects can go both ways, and until it is explained why in the late 1960s the example of, say, the French and Italian labour forces should have more influence on the international scene than that of the Germans or the Americans, we do not really have an explanation of the international transmission of inflationary impulses at all. All we have is a description of one aspect of inflation as it manifests itself on the international level.

6. THE REDISTRIBUTIVE CONSEQUENCES OF INFLATION

At the very outset of this survey we noted that the major reason for paying particular attention to the problem of inflation lay in its consequences.[1] These consequences mainly involve the distribution of income and wealth and it is convenient for purposes of exposition to divide such redistribution up into two categories: that which takes place within the private sector of the economy and that which takes place between the private sector and the government. We will begin by considering the matter of redistribution within the private sector. Analysis here has concentrated on two hypotheses, one concerning wages lag and the other concerning debtor–creditor relationships. In discussing the redistributive consequence of inflation it is, of course, vital to distinguish between inflation that is fully anticipated and inflation that is imperfectly anticipated. If by anticipated we mean not only that a particular rate of inflation is expected by everybody but also that the expectation in question has been acted upon by all concerned, then a fully anticipated inflation can, by definition, have no distributive consequences in the private sector.[2] All bargains, be they about wages

[1] In preparing this section of the paper we have benefited greatly from having access to a draft survey paper (Foster, 1975) on this material prepared by John Foster of the University of Glasgow. The paper in question is part of a recently completed Manchester Ph.D. thesis on the redistributive consequences of owner-occupier housing finance in Britain.

[2] We owe this distinction to Mr Foster, who notes that inflationary redistribution must therefore depend not only on the characteristics of economic agents but also on the characteristics of the assets and liabilities that they hold.

or about borrowing and lending must, on these assumptions, be fully adjusted for inflation in such a way as to ensure that their outcome in real terms is just what it would have been at a fully anticipated zero rate of inflation. The hypotheses about the distributional consequences of inflation with which we are concerned here, therefore, involve the analysis of imperfectly anticipated inflation.

The literature on these hypotheses has been somewhat self-contained, and not without reason. Until recently, most theoretical analysis on inflation dealt with fully anticipated inflation; it was therefore impossible to connect up empirical work on the distributive consequences of imperfectly anticipated inflation with much of the available inflation theory. In consequence, the relevant literature has tended to be heavily empirical with very little theoretical foundation. We have already noted that more recent work, such as that which has incorporated versions of the expectations augmented Phillips curve into complete macro-economic models of the inflationary process, may be looked upon as attempting, among other things, to analyse the evolution of an inflationary process where the various relevant inflation rates are not fully anticipated. The development of theoretical work along these lines brings with it the hope that future studies of the distributive consequences of inflation will be much more integrated with relevant theoretical work on inflation than they have been in the past, but such developments have hardly yet taken place. It is not difficult, though, to point to worth-while lines of investigation.

Let us consider the wages lag hypothesis first of all. It is yet another aspect of the literature on inflation that may be traced back to David Hume. It states that, when inflation is taking place, price rises tend to run ahead of increases in money wages, so that real wages are lower than would be the case with stable prices. In the fully employed economy always assumed in Classical analysis, a lower real wage rate means a lower real wage bill and hence a greater share of a given level of real output going to profits. This in turn means a higher saving (and investment) rate and hence more real growth.[1] Early empirical work of Mitchell (e.g. 1908) on the Greenback era, that of Hamilton (e.g. 1934) on sixteenth- and seventeenth-century Europe, and that of Hansen (1925) on the post-first-world-war inflation in the United States seemed to give a great deal of empirical support to this hypothesis. Hamilton's work in particular was taken up by Keynes (cf. vol. II of the *Treatise*), who laid great stress on the capacity of what he termed "profit inflation" to generate economic growth.

More recent empirical work has seriously undermined the wage lag hypothesis. Studies by Alchian and Kessel (1959), Kessel and Alchian (1960) and Felix (1956) argued that earlier work had made insufficient allowance for the effects of factors other than inflation on the time path of wages, while Hamilton's results in particular were shown to be highly sensitive to small changes in the time period employed in his tests (cf. Kessel and Alchian, 1960). Later work,

---

[1] In Classical economics, of course, the labour force was typically assumed to do no saving. To square this implication of the wage lag hypothesis with more modern approaches to economic theory one would have to postulate a higher saving rate out of profits than out of wages. Moreover, neo-classical growth theory of the type discussed in an earlier section of this paper would have a higher saving rate produce a higher capital–output ratio and a higher level of income rather than a higher growth rate unless there was some embodied technical progress included in the model.

mainly on post-second-world-war United States data (e.g. Bach and Ando, 1957; Bach and Stephenson, 1974; Conard, 1964; Phelps, 1961) but including a study using spectral methods to analyse long runs of British and U.S. data (Cargill, 1969), has produced such mixed results that the only safe conclusion about the wage lag hypothesis must be that it postulates a phenomenon which is certainly not universal, but which may from time to time have happened.[1]

This is all very unsatisfactory and it is easy enough to see why. The wage-lag hypothesis involves the proposition that, during inflation, price adjustment precedes wage adjustment. As we have seen earlier, it has only been in the last decade that we have had work on wage and price formation which recognises that these variables are fixed endogenously to the economic system as part of the activity of firms and households rather than being given by some anonymous "market force" or "auctioneer". One implication of this work must be that the effects of unemployment on income distribution should be an integral part of any study of inflation's consequences, and this fact has been recognised by Scitovsky and Scitovsky (1964) and, more recently, by Nordhaus (1973). However, we have not yet had any rigorous micro analysis of the way in which wage and price setting behaviour are carried on together and interact with one another. We have not had such analysis at the level of the individual firm or industry, let alone for the economy as a whole.[2] We need such analysis in order to provide us with predictions about the circumstances in which we might expect wages to lag behind prices (or vice versa) and until we get it, it is difficult to believe that we are likely to see further progress with empirical work on the wage lag hypothesis.

The debtor–creditor hypothesis has generated more definite results, but here too there is room for a good deal more work; again, in our judgment it is theoretical rather than empirical work that is required. The hypothesis tells us that, if interest rates on assets denominated in terms of money are not fully adjusted to the rate of inflation, then during inflation creditors lose and debtors gain. As early as 1896 Irving Fisher suggested that inflationary expectations would exert a powerful influence on the level of nominal interest rates and produced empirical evidence consistent with this hypothesis.[3] Recent inflationary experience has led to a revival of interest in Fisher's hypothesis and evidence favourable to it has been generated by studies of United States data by Gibson (1960) and Yohe and Karnowsky (1969). Feldstein and Chamberlain (1973) combined Fisher's hypothesis with the Keynesian liquidity prefer-

---

[1] Foster (1975) gives a fuller account of these studies than we have space for here.

[2] It will already be apparent from our account of the so-called "new micro-economics" (pp. 756–7 above) that studies of wage determination (e.g. Mortensen, 1970) take price behaviour for granted, and that those of price setting (e.g. Phelps and Winter, 1970) take wage behaviour for granted. The need to integrate these separate pieces of analysis is widely recognised.

[3] Although such authorities as Keynes (1936), pp. 142–3, and Harrod (1969, 1971) have argued that inflationary expectations drive down the real rate of interest rather than raise the nominal rate. Steindl (1973) builds on Mundell's (1963) analysis of the influence of inflation on the real rate of interest and argues that the effect of anticipated inflation on the real interest rate cannot be predicted *a priori*. Sargent (1973) produces a model in which rising prices and high interest rates go together as a result of being jointly determined by other factors rather than because of the effects of inflationary expectations. In a later (though earlier published) paper (1972) Sargent does incorporate inflationary expectations into his analysis. This later paper is discussed below.

ence approach to interest rate determination, and as far as the United States long-term rate of interest is concerned found that inflationary expectations exerted an important influence on it, particularly after 1967. A recent study by Silveira (1973b) of Brazil shows that expectations heavily influenced bank lending rates there despite legal constraints upon such rates.

Nevertheless, even though there is abundant evidence that inflationary expectations do drive nominal interest rates upwards, it is evident that this does nothing to compensate holders of long-term loans issued before the onset of more rapid inflation. Moreover if we ask how long it takes for rates to change sufficiently to compensate fully for a change in the inflation rate, the answer implicit in all this evidence, at least as far as the United States is concerned, is somewhere in the region of two decades. If this is the case, then there is ample scope for inflation to redistribute wealth from creditors to debtors in the interim, and of course if inflation continuously accelerates the adjustment is always incomplete. Two questions are raised by such a conclusion: who are the debtors and creditors in question, and why do interest rates take so long to adjust?

Overwhelmingly, the losers from inflation appear to be households, and, within the household sector, losses seem to concentrate on the rich and the poor. Middle income groups, having more nominal debt than those at either extreme of the wealth distribution, are less affected (cf. Bach and Stephenson, 1974). There is some suggestion that, in adjusting to inflation, the rich react more quickly than the poor (cf. Tait, 1967) so that they lose relatively less by it. In the private sector, the main gainers from inflation are non-financial corporations, although by no means all corporations are in the position of having more nominal liabilities than assets. The evidence on these matters is, however, overwhelmingly based on United States data and it is not clear to what extent one may generalise from it to other economies.[1]

Why interest rates fail fully to adjust to inflation is a question of considerable analytic interest. There can be two, by no means mutually exclusive, reasons for such failure: first, some or all economic agents can fail to form correct expectations of inflation and second, markets can fail to adjust in such a way as to reflect fully changed expectations. We have already seen above when dealing with the expectations augmented Phillips curve that there is abundant evidence that expectations do indeed lag significantly behind events; this factor must then certainly be part of the answer to the question under discussion here. However, it is implausible to argue that the public take between one and three decades fully to adjust their expectations of inflation to experience, and that is what one would have to believe if he looked to sluggish expectations as the only source of the slowness of interest rates to adjust. Moreover, such an argument would appear to be inconsistent with the evidence generated in Phillips curve type studies, where the lags of expectations behind experience are much shorter.[2] However, the relevant period over which expectations must

---

[1] Once more the reader is referred to Foster (1975) for a fuller account of all this work.

[2] Sargent (1973) shows that, using a first-order error-learning mechanism, the length of the learning process implicit in United States interest rate data is indeed to be measured in decades. We have discussed the results generated by Phillips curve type studies above.

be formed when setting an interest rate on a long-term loan is much longer than that involved in striking a wage bargain. It is quite plausible that the same agents might adjust their expectations of inflation over the next twenty years at a much slower rate than their expectation of the next twelve months' inflation.

Nevertheless, slow market adjustment probably has an important role to play in explaining the slow adaptation of nominal interest rates to inflation. Sargent's (1972) work on a complete macro model of the inflationary process is largely constructed to demonstrate the possibility of this. He notes that one would only expect inflationary expectations necessarily to be fully reflected in the difference between nominal and real interest rates when the capital market was in full equilibrium and then shows, in the context of a macro-economic model based on the IS–LM framework, that interdependence between markets might require that the whole economy be in equilibrium before this result was achieved. Sargent's paper thus focuses, more clearly than any other work of which we are aware, on the interdependence of the short-run dynamics of the inflationary process usually analysed in the context of the inflation–unemployment trade off literature, and the distributional questions hitherto treated in a quite separate branch of the literature, and might be expected to open up an interesting line for future research.[1]

So far we have dealt with the redistributive consequences of inflation within the private sector, but Bach and Stephenson (1974) in particular provide striking evidence that the main gainer from recent inflation is government. In discussing the issues involved here it is once again important to distinguish between perfectly and imperfectly anticipated inflation. The government gains from inflation in three ways. First, inflation reduces the real value of government interest bearing debt.[2] The redistributive mechanism here is exactly the same as that involved in the redistribution between debtors and creditors in the private sector and needs no special analysis. As inflation becomes anticipated, upward pressure is placed on the interest rate that the government must pay on new borrowings. Resistance to this tendency involves government in switching its borrowing away from the public to the central bank and hence in generating further monetary expansion. This feedback from an existing infla-

---

[1] We must not leave the discussion of the behaviour of nominal interest rates in inflationary conditions without referring to the work of Allais (1974) on this matter. He argues that the nominal interest rate in fact reflects what he terms "the psychological rate of interest", essentially the rate of time preference, and postulates that this variable is determined by a weighted sum of past volumes of money expenditure with weights declining as one goes into the past. This postulate of Allais is but one aspect of a body of work in monetary economics, only part of which is available in English (cf. Allais, 1966, 1969), which provides an alternative interpretation of a great deal of empirical evidence to that given by orthodox monetary theory. Like Cagan (1969) these authors find Allais' work difficult to understand. It seems to have no price theoretic foundations, while the empirical predictions that it makes are often difficult to distinguish from those of a more orthodox approach. Nevertheless, at the very least Allais does seem to have provided us with an empirical "law" which describes with considerable accuracy a large body of data. It would be quite wrong to dismiss his work on the grounds that it is difficult to understand and heretical. Work on comparing his theories and their predictions with those of the prevailing orthodoxy in monetary economics is thus badly needed.

[2] Keynes laid considerable stress on this particular redistributive consequence of inflation (cf. for example his discussion of post-world war monetary policy in France in the preface to the French edition of *The Tract*).

tion to the rate of monetary expansion, and thence to further inflation, gets considerable attention in so-called "monetarist" analyses of the inflationary process, analyses which stress the ultimate futility of attempts to keep nominal interest rates at low levels during inflation.

The second source of government gain from inflation is its influence on the real volume of tax payments. Regulations for taxation of income, capital gains, and business profits are usually drawn up on the assumption of price level stability. Hence, as far as income taxation is concerned, allowable deductions are defined in nominal terms while marginal tax rates are progressive with respect to nominal rather than real income. Capital gains taxation is levied upon nominal capital gains rather than real gains, while, as far as corporate taxation is concerned, appreciation of inventories is frequently treated as yielding profits on a par with any other source of corporate income. In all three cases, a rising price level increases the real burden of taxes even if there is no increase in the real value of the base upon which taxation is levied; against this, if payment of taxes is not legally due for a year or more after the middle of the reference year, the real value of the payment is seriously reduced by inflation. The last few years have seen widespread popular discussion of these factors and of schemes to deal with the problems they raise. In particular various schemes for "indexing" tax structures have been canvassed. However, these problems have received little attention in professional economics literature, perhaps because they seem to raise no new theoretical problems.[1] As far as the professional literature on accounting is concerned matters are different, for the tax treatment of nominal gains arising from inflation is just one of the many problems that face accountants in devising helpful conventions for providing and processing information about incomes, both private and business, in an inflationary situation.[2]

The third means whereby inflation redistributes income between the public and government arises from the "tax" that *anticipated* inflation levies on holdings of that part of the non-interest bearing money stock which is the liability of government. This matter has received a good deal of attention recently because the tools with which it can be analysed are precisely those developed by adherents of the modern version of the quantity theory of money, but the analysis of inflation as a tax on cash balances also appeared in the pre-*General Theory* literature (cf. for example chapter 3 of Keynes's *Tract*). The analysis in question starts from the simple proposition that the issue of money is a source of revenue to the issuer. If no interest is paid on money holdings, and if, at a given anticipated rate of inflation, there is a given demand for real balances on the part of the public then, in order to maintain their real balances constant the public must continually acquire new nominal balances. Nominal balances must increase at the rate of inflation, and the issuer of money can obtain a stream of real resources in exchange for these nominal

[1] But there have been pamphlets such as Giersch *et al.* (1974) that deal quite extensively with this matter. Note also that the *National Institute Economic Review* for November 1974 contained some discussion of indexation by Page and Trollope.

[2] For an example of the relevant literature in accounting cf. Carsberg, Hope and Scapens (forthcoming).

balances.[1] Since high powered money is a government liability, increases in the stock of high-powered money represent a source of government revenue.

The value of the resources thus acquired is equal to the product of the inflation rate and the stock of real high powered money balances held and is exactly equivalent to the revenue arising from levying a tax on the ownership of (or equivalently on consuming the services of) any durable good. It is possible to apply the conventional Marshallian welfare analysis of indirect taxation to this aspect of inflation and such analysis was first applied to this problem by Bailey (1956), who, utilising Cagan's estimates of the parameters of the demand for money function, constructed empirical measures of the welfare costs of various rates of inflation.

In comparing these welfare costs to the revenue obtained from inflationary finance, Bailey found them to be relatively high in the cases analysed and concluded that, by the usual standards applied to judging the efficiency of indirect taxation, an inflationary tax on cash balances was inefficient. Subsequent work along these lines has tended to confirm Bailey's initial conclusion, and Pesek's (1960) work on the distributional consequences of taxing cash balances by inflation added further weight to this argument. He showed that such a tax seemed to fall more heavily on the relatively poor than would likely alternative sources of revenue such as sales or income taxes. We find Waud's (1970) argument, that if money-wage rigidity is causing unemployment, then perfectly anticipated inflation can increase welfare by increasing employment, an unconvincing counter to Bailey's position, since in a world in which all price changes are fully anticipated, it is hard to see why there should be wage rigidity in the first place. An analysis of the welfare consequences of imperfectly anticipated inflation which could be used as a basis for dealing with the problem posed by Waud has not, as far as we are aware, been worked out.

Barro (1970, 1972b) developed a sophisticated version of the Baumol–Tobin inventory approach to the transactions demand for money in which the payments period was made an endogenous variable, and was able to give the rather vague notion of the "welfare cost" of inflation more concrete meaning by relating it to the amount of extra time and trouble devoted to trading both between money and interest earning assets and between money and goods. He also suggested that the implementation of the inflationary tax was likely to be, and in the particular cases he studied had been, unstable. If there is a revenue maximising rate of inflation, and if this is exceeded, then the likely response of a government which does not understand the mechanisms at work in inflation would be to increase the rate of monetary expansion in an attempt to increase its revenue – a self-defeating and inherently unstable reaction.[2]

[1] There are two implicit assumptions here. First, zero real growth is assumed. The consequences of taking account of growth are dealt with below. Secondly, it is assumed that in the absence of monetary expansion the nominal interest rate would be zero. This point is also taken up below.

[2] Note that the "instability" here lies in the reactions of the monetary authorities rather than in the behaviour of the public vis-à-vis money holdings. Thus, it is of a different type to that investigated by Cagan (1956) and discussed above (Section 2). Note that Dutton (1971a), in a model of Argentinian inflation, made the rate of monetary expansion an endogenous variable generated by the government's need to satisfy a budget constraint and found that such an hypothesis had considerable explanatory power.

Now the analysis discussed so far begs the question of what it is that the government actually does with the revenue raised by an inflationary tax.[1] The implicit assumption is that it is redistributed to the community for current consumption. However, it seems frequently to be the case, particularly in less-developed countries, that the main purpose of levying taxes, inflationary taxes included, is to finance development programmes. Mundell (1965) and Marty (1967) have analysed, albeit with highly abstract models that incorporate the assumption of perfectly anticipated inflation, some of the issues involved here, for they treat the transfer of resources from the public to the government that is brought about by the inflationary tax as also being a transfer from current consumption to growth generating capital formation. However, their work in no way strengthens the case for inflationary finance. The extra growth generated by the inflation tax, both in terms of income and in terms of government revenue, turns out, given their assumptions, to be small in relation to the costs involved in generating it.

The work of Mundell and Marty studies a potential effect of revenue raising by money creation on an endogenous growth rate. There are also interesting questions to be raised about whether the existence of exogenous growth affects any of the conclusions to be drawn about the revenue raising capacity of inflation. There are potentially heavy overlaps here, of course, with the litera-ture on the role of money in neo-classical growth models. A number of papers (e.g. Tower, 1971; Friedman, 1971; Marty, 1973; Cathcart, 1974) have explicitly addressed questions of the type just raised, and have shown that analysis that abstracts from exogenous growth might be misleading. If real income is constant the government can use its powers of money creation to raise revenue only by generating inflation. However, if real income is growing over time, so is the demand for real balances. The government can obtain revenue simply by meeting the growth in demand for real balances without recourse to any inflation. With a given growth rate in real income, and a given income elasticity of demand for real balances, the amount of revenue raised in this way will depend upon the ratio to real income in which the public hold real balances, but this ratio of course depends inversely upon the rate of infla-tion. This analysis shows that, when this extra source of revenue from money creation is considered, there is even a logical possibility that the revenue maximising rate of inflation might actually be negative given certain, not necessarily implausible parameter values of the demand for money function. The reduction in the real balances to income ratio brought about by inflation subtracts more from the government's ability to raise revenue than can be ob-tained from levying the inflationary tax on the stock of real balances actually held at any moment.

Even this analysis is incomplete, though. It assumes that the only source of revenue to the monetary authority is that which actually accrues from the creation of new nominal balances. But, even if the rate of monetary expansion

---

[1] It also ignores the fact that variations in the inflation rate might affect the real rate of interest. Phelps (1965) investigates this matter, showing that fiscal policy might be used to offset this effect of using monetary policy to impose an inflationary tax.

was zero, the stock of non-interest-bearing high-powered money held by the public is, from the point of view of the monetary authorities, an alternative to having interest-bearing debt outstanding. Thus, the interest they save by having non-interest-bearing high-powered money among their liabilities may be regarded as contributing to their revenue. If this point, due to Auernheimer (1974) and Phelps (1973), is accepted, then the authorities' revenue from the right to issue money is better measured as the nominal interest rate times the real high-powered money stock outstanding than as the rate of monetary expansion times the real money stock. Once again, the effect of this further refinement of the analysis of the influence of money creation on the authorities' revenue is to reduce the rate of inflation compatible with revenue maximisation. Thus the case for an inflationary tax as a means of raising revenue, already weakened by Bailey and Barro's work, is further weakened by the Friedman–Marty and Auernheimer–Phelps results. In the light of all this, it is hard indeed to defend rapid anticipated inflation as a satisfactory form of taxation.

7. CONCLUSIONS

The literature we have surveyed is so diffuse that we are precluded by its very nature from ending this article with any neatly drawn and definitive conclusions. Nevertheless, certain broad themes have run through our discussion, and we shall end our essay by drawing the reader's attention explicitly to them. In doing so we shall highlight what seem to us to be the important unsolved problems in the area. As we shall see, there are important linkages between these problems.

Inflation would not be a problem worth studying if it did not have serious social consequences. We have now seen that the inflationary process can produce important effects on the distribution of income and wealth and on the level of real income and employment. When inflation is not fully anticipated then contracts drawn up in money terms, whether between borrowers and lenders or between employers and employees, yield unexpected and (by at least one party) undesired results. Thus the effectiveness of money as a social institution which facilitates trade and enables contracts to be framed more easily is undermined by unanticipated inflation. Even perfectly anticipated inflation could have adverse consequences, as we have seen, but we would judge these resource allocation effects to be of relatively minor importance compared to the effects on distribution and employment of poorly anticipated variations in the inflation rate.

Here then is an important theme to emerge from the literature: the need to distinguish between fully and less than fully anticipated inflation. If inflation was fully anticipated by all parties the economy could operate consistently at full employment, and there would be no redistribution of income and wealth except between the holders of non-interest-bearing cash balances and those whose liabilities include such balances. The effects on economic welfare of such inflation seem amenable to analysis with the tools of conventional microeconomics. When inflation is poorly anticipated, employment can fluctuate away from its long-run equilibrium level, and apparently arbitrary redistributions of income and wealth take place. Moreover, in this case, there are no tools available to economists to analyse the welfare effects.

Thus we have an important unsolved problem. The analysis of anticipated inflation needs to be so conducted that it covers all the varying extents to which inflation may be anticipated, including unequal expectations and lack of certainty about them. We do not pretend to know how such integration is to be achieved, but a much clearer idea than we have at present of the way in which economic agents form expectations, and of the way in which they change their behaviour in the light of changed expectations, will be required before we can expect to get very far with this problem. It is notable that, in the context of the analysis of inflation, expectations – even if erroneous – are usually treated as if held with certainty, or it is assumed that any variance in expectations does not influence behaviour. There exists a well-developed analysis, based on probability theory, of individual behaviour in the face of risk elsewhere in our subject and there surely are gains to be had from applying this analysis to aspects of the problem of inflation. This at least would be our view, but there are many economists, notably Davidson (1972) and Shackle (1955), who would presumably regard the application of such analysis as misconceived (though possibly better than assuming all expectations to be held with certainty). They would stress that *uncertainty* in the Knightian sense as opposed to risk lay at the root of the problem. Certainly an analysis of behaviour of this kind would provide an interesting alternative to the approach based on probability. There can be no guarantee *ex ante* as to which line of work will prove more fruitful, as a means of replacing the widespread assumption (often unstated) that people's actions are the same as if their expectations were held with certainty.

Analysis of the consequences of inflation is, by its very nature, inevitably concerned with the role of money in the economic system. Inflation is, after all, a sustained fall in the value of money, and as we said at the outset, must be regarded as a fundamentally monetary phenomenon for this reason alone. It does not follow from this that inflation's causes are also inherently monetary, but the evidence which we have cited on the stability of the demand for money function, particularly that generated under inflationary conditions, and the evidence which we have cited on the responsiveness of the inflation rate to excess demand, lends considerable weight to the proposition that sustained expansion of the money supply at a rate in excess of the product of the growth rate of real income and the real income elasticity of demand for money is both a necessary and sufficient condition for sustained inflation.

This, of course, should not be read as implying that only variations in the money supply can have effects on the level of aggregate demand. Swings in business confidence of the type postulated by Wicksell and Keynes can certainly exert an independent influence on aggregate demand, as can fiscal policies. However, we would argue that increases or decreases in aggregate demand from such sources will have only short lived effects on the rate of change of prices unless they also lead to changes in the rate of monetary expansion. But of course they can do just that in certain institutional circumstances, and it may be difficult in practice (for example) to reduce the rate of monetary expansion unless fiscal changes are made. It is the essence of Wicksellian analysis that any attempt to hold down interest rates in the face of an upswing in business confidence will lead to money creation and sustained inflation. It is central to modern work on the role of the government budget constraint in the money supply process that an expansionary fiscal policy met by borrowing from the central bank will result in sustained monetary expansion (cf., for example, Christ (1968), Brunner and Meltzer (1972), Kaldor (1970)). In the light of this work the question as to whether monetary expansion is a unique "cause" of inflation seems to us to be one mainly of semantics, and one that distracts attention from another, more important theme to emerge from our survey, namely that analysis of the inflationary process must involve the study of the whole economic system and not just of one or two markets in isolation. The quantity theory of money might provide one with hypotheses about the behaviour of the money market in the inflationary process, and the Phillips curve with hypotheses about the labour market, but precisely because inflation involves changes in the value of money, its analysis must deal with all markets in which money serves as a means of exchange and a unit of account. That, at least in a developed economy, must mean virtually all markets. The theoretical analysis of fully anticipated inflation in a growing economy recognises this, as does the recent work on what we have termed "complete" models of imperfectly anticipated inflation. As we have seen, work in the latter field is very much in its infancy. We have already noted that progress here is likely to rely on further work on the way in which inflationary expectations interact with economic agents' decisions. Here, we would argue, lies the key to constructing an integrated analysis of the causes and consequences of imperfectly anticipated inflation, a task which must be accomplished before we can expect to see the production of an analytic framework in terms of which all types of inflation can be analysed.

If excessive monetary expansion is a necessary and sufficient condition for sustained inflation, this immediately raises important problems in the analysis of the control of inflation. In developed economies at least the quantity of money is under the control of government, or would be if the government so desired. Why then has it not been controlled recently? How might governments be persuaded to bring monetary expansion under control and to lengthen the time horizon for their monetary policy decisions? These questions are representative of a large group of unsolved problems in the theory of inflation, problems on which the literature we have surveyed casts only a little light. The theoretical literature on the welfare costs of fully anticipated inflationary finance provides a powerful set of arguments against inflation from the point of view of both the government and the community at large. The monetary theory of the balance of payments tells us that a small open economy will find it impossible in the long run to make independent decisions about its money supply or price level while maintaining a fixed exchange rate. This is helpful when it comes to describing, for example, what happened in most economies before 1971, but it does not help us to understand why it happened. Countries which did not like the inflationary pace were not *forced* to maintain fixed exchange rates. But if we do not know why governments generate (or permit) inflation, how can we produce arguments that might persuade them to act against it?

The theoretical arguments against perfectly anticipated inflation are strong indeed, as we have shown above. Thus the prevalence of inflation can only be explained by postulating that Governments believe that there are gains from imperfectly anticipated inflation, or losses from reducing the inflation rate in such a way that the change is not anticipated. Nor is such a view hard to justify in the light of existing literature. First, gains accrue to governments from the effects of inflation on tax revenue and on the value of government debt outstanding, and these are, as we have seen, properly classified as gains from imperfectly anticipated inflation. Moreover, we have also seen that an integral part of the mechanism whereby an imperfectly anticipated inflation accelerates is a fall in unemployment. The gain here, if gain it be, lasts only so long as inflation is unanticipated and hence arises before economic agents perceive the costs involved in achieving it. The same analysis of course leads to the conclusion that slowing down an existing inflation rate imposes costs in terms of higher unemployment before the benefits of such a policy are perceived. Such arguments probably go a long way to explaining the inflationary bias of recent economic policy. Certain observers (e.g. Phelps 1967, 1972) have argued along these lines, and have gone so far as to argue that, once inflation is under way, it might be better to live with it than to cure it.

However, such analysis is tentative, and for a very good reason. Though Phelps (1972) in popularising the ideas first set out in (1967) actually subtitled his book "The Cost Benefit Approach to Monetary Planning", the fact remains that we have no body of analysis analogous to Marshallian or Paretian welfare economics that permits us to discuss coherently the costs and benefits of imperfectly anticipated inflation. We do not even know what an appropriate measure of economic welfare might consist of when we deal with situations in which the outcomes of actions differ from those initially planned. Are we concerned with costs and benefits perceived *ex ante*, or *ex post*? When inflation is imperfectly anticipated these differ.

Once more then we return to what has been the constant theme of this concluding section of our survey. Until we have a much more fully articulated analysis of the formation of expectations and of the interaction of expectations formation and the behaviour of economic agents it is hard to see how we are going to make any significant further progress in understanding inflation. On the other hand, significant progress in this problem area would have implications far beyond the confines of the economics of inflation.

DAVID LAIDLER
MICHAEL PARKIN

University of Western Ontario

REFERENCES

The books and articles listed below are those actually referred to in the text. A more complete bibliography of the literature on inflation, prepared by Geoffrey Hilliard, Andrew Horsman, Linda Ward and Robert Ward is available as a University of Manchester Inflation Workshop Discussion Paper, which may be obtained by writing (enclosing 50p or $ equivalent) to the Secretary, Inflation Workshop, Department of Economics, University of Manchester, Manchester 13.

Abbreviations

AEA	American Economic Association
AEP	Australian Economic Papers
AER (p & p)	American Economic Review (papers and proceedings)
BOEQB	Bank of England Quarterly Bulletin
BOUIES	Bulletin of the Oxford University Institute of Economics and Statistics
CJE	Canadian Journal of Economics
CJEPS	Canadian Journal of Economics and Political Science
EJ	ECONOMIC JOURNAL
FRB	Federal Reserve Board
IER	International Economic Review
JASA	Journal of the American Statistical Association
JES	Journal of Economic Studies
JET	Journal of Economic Theory
JMCB	Journal of Money, Credit and Banking
JME	Journal of Monetary Economics
JOF	Journal of Finance
JPE	Journal of Political Economy
LBR	Lloyds Bank Review
NIER	National Institute Economic Review
OBES	Oxford Bulletin of Economics and Statistics
OECD	Organisation for Economic Co-operation and Development
OEP	Oxford Economic Papers
QJE	Quarterly Journal of Economics
RE Stats	Review of Economics and Statistics
RE Studs	Review of Economic Studies
SAJOE	South African Journal of Economics
SEJ	Southern Economic Journal
SJPE	Scottish Journal of Political Economy
YBESR	Yorkshire Bulletin of Economic and Social Research
YEE	Yale Economic Essays

Ackley, G. (1972). "Observations on Phase II and Wage Controls." *Brookings Papers*, no. 1, pp. 173–90.

AEA & Royal Economic Society. (1965) *Surveys of Economic Theory*. Vol. 1. *Money, Interest and Welfare*. London: Macmillan; New York: St Martin's Press.

Akerlof, G. A. (1969). "Relative Wages and the Rate of Inflation." *QJE*, vol. 83 (3), no. 332, pp. 353–74.

Akyuz, Y. (1973). *Money and Inflation in Turkey 1950–1968*. Political Science Monograph, no. 361. Ankara: Ankara U.P.

Albrecht, W. P. (1966). "The Relationship Between Wage Changes and Unemployment in Metropolitan and Industrial Labour Markets." *YEE*, vol. 6 (2), pp. 279–342.

Alchian, A. A. (1970). In Phelps, E. S. *et al.* "Information Costs, Pricing and Resource Unemployment."

—— and Kessel, R. A. (1959). "Redistribution of Wealth Through Inflation." *Science*, no. 130 (Sept.), pp. 535–9.

—— and Klein, B. (1973). "On a Correct Measure of Inflation." *JMCB*, vol. 5 (1), pp. 173–91.

Alexander, A. J. (1971). "Prices and the Guideposts: The Effects of Government Persuasion on Individual Prices." *R.E. Stats*, vol. 53 (1), pp. 67–75.

Aliber, R. Z. (ed.), (1974). *National Monetary Policies and the International Financial System*. Chicago, London: University of Chicago Press.

Allais, M. (1966). "A Restatement of the Quantity Theory of Money." *AER*, vol. 56 (5), pp. 1123–57.

—— (1969). "Growth and Inflation." *JMCB*, vol. 1 (3), pp. 355–426.

—— (1974). "The Psychological Rate of Interest." *JMCB*, vol. 6 (3), pp. 285–331.

Andersen, L. C. and Carlson, K. M. (1970). "A Monetarist Model for Economic Stabilization." *FRB of St Louis Review*, vol. 52 (4), pp. 7–25.

—— (1972). In Eckstein, O. (ed.). "An Econometric Analysis of the Relation of Monetary Variables to the Behaviour of Prices and Unemployment."

Anderson, P. (1969). "Wages and the Guideposts: Comment." *AER*, vol. 59 (3), pp. 351–54.

Aoki, M. (1967). *Optimisation of Stochastic Systems*. New York: Academic Press.

Archibald, G. C. (1969). "The Phillips Curve and the Distribution of Unemployment." *AER (p & p)*, vol. 59 (2), pp. 124–34.

—— Kemmiss, R. and Perkins, J. W. (1974). In Laidler, D. E. W. and Purdy, D. L. (eds.). "Excess Demand for Labour, Unemployment and the Phillips Curve."

—— and Lipsey, R. G. (1958). "Monetary and Value Theory: A Critique of Lange and Patinkin." *R.E. Studs*, vol. 26 (69), pp. 1–22.

Arrow, K. (1959). "Towards a Theory of Price Adjustment." In Abramovitz, M. (ed.), *The Allocation of Economic Resources*. Stanford: Stanford U.P.

Artis, M. J. and Lewis, M. K. (1975). "The Demand for Money in the U.K. 1963–1973." *Manchester School* (forthcoming).

Ashenfelter, O. C. and Johnson, G. E. (1969). "Bargaining Theory, Trade Unions and Industrial Strike Activity." *AER*, vol. 59 (1), pp. 35–49.

—— —— and Pencavel, J. H. (1972). "Trade Unions and the Rate of Change of Money Wage Rates in United States Manufacturing Industry." *RE Studs*, vol. 39 (1), no. 117, pp. 27–54.

Auernheimer, L. (1974). "The Honest Government's Guide to Inflationary Finance." *JPE*, vol. 82 (3), pp. 598–606.

Bach, G. L. and Ando, A. (1957). "The Redistributional Effects of Inflation." *RE Stats*, vol. 39 (1), pp. 1–13.

—— and Stephenson, J. B. (1974). "Inflation and the Redistribution of Wealth." *RE Stats*, vol. 56 (1), pp. 1–13.

Bailey, M. J. (1956). "The Welfare Cost of Inflationary Finance." *JPE*, vol. 64 (2), pp. 93–110.

Ball, R. J. (1962). "The Prediction of Wage-Rate Changes in the United Kingdom Economy 1957–1960." *EJ*, vol. 72 (285), pp. 27–44.

—— (1964). *Inflation and the Theory of Money*. Chicago, Ill.: Aldine Publishing Co.

—— and Duffy, M. (1972). In Eckstein, O. (ed.). "Price Formation in European Countries."

Balogh, T. (1970). *Labour and Inflation*. London: The Fabian Society.

Bank of England (1970). "The Importance of Money." *BOEQB*, vol. 10 (2), pp. 159–98.

Barret, R. J., Gray, M. R. and Parkin, J. M. (1975). "The Demand for Financial Assets by the Personal Sector of the U.K. Economy." In Renton, G. A. (ed.), *Modelling the Economy*. London: Heinemann Educational (for SSRC).

Barro, R. J. (1970). "Inflation, the Payments Period and the Demand for Money." *JPE*, vol. 78 (6), pp. 1228–63.

—— (1972a). "A Theory of Monopolistic Price Adjustment." *RE Studs*, vol. 39 (1), no. 117, pp. 17–26.

—— (1972b). "Inflationary Finance and the Welfare Cost of Inflation." *JPE*, vol. 80 (5), pp. 978–1001.

—— and Grossman, H. I. (1971). "A General Disequilibrium Model of Income and Employment." *AER*, vol. 61 (1), pp. 82–93.

—— —— (1974). "Suppressed Inflation and the Supply Multiplier." *RE Studs*, vol. 41 (1), no. 125, pp. 87–104.

Baxter, J. L. (1973). "Inflation in the Context of Relative Deprivation and Social Justice." *SJPE*, vol. 20 (3), pp. 262–82.

Behrend, H. (1964). "Price and Incomes Images and Inflation." *SJPE*, vol. 11 (2), pp. 85–103.

—— (1966). "Price Images, Inflation and National Incomes Policy." *SJPE*, vol. 13 (3), pp. 273–96.

Bhatia, R. J. (1961). "Unemployment and the Rate of Change of Money Earnings in the U.S. 1900–1958." *Economica* (NS), vol. 28 (111), pp. 286–96.

Bishop, R. L. (1963). "Game Theoretic Analyses of Bargaining." *QJE*, vol. 77 (4), no. 309, pp. 559–602.

J. Black (1975), "A Dynamic Model of the Quantity Theory." In Parkin, J. M. and A. R. Nobay (eds.). *Current Economic Problems*, Cambridge: Cambridge University Press, 1975.

Bodkin, R. G. (1966). *The Wage-Price-Productivity Nexus*. Philadelphia, Penn.: University of Pennsylvania Press.

Bosworth, B. (1972). "Phase II: The U.S. Experiment with an Income Policy." *Brookings Papers*. no. 2, pp. 343–83.

Bowen, W. G. (1960a). *Wage Behaviour in the Postwar Period: An Empirical Analysis*. Princeton, N.J.: Princeton U.P.

Bowers, J. K., Cheshire, P. C. and Webb, A. E. (1970). "The Change in the Relationship Between Unemployment and Earnings Increases." *NIER*, no. 54, pp. 44–63.

Box, G. E. P. and Jenkins, G. H. (1970). *Time Series Analysis: Forecasting and Control*. New York: Holden Day.

Brechling, F. P. R. (1968). "The Trade-Off Between Inflation and Unemployment." *JPE*, vol. 76 (4), pp. 712–37.

—— (1972). In Parkin, J. M. and Sumner, M. T. (eds.). "Some Empirical Evidence on the Effectiveness of Prices and Income Policies." Ch. 2, pp. 30–47.

—— (1973). "Wage Inflation and The Structure of Regional Unemployment." (Reprinted in Laidler, D. E. W. & Purdy, D. L. (eds.) 1974.) *JMCB*, vol. 5 (1), pp. 355–79.

Bresciani-Turroni, C. (1968). *The Economics of Inflation: A Study of Currency Depreciation in Postwar Germany.* New York: Kelly (earlier editions 1931, 1937).

Brock, W. (1972). "On Models of Expectations That Arise From Maximisation Behaviour of Economic Behaviour Over Time." *JET*, vol. 5 (3), pp. 348–76.

Bronfenbrenner, M. (1950). "Trade Unions, Full Employment and Inflation-Comment." *AER*, vol. 40 (5), pp. 622–4.

—— and Holzman, F. D. (1963). "A Survey of Inflation Theory." *AER*, vol. 53 (4), pp. 593–661. (Reprinted in AEA and Royal Economic Society, 1965.)

Brown, A. J. (1955). *The Great Inflation, 1939–1951.* London: Oxford U.P.

Brunner, K. (1951). "Inconsistency and Indeterminacy in Classical Economics." *Econometrica*, vol. 19 (2), pp. 152–73.

—— (1974). In Aliber, R. Z. (ed.). "Monetary Management, Domestic Inflation, and Imported Inflation."

—— (1975). In Parkin, J. M. and Zis, G. (eds.). "A Fisherian Analysis of World Inflation."

—— Fratianni, M., Jordan, J. L., Meltzer, A. H., and Neumann, M. J. M. (1973). "Fiscal and Monetary Policies in Moderate Inflation." *JMCB*, vol. 5 (1), pp. 313–53.

—— and Meltzer, A. H. (1971). "The Uses of Money: Money in the Theory of an Exchange Economy." *AER*, vol. 61 (5), pp. 784–805.

—— —— (1972). "Money, Debt and Economic Activity." *JPE*, vol. 80 (5), pp. 951–77.

—— —— (1973). "Mr Hicks and the Monetarists." *Economica* (NS), vol. 40 (no. 157), pp. 44–59.

—— —— (eds.) (1975). *Proceedings of the Conference on Wage and Price Controls at Rochester University, New York, October* (1973).

Burmeister, E. and Phelps, E. S. (1971). "Money, Public Debt, Inflation and Real Interest." *JMCB*, vol. 3 (2), pp. 153–82.

Burns, M. E. (1972). "Regional Phillips Curves: A Further Note." *BOUIES*, vol. 34 (3), pp. 295–307.

Burrows, P. and Hitiris, T. (1972). "Estimating the Impact of Incomes Policy." *Bulletin of Economic Research*, 24 (1), vol. pp. 42–51. (Reprinted in Parkin, J. M. and Sumner, M. T. (eds.) 1972.)

Cagan, P. (1956). In Friedman, M. (ed.): "The Monetary Dynamics of Hyperinflation."

—— (1965). *Determinants and Effects of Changes in the Stock of Money 1870–1960.* New York: Columbia U.P. (for NBER).

—— (1968). In Rousseas, S. W. (ed.): "Theories of Mild, Continuing Inflation: A Critique and Extension."

—— (1969). "Allais' Monetary Theory: Interpretation and Comment." *JMCB*, vol. 1 (3), pp. 427–32.

Campbell, C. D. (1970). In Meiselman, D. (ed.): "The Velocity of Money and the Rate of Inflation: Recent Experiences in South Korea and Brazil."

Cargill, T. F. (1969). "An Empirical Investigation of the Wage-Lag Hypothesis." *AER*, vol. 59 (5), pp. 806–16.

Carlson, J. A. and Parkin, J. M. (1975). "Inflation Expectations." *Economica*, (NS) vol. 42 (166), pp. 123–38.

Carsberg, B. V., Hope, A. J. B. and Scapens, R. W. (eds.). (Forthcoming.) *Studies in Accounting for Inflation.* Manchester: Manchester U.P.

Cathcart, C. D. (1974). "Monetary Dynamics, Growth and the Efficiency of Inflationary Finance." *JMCB*, vol. 6 (2), pp. 169–90.

Christ, C. F. (1968). "A Simple Macroeconomic Model With a Government Budget Constraint." *JPE*, vol. 76 (1), pp. 53–67.

Christenson, C. L. (1954). "Variations in the Inflationary Force of Bargaining." *AER* (*p & p*), vol. 44 (2), pp. 347–62.

Claassen, E. and Salin, P. (eds.) (1972). *Stabilisation Policies in Interdependent Economies.* Amsterdam: North-Holland.

Clayton, G., Gilbert, J. C. and Sedgwick, R. (eds.) (1971). *Monetary Theory and Monetary Policy in the 1970's.* London: Oxford U.P.

Clower, R. W. (1965). In Hahn, F. H. and Brechling, F. P. R. (eds.). "The Keynesian Counter-Revolution: A Theoretical Appraisal." (Reprinted in part in Clower, R. W. (ed.) 1969.)

—— (ed.) (1969). *Monetary Theory.* Harmondsworth: Penguin Education.

—— Burstein, M. L. (1960). "On the Invariance of Demand for Cash and Other Assets." *RE Studs*, vol. 28 (57), pp. 32–6.

Coddington, A. (1966). "A Theory of the Bargaining Process: Comment." *AER*, vol. 56 (3), pp. 522–30 (reprinted in Coddington, A., 1968).
—— (1968). *Theories of the Bargaining Process*. London: Allen & Unwin.
Commission on Money and Credit. (1964). *Inflation, Growth and Unemployment*. Englewood Cliffs, N.J.: Prentice-Hall.
Conard, J. W. (1964). In Commission on Money and Credit. "The Causes and Consequences of Inflation."
Connolly, M. B. and Swoboda, A. K. (1973). *International Trade and Money*. London: Allen & Unwin.
Corry, B. A. and Laidler, D. E. W. (1967). "The Phillips Relation: A Theoretical Explanation." *Economica* (NS), vol. 34 (134), pp. 189–97.
Cowling, K. and Metcalf, D. (1967). "Wage–Unemployment Relationships: A Regional Analysis for the U.K. 1960–1965." *BOUIES* 29 (1), pp. 31–9.
Cross, J. G. (1965). "A Theory of the Bargaining Process." *AER*, vol. 55 (1), pp. 67–94.
—— (1966). "A Theory of the Bargaining Process – Reply." *AER*, vol. 56 (3), pp. 630–33.
Cross, R. B. and Laidler, D. E. W. (1975). In Parkin, J. M. and Zis, G. (eds.). "Inflation, Excess Demand and Expectations in Fixed Exchange Rate Open Economies: Some Preliminary Empirical Results."
Davidson, P. (1972). *Money and the Real World*. London: Macmillan.
Deaver, J. V. (1970). In Meiselman, D. (ed.). "The Chilean Inflation and the Demand for Money."
Dicks-Mireaux, L. A. (1961). "The Inter-Relationship Between Cost and Price Changes, 1945–1959: A Study of Inflation in Postwar Britain." *OEP* (NS), vol. 13 (3), pp. 267–92.
—— and Dow, J. C. R. (1959). "The Determinants of Wage Inflation in the United Kingdom, 1946–1956." *Journal of the Royal Statistical Society*, series A (General), vol. 122 (2), pp. 145–84.
Diz, A. C. (1970). In Meiselman, D. (ed.). "Money and Prices in Argentina, 1935–1962."
Dornbusch, R. and Frenkel, J. A. (1973). "Inflation and Growth: Alternative Approaches." *JMCB*, vol. 5 (1), pt. 1, pp. 141–56.
Dow, J. C. R. (1956). "Analysis of the Generation of Price Inflation." *OEP* (NS), vol. 8 (3), pp. 252–301.
—— and Dicks-Mireaux, L. A. (1958). "The Excess Demand for Labour." *OEP* (NS), vol. 10 (1), pp. 1–33.
Duck, N. W., Parkin, J. M., Rose, D. and Zis, G. (1975). In Parkin, J. M. and Zis, G. (eds.). "The Determination of the Rate of Change of Wages and Prices in the Fixed Exchange Rate World Economy: 1956–1970."
Dutton, D. S. (1971a). "A Model of Self-Generating Inflation: The Argentine Case." *JMCB*, vol. 3 (2), pt. 1, pp. 245–62.
—— (1971b). "The Demand for Money and the Price Level." *JPE*, vol. 79 (5), pp. 1161–70.
Eagly, R. V. (1965). "Market Power as an Intervening Mechanism in Phillips Curve Analysis." *Economica* (NS), vol. 32 (125), pp. 48–64.
Eatwell, J., Llewellyn, J. and Tarling, R. (1974). "Money Wage Inflation in Industrial Countries." *RE Studs*, vol. 61 (4), no. 128, pp. 515–23.
Eckstein, O. (ed.) (1972). *The Econometrics of Price Determination, Conference*. Washington, D.C.: Board of Governors of the Federal Reserve System and the S.S.R.C.
—— and Fromm, G. (1968). "The Price Equation." *AER*, vol. 58 (5), pt. 1, pp. 1159–84.
Edgren, G., Faxen, K. O. and Odhner, G. E. (1969). "Wages Growth and the Distribution of Income." *Swedish Journal of Economics*, vol. 71 (3), pp. 133–60.
Feige, E. L. (1974). In Johnson, H. G. and Nobay, A. R. (eds.). "Alternative Temporal Cross-Section Specifications of the Demand for Demand Deposits."
—— and Parkin, J. M. (1971). "The Optimal Quantity of Money, Bonds, Commodity Inventories and Capital." *AER*, vol. 61 (3), pt. 1, pp. 335–49.
Feldman, A. M. (1973). "Bilateral Trading Processes, Pairwise Optimality and Pareto Optimality." *RE Studs*, vol. 40 (4), no. 124, pp. 463–73.
Feldstein, M. and Chamberlain, G. (1973). "Multimarket Expectations and the Rate of Interest." *JMCB*, vol. 5 (4), pp. 873–902.
Felix, D. (1956). "Profit Inflation and Industrial Growth: The Historic Record and Contemporary Analogies." *QJE*, vol. 70 (3), no. 320, pp. 441–63.
Fiedler, E. R. (1972). "The Price–Wage Stabilisation Program." *Brookings Papers*, no. 1, pp. 199–206.
Fisher, D. (1970). "The Instruments of Monetary Policy and the Generalized Trade-Off Function for Britain, 1955–1968." *Manchester School*, vol. 38 (3), pp. 209–22.
Fisher, I. (1896). "Appreciation and interest." *AEA Publications, Series Three* (II), Aug., pp. 331–442.
—— (1911). *The Purchasing Power of Money*. Macmillan, New York. (Latest edition, A. M. Kelly, New York, 1963.)
—— (1926). "A Statistical Relation Between Unemployment and Price Changes." *International Labour Review* (reprinted as "I Discovered the Phillips Curve," *JPE*, vol. 81 (2), pt. 1, Mar./Apr. 1973), pp. 496–502.

Flanagan, R. J. (1973) "The U.S. Phillips Curve and International Unemployment Rate Differentials." *AER*, vol. 63 (1), pp. 114–31.

Foldes, L. (1964). "A Determinate Model of Bilateral Monopoly." *Economica* (NS), vol. 31 (121), pp. 117–31.

Foley, D. K. and Sidrauski, M. (1971). *Monetary and Fiscal Policy in a Growing Economy*. New York: Macmillan.

Foster, J. I. (1973). "The Behaviour of Unemployment and Unfilled Vacancies: Great Britain 1958–1971 – A Comment." *EJ*, vol. 83 (329), pp. 192–201.

—— (1974). In Laidler, D. E. W. and Purdy, D. L. (eds.). "The Relationship Between Unemployment and Vacancies in Great Britain (1958–1972): Some Further Evidence."

—— (1975). "The Redistributive Effects of Inflation – Questions and Answers." University of Manchester. Inflation Workshop Discussion Paper, no. 7504.

Friedman, M. (ed.) (1956). *Studies in the Quantity Theory of Money*. Chicago, Ill.: University of Chicago Press.

—— (1959). "The Demand for Money – Some Theoretical and Empirical Results." *JPE*, vol. 67 (4), pp. 327–51.

—— (1966). "Interest Rates and the Demand for Money." *Journal of Law and Economics*, vol. 9 (reprinted in Friedman, M. 1969).

—— (1968). "The Role of Monetary Policy." *AER*, vol. 58 (1), pp. 1–17.

—— (1969). *The Optimum Quantity of Money*. Chicago, Ill.: Aldine Press.

—— (1970). *The Counter-Revolution in Monetary Theory*. London: *IEA* (for Wincott Foundation) Occasional Paper, no. 33.

—— (1971). "Government Revenue From Inflation." *JPE*, vol. 79 (4), pp. 846–56.

—— (1972). "Comments on the Critics." *JPE*, vol. 80 (5), pp. 906–50.

—— and Schwartz, A. J. (1963). *A Monetary History of the United States, 1867–1960*. Princeton, N.J.: Princeton U.P. (For N.B.E.R.)

Fromm, G. and Taubman, P. (1968). *Policy Simulations With an Econometric Model*. Washington, D.C.: The Brookings Institution.

Gallaway, L. E. (1958). "The Wage-Push Inflation Thesis, 1950–1957." *AER*, vol. 48 (5), pp. 967–72.

—— Koshal, R. K. and Chapin, G. L. (1970). "The Relationship Between the Rate of Change in Money Wage Rates and Unemployment Levels in South Africa." *SAJOE*, vol. 38 (4), pp. 367–73.

Gibson, W. (1970). "Price Expectations Effects on Interest Rates." *JOF*, March.

Giersch, H. *et al.* (1974). *Essays on Inflation and Indexation*. Washington, D.C.: American Enterprise Institute for Public Policy Research.

Godfrey, L. (1971). In Johnson, H. G. and Nobay, A. R. (eds.). "The Phillips Curve: Incomes Policy and Trade Union Effects." (Abridged and Amended in Parkin, J. M. and Sumner, M. T. (eds.), 1972.)

—— and Taylor, J. (1973). "Earnings Changes in the U.K. 1954–1970: Excess Labour Supply, Expected Inflation and Union Influence." *BOUIES*, vol. 35 (3), pp. 197–216.

Godley, W. A. H. and Nordhaus, W. D. (1972). "Pricing in the Trade Cycle." *EJ*, vol. 82 (327), pp. 853–82.

—— and Rowe, D. A. (1964). "Retail and Consumer Prices." *NIER* (30), pp. 44–57.

Goldman, S. M. (1972). "Hyperinflation and the Rate of Growth in the Money Supply." *JET*, vol. 5 (2), pp. 250–57.

Gordon, D. F. and Hynes, A. (1970). In Phelps, E. S. *et al.* "On the Theory of Price Dynamics."

Gordon, R. J. (1971). "Inflation in Recession and Recovery." *Brookings Papers*, no. 1, pp. 105–58.

—— (1972). "Wage-Price Controls and the Shifting Phillips Curve." *Brookings Papers*, no. 2, pp. 385–421.

—— (1973). "The Response of Wages and Prices to the First Two Years of Controls." *Brookings Papers*, no. 3, pp. 765–79.

Gray, M. R. (1975). "Inflation Expectations and the Accelerationist Controversy." University of Manchester Inflation Workshop Discussion Paper, no. 7507 (mimeo).

—— and Parkin, J. M. (1974). "Discriminating Between Alternative Explanations of Inflation." University of Manchester Inflation Workshop Discussion Paper, no. 7414 (mimeo).

—— Ward, R. and Zis, G. (1975). In Parkin, J. M. and Zis, G. (eds.). "World Demand for Money." (Forthcoming.)

Griffin, K. B. (1962). "A Note on Wages Prices and Unemployment." *BOUIES*, vol. 24 (3), pp. 379–85.

Gronau, R. (1971). "Information and Frictional Unemployment." *AER*, vol. 61 (3), pt. 1, pp. 290–301.

Gujarati, D. (1972a). "The Behaviour of Unemployment and Unfilled Vacancies: Great Britain, 1958–1971." *EJ*, 82 (325), pp. 195–204.

—— (1972b). "A Reply to Mr Taylor." *EJ*, vol. 82 (328), pp. 1365–68.

Gustman, A. (1972). "Wage Bargains and the Phillips Curve – Re-examination." *QJE*, vol. 86 (2), no. 343, pp. 332–38.

Hague, D. C. (ed.) (1962). *Inflation*. London: Macmillan.

Hahn, F. H. and Brechling, F. P. R. (eds.) (1965). *The Theory of Interest Rates*. London: Macmillan.

Hamermesh, D. S. (1970). "Wage Bargains, Threshold Effects, and the Phillips Curve." *QJE*, vol. 84 (3), no. 336, pp. 501–17.

—— (1972a), "Wage Bargains, Threshold Effects, and the Phillips Curve: Reply." *QJE*, vol. 86 (2), no. 343, pp. 339–41.

—— (1972b), "Market Power and Wage Inflation." *SEJ*, vol. 39 (2), pp. 204–12.

Hamilton, E. J. (1934). *American Treasure and the Price Revolution in Spain, 1501–1650*. Cambridge, Mass.

Hancock, K. J. (1966). "Earnings Drift in Australia." *Journal of Industrial Relations*, vol. 8 (2), pp. 128–57 (reprinted in Isaac, J. E. and Ford, G. W. (eds.), 1967).

Hansen, A. H. (1925). "Factors Affecting the Trend in Real Wages." *AER*, vol. 15 (1), pp. 27–42.

—— (1953). *A Guide to Keynes*. New York: McGraw-Hill.

Hansen, B. (1951). *A Study in the Theory of Inflation*. London: Macmillan.

—— (1957). In Dunlop, J. T. (ed.). "Full Employment and Wage Stability." (Reprinted 1966.)

—— (1970). "Excess Demand, Unemployment, Vacancies and Wages." *QJE*, vol. 84 (1), no. 334, pp. 1–23.

Harrod, R. F. (1969). *Money*. London: Macmillan.

—— (1971). In Clayton, G., Gilbert, J. C. and Sedgwick, R. (eds.). Discussant's Comments on Paper by M. Friedman.

—— (1972). In Hinshaw, R. (ed.). "The Issues: Five Views."

Harsanyi, J. C. (1966). "Approaches to the Bargaining Problem Before and After the Theory of Games: A Critical Discussion on Zeuthen, Hicks and Nash." *Econometrica*, vol. 24 (2), pp. 144–57.

Hayek, F. A. (1933). *Monetary Theory and the Trade Cycle*. London: Jonathan Cape.

Helliwell, J. F. et al. (1971). *The Structure of RDX2*. Bank of Canada Staff Research Papers, no. 7 (2 parts).

Hicks, J. R. (1932). (2nd ed., 1963.) *The Theory of Wages*. London: Macmillan.

—— (1937). "Mr Keynes and the 'Classics': A Suggested Interpretation." *Econometrica*, vol. 5 (2), pp. 147–59.

—— (1974). *The Crisis in Keynesian Economics*. Oxford: Blackwell.

—— (1975). "The Permissive Economy." In *Crisis '75 . . . ?* IEA Occasional Paper Special, no. 43, London: IEA.

Higgins, C. I. (1973). "A Wage-Price Sector for a Quarterly Australian Model." In Powell, A. A. and Williams, R. A. (eds.).

Hines, A. G. (1964). "Trade Unions and Wage Inflation in the United Kingdom, 1893–1961." *RE Studs*, vol. 31 (3), no. 88, pp. 221–52.

—— (1968). "Unemployment and the Rate of Change of Money Wage Rates in the United Kingdom 1862–1963: A Reappraisal." *RE Stats*, vol. 50 (1), pp. 60–7.

—— (1969). "Wage Inflation in the United Kingdom 1948–1962: A Disaggregated Study." *EJ*, vol. 79 (313), pp. 66–89.

—— (1971). In Johnson, H. G. and Nobay, A. R. "The Determinants of the Rate of Change of Money Wage Rates and the Effectiveness of Incomes Policy."

—— (1972). "The Phillips Curve and the Distribution of Unemployment." *AER*, vol. 62 (1), pp. 155–60.

Hinshaw, R. (ed.) (1972). *Inflation as a Global Problem*. London: Johns Hopkins Press.

Holmes, J. M. and Smyth, D. J. (1970). "The Relationship Between Unemployment and the Excess Demand for Labour: an Examination of the Theory of the Phillips Curve." *Economica* (NS), vol. 37 (147), pp. 311–14.

Holt, C. C. (1970a). In Phelps, E. S. et al.. "Job Search, Phillips' Wage Relation and Union Influence: Theory and Evidence."

—— (1970b). In Phelps, E. S. et al. "How Can the Phillips Curve be Moved to Reduce Both Inflation and Unemployment?"

Hu, T-W. (1971). "Hyper-Inflation and the Dynamics of the Demand for Money in China, 1945–1949." *JPE*, vol. 79 (1), pp. 186–95.

Hymans, S. H. (1972). In Eckstein, O. (ed.). "Prices and Price Behaviour in Three Econometric Models."

—— (1963). "A Survey of Theories of Inflation." *Indian Economic Review*, vol. 6 (4). (Reprinted in Johnson, H. G., 1967b.)

Johnson, H. G. (1967a). In Johnson, H. G. "Money in a Neo-Classical One-Sector Growth Model."

—— (1967b). *Essays in Monetary Economics*. London: Allen and Unwin.

—— (1972). "Inflation and the Monetarist Controversy." Amsterdam: North-Holland.

—— (1973). "Secular Inflation and the International Monetary System." *JMCB*, vol. 5 (1), pt. II, pp. 509–20.

Johnson, H. G. and Nobay, A. R. (eds.) (1971). *The Current Inflation.* London: Macmillan.
—— —— (1974). (eds.). *Issues in Monetary Economics.* London: Oxford U.P.
Johnston, J. (1972). "A Model of Wage Determination Under Bilateral Monopoly." *EJ*, vol. 82 (327), pp. 837–52 (reprinted in Laidler, D. E. W. and Purdy, D. (eds.), 1974).
—— and Timbrell, M. C. (1973). "Empirical Tests of a Bargaining Model of Wage Rate Determination." *Manchester School*, vol. 41 (2), pp. 141–67 (reprinted in Laidler, D. E. W. and Purdy, D. (eds.), 1974).
Jones, A. (1972). *The New Inflation: The Politics of Prices and Incomes.* London: Penguin Books and Andre Deutsch.
De Jong, F. J. (1973). *Developments of Monetary Theory in the Netherlands.* Rotterdam: Rotterdam U.P.
Jonson, P. D., Mahar, K. L. and Thompson, G. J. (1975). "Earnings and Award Wages in Australia." Reserve Bank of Australia discussion paper.
Kaldor, N. (1970). "The New Monetarism." *LBR*, no. 97, pp. 1–18.
Kaliski, S. F. (1964). "The Relation Between Unemployment and the Rate of Change of Money Wages in Canada." *IER*, vol. 5 (1), pp. 1–33.
—— (1972). *The Trade-Off Between Inflation and Unemployment: Some Explorations of the Recent Evidence for Canada.* Ottawa: Economic Council of Canada Special Study, no. 22.
Kaun, D. E. (1965). "Wage Adjustments in the Appalachian States." *SEJ*, vol. 32 (2), pp. 127–36.
—— (1970). "The Relation Between Wages and Unemployment in U.S. Cities 1955–1965." *Manchester School*, no. 38 (1), pp. 1–14.
Kessel, R. A. and Alchian, A. A. (1960). "The Meaning and Validity of the Inflation-Induced Lag of Wages Behind Prices." *AER*, vol. 50 (1), pp. 43–66.
Keynes, J. M. (1923). *A Tract on Monetary Reform.* London: Macmillan.
—— (1930). *A Treatise on Money.* Vol. II. *The Applied Theory of Money.* London: Macmillan.
—— (1936). *The General Theory of Employment, Interest and Money.* London: Macmillan.
Kirkpatrick, C. H. and Nixson, F. I. (1974). "The Origins of Inflation in Less Developed Countries." University of Manchester Inflation Workshop Discussion Paper, no. 7413 (mimeo).
Klein, L. R. and Ball, R. J. (1959). "Some Econometrics of the Determination of the Absolute Level of Wages and Prices." *EJ*, vol. 69 (275), pp. 465–82.
—— and Evans, M. K. (1967). *The Wharton Econometric Forecasting Model.* Philadelphia, Penn.: University of Pennsylvania Press.
—— and Goldberger, A. S. (1955). *An Econometric Model of the United States 1929–1952.* Amsterdam: North-Holland.
Knight, K. G. (1972). "Strikes and Wage Inflation in British Manufacturing Industry 1950–1968." *BOUIES*, vol. 35 (3), pp. 281–94.
Knowles, K. G. J. C. and Winsten, C. B. (1959). "Can the Level of Unemployment Explain Changes in Wages?" *BOUIES*, vol. 21 (2), pp. 113–20.
Koshal, R. K. and Gallaway, L. E. (1971). "The Phillips Curve for West Germany." *Kyklos*, vol. 24 (2), pp. 346–9.
Kuh, E. (1959). "Profits, Mark-Ups and Productivity: an Examination of Corporate Behaviour Since 1947." Study Paper no. 15, Studies of Employment, Growth and Price Levels, Washington, D.C.: U.S. Joint Economic Committee.
—— (1967). "A Productivity Theory of Wage Levels – An Alternative to the Phillips Curve." *RE Studs*, vol. 34 (4), no. 100, pp. 333–60.
Kuska, E. A. (1966). "The Simple Analytics of the Phillips Curve." *Economica* (NS), vol. 33 (132), pp. 462–7.
Laidler, D. E. W. (1966). "The Rate of Interest and the Demand for Money – Some Empirical Evidence." *JPE*, vol. 74 (6), pp. 545–55.
—— (1969a). *The Demand for Money: Theories and Evidence.* Scranton, Pa.: International Textbook Co.
—— (1969b). "Money, Wealth and Time Preference in a Stationary Economy." *CJE*, vol. 2 (4), pp. 526–35.
—— (1972). "On Wicksell's Theory of Price-Level Dynamics." *Manchester School*, vol. 40 (2), pp. 125–44 (reprinted in Laidler, D. E. W., 1975).
—— (1973a). "The Influence of Money on Real Income and Inflation: A Simple Model With Some Empirical Tests for the United States, 1953–1972." *Manchester School*, vol. 41 (4), pp. 367–95 (reprinted in Laidler, D. E. W., 1975).
—— (1974). "Information, Money and the Macroeconomics of Inflation." *Swedish Journal of Economics*, vol. 76 (1), pp. 27–42 (reprinted in Laidler, D. E. W., 1975).
—— (1975a). *Essays on Money and Inflation.* Manchester and Chicago: Manchester U.P. and Chicago U.P.
—— (1975b). "Price and Output Fluctuations in an Open Economy." In Laidler, D. E. W. (1975a).
—— and Purdy, D. (eds.) (1974). *Labour Markets and Inflation.* Manchester and Toronto: Manchester U.P. and Toronto U.P.
Lapkin, D. T. (1950). "Trade Unionism, Full Employment and Inflation – Comment." *AER*, vol. 40 (4), pp. 625–7.

Lerner, E. (1956). In Friedman, M. (ed.). "Inflation in the Confederacy, 1861–1865."

Leslie, D. G. (1973). "A Note on the Regional Distribution of Unemployment." *OBES*, vol. 35 (3), pp. 233–7.

Lipsey, R. G. (1960). "The Relationship Between Unemployment and the Rate of Change of Money Wage Rates in the U.K. 1862–1957: A Further Analysis." *Economica* (NS), vol. 27 (105), pp. 1–31.

—— and Parkin, J. M., (1970). "Incomes Policy: A Reappraisal." *Economica* (NS), vol. 37 (146), pp. 115–38 (reprinted in Parkin, J. M. and Sumner, M. T. (eds.), 1972).

—— and Steuer, M. D. (1961). "The Relation Between Profits and Wage Rates." *Economica* (NS), vol. 28 (110), pp. 137–55.

Lucas, R. E. Jnr. (1972a). In Eckstein, O. (ed.). "Testing the Natural Rate Hypothesis."

—— (1972b). "Expectations and the Neutrality of Money." *JET*, vol. 4 (2), pp. 103–24.

—— (1973). "Some International Evidence on Output-Inflation Trade Offs." *AER*, vol. 63 (3), pp. 326–34.

—— and Rapping, L. A. "Price Expectations and the Phillips Curve." *AER*, vol. 59 (3), June (1969), pp. 342–50 (reprinted in Phelps, E. S. *et al.*, 1970).

MacKay, D. I. (1972). "Redundancy and Re-Engagement: A Study of Car Workers." *Manchester School*, vol. 40 (3), pp. 295–312.

—— and Hart, R. A. (1974). "Wage Inflation and the Phillips Relationship." *Manchester School*, vol. 42 (2), pp. 136–61.

—— and Reid, G. L. (1972). "Redundancy, Unemployment and Manpower Policy." *EJ*, vol. 82 (328), pp. 1256–72.

Marris, S. (1972). In Claassen, E. and Salin, P. (eds.), "World Inflation – Panel Discussion."

Marty, A. L. (1964). "The Real Balance Effect: An Exercise in Capital Theory." *CJEPS*, vol. 30 (3), pp. 360–7.

—— (1967). "Growth and the Welfare Cost of Inflationary Finance." *JPE*, vol. 75 (1), pp. 71–6.

—— (1973). "Growth, Satiety and the Tax Revenue From Money Creation." *JPE*, vol. 81 (5), pp. 1136–52.

McCallum, B. T. (1970). "The Effect of Demand on Prices in British Manufacturing: Another View." *RE Studs*, vol. 37 (1), no. 109, pp. 147–55.

—— (1973). "Freidman's Missing Equation; Another Approach." *Manchester School*, vol. 41 (3), pp. 311–28.

—— (1975). "Rational Expectations and the Natural Rate Hypothesis: Some Evidence for the United Kingdom." *Manchester School*, vol. 43 (1), pp. 55–67.

Meiselman, D. (ed.). (1970). *Varieties of Monetary Experience*. Chicago, Ill.: University of Chicago Press.

De Menil, G. (1971). *Bargaining, Monopoly Power versus Union Power*. Cambridge, Mass.: M.I.T. Press.

—— (1974). "Aggregate Price Dynamics." *RE Stats*, vol. 51 (2), pp. 129–41.

Metcalf, D. (1971). "The Determination of Earnings Changes: A Regional Analysis for the U.K., 1960–1968." *IER*, vol. 12 (2), pp. 273–82.

Mitchell, W. C. (1908). *Gold, Prices and Wages Under the Greenback Standard*. Berkeley, Calif.

Modigliani, F. (1944). "Liquidity Preference and the Theory of Interest and Money." *Econometrica*, vol. 12 (1), pp. 45–88.

—— (1963). "The Monetary Mechanism and its Interaction With Real Phenomena." *RE Stats*, vol. 45 (1), pt. II (suppl.), pp. 79–107.

—— and Tarantelli, E. (1973). "A Generalization of the Phillips Curve for a Developing Country." *RE Studs*, vol. 40 (2), no. 122, pp. 203–24.

Mortensen, D. T. (1970). "Job Search, the Duration of Unemployment and the Phillips Curve." *AER*, vol. 60 (5), pp. 847–62, reprinted in Phelps, E. S. *et al.* (1970).

Morton, W. A. (1950). "Trade Unionism, Full Employment and Inflation." *AER*, vol. 40 (1), pp. 13–39.

Mulvey, C. and Trevithick, J. A. (1974). "Some Evidence on the Wage Leadership Hypothesis." *SJPE*, vol. 21 (1), pp. 1–12.

Mundell, R. A. (1963). "Inflation and Real Interest." *JPE*, vol. 71 (3), pp. 280–3.

—— (1965). "Growth, Stability and Inflationary Finance." *JPE*, vol. 73 (2), pp. 97–109.

—— (1968). *International Economics*. New York: Macmillan.

—— (1971). *Monetary Theory: Inflation, Interest and Growth in the World Economy*. Pacific Palisades, Calif.: Goodyear Publishing Co.

Muth, J. F. (1960). "Optimal Properties of Exponentially Weighted Forecasts." *JASA*, vol. 55 (290), pp. 299–306.

—— (1961). "Rational Expectations and the Theory of Price Movements." *Econometrica*, vol. 29 (3), pp. 315–35.

Nash, J. F. Jnr. (1950). "The Bargaining Problem." *Econometrica*, vol. 18 (2), pp. 155–62.

—— (1953). "Two Person Co-Operative Games." *Econometrica*, vol. 21 (1), pp. 128–40.

Neild, R. R. (1963). *Pricing and Employment in the Trade Cycle*. London: Cambridge U.P. (for N.I.E.S.R.).

Nevile, J. W. (1970). *Fiscal Policy in Australia: Theory and Practice*. Melbourne: Cheshire.

Niehans, J. (1969). "Money in a Static Theory of Optimal Payment Arrangements." *JMCB*, vol. 1 (4), pp. 706–26.

Nobay, A. R. (1974). In Johnson, H. G. and Nobay, A. R. (eds.). "A Model of the United Kingdom Monetary Authorities' Behaviour 1959–1969."

Nordhaus, W. D. (1972a). In Eckstein, O. (ed.). "Recent Developments in Price Dynamics."

—— (1972b). "The World-Wide Wage Explosion." *Brookings Papers*, no. 2, pp. 431–63.

—— (1973). "The Effects of Inflation on the Distribution of Economic Welfare." *JMCB*, vol. 5 (1), pt. ii, pp. 465–504.

—— (1975). "Political Business Cycle." *RE Studs* (forthcoming).

OECD (1970). *Inflation: The Present Problem*. Paris: OECD.

Ostroy, J. M. (1973). "The Information Efficiency of Monetary Exchange." *AER*, vol. 63 (4), pp. 597–610.

Packer, A. H. and Park, S. H. (1973). "Distortions in Relative Wages and Shifts in the Phillips Curve." *RE Stats*, vol. 55 (1), pp. 16–22.

Page, S. A. B. and Trollope, S. (1974). "An International Survey of Indexing and its Effects." *NIER* (70), pp. 46–59.

Paish, F. W. (1962). *Studies in an Inflationary Economy – The United Kingdom, 1948–1961*, 2nd ed. (1966). London: Macmillan.

Parkin, J. M. (1970). "Incomes Policy: Some Further Results on the Rate of Change of Money Wages." *Economica* (NS), vol. 37 (148), pp. 386–401 (reprinted in Parkin, J. M. and Sumner, M. T. (eds.), 1972).

—— (1973a). "The 1973 Report of the President's Council of Economic Advisers: A Critique." *AER*, vol. 63 (4), pp. 535–45.

—— (1973b). "The Short Run and Long Run Trade-Off Between Inflation and Unemployment in Australia." *AEP*, vol. 12, pp. 127–44.

—— (1974). In Aliber, R. Z. (ed.). "Inflation, the Balance of Payments, Domestic Credit Expansion and Exchange Rate Adjustments."

—— and Sumner, M. T. (eds.). (1972). *Incomes Policy and Inflation*. Manchester and Toronto: Manchester U.P. and Toronto U.P.

—— Sumner, M. T. and Jones, R. A. (1972). In Parkin, J. M. and Sumner, M. T. (eds.). "A Survey of the Econometric Evidence of the Effects of Incomes Policy on the Rate of Inflation."

—— Sumner, M. T. and Ward, R. (1975). In Brunner, K. and Meltzer, A. H. (eds.). "The Effects of Excess Demand, Generalised Expectations and Wage-Price Controls on Wage Inflation in the U.K." (Forthcoming.)

—— and Zis, G. (eds.) (1975). *Inflation in the World Economy*.

Parkinson, J. R. (1958). "Wage Stability and Employment." *SJPE*, vol. 5 (2), pp. 85–98.

Patinkin, D. (1956). *Money, Interest and Price – an Integration of Monetary and Value Theory*. Evanston Ill.: Row Peterson (2nd ed., New York: Harper and Row).

—— (1969). "The Chicago Tradition, the Quantity Theory and Friedman." *JMCB*, vol. 1 (1), pp. 46–70 (reprinted in Patinkin, D, 1972a).

—— (1972a). *Studies in Monetary Economics*. New York, Harper and Row.

—— (1972b). In Patinkin, D. "Monetary and Price Developments in Israel, 1949–1953."

—— (1974). In Johnson, H. G. and Nobay, A. R. (eds.). "Keynesian Monetary Theory and the Cambridge School."

Paunio, J. J. (1961). *A Study in the Theory of Open Inflation*. Helsinki: Bank of Finland.

Pencavel, J. H. (1970). "An Investigation into Industrial Strike Activity in Britain." *Economica* (NS), vol. 37 (147), pp. 239–56.

Perry, G. L. (1964). "The Determinants of Wage Rate Changes and the Inflation-Unemployment Trade-Off for the United States." *RE Studs*, vol. 31 (4), no. 88, pp. 287–308.

—— (1966). *Unemployment, Money Wage Rates and Inflation*. Cambridge, Mass.: M.I.T. Press.

—— (1967). "Wages and the Guideposts." *AER*, vol. 57 (4), pp. 897–904.

—— (1969). "Wages and the Guideposts – Reply." *AER*, vol. 59 (3), pp. 365–70.

—— (1970). "Changing Labor Markets and Inflation." *Brookings Papers*, no. 3, pp. 411–41.

—— (1972). "Controls and Income Shares." *Brookings Papers*, no. 1, pp. 191–4.

Pesek, B. P. (1960). "A Comparison of the Distributional Effects of Inflation and Taxation." *AER*, vol. 50 (2), pp. 147–53.

Petersen, D. W., Lerner, E. M. and Lusk, E. J. (1971). "The Response of Prices and Incomes to Monetary Policy: an Analysis Based Upon a Differential Phillips Curve." *JPE*, vol. 79 (4), pp. 857–66.

Phelps, E. S. (1961). "A Test For the Presence of Cost Inflation." *YEE*, vol. 1.

—— (1965). "Anticipated Inflation and Economic Welfare." *JPE*, vol. 73 (1), pp. 1–17.

—— (1967). "Phillips Curves, Expectations of Inflation and Optimal Unemployment Over Time." *Economica* (NS), vol. 34 (135), pp. 254–81.

Phelps, E. S. (1968). "Money Wage Dynamics and Labour Market Equilibrium." *JPE*, vol. 76 (4), pt. II, pp. 678–711. (Amended reprint in Phelps, E. S. *et al.* (1970).)
—— (1972). *Inflation Policy and Unemployment Theory: The Cost-Benefit Approach to Monetary Planning.* New York: W. W. Norton & Co.
—— (1973). "Inflation in a Theory of Public Finance." *Swedish Journal of Economics*, vol. 75, pp. 67–82.
—— *et al.* (1970). *The Microeconomic Foundations of Employment and Inflation Theory.* New York: W. W. Norton & Co.
—— and Winter, S. G. Jnr. (1970). In Phelps, E. S. *et al.* "Optimal Price Policy Under Atomistic Competition."
Phelps-Brown, E. H. (1971). "The Analysis of Wage Movements Under Full Employment." *SJPE*, vol. 18 (3), pp. 233–43.
Phillips, A. W. (1958). "The Relationship Between Unemployment and the Rate of Change of Money Wage Rates in the U.K. 1861–1957." *Economica* (NS), vol. 25 (100), pp. 283–99.
Pierson, G. (1968). "The Effect of Union Strength on the U.S., Phillips Curve." *AER*, vol. 58 (4), pp. 456–67.
Pigou, A. C. (1917). "The Value of Money." *QJE*, vol. 32 (1), pp. 38–65.
Pissarides, C. A. (1972). "A Model of British Macroeconomic Policy, 1955–1969." *Manchester School*, vol. 40 (3), pp. 245–59.
Pitchford, J. D. (1956/7). "Cost and Demand Elements in the Inflationary Process." *RE Studs* 24 (64), pp. 139–48.
—— (1961). "The Inflationary Effects of Excess Demand for Goods and Excessive Real-Income Claims." *OEP* (NS), vol. 13 (1), pp. 59–71.
—— (1963). *A Study of Cost and Demand Inflation.* Amsterdam: North Holland.
—— (1968). "An Analysis of Price Movements in Australia, 1947–1968." *AEP*, vol. 7 (2), pp. 111–35.
Polak, J. J. (1957/8). "Monetary Analysis of Income Formation and Payments Problems." *IMF Staff Papers*, vol. 6, pp. 1–50.
Powell, A. A. and Williams, R. A. (eds.) (1973). *Econometric Studies of Macro and Monetary Relations.* Amsterdam: North-Holland.
Purdy, D. L. and Zis, G. (1973). "Trade Unions and Wage Inflation in the U.K.: A Reappraisal." In Parkin, J. M. (ed.), *Essays in Modern Economics.* London: Longmans (reprinted in Laidler, D. E. W. and Purdy, D. L. (eds.), 1974).
—— —— (1974). In Laidler, D. E. W. and Purdy, D. L. (eds.). "On the Concept and Measurement of Union Militancy."
Radcliffe Committee (1959). *Report on the Working of the Monetary System.* London: H.M.S.O.
Raiffa, H. (1953). "Arbitration Schemes for Generalised Two Person Games." In Kuhn, H. W. and Tucker, A. W. (eds.), *Contributions to the Theory of Games II.* Princeton, N.J.: Princeton U.P.
—— and Schlaifer, R. (1961). *Applied Statistical Decision Theory.* Boston, Mass.: Harvard Business School.
Reddaway, W. B. (1965). "Reasons for Rising Prices." University of Cambridge, Department of Applied Economics, Reprint Series, no. 230, London: Cambridge U.P.
—— (1966). "Rising Prices for Ever?" *LBR*, no. 81, pp. 1–15.
Reuber, G. L. (1964). "The Objectives of Canadian Monetary Policy, 1949–61: Empirical 'Trade-Offs' and the Reaction Function of the Authorities." *JPE*, vol. 72 (2), pp. 109–32.
Ripley, F. C. and Segal, L. (1973). "Price Determination in 395 Manufacturing Industries." *RE Stats*, vol. 53 (3), pp. 263–71.
Robertson, D. H. (1961). *Growth, Wages, Money.* London: Cambridge U.P.
Rose, D. E. (1972). "A General Error-Learning Model of Expectations Formation." University of Manchester Inflation Workshop Discussion Paper, no. 7210 (mimeo).
Rousseas, S. W. (ed.) (1968). *Proceedings of a Symposium on Inflation: its Causes, Consequences and Control.* Wilton, Conn.: The Calvin K. Kazanjian Economics Foundation Inc.
Routh, G. (1959). "The Relationship Between Unemployment and the Rate of Change of Money Wage Rates in the U.K. 1861–1957: Comment." *Economica* (NS), vol. 26 (104), pp. 299–315.
Runciman, W. G. (1966). *Relative Deprivation and Social Justice.* London: Routledge & Kegan Paul.
Rushdy, F. and Lund, P. J. (1967). "The Effect of Demand on Prices in British Manufacturing Industry." *RE Studs*, vol. 34 (3), no. 99, pp. 361–73.
Samuelson, P. A. and Solow, R. M. (1960). "Analytical Aspects of Anti-Inflation Policy." *AER (p & p)*, vol. 50 (2), pp. 177–94.
Sargan, J. D. (1964). "Wages and Prices in the United Kingdom." In Hart, P. E., Mills, G. and Whittaker, J. K. (eds.), *Econometric Analysis for National Economic Planning.* London: Butterworths.
Sargent, T. J. (1971). "A Note on the 'Accelerationist' Controversy." *JMCB*, vol. 3 (3), pp. 721–5.
—— (1972). "Anticipated Inflation and the Nominal Rate of Interest." *QJE*, vol. 86 (2), no. 343, pp. 212–25.
—— (1973). "Interest Rates and Prices in the Long Run." *JMCB*, vol. 5 (1), pt. II, pp. 385–449.

Sargent, T. J. and Wallace, N. (1973). "Rational Expectations and the Dynamics of Hyperinflation." *IER*, vol. 14 (2), pp. 328–50.

Saunders, P. G. and Nobay, A. R. (1972). In Parkin, J. M. and Sumner, M. T. (eds.), "Price Expectations, the Phillips Curve and Incomes Policy."

Scarfe, B. L. (1973). "A Model of the Inflation Cycle in a Small Open Economy." *OEP* (NS), vol. 25 (2), pp. 192–203.

Schultze, C. L. and Tryon, J. L. (1965). "Prices and Wages." In Duesenberry, J. S. *et al*. *The Brookings Quarterly Econometric Model of the U.S.* Chicago: Rand McNally.

Scitovsky, T. and Scitovsky, A. A. (1964). "Inflation vs. Unemployment – Examination of Their Effects." In Commission on Money and Credit.

Shackle, G. L. S. (1955). *Uncertainty in Economics and Other Reflections*. London: Cambridge U.P.

Sharot, T. (1973). "Unemployment Dispersion as a Determinant of Wage Inflation in the United Kingdom 1925–1966. A Note." *Manchester School*, vol. 4 (3), pp. 225–28.

Sidrauski, M. (1967). "Rational Choice and Patterns of Growth in a Monetary Economy." *AER* (*p & p*), vol. 57 (2), pp. 534–44.

Silveira, A. M. (1973*a*). "The Demand for Money: The Evidence from the Brazilian Economy." *JMCB*, vol. 5 (1), pt. 1, pp. 113–40.

—— (1973*b*). "Interest Rates and Rapid Inflation: The Evidence from the Brazilian Economy." *JMCB*, vol. 5 (3), pp. 794–805.

Simler, N. J. and Tella, A. (1968). "Labour Reserves and the Phillips Curve." *RE Stats*, vol. 50 (1), pp. 32–49.

Sims, C. A. (1972). "Money, Finance, and Causality." *AER*, vol. 62 (4), pp. 540–52.

Sjaastad, L. (1975). In Parkin, J. M. and Zis, G. (eds.), "Why Stable Inflations Fail."

Slichter, S. H. (1954). "Do Wage-Fixing Arrangements in the American Labour Market Have an Inflationary Bias?" *AER* (*p & p*), vol. 44 (2), pp. 322–46.

Solow, R. M. (1956). "A Contribution to the Theory of Economic Growth." *QJE*, vol. 70 (1), no. 278, pp. 65–94.

—— (1968). In Rousseas, S. (ed.), "Recent Controversies on the Theory of Inflation: An Eclectic View."

—— (1969). *Price Expectations and the Behaviour of the Price Level*. Manchester, Manchester U.P.

Starr, R. M. (1972). "Exchange in Barter and Money Economies." *QJE*, vol. 86 (2), pp. 290–302.

Stein, J. L. (1974). "Unemployment, Inflation and Monetarism." *AER*, vol. 64 (5), pp. 867–87.

Steindl, F. G. (1973). "Price Expectations and Interest Rates." *JMCB*, vol. 5 (4), pp. 939–49.

Stephens, J. K. (1974). "A Note on Non-Synchronous Decisions and the Phillips Curve." *JES*, vol. 6 (1/2), pp. 19–64.

Swan, T. W. (1956). "Economic Growth and Capital Accumulation." *ER*, vol. 32 (163), pp. 334–61.

Tait, A. A. (1967). "A Simple Test of the Redistributive Nature of Price Changes for Wealth Owners in the U.S. and U.K." *RE Stats*, vol. 49 (4), pp. 651–5.

Taylor, J. (1970). "Hidden Unemployment, Hoarded Labour, and the Phillips Curve." *SEJ*, vol. 37 (1), pp. 1–16.

—— (1972). In Parkin, J. M. and Sumner, M. T. (eds.), "Incomes Policy, the Structure of Unemployment and the Phillips Curve: the United Kingdom Experience, 1953–1970.".

—— (1975). In Parkin, J. M. and Nobay, A. R., *Contemporary Issues in Economics*. Manchester, Manchester. U.P. "Wage Inflation, Unemployment and the Organised Pressure for Higher Wages in the U.K. 1961–1971."

Thirlwall, A. P. (1969). "Demand Disequilibrium in the Labour Market and Wage Rate Inflation in the United Kingdom." *YBESR*, vol. 21 (1), pp. 65–76.

—— (1970). "Regional Phillips Curves." *BOUIES*, vol. 32 (1), pp. 19–32.

Thomas, R. L. (1973). "Unemployment Dispersion as a Determinant of Wage Inflation in the United Kingdom, 1925–1966: Reply." *Manchester School*, vol. 41 (3), pp. 229–34.

—— (1974). In Laidler, D. E. W. & Purdy, D. L. (eds.), "Wage Inflation in the U.K. – A Multi-Market Approach."

—— and Stoney, P. J. M. (1970). "A Note on the Dynamic Properties of the Hines Inflation Model." *RE Studs*, vol. 37 (2), no. 110, pp. 286–94.

—— —— (1971). "Unemployment Dispersion as a Determinant of Wage Inflation in the United Kingdom, 1925–1966." *Manchester School*, vol. 39 (2), pp. 83–116 (reprinted in Parkin, J. M. and Sumner, M. T. (eds.), 1972).

Throop, A. W. (1968). "The Union–Non Union Wage Differential and Cost-Push Inflation." *AER*, vol. 58 (1), pp. 79–99.

—— (1969). "Wages and the Guideposts: Comment." *AER*, vol. 59 (3), pp. 358–65.

Tinbergen, J. (1951). "An Economic Policy for 1936." In *Business Cycles in the United Kingdom, 1870–1914*. Amsterdam: North-Holland.

Tobin, J. (1965). "Money and Economic Growth." *Econometrica*, vol. 33 (4), pp. 671–84.

—— (1972). "Inflation and Unemployment." *AER*, vol. 62 (1), pp. 1–18.

Tower, E. (1971). "More on the Welfare Cost of Inflationary Finance." *JMCB*, vol. 3 (4), pp. 850–60.

Toyoda, T. (1972). "Price Expectations and the Short Run and Long Run Phillips Curves in Japan, 1956–1968." *RE Stats*, vol. 54 (3), pp. 267–74.

Turner, H. A. and Jackson, D. A. S. (1970). "On the Determination of the General Wage Level – A World Analysis: Or 'Unlimited Labour Forever'." *EJ*, vol. 80 (320), pp. 827–49.

Turnovsky, S. J. (1969). "A Bayesian Approach to the Theory of Expectations." *JET*, vol. 1, pp. 220–7.

—— (1970). "Empirical Evidence on the Formation of Price Expectations." *JASA*, vol. 65, pp. 1441–54.

—— (1972). "The Expectations Hypothesis and the Aggregate Wage Equation: Some Empirical Evidence for Canada." *Economica* (NS), vol. 39 (153), pp. 1–17.

—— (1974). "On the Role of Inflationary Expectations in a Short-Run Macro-Economic Model." *EJ*, vol. 84 (334), pp. 317–37.

—— and Wachter, M. L. (1972). "A Test of the Expectations Hypothesis Using Directly Observed Wage and Price Expectations." *RE Stats*, vol. 54 (1), pp. 47–54.

Turvey, R. (1951). "Some Aspects of the Theory of Inflation in a Closed Economy." *EJ*, vol. 61 (243), pp. 531–43.

Ulman, L. and Flanagan, R. J. (1971). *Wage Restraint: A Study of Incomes Policies in W. Europe*. Los Angeles, London: University of Los Angeles Press.

Vanderkamp, J. (1972). "Wage Adjustment, Productivity and Price Change Expectations." *RE Studs*, vol. 39 (1), no. 117, pp. 61–72.

—— (1975). "Inflation: A Simple Friedman Theory With a Phillips Twist." *JME*, vol. 1 (1), pp. 117–22.

Viner, J. (1937). *Studies in the Theory of International Trade*. New York, London: Harper Bros.

Wachter, M. L. (1969). "Wages and the Guideposts: Comment." *AER*, vol. 59 (3), pp. 354–8.

Walters, A. A. (1971). "Consistent Expectations, Distributed Lags and the Quantity Theory." *EJ*, vol. 81 (322), pp. 273–81.

Ward, R. and Zis, G. (1974). "Trade Union Militancy as an Explanation of Inflation: an International Comparison." *Manchester School*, vol. 42 (1), pp. 44–65.

Watanabe, T. (1966). "Price Changes and the Rate of Change of Money Wage Earnings in Japan, 1955–1962." *QJE*, vol. 80 (1), no. 318, pp. 31–47.

Waud, R. N. (1970). "Inflation, Unemployment and Economic Welfare." *AER*, vol. 60 (4), pp. 631–41.

Weidenbaum, M. L. (1972). "New Initiatives in National Wage and Price Policy." *RE Stats*, vol. 54 (3) pp. 213–34.

Wicksell, K. (1962). *Interest and Prices*. London: Cass Reprint of Economics Classics. (First published, 1898: First English Edition, 1936.)

Wiles, P. (1973). "Cost Inflation and the State of Economic Theory." *EJ*, vol. 83 (330), pp. 377–98.

Williamson, J. (1970). "A Simple Neo-Keynesian Growth Model." *RE Studs*, vol. 37 (2), no. 110, pp. 157–71.

Wilson, T. (1961). *Inflation*. Oxford: Blackwell; Cambridge, Mass.: Harvard U.P.

Yohe, W. P. and Karnosky, D. S. (1969). "Interest Rates and Price Level Changes 1952–1969." *FRB* of St Louis Review, vol. 51 (12).

Zeuthen, F. (1930). *Problems of Monopoly and Economic Warfare*. London: Routledge.

V

A SURVEY OF INTERNATIONAL
COMPARISONS OF PRODUCTIVITY [1,2]

I. B. KRAVIS

I. INTRODUCTION

Productivity is the ratio of output to one input such as labour services or to inputs taken in their totality. Since economics is in its very essence concerned with the organisation of inputs (scarce means) to produce outputs (satisfy human wants), comparisons of productivity go to the heart of the assessment of economic performance. By far the most common form of comparisons is over

[1] This is the ninth of a series sponsored jointly by the Social Science Research Council and the Royal Economic Society.

[2] I have greatly benefited from the advice of Solomon Fabricant in preparing this article. I am grateful too to David Teece, who helped organise the data and to Alicia Civitello and Helen Hirschfeld who did most of the statistical work. Christopher Clague and Laszlo Drechsler were helpful with source materials. I wish to thank Mr Drechsler, D. J. Daly, E. Denison, J. Mairesse, F. Nyitrai and members of the Joint Committee of the Royal Economic Society and the Social Science Research Council, especially Professors Champernowne and Reddaway, for their helpful criticisms of earlier drafts.

time in a given country.[1] We are concerned here, however, with the less frequently made comparisons between countries.

At one level, international comparisons of productivity measure the relative fruitfulness of different economies without regard to causes. Thus, in aggregate comparisons referring to GDP or GNP, output is usually related to total population. The resulting comparisons measure differences in real *per capita* product of different economies, but they do not in themselves throw any light on the reasons for the differences. One country may have a high *per capita* product because its land flows with milk and honey (or oil), and another because its people are industrious.

At a more analytical level, productivity comparisons are aimed at measuring the relative efficiency with which resources are used to obtain output. This becomes a much more complex exercise than the simple comparisons of output per unit of input; there can be an almost endless chain of measures designed to ensure that precisely the same outputs in each country are related to precisely the same inputs. If we were able to standardise all the outputs and take account of all the inputs, including not only labour and capital but technological and managerial, climate and natural resources elements, there should be no remaining differences in productivity or if there were they might, as Professor Fabricant has pointed out, simply represent differences in the rate of return. From this standpoint international productivity comparisons can be viewed as an effort to explain the observed differences in *per capita* GDP.

In practice, international productivity comparisons are not so ambitious. Most frequently, output per unit of labour input is compared for a pair of countries across a number of different industries. Sometimes explanations for the observed differences are sought in such factors as the amount of capital and the scale of production, but such efforts have met only limited success.

The inter-industry differences in relative productivity are themselves of interest and importance, even if they cannot be fully explained. They should help to explain international differences in price structure and hence in comparative advantage.

Because productivity comparisons are so closely related to the core of economics, it is not surprising that they have a long history. They go back, at least in the form of comparisons of total product *per capita*, to the very beginnings of modern economics. Gregory King's initial comparisons of the national income and expenditure of England, France and Holland in 1688 and 1695 were followed by comparisons by Mulhall and Colin Clark, to mention only a few of the landmark estimates.[2] There are, too, a large number of scattered productivity comparisons for particular sectors and individual industries, many of them designed to provide guidance for legislative or administrative decisions with respect to tariffs.[3]

[1] For surveys of time to time comparisons see Nadiri (1970, 1972).
[2] For an account of the history of national accounts estimates, including international comparisons, see Studentski (1958).
[3] See, for example, the excerpt from a U.S. Tariff Commission report "Wages and Productivity in Glass Tableware Industry of Czechoslovakia and United States", *Monthly Labor Review*, May 1933, pp. 1059–61.

This survey concentrates for the most part on productivity comparisons of recent decades. No effort is made to provide a statistical compendium of all the estimates that have been prepared or even a complete catalogue of all the studies, but an attempt is made to provide good coverage of the major studies. Beyond the mere summary of the results of these studies, a limited attempt is made to assess the meaning of the results when the studies are considered as a whole.

II. METHODS

International comparisons of productivity may relate to entire economies, to major sectors (e.g. agriculture or manufacturing), or to specific industries (e.g. textiles or steel).[1] In any of these cases the ratio of net output to input for one country is compared to the corresponding ratio for another country. The formula, based on Geary's net output index, may be set out as follows:

$$\frac{\Sigma G_i P_G - \Sigma M_i P_M - \Sigma K_i P_K}{\Sigma G_j P_G - \Sigma M_j P_M - \Sigma K_j P_K} \div \frac{\Sigma N_i}{\Sigma N_j}, \qquad (1)$$

where the Gs represent gross output, the Ms intermediate consumption of materials and services,[2] the Ks capital consumed, the Ps the common set of prices used in the comparisons, the Ns the services of labour or other factors, and i and j two countries. The expression preceding the division sign represents relative net outputs in the two countries, and that following the division sign relative flows of inputs. Measurement difficulties relating to net output, to be described presently, preclude the use of this formula precisely, and all productivity studies represent an approximation of some kind.

A. *Aggregate Comparisons*

A distinction may be made at the outset between studies that compare productivity for whole economies and those that address themselves to specific sectors or industries. The former generally seek to compare output by converting the money value of net output in one country to the currency of the other country. The easy way to accomplish this is by means of official or prevailing exchange rates.[3] However, it is by now widely appreciated that this procedure, though still widely followed, gives misleading results because exchange rates do not necessarily reflect the relative purchasing power of different currencies. For example, in the outcome of the first phase of the United Nations International

---

[1] For a more extended discussion of methodological issues, particularly with respect to comparisons for particular industries, see Conference of European Statisticians, *Methodological Problems . . .* (1971). This document was prepared by the Secretariat of the U.N. Economic Commission for Europe with the assistance of Mr J. Kux. Other authoritative treatments are those by L. Rostas (1948, chap 2) and S. Fabricant (1968, vol. 12, pp. 523–36).

[2] For convenience, intermediate consumption will henceforth be referred to simply in terms of "materials" though externally purchased services are also included.

[3] *Per capita* product comparisons based entirely or largely on official exchange rates are published by the United Nations and the International Bank for Reconstruction and Development. The U.N. publishes *per capita* comparisons of GDP based on conversion via exchange rates in its *Yearbook of National Account Statistics* and in the January issue of the *Monthly Bulletin of Statistics*. The IBRD publishes estimates of GNP *per capita* in successive editions of the *World Bank Atlas of Per Capita Product and Population*, also relying, for the most part, on exchange rates, and including estimates for a number of socialist and developing countries which do not supply GNP or GDP figures to the U.N.

Comparison Project (ICP), the 1970 *per capita* real GDP relative to the United States ranged from 16 % higher than that indicated by the exchange conversion in the case of West Germany to 249 % higher in the case of India.[1]

What must be done to obtain reliable comparisons is to value the outputs of the countries at a common set of prices. In binary comparisons (between pairs of countries) the usual practice is to value the outputs of both countries first in the prices of the one and then in the prices of the other. We return to the question of the difference in the results in a moment.

Of course there is no problem in valuing each country's quantities at its own prices – its expenditure data do exactly that. The valuation of a country's quantities at another's prices is usually derived from its expenditure data and a set of price comparisons. For example, the term $P_j Q_i$ where the Ps and Qs are prices and quantities for a particular type of good and i and j are two countries, may be obtained by dividing i's expenditure $(P_i Q_i)$ by the purchasing power parity or price ratio (P_i/P_j) for that type of good. The overall quantity comparison is then given by the ratio $(\Sigma P_j Q_i)/(\Sigma P_j Q_j)$

The alternative to this procedure of using price comparisons to derive the quantity comparisons is to make the quantity comparisons directly.[2] In this case the numerator term $(P_j Q_i)$ for the overall comparison $(\Sigma P_j Q_i)/(\Sigma P_j Q_j)$ can be derived for the individual types of products by multiplying the Q_i/Q_js by the appropriate $P_j Q_j$s. The comparison is a weighted average of the Q_i/Q_js, with weights equal to $P_j Q_j$ for the various items.

Greater use has been made of the price comparison method because there are reasons for thinking that within most categories sampling errors will be smaller for a sampling of prices than for a sampling of quantities.[3]

The sample of goods selected for price or purchasing power comparisons is usually stratified to correspond to the categories of gross product for which separate expenditure figures can be obtained in both (or all) the countries being compared. In the Gilbert and Kravis study (1954) and most studies of this type, the categories for which the price comparisons were made represented subdivisions of final expenditures of GNP or GDP. In the U.N. ICP, for example, the expenditures of GDP were subdivided into about 150 categories (e.g. rice; eggs; fresh vegetables; men's footwear; local transport services; toilet articles; industrial buildings; roads, streets, and highways; trucks, buses, and trailers; electrical transmitting equipment; and government employees in professional occupations).

The quality of the comparisons is critically affected by the care which is taken to identify products of identical or equivalent quality for pricing in different countries. Exchange of samples and visits by experts to the participating countries are necessary to assure reliable results. Once the identity of

---

[1] Kravis, Kennessey, Heston and Summers. The corresponding deviations for seven other countries covered by the study may be derived by comparing the figures in columns (3) and (6) in Table 1.

[2] In the ICP, for example, direct quantity comparisons for the services of teachers and physicians were preferred over the indirect ones derived from price comparisons. In such cases, expenditures are used in conjunction with the quantity comparisons to derive the price comparisons. See Kravis, Kennessey, Heston and Summers (1975, chap. 2).

[3] See Kravis *et al.* (1975, chap. 2, section B).

each sample item is determined, it is necessary to obtain its national average price. The price concept that is used must be consistent with that embodied in the national accounts expenditure figure (so as to maintain the relation that expenditure equals price times quantity). Prices and expenditures may be recorded in each country's own currency.

The quality of the comparisons is also dependent on the quality of the expenditure data. There is no reason to believe that errors in the totals for GDP will or will not tend to be offsetting for given pairs of countries; if one of the countries fails to include some outputs in its GDP estimates while the other has full coverage, the results will be that much in error. On the other hand, errors in the allocation of total GDP to particular expenditure categories may have relatively little impact on the comparison for overall GDP. However, if, as in the ICP, comparisons are desired not only for total GDP but also for the subaggregates, it is important to have the GDP for each country accurately distributed to the categories set out in the classification scheme that is chosen for the comparisons.

The practical consequence of these rather onerous requirements for reliable comparisons is that they generally require the active participation of the statistical authorities of the individual countries, and that only a small number of such studies based on the necessary price field work have been carried out.

The several studies meeting these requirements vary somewhat in the methods of obtaining the price comparisons for the individual categories (e.g. weighted versus unweighted averages for the different price comparisons within a given category) and in the methods of aggregating the results for the individual categories to higher levels such as food, consumption and GDP.

In the studies of the Organization for European Economic Cooperation (1954, 1958), United Nations (1975) and the Council for Mutual Economic Assistance[1] a "star" pattern of binary comparisons was carried out. A single country (the United States in the first two and the Soviet Union in the third study) was selected as the base country (the centre of the star) and each of the other countries (the points of the star) was compared with the base country. In each binary comparison the price and quantity indexes for the individual categories were aggregated, once with the base country's weights and again with own-country weights.

A disadvantage of this approach is not only that it gives two answers, but also that the results are not in general transitive. That is, it will not necessarily be true that the results of a direct comparison of country i and j would be identical with the results derived from the comparison of each with the base-country.[2] In order to meet this difficulty, some of the studies, including the recent U.N. study, offer not only the traditional binary comparisons but also what have been called "multilateral" comparisons. Multilateral comparison methods differ considerably one from the other, but they have in common an

---

[1] This study has not been published but the results have been cited in U.N. Economic Commission for Europe (1970), p. 120.

[2] They would be necessarily transitive only if a uniform set of items entered into all the comparisons and if a single set of weights (presumably the base country's or some average of all the countries) were used.

element of simultaneity in their treatment of three or more countries. They are characterised by transitive results, and sometimes by the property of base-country invariance, which reduces the role of the base-country to that of a *numéraire*.[1]

The differences between base-country and own-country weighting have, like the analogous differences between Laspeyres and Paasche indexes in inter-temporal comparisons, been widely discussed and need not be dwelt upon at length. However, it may be worth calling attention to the tendency for the relative quantity index of a given country (real GDP, for example, compared to that of a base-country) to be higher when base-country price weights are used than when its own-country price weights are used. This "Gerschenkron effect", as it has been called in the intertemporal context, arises in international comparisons from the fact that each country's quantity structure (which covers exports as well as the home market) adapts itself to the country's own price structure, the quantities tending to be relatively large where prices are low and relatively small where prices are high. Hence, valuation of the quantities by a set of foreign prices tends to inflate their aggregate value. In the nine binary comparisons in the U.N. ICP study, the ratio of base-weighted to own-weighted indexes varied from 1·8 for the United Kingdom to 2·15 for Kenya (with the United States the base-country in all comparisons). The size of the index spread is positively correlated with differences in the extent of the dissimilarity between the base-country and own-country price structures. Since price structure dissimilarity is correlated with differences in *per capita* income, the index spread is also correlated with *per capita* income differences.[2]

Despite the differences between the own-weighted and base-weighted results, we have entered only the geometric mean of the two in our summarisations of the overall studies and of the sector and industry comparisons.[3] This "ideal" index, as it was called by Irving Fisher, is difficult to defend on theoretical grounds, but the convenience of offering a single compromise answer has earned it wide usage (Samuelson, 1974).

The use of the Fisher index is moreover quite in keeping with the approximate character of the relationships we shall be summarising. While the several studies from which the data are drawn are similar in purpose and general design, they differ significantly in method and detail. Some refer to GNP, some to GDP, and others to material product.[4] In addition, price comparisons in the case of Latin American countries include only the capital cities (Braithwaite, 1968). Finally, the variety of reference dates adopted in the different studies is so great that we have adopted the practice of ignoring small differences (as much as 5–7 years).

[1] See Kravis *et al.* (1975, chap. 5).

[2] For a discussion of these empirical relationships see Kravis *et al.* (1975, chap. 3 and 15). The classical formulation of the relationship between Laspeyres and Paasche indexes is that of Bortkiewicz. See Staehle (1934, pp. 14–17). The original Bortkiewicz article is in *Nordisk Statistisk Tidskrift*, vol. 2, 1923.

[3] The figure for Canada entered in column (6) of Table 1, for example, is the result of taking the geometric mean of the index based on Canadian price weights and the index based on U.S. price weights.

[4] For a brief description of the material product system used by the socialist countries of eastern Europe, see U.N. *Yearbook of National Accounts* (1970).

All these theoretical and practical sources of incomparability mean that little weight can be given to small differences in productivity that emerge from our analysis of the various studies. The figures can, at best, supply an approximate measure of the differences subject to margins of error that may be wide when the results of the different investigations are compared.

Comparisons of GDP *per capita*, as noted earlier, simply provide information about the relative fruitfulness of the countries without seeking to explain the reasons for the differences. A step from these welfare-type comparisons towards efficiency-oriented comparisons involves the substitution of economic inputs such as labour or capital in the denominator of the productivity ratio in lieu of population. Sectoral and industry comparisons are necessarily cast in terms of specific inputs, and we discuss the alternatives in connection with our consideration of these kinds of studies.

B. *Sectoral and Industry Comparisons*

1. *Concepts of Output and Input.* Sectoral and industry comparisons, like the overall comparisons, require that an index of relative outputs be constructed, but the approach to the measurement of output is more circumscribed.

In the comparisons of total product, the major studies have, with but one exception, followed the final expenditure approach of the Gilbert and Kravis study. The exception was provided by Paige and Bombach (1959), who in a companion study to Gilbert and Kravis, compared the GNP of the United Kingdom and the United States by aggregating comparisons of net output for the individual industries comprising GNP.[1] Their study produced U.K./U.S. results for 1950 that showed *per capita* output in the United States 78 % higher than that of the United Kingdom when U.K. weights were used and 51 % higher when U.S. weights were used; the corresponding margins of U.S. superiority on the final expenditure approach used by Gilbert and Kravis were 104% and 59% respectively.

From the standpoint of comparisons of total GNP or GDP, the final expenditure approach is much simpler to carry out than the individual industry or industry-of-origin approach. The reason is that the concentration on final products automatically nets out all the intermediate goods; the aggregate value of final expenditures provides an unduplicated total of the output of the economy. Further, the final products themselves consist almost entirely of readily identifiable commodities and services for which prices can be observed and compared. This total of the expenditure on these products is not, to be sure, *exactly* what we would like conceptually. It includes not only factor rewards which we want included, but also the value of capital consumed and of

---

[1] The Paige and Bombach study is the classic treatment of the theory and practice of comparisons based on the industry-of-origin approach. For some of the problems discussed in the ensuing paragraphs, see particularly pages 80 ff. and 105. An earlier paper discussing the conceptual problems of both the final expenditure and industry-of-origin approaches is Reddaway (1951). It should be noted that Paige and Bombach assess the balance between the final expenditure approach and the industry-of-origin approach as a means of comparing total GDP somewhat more favourably to the latter, especially for countries with similar production structures, than the present writer. However, the present writer must agree that the industry-of-origin approach is much more valuable for productivity studies because of the detail it provides for individual industries.

indirect taxes less subsidies which we do not want included. But capital consumption is difficult to measure and indirect taxes less subsidies are usually not of great importance. Hence, analysts generally take GDP or GNP as being the best available approximation to the desired output measure, even though net national product or national income may be more appropriate conceptually.

When it comes to measuring the output of a sector or industry – whether for its own sake or eventually to aggregate to total GDP or GNP – we no longer have the option of choosing between the two approaches. Even if we maintain our tolerance of the unwanted inclusion of capital consumption and indirect taxes less subsidies, it is still necessary to deduct from the gross value of the outflows of products of each industry the industry's purchases of materials and services from other industries in order to obtain an estimate of its contribution to the GDP. The net output of an industry is thus an abstract concept. It is an intangible residual, which eludes a simple comparison (with respect to either prices or quantities) between two situations. Comparison requires that both the material inputs and the gross outputs of the two situations be valued at a common set of prices – hence the common term "double deflation" for this approach.[1] Actually, if the formula given in (1) on page 3 were applied fully the term "triple deflation" might be more appropriate.[2]

Indeed, even double deflation has seldom been attempted. Apart from the more burdensome extent of the price comparisons, the method has the disadvantage that the error in net output may exceed that in either gross output or purchased inputs since net output is the difference between the two; the higher the share of intermediate product in gross output, the more sensitive will the error in net output be to errors in either of the basic terms.

Because of these difficulties, all productivity studies use an approximation of some kind to a net output index rather than the double deflation method. The farthest departures from the conceptual requirements are represented by comparisons which use either gross outputs or selected inputs as indicators of net output. The studies of Rostas (1948) and Frankel (1957) are examples of reliance on gross output. (Rostas and Frankel both used physical quantities as output indicators; other studies, as noted below, have used gross output in monetary terms.) Illustrations of the much less common use of input indicators can be found in Paige and Bombach; they relied on such indicators *only* for industries in which inputs tended to be homogeneous and outputs heterogeneous (e.g. furniture and rubber footwear). The assumption underlying the use of both gross output and input indicators is that the proportion of net output to gross output is the same in the countries being compared: this is a much more dangerous assumption to make in inter-country comparisons than in intertemporal comparisons within a country, because the method of production is more likely to be fundamentally different, and the same is true of the usage of intermediate products bought from other industries. In other studies, closer approximations to the theoretical concept are represented by efforts to deduct

[1] Paige and Bombach use the somewhat broader term "double indicator" for this approach, reflecting the fact that for some industries they deflate expenditure via price comparisons, while for others they make direct quantity comparisons. See note 2, p. 4.

[2] On this issue, see Gilbert and Kravis (1954), p. 62.

at least a part of material inputs; examples are the Netherlands/United Kingdom (1966), Czechoslovakia/France (1969), and Paige–Bombach studies. Another approximation method, used by Maizels (1958), is to divide the ratio (e.g. country i to country j) of net output in national currencies by the purchasing power parity for gross output. This method allows for differences in the ratio of net to gross output between the countries, but assumes the price relationships for outputs and intermediate inputs are the same. In a number of the studies, notably that of Paige and Bombach, the approximation method selected varied from industry to industry, the purpose being to select the most appropriate method in each case.

Although net output is in principle the output concept used in the great majority of productivity comparisons, occasionally gross output is employed in its own right rather than as a proxy for net output. Among the studies summarised below, those by Heath (1957) and West (1971) include comparisons based on gross output. The use of gross output, as West points out (1971, p. 4), not only reduces the error in the output comparisons, but has analytical advantages in that fuels and materials can be treated like factor inputs and the relative efficiency in their use can be assessed. The recent increases in the prices of fuel call attention to the possibilities of substitutability between intermediate inputs and primary inputs and hence to the attractiveness of gross output as the appropriate concept for efficiency-oriented comparisons of productivity.

The general practice, however, has been to relate net output to one or more of the primary factors, most often to labour but occasionally to land and capital and still less frequently to all factors combined.

The conceptual and measurement difficulties on the factor input side are fully as great as those encountered with respect to output, though they have generally received less attention in the productivity comparisons. Even if outputs are related only to labour inputs, the index number problems are in principle symmetrical to those encountered on the output side. Just as in most industries there are heterogeneous outputs which must somehow be combined in order to make possible a comparison of industry outputs between two countries, so there are different qualities of labour services, each with its own quantity, which must be combined to produce an input comparison. In a few studies, account is taken of the lower wages of female workers (e.g. Heath), but the more usual practice is to relate outputs simply to the quantity of labour services without any differentiation with respect to quality composition of the inputs.

Even if the quality factor is ignored, there are serious problems about how the quantity of labour services ought to be measured. The ideal is to include all the people whose work has contributed to the industry's output (whether male or female, adult or juvenile, manual or non-manual, regular or casual, employee or working proprietor, etc.) but to allow a "discount" for part-timers and people who only work part of the year; if some of these categories are omitted on grounds of inadequate data (e.g. females or family helpers in agriculture), then the productivity estimate will be biased upwards for those countries in which there is a higher-than-usual proportion of such workers.

Whether or not an allowance should be made for the length of the working week, short-time and over-time, holidays and sickness is more debatable, since this depends on the object of the comparison.

Neither the quality nor the coverage problem has been adequately treated in most studies. Where the quality problem is recognised, it is usually as an explanatory factor to account for differences in "labour" productivity measured per unit of undifferentiated input. With respect to the coverage question, one can count on the inclusion of wage earners, and the treatment of salaried employees is usually described. However, the handling of such groups as proprietors, family workers, part-time labour and apprentices and of absences is often left ambiguous. The treatment of these inputs can have a large impact on productivity comparisons for agriculture, particularly for countries in which family farms are important.

In some studies, output is related not only to the gainfully occupied or to all employees but also to a subset designed to delimit the group to those actually engaged in physical production of commodities, such as "wage earners", "operatives", or "production workers". In the summaries of the results of productivity studies in the following sections, we have in such instances chosen to work with the more inclusive manpower concept. The differences in productivity ratios between those based on gainfully occupied or employees and those based on a narrower group are usually small, but where there is a notable difference more credence can be placed in the former. The reason is that the demarcation of the subsets may vary from one country to another; the absence of clear definitions in the reports of some of the studies does not inspire confidence in the attention given to comparability in this respect.

All of the above versions of labour inputs are cast explicitly or implicitly in the form of man-years. Since a man-year may represent different flows of labour services depending upon weekly hours, vacations, etc., comparisons are occasionally offered also in terms of man-hours and for the coal industry at least in terms of man-shifts. This sometimes leads to substantial differences in the result. In the case of Frankel's comparisons for pig iron, for example, the U.S./U.K. productivity index is 491 on a per man-hour basis and 417 on a per employee basis (U.K. = 100). For efficiency-oriented productivity comparisons, man-hours as a measure of labour input is preferable to the number of persons or man-years. However, the man-hour figures are harder to obtain and are apt to be subject to greater error. Also, man-years have the advantage of indicating the industry's absorption of the nation's supply of workers.

Conceptually, the ideal approach to inputs of capital is similar to that of labour. In order to construct an index of capital inputs, we would like to have for each physical kind of capital (each kind of machine, building, etc.) the quantity of its services provided (in hours or years) and its rental price (per hour or year); moreover the units in which quantities were measured would have to be so defined as to ensure comparability between the countries (Griliches and Jorgenson, 1966; Barna, 1959). This is far removed from what is really available to producers of productivity comparisons, and it is no wonder that capital inputs have been included only in a few comparisons and then usually for a limited number of industries (Czechoslovakia/Hungary, Czecho-slovakia/France and Yugoslavia/Hungary). In these cases, it has been capital stocks (sometimes only machinery) that have been compared, the implicit or explicit assumption being that the flows of capital services are proportionate to the stocks, and the main purpose has been to explain labour productivity rather than to analyse the productivity of capital or total factor productivity. The concepts of capital, the sources, and the methods of achieving comparable valuations of the capital stocks of the two countries, taking account of the different types and vintages of equipment are described only briefly, and it is difficult to assess this work. The possibility of errors in such comparisons is perhaps suggested by Barna's report some years ago that his estimates of the replacement cost new of fixed assets in U.K. manufacturing in mid-1955, derived from valuations for fire insurance, were 51 % higher than another set of estimates based on asset length of life implied by depreciation rates for income-tax purposes (Barna, 1959, p. 53).[1]

In view of all these difficulties, it is not surprising to find that proxies for capital services such as horse-power, fuel consumption, or electric energy consumption have been employed,[2] sometimes along with direct measures of capital stocks. The rationale is that a measure of the degree of mechanisation, one important aspect of capital, is provided. The disadvantage of such proxies is, of course, that the contributions of various types of equipment and machines to output cannot be assumed to be proportionate to their horse-power or to their consumption of energy.

In comparisons of agricultural productivity, output is often related to land as well as to labour and capital. Such comparisons clearly ought to allow for the very large inter-country differences in the average *quality* of the land, even where it is recorded under the same statistical heading (e.g. "pasture" or "arable"), but this is seldom if ever done. One is, however, compelled to adopt some way to combine pasture land and arable land into a single input. Hayami and associates in the estimates cited below simply added the two types of land, while Denison (1967, p. 184) regarded 3 acres of pasture land as equivalent to 1 acre of arable land. The former equated the two types of land partly on the grounds that a farmer can alter the proportions devoted to the two uses by changing farming methods and altering the intensity of cultivation (p. 19). While in some situations this assumption may be warranted, in others it is far from the mark; vast areas of the Australian out-back, for example, barely deserve to be included as "pasture".

In inter-temporal studies such comparisons of "partial" productivity, which relate output to a single factor of production such as labour or capital, have

---

[1] Mention should also be made of West's use of the "Giffen method", which derives the value of the capital stock of each industry in each country by capitalising the flow of property incomes (non-wage value added) by industry-specific rates of return. As actually used by West, the Giffen method is mainly a means of obtaining industry-wide capital estimates by blowing up capital reported by corporations for tax purposes by the ratio of (*a*) industry-wide property income to (*b*) property income reported by corporations in the industry. (See West, 1971, p. 75.)

[2] For the use of horsepower, see Rostas (1948), Heath (1957) and Maizels (1958); fuel inputs, Frankel; electric energy, studies for Austria/Hungary, Czechoslovakia/France, Czechoslovakia/Hungary, and Yugoslavia/Hungary.

been supplemented in recent years by comparisons of "total" productivity which relate output to total factor inputs. Different factor inputs generally have been combined with weights based on factor shares in income (taken as representing marginal productivities and hence contributions to output) (Denison, 1967). Sometimes, however, a parameter of a production function has been used to estimate overall differences in productivity.[1]

The lack in most international studies of measures of capital produces a corresponding absence of measures of total factor productivity. Our presentation of the results of the industry-by-industry comparisons is thus necessarily cast in terms of labour productivities.

Obviously, comparisons of labour productivity are of great interest from a welfare standpoint. Man is after all the focus of economic activity and output per man or per man-hour is an important measure of the return of economic activity to human effort. Partial productivity measures also assume a strategic character in situations in which a particular factor is the limiting element for economic growth. Land, labour and even seed have played this role in agriculture in different places and times (Hayami, Ruttan and Southworth), and perhaps the quadrupling of fuel prices in 1973–4 will add still another input to this list. More generally, labour input looms so large in importance relative to other inputs in the economy as a whole and in most major sectors that one can expect a significant correlation between indexes of labour productivity and indexes of total factor productivity. In the West study, for example, the (Spearman) rank correlation between the two types of indexes for 24 manufacturing industries[2] was 0·43; this is significant at the 5% level but does not of course imply that one measure is a good substitute for the other. For manufacturing as a whole the difference between the indexes was less than 2% and in 14 of the 24 individual industries the difference was less than 10%. There is the possibility, however, that the differences between labour productivity and total factor productivity may be systematically related to income levels for countries and to the size of the elasticity of substitution between labour and capital in individual industries. For example, low wage countries may show up less favourably in terms of labour productivity than in terms of total factor productivity if factor proportions are really sensitive to factor prices (Clague, 1967).

But efforts at the international comparison of total factor productivity are bound to involve great uncertainties in view of measurement problems with respect to capital and hence to introduce margins of error that are larger than those to be expected in comparisons of labour productivity. In these circumstances, the optimal research strategy for international comparisons may be to

[1] See Arrow, Chenery, Minhas and Solow (1961) for the use of the "efficiency parameter" in the CES production function for Japan/U.S. comparisons. Their procedure rests on the assumption of (Hicks) neutral differences in the efficiency of factor use across countries (i.e. equal marginal rate of substitution between capital and labour for each industry across countries for each capital–labour combination). For a challenge to this hypothesis see Gupta (1968) and for a reply see Minsol (1968).

[2] Calculated from West (1971), p. 43. Actually, what we refer to here as total factor productivity is based on inputs of labour and capital only. The numerator of the productivity ratios is gross output. If petroleum refining, in which Canadian labour productivity relative to U.S. is next to the highest and Canadian total factor productivity near the lowest, is excluded, the rank correlation rises to 0·57.

continue to produce comparisons of labour productivity and to treat capital services as one of the external variables in terms of which it is sought to explain the results. This is what a number of the studies have done and it is hard to fault them on this score,[1] pending substantial improvements in the measurement of capital stocks and their international comparison.

2. *Sample versus Global Comparisons.* The productivity comparisons that we have been discussing have been based mainly on aggregate data for entire industries such as those provided by census statistics; these may be referred to as "global" comparisons. Another group of studies, which may be labelled "sample" comparisons, are based on information from a sample of individual plants or firms, usually collected especially for this purpose.[2]

In the sample studies great care can be taken to define comparable outputs and to take account of such differences in labour inputs as young workers versus experienced workers, workers on piece rates versus those on time rates, the age and quality of the equipment of the factory, and the rate of utilisation. Productivity comparisons in these studies are sometimes made for the detailed operations as well as for the total output of the selected product. For example, a comparison of the labour time required to produce Goodyear welt footwear in a number of factories in Denmark, France, the Netherlands and the United Kingdom was carried out in terms of forty different operations (Carrie, 1956). Sample studies are often undertaken as an aid to the management of individual firms, rather than for the overall assessment of the performance of an entire industry. From the overall assessment point of view, these studies have the disadvantage that the sample depends upon the existence of factories in different countries that produce very similar outputs and upon the willingness of their managements to cooperate. Such factories may not be representative of the industry as a whole in either (or any) of the countries with respect to productivity-determining factors such as size, amount and quality of capital, quality of labour force, etc. There is also the practical obstacle that special field work is necessary in each country. On the other hand, such comparisons if they can include a number of different firms in each country provide an opportunity to compare the extent of intra-national variations in productivity with inter-national differences. Examples of well-known sample studies in addition to the Goodyear welt footwear study reported by Carrie are the studies of diesel engines by Baranson (1969) and of electrical equipment by Cilingiroglu (1969).

The global studies have the merit of providing a comprehensive view of the industry in each country, but such studies cannot go as far as the sample

---

[1] This is a pragmatic judgment. Its disadvantage is that the treatment of the relative quantity of capital as an explanatory variable includes in the measured difference in labour productivity, differences produced both by (a) differences in factor proportions between the two countries due to differences in factor prices and by (b) differences in labour productivity at given factor proportions. It would, of course, be desirable to keep these influences separate.

[2] The terms are those of Rostas (1948, pp. 7–10) but he confined the use of the term global to comparisons based on physical indicators. Another type of survey that has occasionally been undertaken is directed to multinational firms. The firms may be requested to compare labour and other costs per unit of output, or labour time per unit of output, and sometimes to describe the reasons for the differences. See, for example, Kreinin (1965). Productivity comparisons based on subsidiaries and parent companies, while of interest in themselves, may not yield the same results as comparisons between all plants in a given industry in the host country and in the parent country.

comparisons in tracing all the elements producing differences in the observed levels of productivity. In careful global studies of a comprehensive character, such as those of Rostas and the more recent studies carried out under the aegis of the Conference of European Statisticians (1969, 1970, 1971), efforts have been made to examine such contributing factors as the scale of operations, the extent of capital equipment, the rate of utilisation, and even in a few cases the quality of the labour force, but usually the detail necessary to correlate these influences with the output of particular products is lacking. (See Part V for a discussion of the role of these factors in explaining international differences in productivity for various industries.)

3. *Physical versus Monetary Indicators of Output.* The sample studies usually identify a particular product or process, and, by selecting plants or parts of plants engaged solely or largely in that activity, are able to make the comparisons in terms of narrowly defined physical outputs. Most of the more ambitious global studies from the classic contribution of Rostas onwards are also based mainly on comparisons of physical outputs. Of course the possibility of comparing physical outputs from production data in two or more countries is limited in principle to industries which produce a relatively homogeneous output. Ideally, for the purpose of such a study the industry's output should consist of a single product which is of uniform quality in the countries being compared.

There are not many industries in which these optimal conditions are found and global studies based on physical indicators of output must find ways to circumvent this limitation. It is not a great extension of the method to employ it when there is more than one homogeneous product produced by the industry, although it is then necessary to weight the quantity ratios for the several products to obtain the quantity ratio for the industry as a whole. In principle, the net value of the output of each product should constitute the weights, but when, as is often the case, such data are not available, gross values or the amounts of labour employed on each product may be used as weights. Whatever type of weights is chosen, those drawn from the data of each country in the comparison are customarily used in turn. Differences of 20 % in the two sets of results are not uncommon in productivity comparisons for individual industries.

Similar considerations apply when it is desired to aggregate the quantity or productivity ratios for various industries to provide comparisons for say "light industry" or manufacturing as a whole.

Global studies using physical output indicators do not in practice limit themselves closely to industries producing one or a few homogeneous products. For example, Rostas included steel works and rolling mills and Frankel included motor vehicles. For motor vehicles Frankel used the number of passenger cars, trucks and other commercial vehicles and agricultural and industrial tractors as a quantity measure, and as an alternative, the number of passenger cars alone, each measure being used without adjustment for differences in quality.

Of course, if in a comparison between two countries one does not have a higher quality level than the other for products in general, the errors for individual industries will tend to be offsetting. It is also true that, from the standpoint of the results of a given industry, quality differences attributable solely to material inputs do not matter since it is the processing or value added that is in principle being compared.

It is often recognised that these defences against the problems posed by possible incomparabilities in quality are not adequate and efforts are sometimes made to take account of quality differences. For example, Frankel obtains a U.S./U.K. output per worker index of 166 for building brick, but he then converts the output for both countries to bricks of equivalent size and estimates the corrected ratio to be 111. In the Czechoslovakia/Hungary comparison such adjustments were made for about a quarter of total production (Conference, 1971, *Methodological . . .*, p. 22). For the most part, however, the global studies tend to ignore the possibility of quality differences and simply to assume that products with similar descriptions (e.g. "passenger cars", "generators", "men's shoes", etc.) are equivalent in quality in the countries being compared. The error introduced in this way is likely to be related to the extent of the difference in industrial sophistication between the countries, and thus to bias upwards the measured productivity of low-income countries.

Another problem encountered in global studies using physical output indicators is that the products selected to form the quantity ratios usually fail to represent fully the industry's output in either country. Of course, if the sample of quantity ratios is representative, this problem does not arise. In actuality, incomplete coverage by the quantity ratios can be an important source of error in productivity comparisons for industries with a variegated product mix that is different for the countries being compared. The problem is usually resolved by finding some means of blowing up the output of each country to provide full coverage. In some studies the blow-up ratio is the proportion of the industry's labour inputs producing the covered output; the assumption is, of course, that the productivity for the non-covered part equals productivity for the covered part. This blow-up ratio requires knowledge of the labour inputs represented by the included commodities versus those represented by the excluded ones. Rostas and some others who relied upon physical indicators of output converted the omitted products into units of the representative products (i.e. those used as the quantity indicators) on the basis of relative prices.[1]

The global studies that use monetary indicators of output are similar to the aggregate comparisons described earlier in that the relative quantity of output is derived from data on the relative value of output and the relative prices or purchasing powers of the currencies of the countries being compared.

In the studies preceding Rostas' work, including some very widely cited ones, it was not unusual to derive the relative quantities simply from the value of gross output in each country and the exchange rate. Indeed, there are a number

[1] For a catalogue of many of the possible incomparabilities that may bias productivity comparisons see Snow's critique of Rostas' study.

of recent studies in which the same thing has been done, but we have not, for the most part, included them in our analyses.[1] The objection to the use of the exchange rate is not only that it may not reflect the correct overall purchasing power parity between two currencies but also that it fails to take account of the fact that the relative purchasing power of one currency *vis-à-vis* another will normally differ for different products and industries.[2]

The validity of productivity comparisons based on monetary indicators of output rests to a large degree on the quality of the price comparisons. If the price comparisons are based on average values derived from census data, as is sometimes the case, the quality problems are very much like those associated with the use of quantity indicators.

A careful price comparison, on the other hand, has substantial advantages which may not have been given enough weight in international productivity comparisons. There is no need here to restrict the sample to items for which output quantities and labour inputs are available on a product basis. The greater freedom in choosing representative items provides a better opportunity to establish quality equivalence between the two countries. Also, as suggested earlier in connection with aggregate comparisons, the sampling variance of price ratios (country i to country j) for different products within an industry is likely to be smaller than that of the quantity ratios.

4. *Treatment of the Composition Effect.* The studies also differ with respect to their treatment of the "composition effect"; that is, the effect of the varying output mix of the industries being compared in the two or more countries. Formula (1) as written indicates that an output index is to be divided by an input index, and this is the most common practice and what for the most part we have been assuming. This means, however, that a country with a relatively large proportion of high net-output-per-worker products will emerge with higher overall productivity in a given industry than a country with a lower proportion of such products, even if productivity per worker is the same in the two countries for each individual product. The alternative is to form the international productivity ratios for each of the individual products and to aggregate with one or more common sets of weights. This would produce a productivity comparison for an identical composition of output; the overall productivity index would in this case necessarily be 100 if the productivity of the two countries were equal in each individual product. The difficulty with this approach, however, is that it requires data on labour input for each product. (Establishment-basis data, which are the kind generally available, usually do not link inputs to particular products.) Among the studies we subsequently summarise, the Netherlands/U.K. comparison calculated both kinds of indexes. When Dutch price weights were used for these 1958 comparisons, the net output per worker in the United Kingdom as a percentage of that of the Netherlands in the tobacco industry was 73 for a fixed (U.K.) output composition and 118 when the product mix was allowed to affect the result; the

---

[1] See note 1, p. 31.
[2] For further comment on the use of exchange rates in productivity comparisons, see the discussion of the data in Table 6.

corresponding figures for milk were 93 and 109 and for knitted fabrics, 97 and 100.[1]

It would be desirable to present both fixed-composition and varying-composition productivity comparisons for each industry, and similar considerations apply with respect to the mix of industries (Kuznets, 1957). As a practical matter, however, it is much more difficult to isolate the composition effect with industries than among industries, and we can expect that productivity comparisons will continue to incorporate product mix effects more often than not.

5. *Problems of Comparing the Results of Different Studies.* It is not always easy to ascertain which of the general methods has, in fact, been applied in particular cases. Very few of the studies set out their methods for each particular industry in full detail as Paige and Bombach, for example, have done. In actual practice one method often takes on some attributes of another. For example, quantity ratios based on physical indicators of output are sometimes adjusted, as noted above, by monetary values to take account of portions of the output of the industry in the two countries not covered by the selected industries. Frankel also used value figures to eliminate from his quantity figures the outputs of secondary products properly classified to other industries, to adjust for inventory changes, and to adjust the employment figures to match the physical output data, as well as for the purpose of converting the other products produced by an industry into the "typical" product common to both countries. It is also quite common for value weights to be used in aggregating quantity ratios based on physical output indicators.

A difficulty that is encountered in comparing the results of the different studies is that the scope of the industry for which comparisons are made is often left unclear. The term "chemicals", for example, is used as a classification in a number of studies without any indication about its commodity or industrial coverage. It would help readers to have the results indicated in terms of the *International Standard Industrial Classification of All Economic Activities* (ISIC).[2]

In view of all of the sources of differences the extent to which roughly similar results are obtained by different studies when they overlap in country, time and industry coverage is surprising. While the comparable indexes sometimes differ in individual cases by substantial margins the overall impression is one of similarity. However, the reader should bear in mind the propensity of economists to issue the necessary caveats (as in the preceding paragraphs) and then to ignore them (as in the ensuing ones).

---

[1] The study, by the Netherlands Central Bureau of Statistics, attempted to produce four sets of estimates. One pair was based on Dutch price weights using first the composition of Dutch output and secondly the composition of U.K. output. The second pair was based on U.K. price weights, again alternating between the Dutch and U.K. structure of production. In only two of the 26 comparisons did it prove possible to give all four results (for public gas supply and for public electricity supply).

[2] This was one of the purposes of the multilateralisation of three binary comparisons reported upon in a document of the Conference of European Statisticians (1972). An alternative followed by West is to set out side by side the detailed composition of each industry being compared in terms of the industrial classification used by each of the included countries (see West, Appendix A).

III. DIFFERENCES IN *PER CAPITA* OUTPUT

Only a limited number of international comparisons of real *per capita* output have been based on extensive field work to make the essential price comparisons. The results of these studies are summarised in Table 1.

The first were the Organization for European Economic Cooperation (OEEC) studies by Gilbert and Kravis and by Gilbert and Associates comparing the *per capita* GNP of eight western European countries with the United States for 1950 and 1955. To the 1950 results, which are entered in the table, we have added Finland and Sweden, linking them via Denmark, on the basis of a Scandinavian study comparing living costs in capital cities for April 1952. Because the comparisons for Latin America and Eastern Europe, described in the next paragraphs, refer to 1960, Edward Denison's extrapolations of the OEEC results, on a national income basis, are also presented.

A study based largely on the OEEC methods but with the price comparisons confined to the capital cities was carried out by the Economic Commission for Latin America (ECLA) under the direction of S. Braithwaite (1968) with 1960 as the reference year. The purchasing power comparisons were linked to the United States through prices collected in Houston and Los Angeles, and it is in this form, relative to the United States, that the ECLA comparisons of real GDP *per capita* are summarised in Table 1. Australia is linked into the 1960 comparisons via the United Kingdom on the basis of Haig's study for 1958.

Another important investigation, about which much less is known in the West, involves some very careful and detailed comparisons of purchasing power and real material product for the socialist countries of Eastern Europe by the Council for Mutual Economic Assistance (CMEA). The figures in Table 1 for these countries are based on a study relating to 1963, but there have also been investigations for 1966 and other years. The CMEA comparisons are linked to the United States in Table 1 on the basis of Professor Bergson's comparison of Soviet and U.S. national income *per capita* for 1960 (1968, p. 89).

The most recent of the major studies is the United Nations International Comparison Project (ICP) which has been carried on by the U.N. Statistical Office and a group at the University of Pennsylvania in co-operation with the International Bank for Reconstruction and Development (IBRD). The first phase of the U.N. project produced 1970 comparisons of GDP *per capita* for ten countries, which were selected so as to provide for methodological purposes a varied sample of countries with respect to income level, location, and social and economic structure.[1] The Statistical Office of the European Economic Community (EEC) organised a closely co-ordinated study of the (then) six common market countries.[2] The results of the UN and EEC studies are shown in Table 1. The other 1970 comparison, for mainland China, is linked to the United States on the basis of Professor Swamy's (1973) comparison of China and India (India being compared with the United States in the UN study).

---

[1] See Kravis *et al.* (1975). The comparisons are being extended to more than 30 countries for 1975.
[2] See Paretti, Krijnse-Locker and Goybet (1970).

Table I

International Comparisons of Product per capita

(U.S. = 100.)

	Per capita product via exchange rate			Real per capita product		
	1950 (1)	1960 (2)	1970 (3)	1950 (4)	1960 (5)	1970 (6)
North America						
U.S.	100	100	100	100	100	100
Canada	75	71	—	75	77	—
Europe						
OECD countries						
Belgium	43	44	55	52	57	72
Denmark	37	46	—	55	63	—
Finland	39	—	—	39	—	—
France	35	45	60	46	58	75
Germany (Fed. Rep.)	26	44	64	37	64	75
Italy	16	25	35	25	33	46
Netherlands	27	35	51	45	52	72
Norway	34	42	—	52	55	—
Sweden	49	—	—	58	—	—
U.K.	37	49	45	55	64	60
CMEA countries						
Bulgaria	—	—	—	—	34	—
Czechoslovakia	—	—	—	—	44	—
Germany (Dem. Rep.)	—	—	—	—	53	—
Hungary	—	—	22	—	34	40
Poland	—	—	—	—	34	—
Romania	—	—	—	—	25	—
Soviet Union	—	—	—	—	38	—
Latin America						
Argentina	—	20·2	—	—	31·3	—
Bolivia	—	3·7	—	—	5·9	—
Brazil	—	9·0	—	—	10·4	—
Chile	—	21·8	—	—	23·7	—
Colombia	—	9·3	7·0	—	12·1	15·9
Costa Rica	—	13·5	—	—	17·0	—
Dominican Republic	—	8·6	—	—	9·1	—
Ecuador	—	7·8	—	—	11·0	—
El Salvador	—	8·2	—	—	10·1	—
Gautemala	—	9·8	—	—	10·5	—
Haiti	—	2·6	—	—	3·4	—
Honduras	—	7·0	—	—	7·5	—
Mexico	—	12·5	—	—	18·7	—
Nicaragua	—	8·2	—	—	8·8	—
Panama	—	15·0	—	—	17·1	—
Paraguay	—	5·8	—	—	9·2	—
Peru	—	7·5	—	—	12·2	—
Uruguay	—	17·2	—	—	30·7	—
Venezuela	—	37·6	—	—	29·2	—
Asia and Africa						
Australia	—	56	—	—	69	—
China	—	—	—	—	—	5·2
India	—	—	2·0	—	—	7·1
Japan	—	—	42·0	—	—	62·0
Kenya	—	—	3·0	—	—	5·7

For Notes and Sources see next page.

The estimates of real *per capita* product produced by these studies may be found in columns 4–6. They may be compared with the estimates derived by exchange rate conversions which are shown in columns 1–3. The latter are included for comparison with the real figures, despite our earlier criticisms, because they are so commonly used.

The general impressions about rough orders of magnitudes of the figures on real *per capita* product may be summarised quickly. For 1960, the year for which we have the largest number of estimates, the *per capita* gross products of the Western European countries and Australia vary between one-half and two-thirds that of the United States, except in the case of Italy (one-third). For the eastern European countries relative output *per capita* ranges roughly from one-fourth to one-half that of the United States. For the Latin American countries the ratio is from 3 % to 30 %. Data for 1960 are not available for the few Asian

---

Columns (1)–(3)   NOTES AND SOURCES (*For Table 1*)

Columns (1) to (3) are from data in IMF, *International Financial Statistics*; they are given only to show their downward bias compared with cols. (4)–(6).

Canada

Columns (4) and (5) are obtained from columns (1) and (2) by division by purchasing power parities taken from Appendix by E. C. West to D. Walters (1968). The geometric mean of the Canadian- and U.S.-weighted PPPs was used.

OECD Europe

1950   GNP *per capita* data. Data for all except Finland and Sweden from Gilbert and Associates (p. 28). In column (5) the figures represent the geometric mean of the results using U.S. and European price weights. Finland and Sweden linked in via Denmark on the basis of comparisons of the cost of living in the capital cities for April 1952. Geometric means of the Denmark- and own-weighted cost of living comparisons were used to deflate the GNP *per capita* of each country. Cf. Statistical Reports of the Northern Countries.

1960   Column (5) from extrapolations by E. Denison, p. 22, of the Gilbert and Associates estimates. The Denison data are on a national income basis; the geometric mean of U.S. and European price weights has been entered in column (5).

1970   France, Germany, Italy and U.K. from multilateral comparisons of GDP by U.N. International Comparison Project (Kravis, Kenessey, Heston and Summers, table 1–3). Belgium and Netherlands linked in through France on the basis of comparisons by Paretti, Krijnse-Locker and Goybet (table 1–1). The EEC comparisons using EEC weights were employed for this purpose.

CMEA countries

Soviet Union/U.S. is the geometric mean of Soviet- and U.S.-weighted comparisons of net national product by A. Bergson (1968, p. 89). The other CMEA countries are linked to the United States via the Soviet Union on the basis of CMEA comparisons of 1963 material national income *per capita* among the socialist countries. The data used here are cited with the Soviet Union as the base country in U.N. Economic Commission for Europe (1970), p. 144.

Latin America

Comparisons represent ECLA data reported by S. N. Braithwaite. The figures in column (5) represent the geometric mean of Latin American and U.S. weights for DGP *per capita*.

Asia and Africa

The figures for Australia, from Haig's comparison of GDP for 1958, are linked via the United Kingdom. The figures for India, Japan and Kenya are from the UN ICP and are on the same basis as noted above for the 1970 comparisons of the OECD countries of Europe. China was linked into the other countries on the basis of Professor Swamy's China–India comparisons of net domestic product (1973, table 37). Net domestic product *per capita* was derived by using the population estimates for China cited by Swamy (table 2) and a population estimate for India from IMF (*op. cit.*). The results of the China–India comparisons of GDP *per capita* were 72·6 for 1970, 78·3 for 1960 and 89.9 for 1952.

Table 2

Net Domestic Product per Occupied Person, Four Countries Compared with the United States, three periods

(U.S. = 100.)

	France	Germany	Sweden	U.K.
1905–11	—	55	61	92
1924–30	—	55	65	69
1952–59	61	48	65	61

Averages for period indicated are derived from figures in local currency by deflating by relative cost of a composite unit of consumables used by Phelps Brown and Browne to deflate wages. These relative costs, estimated with the United Kingdom as the base country, referred to 1905 (1909 in the case of the U.S./U.K.), 1930/1 or January 1931 and 1953. Phelps Brown and Browne stress the narrow coverage of the underlying price comparison; especially for the first period. The geometric mean of the results of applying U.K.- and own-weighted cost of consumables was used in each case for the first two periods; the spreads between the two indexes was 4 or 5 percentage points in the first period and 6 points for Germany, 10 for Sweden and 14 for the United States in the second period. For the third period, no index spread is reported here because Phelps Brown and Browne used price comparisons made by the Statistical Office of the Federal German Republic in which geometric means were taken of German-weighted and other country-weighted indexes. Phelps Brown and Browne did not include Sweden in the 1905 price comparisons; the purchasing power par for Sweden/U.K. was assumed in this case to be the same as exchange rate (see E. H. Phelps Brown, 1973, table 1).

Source: E. H. Phelps Brown and M. H. Browne (1968, pp. 46, 201–2, 274–5, except as noted).

and African countries included in the table, but it is clear that Japan would fall in the western European league or in the upper ranges of the eastern European group. Canada, with three-quarters of the U.S. product *per capita*, is the highest income country other than the United States.

The broad results refer to a middle year between 1950 and 1970, the reference dates for two of the major studies covering western European countries and the United States. A comparison of the 1950 and 1970 figures quantifies the substantial changes in the relative position of the United States *vis-à-vis* western Europe over the two intervening decades that has been widely noted and commented upon. All six of the European countries for which comparisons with the United States are available for the two dates improve their position relative to the United States with the relative gains of Italy and Germany being the greatest.

It may be noted that the real product estimates obtained as a result of purchasing power parity comparisons produce higher *per capita* incomes for most countries relative to that of the United States than are produced by comparisons via exchange rates (e.g. compare columns (2) and (5)). Furthermore there is a strong tendency for conversions via the exchange rate to show a bigger understatement for low-income countries than for higher income countries. In the 1970 comparisons, for example, the real product *per capita* is three times that suggested by the exchange rate in the case of India and two times in the case of Kenya, while for France and Germany the differences fall in the 15–25 % range.

For the period before World War II there were some sporadic efforts at careful price comparisons, though limited in commodity coverage. These have been used to derive the comparisons in Table 2 for three European countries with the United States for as far back as 1905–11. Unlike the data in Table 1, these estimates are based on price comparisons for consumers' goods only.[1] We would have preferred that for this section of our paper the results be based on total population rather than occupied persons, but it is doubtful whether the difference has a substantial impact on the figures. The figures suggest that during the first half of the twentieth century relative output per occupied person in the United States, Germany, and Sweden did not change very radically (the drop for Germany from 55 % of the United States in the 1920s to 48 % in the 1950s may well be due to the impact of World War II). The other notable feature of these data is the relative decline in the United Kingdom, caused by faster growth rates in the other countries. For the final period in the table, 1952–9, the figures for Germany and the United Kingdom seem to fit in very well with the data in Table 1, but the estimate for France seems high relative to the Table 1 figures.

The estimates in Tables 1 and 2 summarise the only studies based on extensive field work in making price comparisons. There have been a number of studies by individual scholars which have relied on data available in published sources. Mention should be made of the pioneering work of Colin Clark (1940), and of the estimates of *per capita* GDP at 1965 U.S. prices by Angus Maddison (1970, p. 18) for nearly a dozen countries in 1870 and for nearly thirty countries in 1956 with estimates for three intermediate years. Finally, there have been a number of efforts to estimate relative GDP or consumption *per capita* from various indicators, such as the amount of newsprint consumed and telephones installed. The work of Beckerman and Bacon (1970) is perhaps the most widely cited in this category; in one version, *per capita* consumption comparisons are offered for 72 countries with 1960 as the reference year.[2] There have also been a number of efforts to cover additional countries by extrapolating the relationship between the exchange-rate-derived estimates of GDP *per capita* and real GDP *per capita* on the basis of the OEEC and other studies.[3] The number of estimates of real GDP of the OEEC and UN ICP type is probably too small to provide adequate benchmarks for these efforts and certainly too small for their proper assessment.

IV. DIFFERENCES IN PRODUCTIVITY: AGGREGATE LEVEL

The large differences in *per capita* product observed in Table 1 represent the net result of the varied influences affecting what the people of each country are able to wrest from their environment. Some of these explanatory factors are natural, others the result of historical development; prominent among them are natural resource endowment (including climate), acquired physical

---

[1] However, this is true also of the estimates for Finland and Sweden in Table 1.

[2] See also Beckerman (1966) and Beckerman and Bacon (1966), the former containing brief summaries of earlier direct comparisons of real product and of short cut estimates based on the indicator approach.

[3] See the series of interchanges between David and Balassa. See also Summers and Ahmad (1974).

and human capital, and the efficiency with which inputs are used to obtain output.

The purpose of productivity comparisons is to help identify these factors and to ascertain their relative roles. More specifically, productivity comparisons may be used to illuminate the reasons for differences in *per capita* output by standardising the inputs and even some of the circumstances in which the inputs are used (e.g. size or scale of operations). In this way the extent to which observed differences *per capita* are attributable to differences in *per capita* input and to specified attendant circumstances can be ascertained.

A. *Labour Productivity Comparisons*

The first and most commonly taken step to explain the international differences in *per capita* income is to take account of the number of persons engaged in producing output. Doubtless some incomparabilities are introduced here because of country to country differences in the concepts used and the practices employed to measure the number of persons engaged in economic activity. As already noted, the statistical treatment of part-time workers and family workers, particularly those in agriculture, create problems that are handled in different ways in different countries.

The effects of shifting from a *per capita* basis to a per person employed basis in a number of developed countries may be seen in Table 3 by comparing columes 1 and 2.[1] The figures in column 1 are drawn from similar sources to the 1960 data in Table 1. However, following Denison, who is the main source of figures in Table 3, the estimates in this table are based on U.S. price weights rather than the geometric means of own- and U.S.-price weighted quantity indexes. When the national income estimates, based on U.S. price weights, are divided by the number of persons employed rather than by the population, the income gap between Canada and the United States narrows, but in the case of the other countries it generally widens, sometimes by substantial amounts. Compared to the United States the seven countries of north-west Europe as a whole had larger fractions of their labour forces engaged in employment; thus, output per person employed is lower relative to the United States than output *per capita*. It is interesting to note, however that the differences among the countries of northwest Europe tend to diminish; on a *per capita* basis, the figures for the seven countries range from 61–73 % of the U.S. national income, but on a per person employed basis, the range was only 58–65 %.

Part of the difference in productivity per person employed might be due to differentials in hours of work. Data on hours worked are sketchy in most countries, except in manufacturing, but in column 3 comparisons of productivity per man-hour are presented. The average employed person worked more hours per week in all the other countries than in the United States so that output per man-hour was lower still, relative to the United States, than output per person employed. Once again the variation in productivity levels among the seven countries of north-west Europe is reduced when the comparisons are

---

[1] "Persons employed" refers to all members of the labour force other than the unemployed;i includes proprietors as well as wage and salary workers.

Table 3

International Comparisons of Labour, Capital and Total Factor Productivity, 1960

	National income* per					
	Capita (1)	Person employed (2)	Man-hour (3)	Unit of labour input (4)	Unit of capital input (5)	Unit of total input† (6)
U.S.A.	100	100	100	100	100	100
Canada	73	82	79	82	90	83
Northwest Europe	69	59	53	60	119	66
Belgium	61	61	55	62	103	67
Denmark	71	58	55	61	103	66
France	66	59	53	60	122	66
Germany	73	59	53	61	134	68
Netherlands	61	65	57	60	107	66
Norway	64	59	55	59	87	63
U.K.	72	59	54	60	116	66
Italy	43	40	36	43	140	50
Soviet Union	50	38	36	49	64	51

Cols. (1) and (2). European countries from Denison, tables 2–4; Canada from Walters (1968), table 10; Soviet Union from Bergson (1968), p. 89. Later work by Walters (1970) indicates that revisions in the Canadian accounts raised the ratio of Canadian to U.S. real GDP per person employed by 4·7%. (Compare Table 10 in Walters (1968) with table 21 in Walters (1970).)

Col. (3). Col. (2) ÷ relative annual hours worked per employed person. Hours data from Denison Table 6–4, col. 14; Walters Table 22; and Bergson (1972), p. 124.

Col. (4). Col (2) ÷ quality-adjusted labour inputs per person (adjusted for hours, education, and age-sex composition). Quality-adjusted labour inputs from Denison, tables 15–6, line 3; Walters, table 73; and Bergson (1972), p. 124.

Col. (5). Col. (2) ÷ total capital per person (inc. dwellings, international assets, structures, and equipment, and inventories, but excluding land). Capital per person from Denison, tables 15–6, line 7; Walters, table 73; and Bergson (1968), p. 9. Bergson's comparison of Soviet/U.S. capital excludes foreign assets and capital used in housing, government, health and education.

Col. (6). From Denison, tables 15–6, line 14; Walters, table 73; and in case of Soviet Union weighted geometric average of cols. (4) and (5) with weights of 0·86 and 0·14 based on Denison, p. 38 (U.S. weights for 1960–2, exc. housing, foreign assets, and land). The Denison estimates include inputs of land while the others do not; however, the variation in land inputs per person employed and the relative weight of land inputs were so small that the figures based on inputs of only labour and capital would be substantially the same.

* Comparisons based on U.S. price weights.
† Based on U.S. weights for different factor inputs.

shifted to a more refined input basis; in this case the range is only 53–57 % of the United States.

A final refinement in the measurement of labour productivity is to relate output not simply to man-hours but to quality-adjusted man-hours. Productivity comparisons on this basis are presented in column (4), "quality" being defined in terms of level of education and age–sex composition. When the necessary downward adjustments are made in European countries for the relative quality of the labour inputs, the output per unit of labour input rises relative to the United States, and the range is narrowed by a further point to 59–62 %.

B. *Capital Productivity*

In column (5) of Table 3 output is related to capital rather than to labour. International comparisons of capital stocks are, as already noted, open to grave conceptual problems and also subject to very substantial margins of error, but the fact that European productivity in terms of capital turns out to be generally higher than in the United States certainly is a plausible result. The fact that this index is always higher than that for labour productivity is plausible if we are willing to believe that labour is more expensive relative to capital in the United States than in Europe. In this event, even if both areas had identical production functions, the capital/labour ratio would be higher in the United States, and therefore the ratio of Europe to U.S. output per unit of capital would be higher than the ratio of Europe to U.S. output per unit of labour. Another factor is that fuller utilisation of capacity in Europe tended to raise European productivity since output is divided by the stock of capital rather than the flow of capital services.[1]

Denison's estimates of total factor productivity are shown in column (6). It can be seen that the resulting figures are close to those based on labour inputs alone (column 4). This is due to the relatively great importance of labour in total factor inputs.

C. *Explanations*

The most systematic and imaginative effort to explain the reasons for international differences in overall national productivity is that of Denison. Using the estimates in Gilbert and Associates, he found that national income per employed person in eight countries of north-western Europe was 41 % lower than in the United States in 1960. Denison then sought to assign this gap to differences in various inputs and to factors that produced differences in output per unit of input. A little over one-quarter (11·3 percentage points) of the gap was due to lower factor input per person employed in Europe – mainly (9·7 points) less capital input. Not much of the gap was attributable to labour input per person employed because longer hours of work in Europe tended to be offset by less education. The remaining three-quarters (29·7 points) represented the difference between north-western Europe and the United States in output per unit of input; most (23·7 points) of this difference could not be explained and had to be attributed to "lag in the application of knowledge, general efficiency, and errors and omissions" (Denison, 1967, p. 332). The part that could be explained was accounted for mainly by economies of scale, at the levels of both national and local markets (4·9 points).

Not only the amount of capital per worker but also its vintage is sometimes cited as a factor accounting for productivity differences (though the distinction depends on the method used for valuing old capital). Heath, for example,

---

[1] Greater irregularity in the pressure of demand in the U.S. reduced the superiority of U.S. output per employed person over that of north-west Europe (amounting to a net figure of 41 %) by 1·6 percentage points (Denison, 1967, p. 332). For further discussion of the sources of the differences, see section of text headed "Explanations".

suggested that the greater modernity of Canadian equipment was responsible for the fact that labour productivity was higher in Canada than in Britain in 1948 (1957, p. 686). However, doubt has recently been cast on the hypothesis that new factories necessarily embody the most efficient technology (Gregory and James).

V. DIFFERENCES IN PRODUCTIVITY FOR MAJOR SECTORS AND INDUSTRIES

International comparisons of productivity for specific sectors and industries are numerous and scattered. We have almost of necessity confined ourselves to the major studies that have found their way into reports which have received fairly wide circulation, and in presenting the results we follow the principle that the main additional insight we can hope to obtain is the extent and nature of the deviations shown by individual industries from the overall averages represented by the aggregates. Productivity comparisons for major sectors such as agriculture and manufacturing are, however, important in themselves and we can and do present such data.

The theory of comparative advantage, to take an important example, turns, at least in its Ricardian version, upon the extent to which relative productivity in different countries differs in individual industries one from the other. For this and other purposes it is of interest to know whether international differences in productivity for particular sectors (or for particular manufacturing industries) have regressed toward the mean differences for the countries as a whole (or for manufacturing as a whole) over time. For example, Keynes once predicted that the diffusion of technology would reduce differences in productivity between industries in various countries and consequently erode the bases for different national comparative advantages. Another interesting hypothesis is that the diffusion of technology is uneven in different industries, and on this account (and perhaps others) larger productivity differences tend to characterise some industries more than others.

It is plausible to think that the dispersion of productivity indexes that we may expect to find in different major economic sectors will vary with the nature of the factors employed in each. International differences in productivity should be least in activities that have a high labour content and require little capital or land. The productivity of an Indian teacher relative to that of his U.S. counterpart may be difficult to measure, but it is very likely to be high compared to the Indian/U.S. productivity ratio for economic activity as a whole. In agriculture, we may expect to find the other extreme. Here, the large variation in the quality and quantity of land available per agricultural worker (whatever the reasons for these variations) is likely to produce great differences in productivity per worker among the countries. In mining, also, it is the bounty of nature that is likely to have a very great influence on the returns to man's efforts. Manufacturing is likely to fall in an intermediate position. Here, man does not work unaided to the same degree that he does in some of the service industries, like education. But neither does he have to rely on what has been

provided solely as the result of good or bad fortune; the tools of the manufacturing worker have a great deal to do with his productivity, but they can be
acquired.

These expectations are in accord with Professor Kuznets' analysis of national
income data. By comparing product per worker in different sectors within each
of about 40 countries, he found that international differences in product per
worker around 1950 were greatest in agriculture and least in the service sectors
(1957, pp. 35–41). Later he came to the same conclusions, working with nearly
60 countries with a reference date around 1960 (1971, pp. 208–14). Kuznets
was interested in differences when countries were arrayed by *per capita* income
level. It will be seen below that cross-country productivity comparisons for
particular sectors also conform to expectations, at least as far as the difference
between agriculture and manufacturing is concerned, even if *per capita* income
is held constant.

A. *Agriculture*

We turn first to agriculture. In Table 4 we show the results of comparisons of
productivity made by Hayami and associates (H & A) for 40 countries. Gross
output for over 50 categories of agricultural products net of agricultural intermediate products such as seed and feed were aggregated on the basis of three sets
of prices. The prices were those of the United States, Japan and India, taken, respectively, as representative of the price structures of "advanced", "midway"
and "initial" stages of economic development. A single composite measure of
output, used in the analysis, was derived by taking the geometric mean of three
resulting output series. The productivity ratio was formed for each country
by relating the output figure to the number of male workers in agriculture.

We must first note two important biases arising out of the definitions and
procedures, the choice of which reflects difficulties over data rather than what is
desirable on economic grounds. First, the failure to deduct inputs of industrial
products (artificial fertilisers, tractor fuel and spares, etc.) means that the output
of advanced countries is overstated, but has little effect on the figures for
developing countries: the comparisons are systematically biased against the
latter. And secondly, the failure to take any account of female workers means
that the comparisons are too flattering for countries which use a lot of female
labour in agriculture.

As it happens, a comparison between the United Kingdom and the
Netherlands is available (see below) which shows how important these biases
can be, even between countries which belong to the same broad class.

The disparities in labour productivities shown in Table 4 are however much
greater than these biases. "Agricultural" output per male worker in the four
most productive countries ranges from nearly 20 to more than 60 times as great
as in the four least productive countries. The differences between the top four,
the traditional larders of Europe, and the next eight countries, seven being in
north-western Europe, is on the average more than 2 to 1.

The differences in labour productivities are not only great but are systematically related to differences in national income *per capita*. For the 19 countries

Table 4

International Comparisons of Land and Labour Productivity in Agriculture, 1957–62

(U.K. = 100.)

	Output per			Output per	
	Hectare	Male worker		Hectare	Male worker
New Zealand	61	322	Chile	25	29
Australia	5	241	Spain	56	28
U.S.	41	226	South Africa	8	26
Canada	30	168	Mauritius	275	26
Belgium	315	120	Japan	385	24
Denmark	237	108	Peru	29	23
Sweden	120	101	Colombia	43	23
U.K.	100	100	Greece	63	22
Netherlands	372	98	Syria	19	21
Argentina	19	91	Brazil	31	21
Germany	206	88	Venezuela	14	19
France	128	81	Taiwan	528	18
Austria	120	72	Portugal	n.a.	17
Finland	104	70	Turkey	30	16
Norway	159	71	Mexico	14	12
Switzerland	163	67	Paraguay	48	11
Israel	95	66	U.A.R.	356	10
Ireland	81	48	Ceylon	147	9
Surinam	230	39	Philippines	97	9
Italy	155	36	India	55	5

Source: Hayami and associates.

"Output" is gross output less agricultural intermediate products. See text. Hectares refer to "agricultural land including permanent meadows and pastures in the year closest to 1960 as reported in FAO's *Production Yearbook*" (Hayami and associates, p. 7), with no allowance for quality variations.

ranging from the United States and Canada to Mexico and Paraguay that are found both in Table 4 and in the 1960 figures for real product *per capita* in Table 1, Spearman's coefficient of rank correlation between labour productivity in agriculture and *per capita* real product is +0·89. The figures thus reflect the association between the reduction of labour requirements in agriculture and the attainment of high overall incomes that has been widely noted in development literature. The land productivities (i.e. outputs per hectare) associated with these labour productivities and income levels differ widely, and largely reflect the varying quality of the land included in the statistics.

The figures indicate that the highest labour productivity countries are engaged in extensive agriculture (i.e. using much land per worker), an inference that would probably hold up even if allowance were made for the relatively large amount of inferior land used in these countries. (An index for hectares per male worker can be obtained by dividing output per male worker by output per hectare.) At the other extreme are countries like Taiwan, Japan and the United Arab Republic with very intensive agriculture, marked by very high outputs per hectare and very low outputs per worker. The land and labour productivities of countries of north-western Europe fall between those of these two groups of countries. A fourth group of countries, including India and a number of Latin American countries, have very low outputs in terms of both land and labour. Hayami and Ruttan, in discussing these phenomena, show that the countries in the first of these four groups with plenty of land and scarce labour ease the scarcity of labour by mechanisation (high tractor horse-power per worker) while those in the second group with scarce land and abundant labour stretch the amount of land with relatively larger fertiliser inputs per hectare (1971, pp. 69 f.).

While the results of this cross-country study of a single sector seem plausible, it is of interest to compare them with the results of cross-industry comparisons for pairs of countries. There are two points of overlap among the studies we have summarised. One is with the Paige–Bombach comparison of the U.S./U.K. for 1950 and the other is with the comparison of the Netherlands/U.K. by the Netherlands Central Bureau of Statistics for 1973.

The Paige–Bombach index for agriculture is 207, a result that is not obviously at variance with the H & A estimate of 226 for 1957–62. According to the Dutch study, however, net output per man in the Netherlands was 152 % of that of the United Kingdom using Dutch price weights and 149 % using U.K. price weights, whereas the H & A estimates show Netherlands output per worker to be less than that of the United Kingdom for the period 1957–62.

Inspection of the data underlying the H & A estimates shows that a large part of this discrepancy springs from the relative grossness of their output concept. The United Kingdom makes much more use of industrial inputs, and if these had been subtracted in comparing Dutch and U.K. outputs H & A would have obtained a ratio for value added which was 30 % higher than the one they actually obtained for "agricultural output".

The narrowness of H & A's labour concept would, however, tell the other way. The Dutch study converted part-time and women working into equivalent man-years, and as these are more important in the Netherlands than in the United Kingdom this raised the ratio of Dutch to U.K. labour above the one that would have been obtained by using only full-time males.[1]

B. *Mining*

Aside from coal mining the estimates are too scattered for any generalisation, but it is not unlikely that other major branches are similar to coal as far as factors affecting productivity are concerned.

Mining productivity is heavily influenced by the richness of the deposits and the ease of access to them. In coal, shortly after World War II, over 20 % of U.S. output came from strip mining where labour productivity is high, while only around 5 % was obtained in this way in Great Britain. The remainder

---

[1] Aside from the difference in "netness" mentioned in the text, there are differences in (*a*) reference dates, (*b*) scope of "agriculture" and (*c*) the concept of labour input. An examination of the underlying data suggests that the first two are unlikely to matter much. The conversion of part-time and women workers to equivalent man-years in the Dutch study should operate so as to make the Dutch estimate of relative productivity in the Netherlands lower if, as seems likely, the ratio of part-time workers and women in the Dutch agricultural labour force was higher than that in the U.K. agricultural labour force.

Table 5

International Comparisons of Labour Productivity in Coal Mining

(U.K. = 100, unless otherwise indicated.)

c. 1910	c. 1935	c. 1950	c. 1965
U.S. (T 11, W) 227 (T 14, W) 245 (R 13, M) 317	U.S. (R 38, M) 381	U.S. (I 49, M) 496 (P 50, E) 382‡§	Czechoslovakia/France*† (K 62, W) 220 (K 62, W) 105
Ruhr (R. 13, M) 92	Ruhr (R 38, M) 132	Germany (Fed. Rep.) (I 49, M) 90	Czechoslovakia/Hungary† (CH 67, E) 361‡ (CH 67, W) 356‡
Upper Silesia (R 13, M) 111	Upper Silesia (R 38, M) 159	—	
Saar (R 13, M) 78	Saar (I 37, M) 89 (R 38, M) 98	Saar (I 49, M) 72	
Prussia (T 11, W) 95 (T 14, W) 103	Germany (Fed. Rep.) (I 37, M) 134	—	
Belgium (T 11, W) 59 (T 14, W) 52	Belgium (I 37, M) 66	Belgium (I 49, M) 54	
France (T 11, W) 72	France (I 37, M) 70	France (I 49, M) 60	
Nova Scotia (T 11, W) 185	Poland (I 37, M) 146	Poland (I 48, M) 118	
New South Wales (T 11, W) 187 (T 14, W) 214	Czechoslovakia (I 37, M) 118	Czechoslovakia (I 48, M) 97	
India (T 11, W) 42 (T 14, W) 47	Netherlands (I 37, M) 150	Netherlands (I 49, M) 119	
	U.S.S.R./U.S.† (G 39, M) 29 (G 39, W) 42	U.S.S.R./U.S.† (G 50, M) 23 (G 50, W) 30	

The material in the parentheses preceding each productivity index provides information on (a) source, (b) reference year and (c) the nature of the input-measure in the denominator of the productivity ratio. The codes used for each are as follows:

(a) *Source:* CH = Conference of European Statisticians WG 21.14. G = Galenson. I = I.L.O. K = Kux, Mairesse, Drechsler. P = Paige and Bombach. R = Rostas. T = Taussig.

(b) *Reference year.* Last two digits of year. (The reference date for the numerator country has been entered in cases where the reference dates differ for the two countries being compared; when the years are not the same they usually differ only by 1 or 2 years.)

(c) *Input measure in the denominator.* E = Employees (or workers). M = Man-shift. W = Wage earners.

General. Output per worker includes both above- and beneath-surface workers. Rostas' output per head was for bituminous coal mines only. Taussig's 1911 comparisons include anthracite as well as bituminous; his 1914 comparison cited here refers to bituminous alone. Taussig's figures show that output per man for bituminous was 40% higher than that for anthracite.

* The first figure is based on a comparison of physical tons per worker; the second figure takes account of the caloric value of the outputs.

† Second country mentioned, rather than the United Kingdom, is the base country.

‡ Ideal index.

§ Based on "ring-fence" method in which a group of related industries is treated as an entity for purposes of measuring inputs and outputs. See Paige & Bombach, pp. 83 f.

came from average depths of 190 feet in the United States and 1170 feet in Great Britain (Frankel, p. 33). This probably does much to explain Taussig's early twentieth-century data showing productivity levels in the new regions of the world two or three times those of areas with a longer history of intensive exploitation of natural resources (see Table 5). Within Europe, the Netherlands, Poland and Czechoslovakia had substantially higher productivity than the Saar, France, and Belgium both before and after World War II. Before the war, coal output per operative in Poland and Czechoslovakia also exceeded that of the United Kingdom, but after the war only the former had a greater productivity, and that by a reduced margin. The other war-torn countries of continental Europe also slipped relative to Great Britain. U.S. productivity relative to Europe in the early post-war years (1949 and 1950) was very much higher than in 1911.

A comparison of the figures for coal mining with those of agriculture in Table 4 may give the impression that the extent of the international differences in productivity is smaller in coal mining than in agriculture. If, however, comparisons are confined to the same set of countries, this is less obvious. For example, the U.S. margin of superiority over Europe is clearly higher in mining than in agriculture.

C. *Manufacturing*

The main studies that we rely upon for a summary of the comparisons of productivity in manufacturing industries are set out in Table 6. We have also examined data from several other studies, but we confine ourselves in this table to studies (a) containing comparisons for more than a half a dozen different industries, (b) involving access to original data of both countries being compared, and (c) not, as concerns post-World War II studies, based on exchange rate conversions of currency.[1]

---

[1] Among the excluded comparisons are a number involving the socialist countries of Eastern Europe that have been summarised by Drechsler, Kux and Nyitrai (1974). Among the more extensive of these were a Hungarian/West German comparison by the Hungarian Central Statistical Office and a comparison of the Soviet Union with France, U.K. and West Germany by A. J. Kac of the Research Institute of the Ministry of Labour of the U.S.S.R. The per worker comparisons for "industry" (manufacturing and mining), taking the denominator country as 100, were as follows:

	1956	1959	1963
W. Germany/Hungary	—	197	187
U.S.S.R./France	119	125	—
U.S.S.R./U.K.	130	152	—
U.S.S.R./Germany	111	118	—

Drechsler *et al.* (1974) reported comparisons for about 30 different industry groupings from the Hungarian study and for about 20 from the Soviet study.

Mention should also be made of a U.S./France comparison by Chandrasekar (1973) covering 19 manufacturing industries; the average index for all the industries was 216 for 1958 and 234 for 1963 when French employment weights were used and 226 and 248, respectively, with U.S. weights.

Unlike the recent studies in Table 6, the above comparisons had to be carried out with an outsider's reliance on published data for at least one of the pairs of countries. In addition, as far as one can tell from his published report, Chandrasekar converts net output in one currency to the other currency at prevailing exchange rates without regard to the relative purchasing powers of the currency or to differences in the composition and quality of the output of the two countries in each industry.

A very careful study of seven manufacturing sectors of France and Germany by Branchu, Grotius,

The list of studies shown in Table 6 is disappointingly thin, with very few relating to years since 1950, despite the greatly increased supply of census material. If, however, we ignore the differences in the methods used in the studies and slur over some of the differences in reference dates, we can group the estimates for the various countries together to obtain a rough summary of the relationships, but there is very little continuity in the countries covered. Using the United Kingdom as the base country where we can, and France in other instances, the results are as follows:

c. 1937 (U.K. = 100)		c. 1950 (U.K. = 100)		c. 1960 (France = 100)	
U.S.	216	U.S.	273	Czechoslovakia	81*
Germany	104	Canada	163	Austria	70
Sweden	103	Netherlands	116	Hungary	53†
U.S.S.R.	86	Australia	96	Yugoslavia	57‡
		Japan	95§		

* Czechoslovakia/France comparison included mining, electricity and gas.
† Czechoslovakia/Hungary comparison included mining and electricity production.
‡ Refers to 1970.
§ Based on U.S./Japan for 1963; Japan/U.K. for 1950 was probably much lower than 95.

We do not have the France/U.K. link for manufacturing; for *per capita* product as a whole, the France/U.K. ratio was 84 in 1950 and 91 in 1960 (see Table 1). If the France/U.K. relationship for manufacturing was the same as the relationship for GDP as a whole, the figures in the right-hand column could be put on a (1960) U.K. basis by deducting about 10%.[1]

There are virtually no overlapping comparisons between these data for manufacturing and those for agriculture in Table 4. For the very few comparisons that can be made between the manufacturing figures and those relating to coal mining in Table 5, the tendency is for smaller international differences in productivity to exist in manufacturing. This is, as argued earlier, a plausible result, but the data are too skimpy and the basis for the comparisons between the sectors too shaky to claim that any very firm conclusion can be drawn.[2]

More broadly, any inferences drawn from the manufacturing comparisons in

---

Temple and Wartenberg (1973) included productivity comparisons, though with one exception they were based on exchange rate conversions. For agricultural machinery, the German/France productivity ratio per person for 1967 rises from 97.4 with exchange rates to 117.5 with price comparisons, and on a per hourly basis from 111.6 to 134.6. In 1969, German output per person varied from 79% of the French in chalk and cement to 109% in foundries; on a per hourly basis the range was from 84% to nearly 119%.

[1] The Kreinin survey mentioned earlier suggests that American firms operating abroad found very little difference between labour requirements per unit of output in the U.K. on one hand, and Italy and France on the other. The median labour productivity ratio, based on the numbers of observations ranging from 28 to 51, was 83 in the U.K., Italy, France and Benelux, and 87 in Germany. In Mexico the productivity index was 80 (24 observations). The reference date was not given in the report, but it presumably was 1963 or 1964. The relatively high figure for Mexico, compared to those in Europe, suggests that the productivity of American firms cannot be considered typical with respect to the productivity of all firms operating in the host country.

[2] The only pair of countries for which the table affords longitudinal comparisons is the U.S. and the U.K. However, it would be hazardous to make any generalisation about the trend in relative manufacturing labour productivities from these data. Yukiyawa's (1975) U.S./Japan estimates for periods before and after the one shown in the table reveal the expected decline in the U.S. margin of superiority for manufacturing as a whole; his indexes are 308 for 1958-9 and 195 for 1967. Some longitudinal

Table 6 must take account of the disparate nature of the underlying studies and the doubtful validity of linking their results. Some of the studies provide comparisons for a dozen broad industry classifications, corresponding roughly to the 2-digit industries in the ISIC, which together account for all of manufacturing. Both of the Flux studies and two of the Rostas studies (lines 3 and 7) are of this character. So too are the Yugoslav–Hungary and the Austria–Hungary comparisons. The other studies referred to in the table involve comparisons of much more narrowly defined industries or products. Although the Paige–Bombach study in this group is comprehensive in its coverage, the more usual situation is that the fraction of manufacturing covered by the included industries is generally quite small; the industries analysed by Frankel, for example, accounted for less than one-fifth of manufacturing employment, both in the United States and the United Kingdom. For the most part, the comparisons of the more aggregated but comprehensive type are based on money values, often converted to a common currency by the suspect method of using exchange rates, while those based on more detailed industries involve quantity comparisons for a limited number of products.

Of course, even the same method may lead to different results when carried out by different analysts. The need for the exercise of judgment in choosing among equally valid compromises at many points in the course of producing time-to-time or place-to-place indexes of quantities or prices is familiar to anyone who has tried his hand at index number construction. But as far as concerns the average level of relative productivity, with one notable exception, the methods used by the studies in the table would appear to be exposed to equal chances of error in either direction; one can identify plenty of possible sources of error, but they may operate sometimes in one direction and sometimes in another. The exception concerns the use of exchange rates to convert output figures to a common currency. We have already observed that exchange rates tend systematically to understate the relative purchasing power of low income countries so that productivity comparisons based on exchange rate conversions of monetary indicators can be expected to exaggerate the productivity of a high income country relative to that of a low income country. The table contains no really low-income countries, but Rostas' two methods show that the result using the exchange rate (line 3) gives the United States a greater margin of superiority over the United Kingdom than the quantity method (line 4).

However, the difference is not great, and it can be said that such overlapping with respect to time and country coverage as is found among the studies in the table suggests that, within the field of developed countries, different approaches and even different authors have obtained roughly similar results for the average for manufacturing as a whole. (See column 4, lines 5 and 6, and 7 and 8, as well as lines 3 and 4.)

---

comparisons, generally for short spans of years, can be found also for particular manufacturing industries. For example, Pratten and Silberston (1967) offer comparisons of labour productivity in the automobile industries of 6 countries for 1955, 1960 and 1965. The indexes varied from 11% (Japan) to 38% (U.K.) of the U.S. in 1955 and from 32% (Japan) to 53% (Italy) of the U.S. in 1965. (The other countries were France and Germany.)

Table 6

Summary of International Comparisons of Productivity in Manufacturing Industries

Line	Author (1)	Date (2)	Countries (3)	Weighted mean index* (4)	Largest number of comparisons for mutually exclusive manufacturing industries			Method† (8)
					Number of industries* (5)	Unweighted mean index* (6)	Coefficient of variation (7)	
			Comparisons of U.S. and U.K.					
1	Flux	1909	U.S./U.K.	226	12	248	0·140	Ex. rate
2	Flux	1929	U.S./U.K.	293	12	316	0·162	Ex. rate
3	Rostas	1937	U.S./U.K.	225	12	229	0·181	Ex. rate
4	Rostas	1937	U.S./U.K.	216‡	33	231	0·493	Quantity
5	Frankel	1947	U.S./U.K.	269‡	36	247	0·478	Quantity
6	Paige–Bombach	1950	U.S./U.K.	273‡	70	280	0·360	Quantity
			Other countries compared with the U.K.					
7	Rostas	1936	Ger./U.K.	111	12	119	0·199	Ex. rate
8	Rostas	1936	Ger./U.K.	104‡	20	102	0·318	Quantity
9	Rostas	1937	Sweden/U.K.	103‡	7	103	0·327	Quantity
10	Heath	1948	Can./U.K.	163‡	14	170	0·184	Quantity
11	Netherlands§	1958	Neth./U.K.	116‡	15	119	0·167	Quantity
			Other countries compared with the U.S.					
12	Galenson	1937	U.S.S.R./U.S.	41‡	11	44	0·330	Quantity
13	West	1963	Can./U.S.	66‡	29	79	0·382	Price
14	Yukizawa	1963	U.S./Japan	286‖	60	350	0·862	Quantity
			Comparisons between other countries					
15	Maizels	1950	Can./Austral.	170‡	21	180	0·420	Price
16	Czech./France§	1962	Czech./France	81‡	33	90	0·230	Quantity
17	Austria/Hung.§	1965	Austria/Hung.	132‡	17	146	0·270	Price
18	Czech./Hung.§	1967	Czech./Hung.	154‡	26	139	0·236	Quantity
19	Yugo./Hung.§	1970	Yugo./Hung.	108‡	14	105	0·155	Quantity

Sources: See References.

* Productivity of numerator country as percentage of that of denominator country. All the unweighted means and the weighted means on lines 10 and 16 have been computed for the present paper; the other weighted means are from the original sources.

† Where the method varied according to industry, the predominately used method is given.

‡ Geometric mean of Paasche and Laspeyres indexes.

§ Studies prepared by official statistical offices of indicated countries; except for Netherlands/U.K. and Yugoslavia/Hungary, the results have been circulated under the aegis of the Conference of European Statisticians.

‖ Sum of U.S. and Japanese employees used to weight the individual productivity indexes.

D. *Differences within Manufacturing*

Each of the studies produced a productivity ratio for each of the industries covered, and the dispersion of the ratios is summarised in the coefficient of variation, which appears in column (7) of Table 6. There are great differences between these figures for the various studies, but they are of little economic interest, as they reflect mainly the different statistical methods used in making the comparisons. Understandably enough, the coefficient of variation tends to be *high* where industries are finely divided. It also tends to be *low* where a single exchange rate is used to compare value figures for net output. This happens because when a single purchasing power parity is used for all industries, the number of currency units required to buy a high-productivity good is exaggerated relative to the number required to buy a low-productivity good. Since in the monetary indicator approach, the relative quantities for the countries being compared are obtained by dividing the ratio of expenditures (in each country's own currency) by the selected purchasing power parity, the relative output of the high productivity industries is underestimated, and the productivity indexes for the individual industries are biased toward the mean. One must also remember that some part of the dispersion between productivity ratios shown in each study reflects statistical errors caused by inaccurate or non-comparable data.

The question remains whether we can draw any inferences from the studies summarised in Table 6 concerning the industrial pattern of international differences in productivity. There is not space here to pursue this question very far. The studies summarised in Table 6 may not in any case provide a substantial enough body of data for the purpose, considering the extent to which special factors in the situations of individual countries and the statistical methods of particular studies may obscure whatever regularities exist.

For U.S.–U.K. comparisons, we can, however, draw on three separate studies based on quantity comparisons which should help to overcome the effects of the particular procedures used in any one. Since we are interested in finding a pattern for the differences in productivity revealed by the three studies, we have made the indexes for detailed industries more comparable among the studies by converting each index to a percentage of the mean index for its study. We then classified these individual "indexes of relative productivity", as we may call them, into the nine (2-digit) divisions of manufacturing provided by the ISIC. A simple average of the indexes falling within each of the divisions was computed and the results were arrayed in diminishing order in Table 7. This averaging of the indexes from all three studies appeared warranted since the industrial pattern of the productivity gaps was not significantly different from one study to another; the coefficient of concordance among the rankings of the eight 2-digit industries for which there was at least one observation in all three of the studies was 0·75.[1]

If the first two divisions, which have only a scattering of observations, are ignored, industries in the fabricated metals and machinery and chemicals

---

[1] This was significant at the 0·01 level (Moroney, p. 338).

Table 7

Relative Productivity Index-Numbers* for U.S./U.K. Comparisons

ISIC division	Brief description	No. of observations	Average value of relative productivity index
34	Paper and printing	5	132
39	Miscellaneous industries	3	129
38	Fabricated metals, machinery	39	123
35	Chemicals, etc.	14	113
37	Basic metals	10	110
33	Wood	2	101
31	Food, beverages, tobacco	30	78
32	Textiles, apparel	26	76
36	Non-metallic minerals	10	70

* In each of the studies of Rostas, Frankel and Paige–Bambach the productivity ratio for each industry is expressed as a percentage of the mean ratio from the same study to give the relative productivity index for that industry, and all these observations for industries within the ISIC division are averaged to give the index for that division.

divisions are revealed to have larger productivity gaps than food, beverages and tobacco; textiles and apparel; and non-metallic minerals. On a purely intuitive level, these results appear to be consistent with the expectation that productivity gaps would be higher in industries where current technology is less widely dispersed than in older, well-established industries where it is apt to be widely available. This notion of the technological characterisation of different industries gets considerable support from international trade statistics, if it can be assumed that LDC export shares will be low for products for which technology is closely held and higher for those for which technology is more dispersed. In 1971 less-developed countries accounted for less than 2 % of the world export of fabricated metals and only around 4½ % of chemicals, while their shares for textiles and basic metals were 19 and 12 % respectively.[1]

We performed a similar exercise for the 267 observations contained in the studies listed in Table 6 which do not rely on a single exchange rate and which apply to comparisons other than the U.S. and the U.K. (It was necessary, of course, to reverse the comparisons in rows 12, 13 and 16 so as to express the higher productivity country as a percentage of the lower.) Chemicals had by far the highest gap (the relative productivity index was 122). The next highest was for fabricated metals and machinery (107) but this was followed by a not very great distance by textiles (104) and food (102). Basic metals, non-metallic minerals and wood all showed below-average margins of superiority in the productivity of the higher productivity country.

[1] GATT (1973, p. 33). No reference in the text is made to LDC shares in world exports of foods, beverages and tobaccos because manufactures of these products are classified with similar primary products in the Standard International Trade Classification. For an explanation of productivity differences based on the diffusion of technology, see Nelson (1968).

E. *Reasons for Differences in Productivity Indexes*

The explanation of differences in the overall labour productivity of entire economies has already been discussed in Section IV. Here our interest is in the reasons for differences in productivity indexes for different manufacturing industries.

It is apparent that productivity comparisons for particular industries for particular pairs of countries can be influenced by a host of special circumstances. Some of these arise out of differences in natural resource endowments, even in the case of manufacturing industries. Rostas reported, for example, that the British pig-iron industry (which shows particularly low productivity compared with the U.S.) required more labour per unit than the U.S. industry because, owing to the low iron content of the ore used, both more ore and more coal had to be handled per unit of output (1948, p. 50). Institutional factors may also have a substantial effect on particular productivity comparisons. Drawing again for an illustration upon Rostas' U.S./U.K. comparison, the U.K. labour productivity relative to that of the U.S. was low in the tobacco industry in part because of the pattern of taxation; a high tax on tobacco collected before manufacture in the United Kingdom led to a considerable expenditure on labour in order to prevent wastage whereas in the United States taxes were levied after manufacture and hence the same impetus was not given to labour-intensive and material-saving modes of production (1948, p. 50). Industry-to-industry differences in restrictive labour practices may not fall in the same pattern in different countries, and these too would create differences in the productivity ratios for different industries.

It is of greater analytical interest, however, to consider what *general* factors there are that may produce *systematic* differences in the productivity indexes – that is, that may make productivity differentials between countries larger in certain industries and smaller in others.

One possibility is that productivity differences may tend to be larger in industries with lesser dispersion of up-to-date technology than in industries with widespread dispersion. This is broadly supported by the nature of the industries which came high and low in the lists in the last section.

Other possibilities may be classified under two headings. One consists of inter-industry differences in the extent of mechanisation or in the amount of capital per worker and the vintage of the capital. Labour productivities ought to be relatively higher in capital-intensive industries in capital-rich countries when they are compared with capital-poor countries, particularly if the industries that are capital intensive in the capital-rich country have high elasticities of substitution between capital and labour. These expectations have not, however, been very much tested. Occasionally a relationship has been found between horse-power or fuel input (as proxy variables for capital) and the productivity differences. Frankel, for example, was able to explain nearly 19 % of the variation in U.K.–U.S. productivity ratios for 26 industries around 1947 by the fuel input per worker ratio (1957, p. 43). More often, however, the association is averred rather than demonstrated quantitatively.

The other set of influences that may affect the industry-by-industry productivity indexes are organisational characteristics of industries such as the
extent of competition, the size of the optimal plant or firm, or the degree of
concentration on a limited number of product variants and the extent of
capacity utilisation, although for present purposes a structural connection
between these influences and certain industries would have to be established.
(Occasional efforts to take the quality of inputs into account may be regarded
as attempts to improve the labour productivity indexes rather than to explain
them.)

A systematic variation between inter-industry differences in labour and
relative size of plant or firm in each industry has not been established in any of
the studies. This once again is a failure that might have been expected since it
would take a knowledge of the size of the optimum plant in each industry in
order to sort out the influence of plant size.

A related factor that is frequently mentioned is the economy of long production runs. This has been cited, for example, in all three studies comparing
the United States and the United Kingdom. The most tangible evidence in
support of a positive role for long production lines in the explanation of productivity differences is to be found in Canadian investigations of reasons for the
higher productivity prevailing in the United States. In one of the more
dramatic examples it was reported that a Canadian firm had to turn out 1,700
different sizes of tyres in a single factory and that this required changing sizes
on a tyre-building machine three or four times a day. In the United States, on
the other hand, a typical tyre plant of the same size would produce only
125 different types and sizes and would produce the same tyre on a given
machine for months at a time (Daly, Keyes and Spence, 1968). From the
present standpoint, the implication is that international productivity differences
should be greater for industries with a highly variegated set of outputs, but this
has not been tested.

One of the relatively few positive findings that emerges from more than one
study is an association between the labour productivity ratios (i.e. productivity
in country i to productivity in country j) for the various industries and the
relative size of the individual industries (i.e. size in i to size in j) as measured
by total output or employment. The difficulty is, however, to know which way
the causation runs. High relative productivity, whatever its cause, is likely to
make the industry large, because the cheapness of its products will increase both
home and export sales: this large size may well further increase productivity,
through economies of scale, etc.

A relationship of this kind is found, with varying degrees of clarity, in the
U.S./U.K. comparisons by Rostas, Frankel, and Paige and Bombach. Rostas'
data yield a rank correlation coefficient (Spearman) of $+0.73$ between the
U.S./U.K. productivity ratios and U.S./U.K. industry output ratios for
31 industries in 1937.[1] Frankel's coefficient of correlation for 37 manufacturing
industries between the same variables is only $+0.11$, but it rises to $+0.70$ when
he excludes the manufactured-ice and ice-cream industries (on grounds that

---

[1] Computed from Rostas (1948, pp. 36, 71).

markets may be local) and petroleum refining (because of the very different relative importance of this industry in the two countries) (1957, pp. 65–6). The coefficient of rank correlation reported by Paige and Bombach for the same variables for 44 selected manufacturing industries in 1950 is +0·789 (1959, p. 70).

A similar relationship between industry size and labour productivity was found in West's Canada/U.S. comparison for 24 manufacturing industries in 1963 (1971, p. 48), and in the Czechoslovakia/France comparison for 50 product groups for 1962 (Conference..., 1971, p. 17), and in Yukizawa's comparisons of 59 products in 1958–9, 1963 and 1967 (1975, p. 21). However, this relationship is not confirmed in the other studies, in some perhaps because they generally subdivide manufacturing into a smaller number of separate industries. In one study, that for Austria/Hungary, there is actually a negative correlation between the two variables for 15 manufacturing industries (Conference..., 1969, tables 3 and 4).

Unfortunately, it cannot be said that the relative importance of the factors relating to capital and to organisation or even their general operation has been established in the body of studies that are available. The observed differences in labour productivity are often ascribed to these causes without supporting evidence in a *post hoc ergo propter hoc* manner. A fuller assessment of the role of these various factors must await the development of better comparative studies of different countries including productivity comparisons and comparative information about the amount, vintage, and degree of utilisation of capital.

There are still some important dimensions of international productivity differences that we have hardly touched on, and others, such as the external diseconomies (smoke, etc.) that may affect true social productivity comparisons, have not even been mentioned. The role of X-efficiency (Leibenstein, 1966) in explaining international differences in labour productivity has frequently been the subject of speculation, though not always under that rubric, but there is little hard information about it.

VI. CONCLUSIONS

Perhaps the most striking fact that emerges from this survey of international productivity comparisons is the lack of cohesiveness of the studies that have been carried out. We have learned quite a lot about the very large differences which exist between countries in GNP per head of population or per occupied person, but these comparisons rest mainly on an approach from the expenditure side. The lack of good studies from the output side means that we are far from even knowing how productivity differences in the individual industries vary around the national mean differences, and still further from an ability to explain the reasons for these differences. The absence of this knowledge weakens our understanding of the reasons why the national means differ.

There is a major need for a better organisation of the resources that are invested in this work. The Conference of European Statisticians has shown the way by sponsoring a series of studies, but even in this instance the co-ordination has had to be very loose and the choice of methods has had to be left to the decisions of the successive pairs of partners in the binary comparisons.[1] Also, the studies have been largely limited to industry.

From a methodological standpoint it would be wise, in the judgment of the present writer, to move in the direction of a greater use of monetary indicators of output and of the price comparisons that must go with them. Reliance on monetary values and prices cannot be avoided even in the physical indicators method. The difference is that physical indicators rely on the *internal* prices of each country. There are few if any industries in which there is a single homogeneous output for which productivity can be compared; the total output of an industry typically is determined by blowing up the output of the representative goods according to the appropriate value ratios. Also, the assumption of uniform average quality for the items listed usually has to be made, which is very dubious indeed where the classification of products is not very detailed. The monetary approach depends on international price comparisons. While these have their own difficulties, this approach probably affords the advantage of making it possible to get better samples of products for each industry, and the value of the whole output of the industry is known.

In principle, it is desirable that total factor productivity rather than merely labour productivity should be compared, but until there is substantial progress in international comparisons of capital inputs, it is probably preferable to continue to stress labour productivity in international comparisons because of the large errors likely to be introduced in the measurement of inputs other than labour.

Other methodological recommendations that will serve to foster better comparisons and to aid in the analytical utility of the results are as follows:

(1) Better allowance for the varying quality of the inputs has to be achieved: some efforts along these lines can be found in the recent European studies, particularly with respect to labour inputs, but only a start has been made.

(2) More attention has to be given to the compositional effects produced by different output mixes. While a number of the studies make qualitative references to the effects of differences in the composition of output on the results that they obtain, there have been only infrequent efforts to deal with this problem in a systematic way.

(3) Productivity comparisons are more useful when presented for a large number of sectors rather than for a few. When all of manufacturing is subdivided into five (or even ten) sectors, the differences in the characteristics of the industry may not be defined sharply enough to make it possible for analysts to sort out the explanations for the productivity differences.

(4) The industries for which comparisons are given should be clearly defined, preferably in terms of the International Standard Industrial Classification.

(5) It might also be fruitful to pay more attention to the internal dispersion of productivity in individual plants and firms around the national average

---

[1] For an effort to convert a series of three binary comparisons to a multilaterial comparison see Conference of European Statisticians (1972).

for given industries. It would be very interesting to know whether within-nation differences in productivity in a particular industry tend to be large or small relative to the international differences.

Turning from methodological to substantive issues, it is a well-known fact that there are large productivity differences among the nations of the world. Though Denison and others have made a start in explaining these differences, usually within the ambit of the developed countries, we still know far too little about how productivity in less developed countries could be raised.

There is some evidence in support of the *a priori* hypothesis that the dispersion of productivity differences tends to be greater in industries based on natural resources such as agriculture and mining and less in manufacturing industries. Within manufacturing, the suggestion has been put forward that differences in labour productivity may be greater in industries in which technological diffusion is more limited and smaller in industries where technology is widely spread. Among other variables, such as the amount of capital per man and scale, only the total size of the market emerges from the studies with any degree of consistency as being associated with the industry-to-industry differences in relative productivity, and there the line of causation probably runs both ways. Further explorations of explanatory factors and particularly efforts at quantification are obviously important items on the agenda for future work.

IRVING B. KRAVIS

University of Pennsylvania

REFERENCES

Arrow, K. J., Chenery, H. B., Minhas, B. S. and Solow, R. M. (1961). "Capital–Labor Substitution and Economic Efficiency." *Review of Economics and Statistics*, vol. 43 (August).
Balassa, B. (1973). "Just How Misleading are Official Exchange Rate Conversions? A Comment," ECONOMIC JOURNAL, vol. 83 (December).
—— (1975). "The Rule of Four Ninths: A Rejoinder." ECONOMIC JOURNAL, vol. 84 (September).
Baranson, J. (1969). *Automotive Industries in Developing Countries*. World Bank Staff Occasional Paper No. 8. Baltimore: Johns Hopkins Press.
Barna, T. (1959). "Alternative Methods of Measuring Capital." In *The Measurement of National Wealth, Income and Wealth* (ed. R. Goldsmith and C. Saunders), series III. Chicago: Quadrangle Books.
Beckerman, W. (1966). *International Comparisons of Real Incomes*. Paris: Development Center of the Organization for Economic Cooperation and Development.
—— and Bacon R. (1966). "International Comparisons of Income Levels: A Suggested New Measure." ECONOMIC JOURNAL, vol. 76 (September).
—— (1970). "The International Distribution of Incomes." In *Unfashionable Economics: Essays in Honour of Lord Balogh* (ed. Paul Streeten). London: Weidenfeld and Nicholson.
Bergson, A. (1971). "Comparative Productivity and Efficiency in the Soviet Union and the United States." In *Comparison of Economic Systems* (ed. Alexander Eckstein). Berkeley: University of California Press.
—— (1968). *Planning and Productivity Under Soviet Socialism*. New York: Columbia University Press.
Braithwaite, S. M. (1968). "Real Income Levels in Latin America." *Review of Income and Wealth* (June).
Branchu, J. J., Grotius, J., Temple, P. and Wartenberg, E. (1973). "Comparaison des charges d'exploitation et de la productivité dans sept secteurs en France et en Republic Federal d'Allemagne." *Les Collections de l'INSEE*, série E, no. 22 (November).
Bureau of Labor Statistics (1968). *An International Comparison of Unit Labor Cost in the Iron and Steel Industry, 1964: United States, France, Germany, United Kingdom*. Washington, D.C.

Carrie, J. (1956). "Plant Level Measurements Methods and Results." *Productivity Measurement*, vol. II (January). European Productivity Agency, Organisation for European Cooperation.

Chandrasekar, K. (1973). "U.S. and French Productivity in 19 Manufacturing Industries." *Journal of Industrial Economics* (April).

Cilingiroglu, A. (1969). *Manufacture of Heavy Electrical Equipment in Developing Countries*. World Bank Staff Occasional Paper, no. 9. Baltimore: Johns Hopkins Press.

Clague, C. (1967). "An International Comparison of Industrial Efficiency: Peru and the United States." *Review of Economics and Statistics*, vol. 49, no. 4 (November).

—— and Tanzi, V. (1972). "Human Capital, Natural Resources and the Purchasing Power Parity Doctrine: Some Empirical Results." *Economia Internazionale*, February.

Clark, C. (1940). *The Conditions of Economic Progress*. London: Macmillan.

Conference of European Statisticians (1969). *Comparison of Industrial Production and Productivity Between Austria and Hungary*, WG. 21/8 (29 January).

—— (1969). *Comparison of Levels of Labor Productivity in Industry Between Czechoslovakia and France*, WG. 21/9 (17 November).

—— (1970). *Bilateral Comparison, as Between the Czechoslovak Socialist Republic and the Hungarian Peoples Republic, of Levels of Labor Productivity in Industry for 1967, and Analysis of the Main Factors Influencing Labor Productivity*, WG. 21/14 (14 February).

—— (1971). *Comparative Study of the Factors of Labor Productivity in Industry in Czechoslovakia and France*, WG. 21/17 (4 January).

—— (1971). *Methodological Problems of International Comparisons of Levels of Labor Productivity in Industry*. New York: United Nations.

—— (1972). *Comparisons of Levels of Labor Productivity in Industry in Austria, Czechoslovakia, France, and Hungary*, Statistical Standards and Studies, no. 24. New York: United Nations.

Daly, D. J., Keys, B. A. and Spence, E. J. (1968). *Scale and Specialization in Canadian Manufacturing*. Staff Study, no. 21. Economic Council of Canada, Ottawa, Canada: Queen's Printer and Controller of Stationery (March).

David, P. A. (1972). "Just How Misleading Are Official Exchange Rate Conversions?" ECONOMIC JOURNAL, vol. 82 (September).

—— (1973). *The Rule of Four-Ninths Upheld: A Rejoinder to Professor Balassa*. Harvard University and Stanford University, Discussion Paper, no. 290 (April). Harvard Institute of Economic Research.

—— (1973)."A Reply to Professor Balassa." ECONOMIC JOURNAL, vol. 83 (December).

Denison, E. F., assisted by J. P. Poullier (1967). *Why Growth Rates Differ*. Washington, D.C.: Brookings Institution.

Drechsler, L., Kux, J. and Nyitrai, F. (1974). *International Comparison of Labour Productivity* (in Hungarian). Budapest Statistical Publisher.

Fabricant, S. (1968). "Productivity." *International Encyclopedia of the Social Sciences*. New York: Macmillan Co. and Free Press.

Fareed, A. E. (1972) "Human–Capital Intensity of U.S. Trade." ECONOMICAL JOURNAL, vol. 82 (June).

Federal Institute for Statistics of Yugoslavia and Hungarian Central Statistical Office (1973). *The Comparison of the Yugoslav and of the Hungarian Industry (Labor Productivity and Structure Comparison), 1969–70*. Budapest, May.

Flux, A. W. (1933). "Industrial Productivity in Great Britain and the United States." *Quarterly Journal of Economics* (November).

Frankel, M. (1957). *British and American Manufacturing Productivity*. Bureau of Economic and Business Research. Urbana: University of Illinois Press.

Galenson, W. (1955). *Labor Productivity in Soviet and American Industry*.

Geary, R. C. (1944). "The Concept of Net Volume of Output with Special Reference to Irish Data." *Journal of the Royal Statistical Society*, parts III–IV.

General Agreement on Tariffs and Trade (1966). *A Study on Cotton Textiles*. Geneva. (July).

—— (1973). *International Trade, 1972*. Geneva.

Gilbert, M. and Kravis, I. (1954). *An International Comparison of National Products and the Purchasing Power of Currencies—A Study of the United States, the United Kingdom, France, Germany, and Italy*. Paris: Organisation for European Economic Cooperation.

—— and Associates (1958). *Comparative National Products and Price Levels*. Paris: Organisation for Economic Cooperation and Development.

Gregory, R. G. and James, D. W. (1973). "Do New Factories Embody Best Practice Technology?" ECONOMIC JOURNAL (December).

Griliches, Z. and Jorgenson, D. (1966). "Sources of Measured Productivity Change: Capital Input." *American Economic Review*, vol. 56 (May).

Gupta, S. B. (1968). "Some Tests of the International Comparisons of Factory Efficiency with the CES Production Function." *Review of Economics and Statistics*, vol. 50 (November).

Haig, B. D. (1968). *Real Product, Income and Relative Prices in Australia and the United Kingdom.* Canberra: Australian National University Press.

Hayami, Y., with Miller, B., Wade, W. and Yamashita, S. (1971). *An International Comparison of Agricultural Production and Productivities.* University of Minnesota Agricultural Experimental Station, Technical Bulletin no. 277.

—— and Ruttan, V. W. (1971). *Agricultural Development.* Baltimore: Johns Hopkins Press.

—— Ruttan, V. W. and Southworth, H.M. (forthcoming). *Agricultural Growth in Japan, Taiwan, Korea, and the Philippines.* Honolulu: University Press of Hawaii.

Heath, J. B. (1957). "British–Canadian Industrial Productivity." ECONOMIC JOURNAL, vol. 67, no. 268 (December).

Hufbauer, G. E. (1970). "The Impact of National Characteristics and Technology on the Commodity Composition of Trade and Manufactured Goods." In *The Technology Factor in International Trade* (ed. R. Vernon). New York: National Bureau of Economic Research.

International Labor Organisation (1951). *Productivity in Coal Mines.* Geneva.

Kendrick, J. (1961). *Productivity Trends in the U.S.* Princeton: Princeton University Press.

—— (1973). *Postwar Productivity Trends in the U.S., 1948–69.* New York: National Bureau of Economic Research.

King, G. (1936). *Natural and Political Observations and Conclusions upon the State and Condition of England* (1696). In *Two Tracts by Gregory King* (ed. G. Barnett). Baltimore: Johns Hopkins Press.

Kravis, I., Kenessey, Z., Heston, A. and Summers, R. (1975). *A System of International Comparisons of Gross Product and Purchasing Power.* Baltimore: Johns Hopkins Press.

Kreinin, M. (1965). "Comparative Labor Effectiveness of the Leontief Scarce-Factor Paradox." *American Economic Review* (March).

Kuznets, S. (1957). "Quantitative Aspects of the Economic Growth of Nations. II. Industrial Distribution of National Product and Labor Force." *Economic Development and Cultural Change*, supplement to vol. 5, no. 4 (July).

—— (1971). *Economic Growth of Nations.* Cambridge, Mass.: Harvard University Press.

Kux, J., Mairesse, J. and Dreschler, L. (1969). "Labour Productivity Comparison Between Czechoslovakia and France." *The Review of Income and Wealth*, series 15, no. 3 (September).

Leibenstein, H. (1966). "Allocative Efficiency versus X-Efficiency." *American Economic Review*, June.

Little, I., Scitovsky, T. and Scott, M. (1970). *Industry and Trade in Some Developing Countries.* London: Oxford University Press.

Maddison, A. (1970). *Economic Progress and Policy in Developing Countries.* York: W. W. Norton and Company.

—— (1967). "Comparative Productivity Levels in the Developed Countries." *Banca Nazionale del Lavoro Quarterly Review* (December).

Maizels, A. (1958). "Comparative Productivity in Manufacturing Industry: A Case Study of Australia and Canada." *Economic Record* (April).

Minsol, A. (1968). "Some Tests of the International Comparisons of Factor Efficiency with the CES Production Function. A Reply." *Review of Economics and Statistics*, vol. 50 (November).

Mitchell, E. J. (1968). "Explaining the International Pattern of Labor Productivity and Wages: A Production Model with Two Labor Inputs." *Review of Economics and Statistics*, vol. 50 (November).

Moroney, M. J. (1953). *Facts from Figures.* London: Penguin Books.

Mulhall, M. G. (1886). *Mulhall's Dictionary of Statistics*, 2nd ed. London: George Routledge.

Nadiri, M. I. (1970). "Some Approaches to the Theory and Measurement of Total Factor Productivity: A Survey." *Journal of Economic Literature* (December).

—— (1972). "International Studies of Factor Inputs and Total Factor Productivity, A Brief Survey." *Review of Income and Wealth*, June.

Nelson, R. R. (1968). "International Productivity Differences." *American Economic Review* (December).

Netherlands Central Bureau of Statistics (1966). "Comparisons of Labor Productivity in the United Kingdom and the Nethierlands, 1958." *Statistical Studies*, no. 18 (January).

Paige, D. and G. Bombach, G. (1959). *A Comparison of National Output and Productivity of the United Kingdom and the United States*. Paris: Organisation for European Economic Cooperation.

Paretti, V., Krijnse-Locker, H. and Goybet, Ph. (1974). "Comparaison réelle du produit intérieur brut des pays de la Communauté Européenne: Parités de prix et rapports de volume, 1970." *Analyse et Prévision*, vol. 17, no. 6 (juin).

Phelps Brown, E. H. (1973). "Levels and Movements of Industrial Productivity and Real Wages Internationally Compared, 1860–1970." ECONOMIC JOURNAL, vol. 83 (March).

—— and Browne, M. H. (1968). *A Century of Pay*. London: Macmillan.

Pratten, C. and Silberston, A. (1967). "International Comparisons of Labour Productivity in the Automobile Industry, 1950–1965." *Bulletin of the Oxford Institute of Economics and Statistics* (November).

Reddaway, W. B. (1951). "Some Problems in the Measurement of Changes in the Real Geographical Product." *Income and Wealth*, series 1 (ed. E. Lundberg). Cambridge: Bowes and Bowes.

Rostas, L. (1948). *Comparative Productivity in British and American Industry*. Cambridge University Press.

Samuelson, P. A. (1974). "Analytical Notes on International Real-Income Measures." ECONOMIC JOURNAL, vol. 84 (September).

Snow, E. C. (1944). "The International Comparison of Industrial Output." *Journal of the Royal Statistical Society*, part 1, vol. 107.

Staehle, H. (1934). "International Comparisons of Food Costs." *International Comparisons of the Cost of Living*. Geneva: International Labor Office, Studies and Reports, series N, no. 20.

Statistical Reports of the Northern Countries (1954). *Cost of Living and Real Wages in the Capitals of the Northern Countries*. Stockholm: K. L. Beckmans Boktryckeri.

Studentski, P. (1958). *The Income of Nations*. New York: New York University Press.

Summers, R. and Ahmad, S. (1974). "Better Estimates of Dollar Gross Domestic Product for 101 Countries: Exchange Rate Bias Eliminated." University of Pennsylvania, Discussion Paper no. 297 (December).

Swamy, S. (1973). "Economic Growth in China and India, 1952–1970: A Comparative Appraisal." *Economic Development and Cultural Change*, vol. 21 (4), part II (July).

Taussig, F. W. (1924). "Labor Costs in the United States Compared with Costs Elsewhere." *Quarterly Journal of Economics* (November).

United Nations, Statistical Papers (1968). *International Standard Industrial Classification of All Economic Activities*, series M, no. 4, rev. 2.

—— Statistical Papers (1961). *Standard International Trade Classification*, series M, no. 34. New York: United Nations.

—— (1970). *Yearbook of National Accounts Statistics*. New York: United Nations.

United Nations Economic Commission for Europe (1970). *Economic Survey of Europe in 1969*, part 1. New York: United Nations.

Walters, D. (1968). *Canadian Income Levels and Growth: An International Perspective*. Staff Study, no. 23, Economic Council of Canada. Ottawa: Queen's Printer.

—— (1970). *Canadian Growth Revisited, 1950–67*. Staff Study, no. 28. Economic Council of Canada. Ottawa: Queen's Printer.

West, E. C. (1971). *Canada–United States Price and Productivity Differences in Manufacturing Industries, 1963*. Staff Study, no. 32. Economic Council of Canada. Ottawa: Queen's Printer.

Yukizawa (1975). "Japanese and American Manufacturing Productivity: An International Comparison of Physical Output per Head." Discussion Paper, no. 087. Kyoto: Kyoto Institute of Economic Research, Kyoto University (March).